T0395778

THE PRICE OF NICE

THE PRICE of NICE

How Good Intentions Maintain Educational Inequity

Angelina E. Castagno

EDITOR

University of Minnesota Press
Minneapolis
London

Copyright 2019 by the Regents of the University of Minnesota

All rights reserved. No part of this publication may be reproduced, stored in a retrieval system, or transmitted, in any form or by any means, electronic, mechanical, photocopying, recording, or otherwise, without the prior written permission of the publisher.

Published by the University of Minnesota Press
111 Third Avenue South, Suite 290
Minneapolis, MN 55401-2520
http://www.upress.umn.edu

Printed on acid-free paper

The University of Minnesota is an equal-opportunity educator and employer.

Library of Congress Cataloging-in-Publication Data
Names: Castagno, Angelina E., editor.
Title: The price of nice: how good intentions maintain educational inequity / Angelina E. Castagno, editor.
Description: Minneapolis: University of Minnesota Press, [2019] | Includes bibliographical references and index. |
Identifiers: LCCN 2019001517 (print) |
    ISBN 978-1-5179-0566-8 (hc) | ISBN 978-1-5179-0567-5 (pb)
Subjects: LCSH: Educational equalization—United States. | Teachers—United States—Attitudes. | Intention— Social aspects—United States. | Education—Social aspects— United States. | Discrimination in education—United States. | Minorities—Education—Social aspects—United States.
Classification: LCC LC213.2 .P744 2019 (print) |
    DDC 379.2/6—dc23
LC record available at https://lccn.loc.gov/2019001517

UMP LSI

*For all those who refuse to be nice
in the presence of injustice*

Contents

INTRODUCTION

Mapping the Contours of Niceness in Education   *ix*
    Angelina E. Castagno

PART I

Niceness in K–12 Schools

  1. On Average, What's the Mean of Nice School Interactions?   *3*
    Frederick W. Gooding Jr.

  2. "It's Not That Easy!" Foundations of Niceness in Enacting
    Multicultural and Social Justice Education   *18*
    Jia-Hui Stefanie Wong

  3. Being Nice to the Elephant in the (Class)Room: Whiteness in
    New Latino Diaspora Nebraska   *37*
    Jessica Sierk

  4. Niceness in Special Education: An Ethnographic Case Study of
    Benevolence, Goodness, and Paternalism at Colina Cedro Charter
    High School   *54*
    Sylvia Mac

  5. Nice Work: Young White Women, Near Enemies, and Teaching
    inside the Magic Circle   *70*
    Sally Campbell Galman

PART II

Niceness in Higher Education

  6. The Perfect Storm of Whiteness, Middle-Classness, and Cis
    Femaleness in School Contexts   *91*
    Joseph C. Wegwert and Aidan/Amanda J. Charles

7. Evaluating Niceness: How Anonymous Student Feedback Forms Promote Gendered and Flawed Value Systems in Academic Labor   110
Kristine T. Weatherston

8. The Role of Niceness in Silencing Racially Minoritized Faculty   127
Cynthia Diana Villarreal, Román Liera, and Lindsey Malcom-Piqueux

9. The Self-Contained Scholar: The Racialized Burdens of Being Nice in Higher Education   145
Colin Ben, Amber Poleviyuma, Jeremiah Chin, Alexus Richmond, Megan Tom, and Sarah Abuwandi

10. Performative Niceness and Student Erasure: Historical Implications   161
Nicholas Bustamante and Jessica Solyom

PART III
Niceness across Schools and Society

11. Community Resistance to In-School Inequities: Disrupting Niceness in Out-of-School Spaces   185
Katie A. Lazdowski

12. "I Want to Celebrate That": How Niceness in School Administrators' Talk Elides Discussions of Racialized School Discipline in an Urban School District   201
Marguerite Anne Fillion Wilson and Denise Gray Yull

13. "It's Better Now": How Midwest Niceness Shapes Social Justice Education   218
Bailey B. Smolarek and Giselle Martinez Negrette

14. Schooling, Structural Niceness, and Not-Nice White Girls   238
Sabina Vaught and Deirdre Judge

15. "She's Such a Nasty Woman": Nice and Nasty as Gendered Tropes   258
Frances J. Riemer

ACKNOWLEDGMENTS   275

CONTRIBUTORS   277

INDEX   281

Introduction

Mapping the Contours of Niceness in Education

Angelina E. Castagno

> Americans are unique because they are nice and friendly.
> —Carrie Tirado Bramen, *American Niceness: A Cultural History*

> History is replete with injury and harm inflicted on others by
> nice people doing nice things.
> —Ian E. Baptiste, "Wages of Niceness: The Folly and Futility of
> Educators Who Strive to Not Impose"

One need not search hard to see Niceness in action, and once Niceness is a concept with which you are familiar, the instances of its functioning may be overwhelming. At the end of the 2017–18 school year, I was casually talking with a teacher at an elementary school in Arizona where I had spent the year facilitating a series of professional development workshops related to equity and inclusion. The teacher noted how she was now more adept at *seeing* "racist behaviors" among her colleagues, but that she struggled to *talk about* them because of her "need to create harmony." This was a White woman working in a school with over 50 percent teachers of color, 65 percent students of color, and a leadership team that was vocally committed to pushing the staff to become more equity oriented—in other words, she worked in what we might call a best-case scenario for challenging the status quo and yet still, here, she was constrained by her own adherence to Niceness.

Most educators are nice people with the best intentions regarding the schooling they provide to students every day. The dictionary definition for *nice* is consistent with conventional understandings of the word; to be nice is to be pleasing and agreeable, pleasant and kind. What counts as nice is determined by people and communities. Thus, there is nothing factual about Niceness. We construct the notion of Niceness, and we connect it to particular behaviors, interactions, and discourses. A nice person is not someone who creates a lot of disturbance, conflict, controversy, or discomfort. Nice people avoid potentially uncomfortable or upsetting experiences, knowledge, and interactions. We do not point out failures or shortcomings in others but rather emphasize the good, the promise, and the improvement we see. Niceness compels us to reframe potentially disruptive or uncomfortable things in ways that are more soothing, pleasant, and comfortable. This avoidance and reframing are generally done with the best intentions, and having good intentions is a critical component of Niceness. In fact, as long as one means well, the actual impact of one's behavior, discourse, or action is often meaningless.

Niceness is incredibly attractive and, at the same time, difficult to critique. But it is precisely this critique that is necessary if educators are to better understand the ways we maintain and advance inequity despite, or in spite of, our best intentions. The challenges associated with critiquing Niceness find resonance in the feminist articulation of the "killjoy" (Ahmed 2010; Aidoo 1977)—that is, one who is perceived as disrupting or ending the joy of others. Ahmed (2010) explains how "in speaking up or speaking out, you upset the situation. That you have described what was said by another as a problem means you have created a problem. You become the problem you create." A killjoy does not ascribe to the norms of Niceness because she knows that doing so means she is complicit in the perpetuation of educational inequity.

Schools are heralded as fundamental to helping anyone—and everyone—achieve the American dream. They have worked—and continue to work—for most educators, who are understandably invested in an institution that provides an avenue for their own success. Schools educate a diverse student body, but diversity and Niceness have been so intertwined that any engagement with diversity is necessarily, almost by definition, *nice*. As Ahmed (2007) notes, we generally have a "desire to hear happy stories of diversity rather than unhappy stories of racism" (164). Diversity in schools has been framed in such a way as to require a stance of inclusion, optimism, and assimilation. These concepts are, in turn, constitutive of the Niceness we see in schools. Despite their good intentions and the general Niceness among educators, most schools in the United States contribute to inequity every day. How does this happen? At the most basic level, that is the question that this book explores.

An Emerging Body of Scholarship

Many readers will be familiar with the cultural construct of the "ugly American" and may wonder how Niceness fits into that global narrative. This is especially pertinent during this particular historical moment during which the U.S. president epitomizes the image of the ugly American and was even so named by a former Mexican president. But Bramen (2017) offers a compelling cultural history of American Niceness and argues that it is a cultural construct with a deep history, despite its relative lack of scholarly exploration. She notes that "the nice American is as pervasive as its negative counterpart, but it has been neither studied nor defined as explicitly. This is partly due to the fact that niceness is assumed to be a national default mode, an obvious and superficial gesture not worthy of serious inquiry. Its banality puts it under the radar of cultural analysis. My fundamental claim is that even though it often goes unnamed as a pattern of behavior, niceness pervades the everyday conduct, assumptions, and discourses of and about Americans" (7). While Bramen offers a historical account of Niceness in American society, *The Price of Nice* narrows the focus to U.S. schools in the current era.

Ladson-Billings pointed to the connection between Niceness and education when she asked "Just What Is Critical Race Theory and What's It Doing in a Nice Field Like Education?" (1998), but her question has yet to be really taken up by educational researchers. I began thinking about Niceness through my research on Whiteness among K–12 teachers in Utah (Castagno 2014). In one of my first interactions with this particular community, a school district administrator handed me a video that had been produced for the district earlier that year titled *We Teach the World*. As I listened to her describe the "diversity in our district" and the various ways the district addressed that diversity, I also observed the standard educator decor on the surrounding office walls—posters addressing every child's ability to learn and succeed, apple and pencil knickknacks, youth artwork, and quotes about leaders who inspire. There was a clear undercurrent of what another district leader called a "culture of nice" in the stories she shared with me.

I spent the next decade talking about this concept of Niceness in my classes with both new and veteran teachers and educational leaders, as well as with colleagues in universities across the United States. The concept seemed to resonate, so that prompted my investigation into if, and how, others had examined Niceness in schools and other sociopolitical institutions. There were a few articles and books that took up the concept, but most of the references to Niceness were in the personal development / self-help bodies of literature. For the most part, those who had explored Niceness had done so from an individual psychological perspective and, as a result, focused on the impacts or implications of Niceness on individual people. Although this was part of how I was thinking about Niceness, it was by no means what I considered the most important part of the phenomenon.

Niceness is most important because of its relational elements and, especially, its material consequences. Being nice is not the same thing as being ignorant or having a lack of awareness. Within a frame of Niceness, oppressive actions are not actually oppressive; they are just hurtful. They are therefore assumed to be the result of individuals who have made bad choices or who just do not know any better. This framing diverts attention away from patterned inequity, structural oppression, and institutional dominance. But structural phenomena cannot be addressed with individual explanations. Inequity thrives when we limit our understanding of it to individual intentions, knowledge, instances, and interactions. Sabina Vaught and Deirdre Judge's chapter in this volume offers an especially poignant illustration of this idea; their ethnographic data point to larger state engagements with Niceness and how those engagements function to maintain the structured, institutionalized power of the state.

My interest in equity finds resonance with Ward's (2017) analysis of Martin Luther King Jr.'s *Letter from Birmingham Jail*. Ward uses King's writing to draw important distinctions between civility as a virtue tied to justice and courage, and Niceness as a defective generalized ethic that is more concerned with maintaining wealth, prestige, social approval, innocence, and comfort. He notes, "Friendly gestures and kind words, unproblematic in the context of morally benign relationships, are seen as sanctimonious ways of preserving one's power and comfort in the context of unjust ones. These efforts at preservation of an unjustly privileged self are aided by wishful thinking (the semblance of hope), an immoderate desire for power, comfort, and the acceptance of others, excessive fear of experiencing the loss of these, and indifference to real disagreement (the semblance of tolerance)" (Ward 2017, 133). Bringing this focus on justice and equity into the educational sphere, Bissonnette (2016) offers an institutionally situated analysis and suggests that teacher education programs have a preference for Niceness that obstructs efforts to actualize culturally responsive teacher preparation. She focuses on the audit culture of teacher education, preservice teachers themselves, teacher educators, and the curriculum and instruction within teacher preparation programs as four key sites where Niceness is visible and operating to reinforce Whiteness. Weaving the thread from Ladson-Billings's 1998 reference, Bissonnette concludes that Niceness "allows [preservice teachers] to offer 'nice,' liberal-oriented insights without truly engaging in the complex, arduous, self-reflection processes culturally responsive teaching requires" (2016, 10).

Baptiste (2008) defines "educational Niceness" as educators' aversion to all forms of imposition. He does not attempt to discern the extent to which Niceness is a widespread phenomenon, but instead attempts to illustrate the phenomenon of Niceness through language and philosophical analysis. He begins with the premise that education is political; he then articulates four fallacies associated with Niceness and four perils of Niceness. The perils include "(a) wrongful assignment of credit or blame, (b) deployment of weak and ineffectual means of coercion, (c) repressive tolerance, and (d) negation or masking of teacher power" (23). In discussing his own lived experiences, Baptiste suggests that educators' advocacy of Niceness is a facade for imposing their values and ideas on others. The chapter in this volume by Joseph C. Wegwert and Aidan/Amanda Charles offers support for this suggestion, as well as for the additional point that Niceness is also a facade for the perpetuation of the status quo of patterned and pervasive educational inequity.

As a whole, teachers and educational leaders are invested in Niceness (Castagno 2014; Goodman 2001; Marshall and Theoharis 2007). My earlier ethnographic research found that Niceness was a key component of the Whiteness that informed diversity-related policy and practice in Salt Lake City schools. Similarly, Alemán's (2009) study in Utah found that educational leaders' political discourse is shaped by Niceness, which ultimately limits their critique of racism and silences the experiences of underrepresented students. Others have also linked Niceness to Whiteness, racial exclusion, and race privilege (e.g., Hartigan 2009, Low 2009, Bissonnette 2016). Much of this research highlights how Niceness is performed, embodied, policed, and taught among both adults and youth in schools. It is done in implicit and explicit ways. But Niceness is not uniformly applied or expected, so context always matters. While my own work has focused on the connections between Niceness and Whiteness in educational spaces, we also have to explore and better understand the intersectional aspects of Niceness. And Niceness isn't limited to the adults in schools. When young people do not adequately learn the norms of Niceness, they experience repercussions and are often disciplined for being overly critical (Goodman 2001). Girls, especially, are socialized and encouraged to be "pleasing" via "a tyranny of niceness" (Deak 2002, Sommers 2005).

Intentionality is important in understanding Niceness. Good intentions have been linked to the perpetuation of inequity in schools (Castagno 2014, Lewis and Diamond 2015), and the role of intentions is not limited to the educational environment. As Bramen (2017) notes of American culture writ large, "Niceness implies that Americans are fundamentally well-meaning people defined by an essential goodness. Even acts of aggression are framed as passive, reluctant, and defensive acts to protect oneself against the potential aggression of another. My point is that American niceness assumes that Americans are decent and good-natured people with the best of intentions. Even if they do serious damage in the world, American niceness means that the damage will be more than likely seen as a mistake" (8). I have advanced a similar argument (Castagno 2014), and there is a growing body of empirical evidence pointing to the connections between educators' well-meaning dispositions and their role in sustaining inequitable educational outcomes. Silence, passivity, denial, and avoidance are all tied to these patterns. So it should come as no surprise that the word *nice* derives from the Latin *nescius*, meaning "ignorant," and the French *nescire*, meaning "not to know." As Sommers (2005) explains, "To be nice means to silence ourselves in some way, and in doing so, we compromise our authenticity and give up freedom to act and speak. On the other hand, niceness may facilitate the shedding of responsibility" (12).

A Sociocultural Mapping of Niceness in Education

This book advances the concept of Niceness as an analytic category that encompasses a wide range of practices and discourses. The concept of Niceness emerged as an in vivo code for me and for many of the authors in *The Price of Nice*, but it is much more than that. It is clear that Niceness is a thing that stands on its own and is pervasive in educational settings. It matters as an analytic category because of the way it maintains and/or produces inequity. Niceness is a shared socioemotional disposition or a way of being. It is about one's emotional state, the emotional state of others, and the behaviors and discourses that support those emotional states. The emotional component of Niceness may help explain why it has elided scholarly critique for so long—indeed, the classic dichotomy between reason and emotion, or between rationality and feeling, has long relegated the latter of these pairs to a place of relative unimportance. At the same time, it may also be this emotional component that contributes to the durability and pervasive commonsense acceptance of Niceness.[1] Unlike some analytic categories, Niceness is something that many people recognize in themselves and others, and something that at least some people actually name themselves. It is not a heady or overly academic concept. It is common enough to be relatable to most people who hear the word, and it is precisely this relatability and commonsense status that has allowed it to go mostly unexplored and uninterrogated.

Niceness is one mechanism for reifying structural arrangements and ideologies of dominance across lines of race, gender, and social class. It functions not only as a shield to protect (White, female) educators from having to do the hard work of dismantling inequity but also as a disciplining agent for those who attempt or even consider disrupting structures and ideologies of dominance. This distinction is important. We can, and should, think about Niceness as embodied by those in more powerful and privileged positions; but we should also think about it as the demand to act nice among those challenging power. The chapters in *The Price of Nice* provide illustrative examples of both of these employments of Niceness in schools.

Through her research with young, White, preservice teachers, Sally Campbell Galman highlights how Niceness includes behaviors such as avoiding conflict, maintaining a feminine look, framing teaching as love, and supporting existing power structures through obedience in chapter 5. But Galman also discusses the work of "nasty" teachers—those women who construct teaching as political work and engage in the difficult tasks of critiquing the status quo and advocating for students when nobody else is doing so. In chapter 11, Katie A. Lazdowski demonstrates that interrupting Niceness can sometimes be an effective approach for interrupting Whiteness. By countering narratives of Niceness directly and publicly, there are opportunities to foster greater racial literacy within schools and other public spaces.

Other chapters take this a step further by exploring the policing functions of Niceness. As just one example, in chapter 9, Colin Ben, Amber Poleviyuma, Jeremiah Chin, Alexus Richmond, Megan Tom, and Sarah Abuwandi highlight how Niceness causes self-containment among students of color; this self-containment is connected to the simultaneous isolation and hypervisibility among students of color in predominantly White institutions of higher education. The disciplining function of Niceness is reminiscent of Frye's (1983) point that oppression requires that you show signs of being happy with the situation in which you find yourself; anything other than smiles and cheerfulness often result in your being perceived as ungrateful, mean, angry, bitter, or even dangerous. Indeed, complying with the norms of Niceness requires great personal costs for people of color. Code-switching is similarly connected to the demand that minoritized and marginalized people engage Niceness, since switching to the dominant codes of power is often performed as a strategic survival mechanism. In chapter 10, Nicholas Bustamante and Jessica Solyom offer a telling counterstory about a young Latino student in a predominantly White law school who wrestles with the norms of Niceness, but who also draws on his own familial and community legacy to guide his journey.

Niceness is both an embodied practice and a set of discursive expectations. It functions as an institutional norm within educational spaces (and other spaces, but that is beyond the scope of this book). Niceness encompasses a range of practices, discourses, and ideologies, and many of the chapters in this book illustrate some of the specific behaviors and practices that make up Niceness in particular settings. This is especially true in the chapters that draw on ethnographic research, since that is a methodology particularly well suited to uncovering microlevel phenomena. At the same time, this book assumes that microlevel patterns are indicative of larger phenomena and it is through these windows that we can better grasp the meaning of Niceness as a larger analytic category. Niceness can be understood as a political practice, much like Brown's (2008) analysis of tolerance, in which she argues that the concept of tolerance individualizes political conflict and power hierarchies; tolerance suggests that we should all simply behave in ways that demonstrate acceptance of others. The problem, of course, is that tolerance obscures pervasive injustices and, therefore, the need for equity. This is where Niceness and tolerance interface — Niceness includes tolerance, as Brown aptly deconstructs it, but Niceness is more than tolerance.

Some may wonder about the extent to which Niceness is conflated with things such as civility, tolerance, and love, but this book suggests that Niceness is operationalized vis-à-vis some of these related concepts. As I read much of the newer scholarly work on race, social class, sexual orientation, and gender identity in education, many of the concepts and findings can be connected through and to what I'm calling Niceness. Consider, for example, the theory and empirical evidence around White fragility, civility, the White savior complex, allyship, and code-switching: each of these concepts is connected to each of the others through Niceness and their functional purpose of maintaining inequity. To elaborate on one of these examples, we can look to DiAngelo's (2018) important discussion of what she calls White fragility. When White people are challenged racially, they tend to experience emotions such as anger, fear, and guilt. These emotions are often paired with defensiveness, argumentation, and/or silence. White fragility is a sort of protective mechanism for maintaining White racial equilibrium. Similarly, Niceness is a mechanism for maintaining White racial equilibrium—that is, it functions to prevent any sort of challenge or tension (disequilibrium) related to power and structural inequity. As the chapters in this book highlight, Niceness is often engaged in racialized contexts and situations, but it is also engaged intersectionally and functions to gloss over inequities related to gender, social class, heteronormativity, and other power hierarchies. White fragility emerges from a rupture in Niceness, which results in conflict, tension, direct communication about inequity, and what some may interpret as "meanness." But viewing these ruptures as mean only makes sense when we understand that White fragility is at play.

In other words, Niceness is an analytic category that encompasses a number of other practices, discourses, and concepts frequently found in educational settings. Aspects of Niceness that are perhaps the most commonplace in schools include silence around issues of racism, homophobia, and sexism; coded language that allows for the discussion of others while not actually naming them as such; and the general avoidance of potentially uncomfortable or controversial conversations so as to not rock the proverbial boat. Chapter 13, by Bailey B. Smolarek and Giselle Martinez Negrette, and chapter 3, by Jessica Sierk, highlight the ways Niceness is embodied through practices such as silence, tolerance, and lack of critical engagement with social issues. In the higher education context, Kristine T. Weatherston's chapter highlights how institutional norms around teaching, grading, and student feedback rely on double standards and reinforce gender bias on college campuses. And in chapter 1, Frederick W. Gooding Jr. examines four distinct cases highlighted in the media at schools across the United States to illustrate how the criteria and definitions of acceptable, nice behavior shift depending on context, identity, and relations to power. It is this sort of nuance that the book collectively conveys.

A sociocultural approach to studying Niceness would be incomplete without a genealogy—that is, a contextualized, historicized analysis—of Niceness. I recommend readers examine Bramen's (2017) cultural history of Niceness for a detailed account of how Niceness was prevalent in nineteenth-century America. Her cultural history focuses on five key engagements with Niceness during this time period: Indigenous forms of welcoming and the subsequent "dangers of hospitality"; Black amiability and the "slave's smile"; the Niceness of Christianity that emerged from a previously harsh conception of an angry Calvinist God; how femininity required Niceness while simultaneously constraining women's behavior and emotional life; and the contradicting images of American Niceness during the U.S. occupation of the Philippines. Future work on Niceness in education could look to key moments such as the early feminization of teaching, the U.S. civil rights movement in schools, and neoliberal trends in education to provide a genealogical unpacking and teasing out of both the meaning of Niceness and the relationship between it and particular historical and cultural moments. Bramen's argument that "the dominant story of American niceness depends, in part, on incorporating the niceness of the oppressed" (37) is consistent with my own observations of Niceness in educational spaces in the twenty-first century that highlight how Niceness is expected of those who occupy marginalized positions within U.S. schools and society.

Niceness is often tied to deficit perspectives about students and communities. In this way, it is also tied to a number of other theories advanced by educational researchers studying inequity. The White savior complex (Emdin 2016; Straubhaar 2014) is a great example: If I believe my students need someone to rescue them from their plight in life, and if I view myself as capable of providing that rescue, then I engage in ways that advance a paternal or maternal relationship and that are often self-serving in the sense that they boost my sense of philanthropy and belief that I am doing good in the world. But my own savior identity relies on the presence of someone (or many someones) who must be saved. In other words, my Niceness requires that I view my students as needing help, as incapable on their own, and/or as missing something that I can provide. This is a classic deficit framework. Deficit frameworks ultimately say that unsuccessful people lack something that is needed to be successful; these take a number of forms, but some of the more common ones in recent years include that students who are unsuccessful lack grit or a growth mind-set. Deficit frameworks are tied to individualism in the sense that they locate issues or problems within individuals. This can be contrasted to a systems analysis or an institutional framework that locates issues and problems within systems, policies, and institutions. Clearly the world does not work in such dichotomous ways, but overly relying on individualized understandings (success depends largely on one's mind-set) sets one on a clear path to deficit beliefs about individuals (they don't have enough grit), which in turn leads one to seek solutions within individuals (they need to try harder, study longer, develop more resilience). These deficit frameworks teach kids to adapt to systems that are broken rather than requiring broken systems to adapt or even be fixed.

Niceness, Meanness, and the Trump Era

Since the election of Trump to the U.S. presidency, many have noticed a more mainstream White supremacist rage that has (re)surfaced across the United States. I wonder if, in fact, this resurgence is actually one of the many unintended consequences of decades of Niceness. The trend of liberal laissez-faire tolerance cannot adequately keep meanness in check. At some point it allows too much.

Thinking about Niceness has taken on a new urgency, as well as some new meaning, in the age of Trump. It now appears to be acceptable for explicit hate speech to be spewed all over our schools, businesses, and public spaces. But it is not okay for resisters, protectors, protestors, and other activists to display their forms of engagement and communication; theirs is *not nice*, anti-American, a riot, divisive. There seems to be a double standard. This was clearly illustrated in the events of August 2017 in Charlottesville, Virginia, and the subsequent responses by the U.S. president and others (Heim 2017). In 2018 this double standard was perhaps no more obvious than in the debates surrounding Colin Kaepernick and multiple other National Football League players kneeling during the national anthem before games as a means of protest against the persistent racial injustices in our country. Many Americans were outraged over these players kneeling, yet these same people simultaneously vigorously defended other demonstrations of free speech in support of causes that aligned with their own interests (the Second Amendment, anti-immigration policies, etc.). As Harper (2018) points out, the policy adopted by the National Football League in May 2018 that requires players to stand for the anthem is squarely about race and is, in fact, a violation of players' First Amendment rights. Future research and cultural analysis should explore new engagements with Niceness in the age of White supremacist rage that we are currently witnessing. It may indeed be one of the (unintended) consequences of Niceness to have allowed this sort of phenomenon to fester.

Overall, though, this book suggests that within schools, and particularly among the adults in schools—the presumed educators—Niceness still rules. There is indeed meanness within educational spaces, and Gooding's chapter, as well as chapter 15, by Frances J. Reimer, point to just a few examples of this. But even in the instances of meanness, we can learn something about the norms of Niceness that are expected, broken, and policed in various ways. It is this nuanced unpacking of Niceness that the chapters in this volume collectively offer.

As we finalized this manuscript in spring 2018, the nation saw a steady pattern of statewide teacher walkouts. They started in West Virginia, then progressed to Oklahoma, Kentucky, Arizona, and Colorado. Teachers, support staff, parents, children, and allied community members came together to demand increased funding for public schools and compensation for those working in them. Educators in the United States are not the usual suspects for such large-scale social movements, and that fact has everything to do with Niceness. As Naomi Shulman shared via social media shortly after Trump was elected president, "Nice people made the best Nazis. My mom grew up next to them. They got along, refused to make waves, looked the other way when things got ugly and focused on happier things than 'politics.' They were lovely people who turned their heads as their neighbors were dragged away. You know who weren't nice people? Resisters."[2]

Even the word *strike* brought about tension among educators and allies in Arizona. When I shared a colleague's social media post about strikes being difficult for everyone, but especially for those who are actually striking, an online debate ensued about the Arizona movement being "a walkout, but not a strike." One commentator noted that "walkout is often used as a less controversial term than strike"—which is exactly the point, and probably why Arizona's educator-leaders were very careful to use the word *walkout* in all of their messaging. Like *resisters*, the word *strike* connotes a stance that is confrontational and even defiant. Resisters, and those who go on strike, are not nice. But educators are nice, traditionally. Even more important, educators occupy ground zero for ensuring that the norms of Niceness are passed on to the next generation.

Niceness is an important mechanism for maintaining the status quo. Schools are institutions that sort children based on race, social class, gender, language, citizenship, ability, and any other number of power-related identity categories. This sorting and selecting feeds the society in which we live—one that is capitalist in nature and requires individuals at various status levels. There is an inherent tension between this functional need of U.S. society and the ideologies of equality and meritocracy on which U.S. schools and society are heralded. So although we continue to propagate the American dream—the notion that anyone can succeed if he or she tries hard enough—most people know this to be far-fetched. This dream may not be impossible, but it is surely not probable. And the probability is even less likely for those who sit on the "wrong side" of certain identity categories. This is where Niceness is particularly useful. Niceness compels educators to focus on the dream, the possibility, and the effort of each individual student. Niceness deters educators from grappling with the red flags that consistently emerge in achievement, behavioral, and other data. Niceness, in other words, both enables avoidance and shields educators from doing the hard work of confronting inequity. The result is the perpetuation of educational inequity.

Niceness is both an institutional norm within schools and an embodied practice among educators. Since the U.S. teaching population remains largely White and female, it follows that Niceness is raced and gendered in particular ways. Niceness takes on specific qualities among White, female educators, but it is not confined to educators who are White women. The nuances of how Niceness is engaged are locally differentiated, but the overall patterns remain firmly in place. In other words, Niceness works at both the individual and institutional levels. Thus, in order to really understand Niceness, we must examine it at each of these levels and also at the intersections of the two. The chapters in this book take up this challenge by exploring Niceness in educational spaces from a sociocultural perspective. Collectively the book unpacks what Niceness looks, feels, and sounds like in educational spaces from elementary school through higher education. *The Price of Nice* specifically engages the following questions:

> How does Niceness both reinforce structural inequity and also disrupt it?

How is Niceness engaged differently by individuals and communities who occupy different relations to power?

When does Niceness work, and to what end?

In all the efforts to advance equity and justice along the educational pipeline, how do we both engage and disrupt Niceness?

What are the personal and institutional costs to maintaining Niceness in schools?

Throughout the chapters we see that Niceness is mobilized as a dominant cultural norm that polices discourse, relationships, policies, and practices in ways that reinforce educational inequity. One of the most critical distinctions that this book offers is between Niceness as a normative practice willingly and purposefully engaged and embodied by educators, and Niceness as an expected—and even policed—practice imposed on those who are inclined to challenge the status quo. This distinction often falls along identity lines. It should not be surprising that Niceness in the first iteration can generally be observed among White, female teachers. Chapter 12, by Marguerite Anne Fillion Wilson and Denise Gray Yull, and chapter 6, by Wegwert and Charles, explore this pattern in depth. Wegwert and Charles's chapter highlights the nuanced intersections between race, class, gender, and sexuality that are engaged through Niceness in teacher preparation, whereas Wilson and Yull's chapter explores how Niceness is taken up by administrators and school board members. Intersectionality is also taken up in chapter 14 through Vaught and Judge's exploration of how Niceness functions through patterned and institutional benevolence.

Opening Up a Conversation

My hope is that this book provides a foundational understanding of Niceness and opens up additional conversation and research into the concept of Niceness. The chapters in *The Price of Nice* interrogate Niceness empirically and conceptually; are grounded in data, personal narrative, and cultural analysis; and are situated at various points along the spectrum, from elementary schools to higher education. Chapter 8, by Cynthia Diana Villarreal, Román Liera, and Lindsey Malcom-Piqueux, provides one example of how Niceness is both an emic and etic concept. In other words, Niceness was a specific concept that was explicitly used by participants in Villareal and colleagues' study, but it was also a more general theme that the authors found throughout their analysis of the data writ large. This is also true in other chapters in this volume; collectively they highlight the ways in which Niceness is raced, gendered, and classed. Notably, Niceness is not always fully ascribed to, but even when Niceness breaks down at the individual or interactional level (i.e., people acting "not nice"), it continues to operate at an ideological and institutional level in service to inequity. Chapter 2, by Jia-Hui Stefanie Wong, and chapter 4, by Sylvia Mac, both offer examples of the ways educators engage Niceness that ultimately reinforce inequity. Wong's research explores this among teachers who self-identify as being committed to social justice, and yet even they engage social justice work in nice ways that their students see right through. Mac's research focuses on special education and suggests that inclusive education is also engaged in nice ways that fail to advance equity for students with disabilities. Ultimately, the present volume turns Niceness on its head to highlight the ways in which it can actually be not nice, good, or healthy for individuals and communities because of the way it maintains, protects, and reinforces educational inequity.

The book is organized loosely around the "sites" in which Niceness is explored: Part I comprises chapters that explore Niceness in K–12 classrooms and schools; Part II investigates Niceness in postsecondary settings; and Part III explores Niceness across educational settings and society. In each of these sections readers will note the multiple and varied ways Niceness is embodied, by whom, and to what ends. Perhaps the most critical distinction is between Niceness as an embodied practice of dominant players and the demands of Niceness placed on those who challenge the system. In many chapters, these two categories overlap. Another critical point that emerges is that although Niceness is often thought about as an individual attribute, a collective reading of the chapters herein clearly demonstrates how Niceness is actually relational and has structural consequences.

The need to understand Niceness is urgent and far reaching; indeed, efforts to reduce educational inequity will continue to fail if we don't understand it. As Baptiste (2008) notes, "Educational niceness . . . is not a humanizing imperative. Rather, it is a deluding phantom—a salacious seduction which might make educators popular with students, and leave them feeling good about themselves, but, which, in the end, might turn out to be the unwitting handmaiden of oppressive hegemony. Until educators rid themselves of their yearning to be nice, until they embrace wholeheartedly their obligation to impose, their educational impact— especially in addressing social inequality—will be severely curtailed" (28). There exists a long legacy of scholars who argue that culturally relevant (Ladson-Billings 1994, 1995), responsive (Castagno and Brayboy 2008; Gay 2000), sustaining (Paris 2012, Paris and Alim 2014), and/or revitalizing schooling (McCarty and Lee 2014) is the path to educational equity. But I agree with Bissonnette (2016), who suggests that Niceness is a barrier to the genuine engagement of these approaches. In her analysis of efforts to advance culturally responsive teacher preparation, she notes that "the opposite of niceness isn't a culture of shaming; rather, its dichotomy is open, critical, and provocative instruction, conversation, and reflexivity" (19). This call for direct communication and "real talk" about oppression has been echoed by others (e.g., Pollock 2005, 2008), as has the related point that those of us in more privileged positions often are able to do this in ways that others cannot.

But direct, honest relationality is not enough if deficit frameworks still pervade. Thus, we must also work to create spaces where deficit ideologies can be unlearned and replaced with ideologies of justice and equity. This work requires both an affective element and a structural one. In other words, emotions are real, and research is clear that emotions often serve as barriers for the kind of equity work that I'm suggesting (Matias 2016). At the same time, understanding the role of emotions does not mean letting people off the hook when the emotional work becomes too great—this, in fact, takes us right back to Niceness. Instead we must acknowledge the emotional, affective elements of Niceness while simultaneously naming the structural components that holds inequity in place.

Notes

1. Many thanks to Peter Demerath for helping me see this important point.

2. Naomi Shulman, Facebook, November 2016. Shulman later elaborated on the comment; see Shulman 2016.

References

Ahmed, S. 2007. "A Phenomenology of Whiteness." *Feminist Theory* 8, no. 2: 149–68.

Ahmed, S. 2010. "Feminist Killjoys (and Other Willful Subjects)." *Polyphonic Feminisms* 8, no. 3. http://sfonline.barnard.edu/polyphonic/ahmed_01.htm.

Aidoo, A. 1977. *Our Sister Killjoy: Or Reflections from a Black-Eyed Squint.* London, England: Longman Press.

Alemán, E., Jr. 2009. "Through the Prism of Critical Race Theory: Niceness and Latina/o Leadership in the Politics of Education." *Journal of Latinos and Education* 8, no. 4: 290–311.

Baptiste, I. E. 2008. "Wages of Niceness: The Folly and Futility of Educators Who Strive to Not Impose." *New Horizons in Adult Education and Human Resource Development* 22, no. 2: 6–28.

Bissonnette, J. 2016. "The Trouble with Niceness: How a Preference for Pleasantry Sabotages Culturally Responsive Teacher Preparation." *Journal of Language and Literacy Education at the University of Georgia* 12, no. 2: 9–32.

Bramen, C. 2017. *American Niceness: A Cultural History.* Cambridge, Mass.: Harvard University Press.

Brown, W. 2008. *Regulating Aversion: Tolerance in the Age of Identity and Empire.* Princeton, N.J.: Princeton University Press.

Castagno, A. E. 2014. *Educated in Whiteness: Good Intentions and Diversity in Schools.* Minneapolis: University of Minnesota Press.

Castagno, A. E., and B. M. J. Brayboy. 2008. "Culturally Responsive Schooling for Indigenous Youth: A Review of the Literature." *Review of Educational Research* 78, no. 4: 941–93.

Deak, J. 2002. "Parents, Girls, and the 'Tyranny of Nice.'" *Independent School* 61, no. 3: 112.

DiAngelo, R. 2018. *White Fragility: Why It's So Hard for White People to Talk about Racism.* Boston: Beacon Press.

Emdin, C. 2016. *For White Folks Who Teach in the Hood . . . and the Rest of Y'all Too: Reality Pedagogy and Urban Education.* Boston: Beacon Press.

Frye, M. 1983. *The Politics of Reality: Essays in Feminist Theory.* Trumansburg, N.Y.: Crossing Press.

Gay, G. 2000. *Culturally Responsive Teaching: Theory, Research, and Practice.* New York: Teachers College Press.

Goodman, J. 2001. "Niceness and the Limits of Rules." *Journal of Moral Education* 30, no. 4: 349–360.

Harper, S. 2018, May 24. "There Would Be No NFL without Black Players. They Can Resist the Anthem Policy." *Washington Post.* https://www.washington post.com/news/posteverything/wp/2018/05/24/there-would-be-no-nfl-without -black-players-they-can-resist-the-anthem-policy/?noredirect=on&utm_term= .0b20fbc0b4f8.

Hartigan, J. 2009. "What Are You Laughing At? Assessing the 'Racial' in U.S. Public Discourse." *Transforming Anthropology* 17, no. 1: 4–19.

Heim, J. 2017, August 14. "Recounting a Day of Rage, Hate, Violence, and Death." *Washington Post.* https://www.washingtonpost.com/graphics/2017/local /charlottesville-timeline/?utm_term=.7c935ff4830e.

Ladson-Billings, G. 1994. *The Dreamkeepers: Successful Teachers of African American Children.* San Francisco: Jossey-Bass.

Ladson-Billings, G. 1995. "Toward a Theory of Culturally Relevant Pedagogy." *American Educational Research Journal* 32, no. 3: 465–91.

Ladson-Billings, G. 1998. "Just What Is Critical Race Theory and What's It Doing in a Nice Field like Education?" *Qualitative Studies in Education* 11, no. 1: 7–24.

Lewis, A., and J. Diamond. 2015. *Despite the Best Intentions: How Racial Inequality Thrives in Good Schools*. New York: Oxford University Press.

Low, S. 2009. "Maintaining Whiteness: The Fear of Others and Niceness." *Transforming Anthropology* 17, no. 2: 79–92.

Marshall, J. M., and G. Theoharis. 2007. "Moving Beyond Being Nice: Teaching and Learning about Social Justice in a Predominantly White Educational Leadership Program." *Journal of Research on Leadership Education* 2, no. 2: 1–31.

Matias, C. 2016. *Feeling White: Whiteness, Emotionality, and Education*. Rotterdam: Sense.

McCarty, T., and T. Lee. 2014. "Critically Culturally Sustaining/Revitalizing Pedagogy and Indigenous Education Sovereignty." *Harvard Educational Review* 84, no. 1: 101–24.

Paris, D. 2012. "Culturally Sustaining Pedagogy: A Needed Change in Stance, Terminology, and Practice." *Educational Researcher* 41, no. 3: 93–97.

Paris, D., and S. Alim. 2014. "What Are We Seeking to Sustain through Culturally Sustaining Pedagogy? A Loving Critique Forward." *Harvard Educational Review* 84, no. 1: 85–100.

Pollock, M. 2005. *Colormute: Race Talk Dilemmas in an American School*. Princeton, N.J.: Princeton University Press.

Pollock, M. 2008. *Everyday Antiracism: Getting Real about Race in School*. New York: New Press.

Shulman, N. 2016, November 17. "No Time To Be Nice: Now Is Not the Moment to Remain Silent." WBUR. https://www.wbur.org/cognoscenti/2016/11/17/the-post-election-case-for-speaking-out-naomi-shulman.

Sommers, E. 2005. *Tyranny of Niceness: Unmasking the Need for Approval*. Toronto: Dundurn.

Straubhaar, R. 2014. "The Stark Reality of the 'White Saviour' Complex and the Need for Critical Consciousness: A Document Analysis of the Early Journals of a Freirean Educator." *Compare: A Journal of Comparative and International Education* 45, no. 3: 381–400.

Ward, I. 2017. "Democratic Civility and the Dangers of Niceness." *Political Theology* 18, no. 2: 115–36.

PART I

Niceness in K–12 Schools

1

On Average, What's the Mean
of Nice School Interactions?

FREDERICK W. GOODING JR.

Is your teacher nice?" While the adjective *nice* can take on many pleasant connotations, for purposes of this writing, the term may have to take on a slightly different meaning. If anything, *nice* within an educational context takes on a more scurrilous flavor when certain analytical rubrics are put in place.

Schooling—especially at the K–12 level—takes on largely two forms: (1) academic instruction inside the classroom, and (2) nonacademic socialization largely outside the classroom. Spring notes that socialization "refers to what students learn from following school rules, interacting with other students, and participating in social events." As contrasted with rote academic learning and rigor, "for some educational leaders, socialization is a powerful means of political control" (Spring 2016, 14). This chapter will analyze the racial implications of student–teacher interactions and how such relationships are leveraged to socialize youth into expecting and reciprocating nice behavior at school.

Before the analysis, it is important to take into account context: K–12 schools in America and the institution of education are heavily influenced by Whites and their shared generational norms. Seeing how the earliest and most influential educational institutions in the United States "were shaped by middle- and upper-class European American men" without interruption until the late 1960s and early 1970s, it is safe to say that "European American norms, ideas, and theories about education are deeply embedded" in the majority of existing educational institutions (Simpson 2003, 127). Even in the modern era, over 82 percent of all public school teachers and over 88 percent of all private school teachers are White, according to data analysis provided by the National Center for Education Statistics (2013).

As "the elementary and secondary educator workforce is still overwhelmingly homogenous" in favor of Whites, according to the U.S. Department of Education (2016, 15), what often goes overlooked is how our nation's educational socialization process is essentially a socialization process into Whiteness. Similarly, any exploration of Niceness in our nation's schools is by default an interrogation of Whiteness. Hence, when "our" students are being socialized within formal school settings, such training and conditioning is based largely on a historic, systemic, and institutionalized White frame of reference, being, and understanding.

It follows that if the education system, as normally run, supports White primacy, then being "nice" merely supports this structure. Pollock (2008, 52) notes that "students are rewarded or punished in education . . . by the simple fact of belonging to a particular racialized group." Pollock reminds researchers that multiple life metrics as affected by race outside school will invariably affect how students perform within a scholastic context—so much so that Pollock (2008, 52–53) has argued that even within an unequal system, "'nice' people can accept and even distribute . . . unfair rewards and punishments."

In other words, "nice" is the polite, willful, superficial suspension of a deeper understanding of this conflict. Many people know that the institution of education has had an explicitly racially problematic beginning, and that many racially destructive policies and philosophies have been actively maintained over the centuries. Yet Alemán (2009) convincingly asserts that being "respectful," "polite," or "nice" in not acknowledging the darker chapters of education's past can serve to silence the voices most desperate to be heard.

Nice to Know

Yet when we consider the generally understood proposition of Niceness, there is likely no other arena where individuals are supposed to be more nice to one another than inside our elementary school classrooms. While not professionally required as a requisite for employment per se, Niceness is often a coveted hallmark of a desired educator. Teachers, as a general rule and especially as a White cultural norm, epitomize Niceness (Bramen 2017, 284). Unlike a delivery person, whose mood and temperament are less relevant to job performance, implicit in becoming a teacher is the unspoken assumption that one will be a *nice* teacher. In other words, many teachers are socialized, trained, and conditioned early in their careers to engage in a style and manner that is "nice" so that they may hopefully be more effective. This concept is fundamental, as many of our nation's mostly White teaching staff does not intentionally try to be mean to students, especially along racial lines. The issue is that with a majority of White teachers present, the entire school environment will most likely be operated by a "White racial frame." Feagin (2013, 14) informs us that such framing emerges when Whites are in control, and it includes "deep emotions, visual images, and the accented sounds of spoken language. Powerful emotions, deep negative feelings, about Americans of color frequently shape how Whites behave and interact," often without any conscious or deliberate action required.

Harris (1993) eloquently argues that Whiteness can actually be viewed as a proprietary right, stemming from the country's origins in taking as property lands already inhabited by Native Americans, and then by "employing" or deploying enslaved Africans as chattel to work and develop these same confiscated lands. In transferring this property right to subsequent generations, many Whites through their educational institutions have consistently obtained broad and positive messaging about their race while simultaneously acquiring broadly negative stereotypes about people of color. In other words, while Whites are not constructively or systematically taught racist ideologies that explicitly prioritize White life at the expense of marginalized people of color, Whites as a collective group nonetheless still learn similar narratives that help them arrive at the same point. Whiteness can be seen as taking on property qualities based on its ability to elicit consistently similar systematic responses along the lines of a "dog whistle" or a "metaphor that pushes us to recognize that modern racial pandering always operates on two levels: inaudible and easily denied in one range, yet stimulating strong reactions in the other" (Lopez 2014, 3). Given the consistent paucity of diversity at the instructor level, cultural norms shared at most schools may generally adhere to those norms commonly shared by Whites. These White teachers may not view themselves as deliberately enacting an agenda to push across "White norms" per se, but in attempting to teach, they will mostly teach what they know. Whiteness is "invisible" (Dyer 1997, 45) and therefore is regarded as "normal," but to a non-White child a distinct difference may be readily discernible early in one's development (Diller 2011, 118).

Thus, this chapter will contain three distinct examples of teachers enforcing Niceness that when put together have implications for understanding Niceness as a mechanism to ironically facilitate inequities for students of color, with the end result being that defending Niceness is actually defending Whiteness to the detriment of all students involved. In other words, we will explore the irony that "being nice" may not really be nice at all.

'Tis Not Nice to Stare

One unique case that illustrates the hazards of not being nice in school comes from Glendale, Ohio. In September 2014, three elementary school students at the private Catholic institution St. Gabriel Consolidated School played a "staring game" whereby they each had to stare at the other without blinking. The three students consisted of two boys and one girl. One boy identified as Black while the other identified as White, and the girl was Asian. It was the Asian female student who complained about the boys' conduct the following day (Grasha 2015).

The story made national headlines because the school handed out suspensions for kids engaging in an activity that is not typically considered dangerous. The

Archdiocese of Cincinnati issued a statement indicating that the Black boy's actions "intimidated the female student and made her feel uncomfortable" (Jones 2015).

The mother of the Black boy, Candice Tolbert, disagreed with her son's suspension and eventually filed a lawsuit to overturn the school's disciplinary action; ultimately, her suit was unsuccessful (WKRC-TV 2016). While the mainstream news media framed the case as a "racial issue," the Black boy's parents nonetheless insisted that their cause was one of due process. The staring incident occurred on Monday, the girl involved made her complaint on Tuesday, and by Tuesday afternoon the school issued its suspension and had the Black boy writing an apology letter. However, the Black boy's parents heard of the problem and the punishment on Wednesday.

It is important to note that another White boy was also disciplined for his involvement in the exact same incident, buttressing the school's claim that race was not a factor. The student handbook clearly listed as grounds for suspension any student "whose presence possesses a continuing danger to persons or property or an ongoing threat of disrupting academic learning" (WLWT-TV 2015). The fact that an Asian girl complained does not alter the analysis significantly insofar that it may appear to be a "minority on minority" case, but given existing narratives that Asians are model minorities triangulated between Blacks and Whites (Kim 1999), the Asian girl's feelings may have been taken seriously only insofar as they were viewed as close to the feelings of White children as a collective group. Even still, with the incident taken on face value alone, the school officials have an unassailable point that the matter was simply disciplinary and not discriminatory. Against the historical backdrop of historically disproportionate rates of Black male suspensions and expulsions, however, this result may require more scrutiny (U.S. Department of Education, n.d.).

In light of high school pranks and hijinks carried out annually by White students that are often viewed as a rite of passage (Associated Press 2012), staring appears to be low on the list of egregious violations. While it would be improper to deny the Asian girl's feelings of intimidation, suspension at this early age may also deny a learning opportunity for all involved.

The full history is unclear, but the general quest for objectivity cannot curtail common sense. Provided that this was the first such incident (and court papers do not indicate that this staring game was part in a longer line of intimidating acts), the suspension on its face is questionable. If the staring was uncomfortable for the student who complained, perhaps a teachable moment was possible to help the offending boys learn and understand the limits of personal space. Yes, it is important for the young men to learn to "play nice," but a suspension for characterizing staring as "a continuing danger" is, perhaps, not nice. Without additional data, it is difficult to conceptualize a brief elementary school stare with no physical contact as a continuing danger. Unless, of course, it is easy to conceptualize the *perpetrator* as a continuing danger.

Naughty or Nice?

The next case comes by way of Brooklyn, New York, in the fall of 2014. A first-grade minority student at the Success Academy charter school was seated in a circle inside Ms. Charlotte Dial's classroom. The teacher was reviewing math problems on an easel and asked the child to complete a task. Apparently after not hearing the answer she desired, Ms. Dial ripped up the student's worksheet and yelled for her to go to the "calm-down chair" and sit. Visibly agitated, Ms. Dial asks another child to complete the problem while cajoling the ejected student: "You're confusing everybody." As the bewildered child dejectedly left the circle, Ms. Dial continued to huff, "There's nothing that infuriates me more than when you don't do what's on your paper" (Taylor 2016).

This incident came to light insofar as it was surreptitiously recorded by a teacher's aide who was also in the classroom. The aide released the video after she left the school out of concern for a growing pattern of not-nice conduct, or "daily harsh treatment of the children" (Taylor 2016).

While all teachers are not alike and all teaching styles do not have to conform to a "soft and cuddly" approach, by most accounts any observer watching the video can safely conclude that the teacher's conduct in the video was not "nice." Yet ten days later the teacher was back on the job. The child's mother initially supported the school, but she changed her mind once she learned of Ms. Dial's return to the classroom. The mother eventually withdrew her child from the school because she felt the teacher's conduct was not only not nice but also potentially destructive for her young child's psyche. Even college football coaches have come under scrutiny for yelling and berating players in public. A first-grade student is likely all the more vulnerable.

Here the story made headlines as well. But the mother of the student involved was incensed because she felt that most of the attention was targeted toward defending the honor of the good teacher who simply had a bad moment. The principal of the Success Charter School, Eva S. Moskowitz, defended the teacher. Other parents defended the teacher. Other teachers defended the teacher. But the question remains: Who defended the child?

The principal, Ms. Moskowitz, who is also a White woman, claimed that Ms. Dial simply lost her cool because she "so desperately wants her kids to succeed and to fulfill their potential." While it is nice for the principal to support her dedicated faculty and staff, it is equally as important to support general principles of not intentionally exposing students to "embarrassment or disparagement."

It is impossible to accurately speculate, but the imagination can run wild as to how such a scenario would play out if a Black teacher were to yell at and berate a White first-grade child, ripping up his or her paper in the process. But the hypothetical would only be complete if the entire educational environment were the same—meaning, if the Black teacher was flanked by a majority Black teaching staff, a Black principal, and a majority Black parent base. In other words, what perhaps may never be accurately measured or assessed is whether the behavior of the teacher is likely "explained" and "given the benefit of the doubt" (at least initially) because the teacher's identity was White and shrouded and protected under the auspices of niceness. For other teachers, this not-so-nice conduct could have easily been a deal-breaker.

Nice Knowing Ya!

Finally, let us consider an example from the state of Arizona. This case involves a teacher leveraging her position to instruct students how to be nice to one another. Several other adults disagreed, resulting in the teacher losing her job, although she claims she did not "mean" any harm.

Pamela Aister, a seventy-year-old fourth-grade teacher and twenty-five-year veteran of the Fountain Hills Unified School District, was monitoring student recess in May 2014 when she noticed a verbal altercation among six students. On closer inspection, Aister saw that five students were "ganging up" on one lone student. As an elementary school teacher, immediate internal alarm bells sounded, as this social dynamic violates every social convention of Niceness, politeness, and proper social decorum.

No twenty-five-year veteran was going to let this moment pass without seizing the opportunity to transform it into a "teachable moment"—meaning, how the teacher could take undesirable conduct and turn it into an example of positive reinforcement for conduct that is desired. In this case, the teacher wanted the conduct to stop and then wanted the five offending children to begin feeling empathy for the isolated student so that such an incident would not be repeated again.

Aister walked over and placed her arm around the victim and stated, "He's in my room now. He's not alone anymore. If you're picking on him, you're picking on me" (Phoenix New Times, 2014). By signaling that the lone boy was no longer isolated, the collective sense of responsibility then shifted back to the five teasing boys to reconsider their treatment of someone who is no longer "othered" but is considered "accepted."

Ideally, as most students are socialized to respect authority figures, and in this case especially with a six-decade age difference between them and their teacher, this should have been signal enough to the young men that the incident was resolved

What's the Mean of Nice School Interactions? 9

now that an authority figure on the school grounds had interrupted their conduct and had both acknowledged and addressed it. Ideally, the teacher's general statement against picking on people would have resonated with complementary home training the students received about how to be nice and how to treat one another. Ideally.

As it so happens, the five students apparently complained to their parents about being disciplined. Their parents, obviously concerned about their children having a nice elementary school experience, went back to school officials and complained. To make a long story short, less than six months later Pamela Aister lost her job.

But, with most of these cases, there is more to the story. How does a seventy-year-old woman and twenty-five-year teaching veteran lose her job? Aister did not yell, did not engage in vitriolic name-calling, did not deliver a physical strike at any time; nor did she stare menacingly or rip up anybody's schoolwork in front of a group of peers. Nevertheless, at a subsequent October 2014 disciplinary hearing where Aister's termination was upheld, the hearing officer listened to testimony from four of the five "bullying boys" in addition to testimony from the victim himself before ultimately siding with the larger group. The hearing officer found that Aister was "heavy-handed and unprofessional, and she did not make the well-being of students the fundamental value of her decision making." The offense Aister committed was that she "engaged in verbally abusive and threatening conduct." (Phoenix New Times, 2014).

On a scale of 1 to 10, with 10 representing the most egregious violations of student–teacher conduct relations, many or most will agree this lone incident as described thus far likely does not land on the upper end of the scale. But yet, Aister was terminated despite traditional contractual safeguards that usually make it difficult to fire teachers (Eltman 2008). Perhaps some more background information may assist. This May 2014 incident was not the first time that Aister's "tough talking ways" were called into question; in 2011 Aister was placed on an improvement plan after her student interactions were deemed to be "negative, demeaning, sarcastic, or inappropriate," and in 2013 she had to meet with the school principal after a student cried after she reprimanded him in front of the class (Phoenix New Times, 2014). These two incidents combined with the "bullying boys" incident suggest that Aister had accrued detractors over her "tough love" style over the years and that this latest incident had enough teeth to finally embarrass her. Aister had in fact built a solid reputation over the years and presented to the hearing officer a petition signed with no fewer than 120,000 signatures, which included plenty of White supporters, seeing how the town of Fountain Hills is over 94 percent White (Phoenix New Times, 2014).

One final detail: one of the "bullying boys" reported that before Aister told his offending group to stop and go away, she told one young man to watch his back and that her intervention "should cure his racist ways" (Phoenix New Times, 2014). Racist ways?

Yes. Aister, as an elderly White female, had intervened after seeing five White males cornering and verbally abusing one, lone African American male—one of only three in the whole school.

Racism does not sound nice. But according to the victim, Malacai Washington, the other five boys (whose names have not been disclosed) made his life at Four Peaks Elementary School "hell on Earth." Washington had been called several racial epithets, including "nigger," "bitch," "monkey ears," and "crackhead" many times before, as well as on that fateful May day.

Ironically, the racially insulting name-calling was not in dispute at the hearing. Thus, when the hearing officer cited the "well-being of students" in her decision, she might as well have said the "well-being of *White* students," as the well-being of an isolated Black victim racially bullied by five White students appeared to factor little into her decision-making. Instead the hearing officer appeared more concerned with Aister's conduct and whether *she herself* was nice enough to the offending bullies. The ultimate disposition of the victim was overlooked. Ironically, Aister intervened because students under her care were not being nice to one another.

In essence, what started off as an intentional act to help a victim of racial bullying led to a vastly different outcome whereby the victimizers ultimately became the final victims within the overarching White racial frame embedded in the school. Worse, what began as a clear racial issue between five White students and one Black one morphed into a political power issue between one elderly White teacher and five sets of younger White parents.

Nevertheless, what unfortunately was overlooked in all of this were the actual feelings of the victim. Despite well-intentioned efforts by White institutional actors to be "fair," within the Whiteness frame the question becomes what, ultimately, the impact on the isolated individual of color was. In 2015, Pixar made an animated movie entitled *Inside Out* that was a phenomenal box office hit. The entire movie revolved around one young White girl and her competing, internal feelings; in fact, her feelings were so important that the entire ninety-four minutes of the movie focused on preserving, valuing, and respecting them. Yet what about this young Black boy in Arizona? His testimony was essentially devalued and invalidated. The hearing officer noted that the principal "also had seen" Malacai Washington be verbally aggressive toward other students in an effort to equate aggressive language with racist language. In other words, Washington—the isolated victim, one of only three Black males in the entire school, and with nothing but words to defend himself—was cast as nullifying any potential emotional damage sustained because he "talked back." Questions abound as to why the principal did not, on observing Washington, stop and inquire to determine whether he was in fact being verbally aggressive or emotionally responsive because others were being racially abusive.

This lack of inquiry was the same rationale used by the hearing officer when articulating Aister's dismissal. The teacher was found to have "failed to ask questions about what actually occurred that day, instead believing that the confrontation was racially motivated based on past incidents. That belief was false" (Phoenix New Times, 2014). Within the Whiteness frame, a "normal" belief may very well be one that is devoid of any overarching, cutting racial critique, as such an approach would not be "nice" to focus on in the name of concentrating on other matters as they are prioritized by other White institutional actors. Hence the hearing officer, as part of the (invisible, yet influential) White racial frame, found it difficult to see racism as a stand-alone explanation of causation. The hearing officer, likely unfamiliar with overt and obvious instances of racism, was unable or unwilling to contextualize the verbal epithets delivered by the group of five as racially problematic. Due to the premium of time, this chapter will not take care to explain the historically consistent disparaging use of "monkey" or "nigger" to denigrate Black identity. If anything, the five White students demonstrated that they have been socialized within the White racial frame accordingly, whereby they not only know of racial epithets but also apparently have *learned* how to use them *appropriately* to disparage or demean another person of color. Such catchphrases were not unwittingly nor spontaneously blurted out during a session of show-and-tell. Where they were learned is unknown. But what is indisputable is that they indeed were learned. Due to the invisibility of Whiteness and Niceness, many Whites face difficulty recognizing more nuanced, subtle, suave, and sophisticated manifestations of ideological narratives that are not as racially explicit but are just as equally problematic (Gooding 2016, 5).

This is where confusion abounds. How does the hearing officer know that such racial accusations are false? This is where Niceness and Whiteness combine to create blindness and unkindness. If Washington was in fact not just ostracized for having holes in his shoes but instead for his visibly identifiable racial identity, then surely some type of consequence is appropriate.

And yet, when the White, racist bully went home and told his White mother about the incident, she was shocked and hurt—not about Washington's feelings or her possible failure as a mother to better educate her own son about not engaging in socially destructive behavior, but about the very insinuation that her son could have engaged in racist behavior. In other words, provided Washington is not fabricating his story of racial harassment, and allowing for the fact that Aister validated his story and existence by witnessing five White boys corner a Black boy and then stopped the inappropriate treatment (which was "not nice," to say the least), there would be no need for this chapter. At issue, however, is not the racist behavior of students not treating another student nicely, but whether the racists themselves were treated nicely enough throughout the process. More alarming is that the hearing officer found that Aister "did not accord the [bullying] students the dignity and respect they deserved" (Phoenix New Times, 2014).

Yet Aister walked over and instinctively felt empathy for the victimized student. Wanting to salvage his dignity and respect, she placed her arm around the young man and stated, "He's in my room now. He's not alone anymore. If you're picking on him, you're picking on me." This symbolic move was meant to signal to the five White boys that although they (and the Black boy) recognized on some instinctive level that the Black boy was outnumbered (in every sense of the word, considering the racial composition of the school), this elderly White woman, as part of the White racial frame, was purposely targeting the Black boy for inclusion. If the White students had accorded Washington such dignity and respect, then perhaps Four Peaks Elementary School would be a nicer environment for learning.

This case raises several questions. First, when is it appropriate and fair to label conduct as racist, and does reticence to do so privilege White offenders over victims? Second, how can school officials address presumptively racist conduct if the White racial frame is generally resistant to labeling anything as racist? Twenty-five years of teaching instinct ought to count for something. Aister observed a hostile situation and sought to intervene. If the teacher had yelled at the bullying boys to "shut the hell up," then this inappropriate verbal command could easily have been addressed. Less facile, however, is getting down to the root of how a team of fourth graders "instinctually" know to isolate a victim and "appropriately" levy contextually sophisticated and historically based insults such as "nigger," "monkey," and "crackhead." Third, if school officials label and address conduct on the part of certain students as racist, what about the buy-in from home? Clearly in Aister's case, the parents of the "bullying victims" felt that Aister was not being nice in how she addressed their children—so much so that they filed a complaint, which triggered an investigation and subsequent disciplinary hearing. There is the old question, If a tree falls in the forest and no one is there to hear it, does it actually make a sound? Following on those lines, does racist conduct occur in our classrooms if parents flat out refuse to acknowledge it? This case, while rooted in Niceness, speaks to a larger question of who has permission to teach about racism. Racism is, perhaps, viewed as more private than sex education. Yet learning about racism is nonetheless taking place.

For instance, Aister saw racist, not-so-nice behavior and intervened. Six months later she was out of a job and the victim was out of the school, while the five White offending students still continued on, their lives relatively unperturbed because their mothers successfully rallied the White racial frame to ensure that their children were treated in a fair and "nice" manner by school officials. While observers may casually say that the five White boys "may not have learned anything" from their experience, this may also be incorrect. *The boys in fact did learn.* They learned that their White racial frame holds power, and their parents exerted this power to manipulate the system in their favor. And they shall likely grow up to do the same one day. While it is inaccurate to state that the five bullying boys learned how to be racist and spout vile and vicious verbal epithets at an isolated victim within a formal classroom setting, they are indeed learning how to be racist through *socialization* within the White racial frame. These youth are learning the limits and consequences of their actions. Here the limitations and consequences for racial name-calling were minimal, and it is therefore likely that this incident will have a minimal effect in changing their behavior. The five White boys learned that they do not have to be nice to Black boys. The boys learned the value of their mothers' White power within a White-dominated and -operated system. More distressing, they learned firsthand that the words they spouted were powerful and true—Blacks are truly less than Whites, at least in the White racial frame in which they live.

Meanwhile, the lesson for Malacai Washington is that if your own words and the words of an older, White sympathetic teacher are inadequate as protection, perhaps you learn to just live with the indignity or leave.

Nicely Put

This chapter highlights three cases from different parts of the country—the Midwest, Northeast, and Southwest. All three cases collectively suggest that the politics of Niceness mask the political reality of meanness against non-White children in a variety of school settings. Additionally, all three cases illustrate how Niceness differentially polices depending on one's position and on context. The facts speak for themselves: When non-Whites engage in behavior adjudged as "not nice" within majority White school settings, swift and severe consequences often follow. The young man at St. Gabriel Consolidated School was suspended immediately because his staring behavior was deemed not to be nice and was classified as a "danger." An appeals court upheld the punishment despite less severe consequences available to help instruct the twelve-year-old boy.

Similarly, when a young first-grade student is not performing nicely, her White teacher has the audacity and authority to berate and demean the child publicly, only to receive public support from her White principal and larger school community. Although all agree that the teacher's conduct was unbecoming, or "not nice," explanations and justifications suddenly abound to mitigate the mean behavior exhibited by the White teacher. Finally, when a young Black male is racially targeted and cornered by five of his peers, the not-so-nice behavior of the boys takes a backseat to the primary issue of whether the intervening teacher was nice enough in her correction of the original offending behavior. Ironically, the bullying boys' mothers were able to successfully use racism as a defense. Because racism is considered such an uncomfortable and touchy subject to Whites within a White-dominated and -operated school environment that equates Niceness with Whiteness, extra care and caution should be used before violating protocols of Niceness in labeling someone or their behavior as racist. In fact, more care was taken to protect the feelings of the racist bullies than the actual victim of the racist behavior, and the victimizers became the victims. More tragically, Black interiority (Mitchell and Taylor 2009, 71) is ignored again and mean, embarrassing, or demeaning behavior can continue against non-Whites because no one has to be nice to someone to whom they have no connection or obligation.

In review, all students are socialized along a White racial frame given the historical and current demographic dominance of Whites within education apparatuses nationwide. This White racial frame interprets Niceness in favor of Whites, even when Whites engage in conduct that is far from nice. As a result, all students learn the power and value of Whiteness—as they are supposed to given education's dual responsibility of providing specialized instruction inside the classroom and extended socialization outside the test-taking activities that only make up a small portion of the K–12 school experience. Lesson learned: 'Tis nice to be White.

In conclusion, these cases bring to mind a quotation from a school official who responded to a bona fide racial controversy at Charter Oak High School in Covina, California. Nine Black students discovered on the day yearbooks were handed out (which was also the last day of school) that their official names were altered without their permission as a "prank." The result was that they received "ghettoized names." As a corrective measure, the victimized Charter Oak students were provided stickers containing their correctly spelled names to hand out to other students to paste in their yearbooks—*if they so chose.*

This result differs markedly from that of an event that occurred at Desert Vista High School in Arizona, where school officials literally decided to glue together carefully planned and sanctioned yearbook pages recounting the infamous incident whereupon six White female students spelled out "NI**ER" in gold lettering on their T-shirts (ABC15.com 2016). The photo prank went viral and raised the requisite debates about free speech and the music genre of hip-hop not shouldering enough responsibility for the popularity of the offending epithet. At Desert Vista, school officials well within the White racial frame were sympathetic to student and parent complaints that the planned two-page recap of the internationally reported event would not be a nice look for the school, as it would potentially open old wounds—not, however, that the offending photo itself enlarged any existing wounds. In other words, the reminder of the racist event would offend the socialization of Niceness or Whiteness inculcated within the White racial framework of the affluent, majority White Phoenix suburb of Ahwatukee. As such, the institutional White framework of the majority White school took initiative and invested resources in protecting the fragile psyches of the White offenders and bystanders who might have been adversely affected from rehashing past embarrassment. Conversely, at Charter Oak, as the Black yearbook victims were outside the White racial frame, the students had to individually shoulder the responsibility of managing the damage of a prank of which they were victim. The ethical duty to correct the "ghettoized" yearbook names was not *a problem*; rather, it was a *Black problem* ironically not visible within the already invisible White racial frame.

What's the Mean of Nice School Interactions?   15

Thus, it is of little surprise that Niceness is primarily reserved for Whiteness within our nation's schools.

After all, Joseph Probst, the president of the Charter Oak Unified School District, summarized the hopeless dynamic non-Whites must learn within a White-dominated and -operated educational system. *Hopeless* is employed as a modifying descriptor only because Blacks and Whites alike are seemingly aware of their inability to change or alter a system not designed to teach true principles of equality anytime soon. "What else can you do?" Probst said. "It would be nice to snap a magic finger, but I think [the replacement sticker solution] was incredibly well done" (Associated Press 2008).

Snap a magic finger? Sounds nice.

References

ABC15.com. 2016, May 6. "Article over Desert Vista High School Racial Slur Controversy Prompts Yearbook Change." ABC15.com. http://www.abc15.com /news/region-phoenix-metro/ahwatukee/article-over-desert-vista-high-school -racial-slur-controversy-prompts-yearbook-change.

Alemán, E. 2009. "Through the Prism of Critical Race Theory: 'Niceness' and Latina/o Leadership in the Politics of Education." *Journal of Latinos and Education* 8, no. 4: 290–311.

Associated Press. 2008, June 27. "Blacks Given 'Ghetto' Names in SoCal Yearbook." Fox News. http://www.foxnews.com/story/2008/06/27/blacks-given -ghetto-names-in-socal-yearbook.html.

Associated Press. 2012, June 6. "Senior Pranks— Where Do You Draw the Line?" Fox News. http://www.foxnews.com/us/2012/06/06/senior-pranks-where -do-draw-line.html.

Bramen, C. T. 2017. *American Niceness: A Cultural History.* Cambridge, Mass.: Harvard University Press.

Diller, J. V. 2011. *Cultural Diversity: A Primer for the Human Services.* 4th ed. Belmont, Calif.: Cengage Learning.

Dyer, R. 1997. *White: Essays on Race and Culture.* New York: Routledge.

Eltman, F. 2008, June 30. "Firing Tenured Teachers Isn't Just Difficult, It Costs You." *USA Today.* http://usatoday30.usatoday.com/news/education/2008–06–30 -teacher-tenure-costs_N.htm.

Feagin, J. 2013. *The White Racial Frame: Centuries of Racial Framing and Counter-framing.* New York: Routledge.

Gooding, F. W., Jr. 2016. *You Mean, There's RACE in My Sports? The Complete Guide for Understanding Race and Sports in Mainstream Media.* Silver Spring, Md.: On the Reelz.

Grasha, K. 2015, October 6. "Suspension Upheld in School 'Staring' Case." Cincinnati.com. http://www.cincinnati.com/story/news/2015/10/06/st-gabriels -suspension-upheld/73481764/.

Harris, C. I. 1993. "Whiteness as Property." *Harvard Law Review* 106, no. 8: 1713–24.

Jones, H. G. 2015, October 6. Extreme Punishment? Boy's Suspension Story Goes Viral." WKRC-TV. http://local12.com/news/local/extreme-punishment -boy39s-suspension-story-goes-viral.

Kim, C. J. 1999, March. "The Racial Triangulation of Asian Americans." *Politics and Society* 27, no. 1: 105–38.

Lopez, I. H. 2014. *Dog Whistle Politics: How Coded Racial Appeals Have Reinvented Racism and Wrecked the Middle Class.* Oxford: Oxford University Press.

Mitchell, A., and D. K. Taylor, eds. 2009. *The Cambridge Companion to African American Women's Literature.* Cambridge: Cambridge University Press.

National Center for Education Statistics, U.S. Department of Education. 2013, August. *Characteristics of Public and Private Elementary and Secondary School Teachers in the United States: Results from the 2011–12 Schools and Staffing Survey.* Washington, D.C.: U.S. Department of Education. https://nces.ed.gov /pubs2013/2013314.pdf.

Phoenix New Times. 2014, October 23. "Teacher Claims She Was Fired for Defending Student against Racist Bullying." http://digitalissue.phoenixnew times.com/publication/index.php?i=230143&m=0&l=&p=8&pre=&ver=html 5#{%22page%22:%228%22,%22issue_id%22:230143}.

Pollock, M. 2008. *Everyday Antiracism: Getting Real about Race in School.* New York: New Press.

Simpson, J. S. 2003. *I Have Been Waiting: Race and U.S. Higher Education.* Toronto: University of Toronto Press.

Spring, J. 2016. *American Education.* New York: Routledge.

Taylor, K. 2016, February 12. "At Success Academy School, a Stumble in Math and a Teacher's Anger on Video." *New York Times.* https://www.nytimes.com /2016/02/13/nyregion/success-academy-teacher-rips-up-student-paper .html?_r=0.

U.S. Department of Education. n.d. "School Climate and Discipline: Know the Data." U.S. Department of Education. https://www2.ed.gov/policy/gen/guid /school-discipline/data.html.

U.S. Department of Education. 2016. *The State of Racial Diversity in the Educator Workforce.* Washington, D.C.: U.S. Department of Education. https:// www2.ed.gov/rschstat/eval/highered/racial-diversity/state-racial-diversity-work force.pdf.

WKRC-TV. 2016, March 14. "Court Rejects Family's Lawsuit after Son Suspended from School for Staring." WKRC-TV. http://local12.com/news/local /court-rejects-familys-lawsuit-after-son-suspended-from-school-for-staring.

WLWT-TV. 2015, October 1. "Staring Showdown Leads to Student Being Suspended, Lawsuit." WLWT-TV. http://www.wlwt.com/article/staring -showdown-leads-to-student-being-suspended-lawsuit/3558501.

2

"It's Not That Easy!"

Foundations of Niceness in Enacting
Multicultural and Social Justice Education

JIA-HUI STEFANIE WONG

Upon entering the building, Chestnut High School's commitment to diversity and equity was quickly visible.[1] Just inside the entrance, signs painted on the wall welcome visitors in English, Hmong, and Spanish. Asian, Black, Latinx, and White students passed each other on their way to classrooms where teachers displayed decor related to social justice, including "Safe Space" signs indicating support for the LGBTQIA community, posters with quotes from activists like James Baldwin and Malcolm X, and artwork with the phrase "Migration Is Beautiful." During lessons, teachers—who are mostly White and of the middle class—discussed inequity and injustice with some frequency. It was not uncommon to see students wearing "Black Lives Matter" T-shirts or encouraging their peers to be politically active. In many ways, Chestnut High School embodied much of what progressive scholars hope to see in schools. Indeed, many educators at Chestnut engaged in practices advocated by scholars of multicultural education (Banks 2014; Sleeter and Grant 2008), which is particularly striking given persistent attacks on multicultural education (May and Sleeter 2010).

Yet a growing body of literature also emphasizes that even schools with commitments to equity are failing to achieve these goals. Rather, good intentions and commitments to being *nice* have facilitated the persistence of inequity in schools (Castagno 2014; Lewis and Diamond 2015). In this chapter, I define practices of Niceness as those that seek to maintain feelings of kindness and agreeableness, to maintain neutrality and balance, and/or to avoid ruffling feathers and creating uncomfortable or controversial situations. Among teachers, Niceness often manifests as a hesitance to discuss issues of inequality and oppression (Castagno 2008; Pollock 2004). Yet not all teachers shy away from engaging in social justice work and instead strive to discuss systemic inequalities in their classrooms. These are topics that typically are not considered nice or polite. As many communities struggle to address persistent educational inequities, schools engaging in some social justice practices are of particular interest. But, as data from Chestnut High School illustrates, such practices are not a silver bullet for challenging oppression in schools.

Despite some efforts to embrace multicultural education, Chestnut also reinforced systems of inequity and injustice. School events largely centered more privileged students; for example, the homecoming pep rally read like a celebration of Whiteness, as several predominantly White sports teams ran into the gym to much fanfare and two mostly White dance groups performed to a medley of popular songs. Educators taught about systemic injustice, but these lessons did not always resonate with all students, and especially not those who are marginalized. These students put their heads down during discussions about mass incarceration or police brutality and complained that the lessons are boring or that they already knew about the topics. Chestnut High School thus reveals some tensions and contradictions in what it means to teach about inequity and social justice to diverse student bodies.

This chapter explores how educational practices can appear to disrupt traditional practices of Niceness in some ways, yet actually continue to engage Niceness in other ways. I argue that schools can challenge systems of power and privilege—which is often seen as *not-nice* behavior—in ways that are still rooted in Niceness. That is, educators continue to engage in practices that avoid conflict and uncomfortable conversations. Educators' explicit desire to challenge inequalities represents some important first steps in dismantling oppression, especially in a political context in which the norms of civility and politeness have been rejected by elected officials. I argue, however, that such commitments are not enough, and it is partially through Niceness that systems of oppression remain in place.

I first provide an overview of the theoretical concepts and bodies of literature on which I draw. I then describe the critical school ethnography that informs the chapter, and I provide a description of the Chestnut High School context. Next, I outline the following findings: (1) educators engage in some not-nice practices that challenge systemic inequities; (2) these practices nonetheless remain rooted in Niceness; (3) many students, especially those from nondominant backgrounds, are not drawn in by nice social justice lessons; and (4) educators' Niceness is sometimes leveraged for the benefit of marginalized students. I conclude by discussing the need to more deeply examine the power of Niceness and Whiteness if we are to better understand how and why inequity persists in schools and to meaningfully challenge systems of oppression.

A Conceptual Framework

This chapter builds on scholarship on critical Whiteness studies, Whiteness and Niceness in education, and multicultural and social justice education. Together these bodies of literature provide context for understanding how Niceness and Whiteness operate through well-meaning multicultural and social justice practices.

Critical Whiteness Studies

Critical Whiteness studies has its roots in the work of scholars of color like Du Bois (1935), who, in attempts to understand and explain racial inequality, turned the lens away from the deficiencies of people of color and onto the role that Whites play in racism. Whiteness studies is distinct from other approaches to race and ethnic studies because it includes the study of the dominant group (Doane 2003). The approach highlights that race and racism are relational. Through the lens of critical Whiteness studies, I am able to examine how systems of oppression award and maintain benefits for privileged groups, which helps explain their persistence.

Whiteness studies scholars emphasize that it is essential to examine Whiteness if we are to understand racial inequality (Doane 2003; Lipsitz 2006). Whiteness was created as a category in order to claim dominance; it is Whiteness that enables and justifies racism (Doane 2003; Giroux 1997; Mills 1997). Notably, Whiteness is understood not just as a category but as a system of racial hierarchy. The use of the terms *Whiteness* or *White supremacy* rather than *racism* is significant, because it names Whites as a group implicated in racism, and makes clear that benefits are conferred through the system (Leonardo 2009). That is, racism or White supremacy not only disadvantages people of color but also rewards Whites with real, material benefits (Du Bois 1935; Leonardo 2009). Because of these benefits, Whites have a possessive investment in Whiteness that allows White supremacy to persist (Lipsitz 2006). To maintain their advantages, Whites devote time and energy into sustaining the system of racial hierarchy. These efforts are undertaken even when Whites mean well (Leonardo 2009). Drawing on critical Whiteness studies in this chapter allows me to examine how well-meaning, social justice–oriented members of a diverse school community ultimately contribute to the perpetuation of White supremacy.

Niceness and Whiteness in Education

I also draw on the notions that Whiteness and Niceness are linked, and Whiteness is upheld through practices of Niceness. As Castagno writes, "A nice person is not someone who creates a lot of disturbance, conflict, controversy, or discomfort. Nice people avoid potentially uncomfortable or upsetting experiences, knowledge, and interactions. We do not point out failures or shortcomings in others but rather emphasize the good, the promise, and the improvement we see. Niceness compels us to reframe potentially disruptive or uncomfortable things in ways that are more soothing, pleasant, and comfortable" (2014, 9). McIntyre similarly describes how Whites' desire to maintain a "culture of niceness" (1997, 46) results in "white talk" that deflects their own roles in structural racism. Through nice talk and actions, the oppressive nature of structures of Whiteness and racism remains unchallenged, because to challenge it would create discomfort and conflict for Whites. Further-more, valuing Niceness allows practices that sustain systems of inequity to become individualized. Behaviors that are rooted in racism can be written off as thoughtless and unkind acts that are disconnected from larger ideologies. These individual actions are much easier to correct than to dismantle the systems that enable them, and thus are much more comfortable problems to confront.

Many scholars have explored how teachers often struggle to understand the complexities and structural dimensions of racism and other inequities. Instead they draw on dominant ways of understanding oppression, such as individualizing explanations for inequality (Abu El-Haj 2006; King 1991). Many teachers fear that explicitly talking about race is racist (Lewis 2003; Pollock 2004), an attitude that is not uncommon in the United States (Bonilla-Silva 2014). When they do recognize racism, educators often fail to understand the ways in which power relations have made such disparities and hierarchies possible (Castagno 2014; Pollock 2004).

A growing body of literature points to the ways that commitments to White-ness and Niceness contribute to educators' struggles to fully engage with how oppression operates. By avoiding discussions of race and what they perceive as uncomfortable and controversial topics, teachers deflect responsibility away from themselves and maintain identities as good, nice, and effective educators—qualities that are also racialized as White (Castagno 2014; Marx 2006). The dedication to Whiteness persists even when educators express a commitment to multicultural-ism. While White teachers may be willing to discuss racial difference, they do so politely, without discussing power differentials, and thus ignore their own participa-tion and benefit from a system that perpetuates racial inequality (Castagno 2014; McIntyre 1997). Such discussions are examples of "White talk," which also enables them to maintain identities as nice. Scholars have also extended this notion of "White talk" and found that Whites in educational spaces who seek to interrogate Whiteness and racism still continue to engage in discourses of Whiteness (Haviland 2008; Hytten and Warren 2003). The lens of Whiteness thus helps to explain why, despite good intentions, efforts to engage multicultural and social justice education sometimes fall short.

Multicultural and Social Justice Education

The modern push for multicultural education developed in the 1960s with the civil rights movement, when activists pointed to the lack of representation of non-White histories, cultures, and knowledges in schools. Since then scholars have articulated and emphasized various goals of multicultural education. These goals include improving self-understanding and curricular relevance for students of color, addressing disparities in schooling, reducing discrimination, promoting understanding of multiple cultures, facilitating participation as global citizens, allowing students to analyze and critique racism and other forms of inequity, and empowering students to work for change and social justice (Banks 2014; Nieto and Bode 2012; Sleeter and Grant 2008).

Engaging in multicultural education is a multifaceted process that goes beyond simple additions to the curriculum and involves broader commitments to school transformation (Banks 2014; Sleeter and Grant, 2008). The complexity of multicultural education has sometimes been ignored, however, and the term has been co-opted and used in ways that scholars of multicultural education did not intend (Sleeter and McLaren 1995). In these iterations of "multicultural" education, schools emphasize more superficial celebrations of diversity, such as food, festivals, and fun (Banks 2014; Nieto and Bode, 2012). In response, some scholars have chosen different terms to reemphasize that they are articulating a vision for educational equity and justice; these have included *culturally relevant pedagogy* (Ladson-Billings 1995), *culturally sustaining pedagogy* (Paris and Alim 2014); *critical multiculturalism* (McLaren 1995), *multicultural social justice education* (Sleeter and Grant 2008), and *social justice education* (Ayers, Quinn, and Stovall 2009; Bell 2007). While each of these approaches draws on different theories and histories, they share a commitment to analyzing and dismantling systems of power in schools and beyond.

Overall, then, multicultural and social justice education emphasize the need to broaden conceptions of knowledge in classrooms, interrogate power and oppression, and work toward justice. I expand this body of literature by offering an example of a school where many educators seek to engage in this type of education.

Research Site and Methodology

Chestnut High School, located in a midsize Midwestern city, is a unique school. While schools across the nation remain racially and socioeconomically segregated (Orfield and Frankenberg 2014), Chestnut's student demographics stand out. The public high school's student population is about 40 percent White, 25 percent Black, 15 percent Latinx, 10 percent Asian, and 10 percent multiracial. Almost a quarter of students are English language learners, over half are from a low-income background, and about 20 percent are in special education. Mirroring national trends, the school's student population has become increasingly racially diverse in the past decade, but its teachers remain predominantly White.

Chestnut is also unique in the goals of its educators. While many teachers emphasize the importance of impartiality and neutrality in their roles (Hess and McAvoy 2015), Chestnut teachers are often explicit about their stances on controversial issues and recognize the need to challenge inequity. Given calls to recognize that teaching is always a political act (Apple 2013) and to infuse critical and social justice work into education (Sleeter and Grant 2008), schools like Chestnut, where educators are committed to these appeals, present important opportunities to gain deeper understandings of how such work plays out in schools.

This chapter draws on data collected as part of a larger study, a critical school ethnography that explores how both students and teachers make sense of persistent inequities and what it means to challenge them. Critical school ethnography enables researchers to see the complex processes involved in students' and teachers' everyday lived experiences at school, and to gain a nuanced understanding of the contexts and systems of power in which these experiences take place (Agar 1996; Castagno 2011; Madison 2005). Data collection for the larger study took place over sixteen months and included:

> **Participant observation in school and community spaces,** including classrooms, club meetings, the cafeteria, and relevant events.

> **Semistructured individual interviews** with students, teachers, and staff. I used purposeful sampling to obtain a diverse range of participants (e.g., across race, gender, and class). I conducted interviews with approximately forty students and twenty-five teachers and staff. Most interviews lasted about an hour.

> **Participant-created documents,** such as student work and class materials provided or created by teachers.

> **School, district, and state documents,** which provided context for school experiences and offered examples of how larger discourses were operating and shaping school life.

Data analysis started once data collection began (Miles and Huberman 1994). Early stages of analysis, which included coding, reflecting, and writing memorandums, informed the focus of subsequent data collection. I also engaged in member checks with participants and discussions with colleagues, which shed light on my understanding of the data. Initial rounds of analysis were inductive and deductive, drawing on extant theories and literature and allowing themes to emerge from the data. Subsequent rounds of analysis involved refining initial ideas and identifying patterns in the data in ways that enabled me to articulate their meanings.

Findings

I argue that at Chestnut High School, (1) educators engaged in some not-nice practices that facilitated some possibilities for challenging injustice; (2) even not-nice practices were rooted in Whiteness and Niceness; (3) students, especially those who were marginalized, resisted these practices of Niceness; and (4) educators' Niceness sometimes provided important support for marginalized students.

Not-Nice Practices

Although scholars have previously found that teachers and students often hesitate to discuss racism and other forms of inequality (Castagno 2014; Lewis 2003; Pollock 2004), Chestnut students and teachers discussed these topics regularly. It was not uncommon to hear references to racial disparities in incarceration rates, frustration about police shootings of unarmed Black men, or discussion about the underrepresentation of students of color in Chestnut's Advanced Placement and honors classes, among other topics. Such practices might be identified as *not-nice* behavior. These are topics are often seen as controversial, as impolite to discuss openly, especially in school.

At Chestnut, vocal support for social justice and marginalized communities was the norm. During the 2015–16 school year, two anti-immigrant bills were proposed in the state legislature. In response, a group of Latinx students at Chestnut organized students to march from the school to meet a larger protest coordinated by a community organization. School administrators were supportive of the students' efforts, even though the march and protest occurred during the school day, and many teachers happily posted flyers about the march in their classrooms. About three hundred Chestnut students assembled outside the school to join the march, and several school staff members assisted in the process. The group included about fifty students enrolled in advanced Spanish classes who attended as part of a field trip organized by some Spanish teachers. Despite the overtly political nature of this trip, the teachers received no pushback from students or parents.

In the same school year, Chestnut also instituted its first all-gender bathroom, and its prom court became gender-neutral. Both changes happened relatively uneventfully, with little explicit resistance within the school community. When proposed state legislation threatened all-gender bathrooms statewide, Chestnut's administrators vowed to maintain the one in their school. The commitment to maintaining a space that contributed to the safety of transgender and nonbinary students—even when doing so might violate state law—is one example of how Chestnut engaged in practices that might be classified as not nice.

The commitment to social justice also extended into classrooms. Many teachers wanted to develop in their students an awareness about issues of social justice, and they designed lessons accordingly. For example, I observed a lesson where social studies students read excerpts of Alexander's *The New Jim Crow* (2012) to learn about racial disparities in incarceration rates, an English class where students discussed racially diverse representation in the media in relation to Morrison's *The Bluest Eye* (1970), and a statistics lesson where students examined local data on graduation rates according to race, gender, and income and then discussed why disparities might exist. Many teachers also urged students to think about what it might mean to work to challenge inequalities. As social studies teacher Maggie Clemens said, "I want them to think of themselves as citizens that can do something to fix a problem or make a problem better, or fight for change, or fight . . . some injustice. I mean, if they learn that and get a little bit of that passion, to me, my job is done, you know?" The encouragement for challenging the status quo reflects beliefs that creating disruption and conflict was sometimes necessary in order to make societal changes.

Not-Nice Behavior Rooted in Niceness

Despite practices that were not nice in some respects, Chestnut continued to operate on a foundation of Niceness. Educators taught about systemic oppression, but did so in a *nice* way. Their lessons were typically made impersonal, filtered through the lens of articles or documentaries, all while eliding the fact that some of their students already had intimate understandings and experiences of injustice. Such experiences would have been uncomfortable to confront, so lessons about oppression were largely contained to the classroom and injustice was mostly discussed as if it affected other people. In this way, even conversations centered on social justice became relatively pleasant and nice.

Often it seemed that the imagined audience of social justice–oriented lessons was relatively privileged students. For example, social studies teacher Nicole Frasier showed her class a documentary that depicted the challenges facing families living in poverty. She recognized that there were students at Chestnut who lived in similar poverty and worried that the film might not be surprising to these students. Ms. Frasier thus demonstrated that she did know that some of her students would not have the same enlightening experience from watching the documentary as others. Yet she still emphasized the value of showing the film, telling me that many students didn't really know about issues of inequality.

After watching the documentary, mostly White, middle-class students participated in the class discussion. They commented that it made them sad that poor families couldn't get ahead even when they were trying hard. The lesson became an exercise in empathy for the individuals portrayed in the film, but it lacked any conversation about how or why these struggles might be connected to the lives of any students in the room. Absent these connections, even a lesson with some social justice aims of educating students about the structural challenges facing poor families became one that was mostly pleasant. Middle-class students were not forced to confront the uncomfortable reality that the families in the documentary could have been the families of some of their peers. Instead, the lesson positioned the issue of poverty as an abstract one and continued to place privileged students at the center.

Discussions about structural advantage and disadvantage, which can often be uncomfortable conversations, were also turned into polite and unobtrusive ones. Uncomfortable with the reality that some of their students were more privileged than others, teachers transformed lessons about systems of power into ones where all students were cast as equally able to talk about their own advantage or disadvantage. This tension was especially apparent during an English class where about half the students were White and the other half were students of color. On this day, teacher Jennifer Nagy, a White woman, introduced the class to McIntosh's piece about White privilege. Ms. Nagy began with a brief overview of the piece, defining "privilege" and highlighting the quote, "I was taught to see racism only in individual acts of meanness, not in invisible systems conferring dominance on my group" (McIntosh 1990, 31). The class then read McIntosh's article, including the list of privileges she has as a White person, after which Ms. Nagy asked students to individually write about the unearned advantages and disadvantages they had. There was little discussion among students about their responses.

It is certainly valuable for young people to reflect on the ways that power and privilege shape their lives, but the design of the lesson is puzzling given the racial demographics of the class. To ask a classroom that includes a dozen White students to read a piece detailing how White privilege operates and then reflect on their *disadvantages* serves to make White students feel more comfortable in the class. When questions are phrased to suggest that all students can equally contribute to conversations about structural advantage and disadvantage, students with relative privilege avoid feelings of discomfort. It is nicer and easier to discuss the issue if everyone can participate, if no group within the classroom is explicitly acknowledged as having more privilege. Furthermore, this approach deprioritizes the needs of students of color in learning about structural racism. Rather, the lesson is designed—perhaps unintentionally—with the needs of White students in mind. Their educational experience, as well as a value on having a balanced lesson, where all students could participate, were given the greatest weight. Thus, even in a classroom where systemic racism was recognized, Whiteness was still placed at the center.

When talking about how to challenge injustice, educators also centered Whiteness. Just after the election of Donald Trump, a Black student asked social studies teacher Cynthia Aldrich what she thought the election meant for race relations. In response, Ms. Aldrich, a White woman, told the class that she thought hate crimes would go up. A few weeks later, I followed up with Ms. Aldrich about this comment, asking if she had had any further discussion with her class about the issue. She replied that she was planning to talk to her students about how to be a good ally in this political climate, explaining that she hoped that she could help them know what to say when they saw something unjust, such as when students were being mean to each other. Similarly, in a conversation I had with teacher Kay Sutton (also a White woman) and two Latinx students, she told them that they should stand up when they saw something racist. It was important to call out racism if we want to fight back, she insisted. Both Ms. Aldrich and Ms. Sutton talked as if their students would be witnesses to harassment or violence, a more palatable situation than envisioning them as possible victims. Furthermore, neither addressed the fact that challenging oppression comes with risks—ones that individuals, particularly those who are marginalized, are not always able to take (Apple 2013; Loutzenheiser 2001).

While these examples are of lessons or interactions with individual teachers, I argue that this pattern persisted throughout the school, and was also informed by broader discourses and dominant ways of thinking. For example, after the protest against the anti-immigrant bills, teachers and students engaged in little discussion about the event, reasons for the protest, or ongoing struggles. They largely did not interrogate why anti-immigrant attitudes and policies persisted, how the Chestnut community might participate in their perpetuation, or how they might continue to challenge these injustices. Elena, a participant who was undocumented, felt that Chestnut's college-going culture marginalized her. She received little support for seeking scholarships open to undocumented students, was frustrated by constant reminders to students to complete Free Application for Federal Student Aid forms, and felt embarrassed when she chose to attend a less selective private college (that offered her a significant scholarship) over the prestigious state university (where she was ineligible for in-state tuition). Students and teachers were willing to speak out against unjust policies in the abstract, but did not fully examine the ways they were implicated in some of these policies. Elena's experience mirrors national, state, and local discourses and policies that render invisible the daily lives and struggles of undocumented immigrants (Gonzales 2016).

On the whole, Chestnut took a *nice* approach to teaching about inequality and social justice. While teachers and students would name structural inequity and oppression as problems, discussions about these issues remained pleasant. Leonardo and Porter (2010) have argued that Whites often talk about race and racism as abstract concepts without recognizing how racism creates everyday violence experienced by people of color. This dynamic played out at Chestnut. Relatively privileged students were not compelled to personally confront oppression or consider that the injustices they were learning about were part of daily life for marginalized individuals, including students they knew. This way of teaching about injustice avoided uncomfortable conversations. Lessons were designed with privileged students at the forefront, and with their comfort prioritized over the needs of more marginalized students. The failure to disrupt this way of teaching—even when the subject matter was about typically not-nice topics—remains a practice of Niceness.

Resisting Niceness

Many students, especially those from nondominant backgrounds, were not drawn in by nice social justice lessons. Rather, they saw how Chestnut's policies and practices still centered Whiteness while marginalizing students of color. They resisted this approach to teaching in a number of ways.

At times students refused to participate in classroom activities that they did not find meaningful. For example, during one English lesson, the class read about and discussed police brutality, particularly as it affected men of color. Many students were not particularly engaged; most did not volunteer to read aloud, and only a few contributed to the discussion. As the class packed up their belongings at the end of the period, I asked a Latinx student sitting near me if she was okay; she had spent most of the class with her head down on her desk or playing with her phone. She responded that she was fine. Wondering if she was put off by the matter-of-fact way of discussing the topic, I asked if it was just that she didn't want to talk about the issue. She shook her head and explained that she thought it was important, but it wasn't anything new. "I already know about it," she said, shrugging. This student's strategy for coping with a lesson that was not designed with her experiences in mind was to withdraw. Her oppositional behavior might be read as a lack of care about the lesson's content, but with her explanation, it was clearly more a rejection of the way the lesson was presented. This response mirrors other literature that illustrates how students sometimes determine that engaging with school is not worth the sacrifices to their identities and commitments (Tuck 2011; Valenzuela 1999).

Other students more subtly resisted supposed social justice lessons. During a history lesson that focused on how stereotypes affected government policies in the 1800s, Maggie Clemens showed a short video about stereotype threat. The clip described how being reminded of stereotypes could affect individuals' test performance, and provided experimental examples including women doing worse on a math test after viewing a commercial portraying a ditzy woman, and Blacks doing better on a golf putting exercise after being told that the test evaluated athletic ability. During the lesson students completed a worksheet, which included a question asking them to provide one example of how stereotypes could be harmful and one of how they could be helpful.

I sat with a group of boys of color as they worked on this assignment. They stumbled when they reached the question about how stereotypes could be helpful. Multiple boys gave examples of how others had stereotyped them, but they were confused as to how these could be anything but harmful. When Ms. Clemens told the class that they should think about the experiments in the video to help them answer how stereotypes might be positive, the boys remained unconvinced. As one Black boy said, "I don't know how a woman crossing the street when she sees me could be helpful." The group decided to leave the answer to that question blank. In attempting to present a balanced and nice lesson about stereotypes, which placed value on a sense of neutrality, Ms. Clemens minimized the impact of some students' experiences of discrimination. The boys saw that their multiple negative experiences were being given equal weight with hypothetical positive experiences.

Subsequently, they refused even a cursory answer to a question that gave credence to the idea that stereotypes could be helpful.

Students acknowledged that members of the Chestnut community explicitly stated their support for challenging injustice. Yet their commitments seemed to lack genuineness or an appropriate vision for change. Keisha, a Black student, explained her frustrations by relaying a story:

> This one teacher, she was like, "Oh yeah! Sit around, guys, and talk about White privilege! Blah blah blah, like it's ever going to change." She said that, and I just had in my head, "Dang! Nobody's really putting any effort into changing things, so maybe it's never going to change." She said it like as a joke, playing around, but I just thought about it. People don't think it's going to change, so people don't want to put the effort into it. And then people who do want to actually do it and put the effort into it are going about it the wrong way. Like they're not being realistic about it! They feel like we can just come together, like, "Kumbaya." *[Laughter.]* It's not that easy!

Keisha and other students like her saw that educators would recognize concepts like White privilege, but they questioned the extent to which these individuals were actually interested in following through on these commitments. In this way Keisha demonstrated a nascent understanding that there are limits to the nice, "Kumbaya" approach to conversations about social justice.

The Benefits of Niceness

Although Niceness usually enabled the persistence of inequity, educators' allegiance to Niceness was sometimes leveraged for the benefit of marginalized students. Often this was manifested as wanting to be kind to students who were struggling under the weight of systems of oppression. While being nice did not necessarily result in fundamental challenges to structural inequality, at times it played an important role in allowing marginalized students to feel safe at school.

The impulse toward Niceness was particularly clear after the election of Trump as president. On the day after the election, many students (and particularly students of color and LGBTQIA students) were distraught, upset, and fearful. Chestnut offered students opportunities to process their feelings, and many educators similarly expressed anger and disappointment. While there were some tensions in the ways various school community members processed their heartbreak and fear, several students told me that they appreciated knowing that their teachers did not support Trump and that it would be much harder to be at a school where they did.

Right after the election, a teacher in California posted the following letter in her classroom, which quickly circulated on social media:

Dear undocumented students,

In this classroom, there are no walls. You belong here. You are loved.

Dear black students,

In this classroom, YOUR life matters. You are loved.

Dear Muslim students and students of Middle Eastern descent,

We know you are not terrorists. You are loved.

Dear Mexican students,

You are not rapists or drug dealers. You are loved.

Dear female students,

Men cannot grab you. Men WILL respect you—demand it. You are loved.

Dear LGBTQ students,

You are perfect just as you are. You are loved.

Dear all students,

We will get through this day, this year, together. We will respect each other and learn from one another. You are a beloved part of this country and community.

A few days after the election, some Chestnut teachers attached copies of the letter to their classroom doors. The following week, large, laminated posters of the letter appeared on walls in common spaces throughout the school, and a teacher told me that this had been the principal's idea. Although Chestnut educators struggled in some ways to discuss the election results with their students, they also embraced a sense of wanting to comfort those young people who felt most vulnerable.

Even though practices of Niceness typically did not serve the needs of marginalized students, there were also times where teachers' desire to be kind and compassionate benefited these students in some ways. Especially in a transformed political climate, where the very humanity of marginalized individuals and communities was under attack, Chestnut educators' willingness to prioritize their students' feelings of safety was significant and meaningful.

Discussion and Implications

Too often in schools, the needs of relatively privileged students are prioritized over those who are more marginalized. Scholars have long documented how school policies and practices dehumanize students of color (e.g., Ferguson 2000), LGBTQIA students (e.g., Pascoe 2007), working-class students (e.g., Willis 1977), immigrant students (e.g. Valenzuela 1999), and others. But it is only more recently that educational researchers have also turned attention to the ways that these patterns persist even when schools are explicit in their commitments to the contrary. The findings in this chapter suggest that one way that dominance remains in place is through practices of Whiteness and Niceness. By remaining committed to principles of Niceness, including avoiding discomfort, using a discourse of connections, and maintaining neutrality, Chestnut continued to contribute to inequity.

Nice people avoid uncomfortable situations. While some educators do so by sidestepping conversations about race and inequity altogether, this chapter illustrates that teachers can maintain an air of pleasantness even when discussing these topics with students. They accomplish this by talking about power and privilege as relatively abstract concepts rather than ones that have meaning within the classroom and in their students' lives. In this way, oppression becomes depersonalized— even though it is deeply personal to those most subject to its forces. While it is certainly important for educators to create spaces in which students can feel comfortable when discussing issues of injustice, the findings of this chapter raise an essential question: Whose comfort are we concerned with? Leonardo and Porter (2010) argue that attempts to create safe spaces in which to talk about race often assume that the safety of both White students and students of color is equally important, which results in violence being inflicted on students of color. At Chestnut, the desire to keep classroom discussions pleasant resulted in greater comfort for White students, but greater *discomfort* for students of color. To transform these lessons, educators must interrogate whose needs are being prioritized as they design social justice–oriented curricula, including how they structure discussions about issues of inequity. They should deeply consider the potential impacts of classroom activities on individuals who are most directly affected by the inequities being discussed.

Educators who are committed to Niceness engage in a human relations approach to multicultural education (Sleeter and Grant, 2008), or what Hytten and Warren (2003) term a "discourse of connections." They seek to emphasize the commonalities and shared experiences among all humans. At Chestnut this compulsion contributed to sustaining inequity in situations where teachers implied that all students were in some ways disadvantaged, or hoped that simply by coming together, communities could fight injustice. It also served to minimize the oppression faced by some students by suggesting all individuals could relate to certain elements of it. But educators also drew on this sense of connection and empathy to comfort students who were terrified at the prospect of a country where policies espoused by Trump might become law. Teachers should carefully consider if and when it is appropriate to emphasize commonalities among humans, and also when they must recognize the diversity of experiences. They should listen to marginalized individuals and communities, including their students, and reflect on whether their lessons are designed in ways that make these voices and stories central, or if the activities serve instead to privilege the gaze of the dominant group.

Finally, even though teachers may make their stances explicit in some ways, they can also struggle to leave behind the idea that educators should be neutral. The impulse to maintain neutrality and balance is a characteristic of Niceness and one way that Whiteness remains in place. Even as teachers call out structural inequity, they continue to maintain a sheen of impartiality, such as when they seek to see the positive and negative aspects of stereotypes, or see all students as equally able to stand up to injustices they witness or experience. If we are to truly engage in social justice education, teachers must ask themselves why they value neutrality, and who truly benefits from a neutral approach to teaching.

Conclusion

Across the nation, educators, researchers, students, parents, and the public are deeply troubled by persistent disparities in educational experiences, opportunities, and achievement. Yet as this chapter illustrates, fighting for justice is a complex process, and there is still significant work to be done to dismantle systems of power and privilege in schools.

This research has implications for educators who are committed to creating more equitable schools. It illustrates that practices of Whiteness and Niceness are so deeply ingrained that they persist even when school communities express commitments to challenge these structures. As a result, the needs and safety of marginalized students are often deprioritized. Schools and educators invested in challenging oppression should thus consider how even well-meaning multicultural and social justice efforts might contribute to persistent inequities.

This chapter also has implications for teacher education. White middle-class educators often learn about inequity in relatively homogeneous spaces that are designed for *them*; they then teach about it in similar ways, even though the schools where they teach may be very different from their teacher education contexts. Teacher education programs should consider how they might better prepare preservice teachers not only to understand structural inequity but also to teach about these issues to different groups of students.

If we are to dismantle systems of oppression in schools and beyond, we need more than commitments to multiculturalism, social justice, and good intentions. It is also essential to interrogate how Whiteness operates, including through practices that appear to be nice or otherwise innocuous. To truly work toward more just and equitable schools, we must decenter Whiteness and privilege marginalized students and perspectives.

Note

1. The name of the school and names of people are pseudonyms.

References

Abu El-Haj, T. R. 2006. *Elusive Justice: Wrestling with Difference and Educational Equity in Everyday Practice.* New York: Routledge.

Agar, M. H. 1996. *The Professional Stranger: An Informal Introduction to Ethnography.* 2nd ed. San Diego: Academic Press.

Alexander, M. 2012. *The New Jim Crow: Mass Incarceration in the Age of Colorblindness.* New York: New Press.

Apple, M. W. 2013. *Can Education Change Society?* New York: Routledge.

Ayers, W., T. M. Quinn, and D. Stovall, eds. 2009. *Handbook of Social Justice in Education.* New York: Routledge.

Banks, J. A. 2014. *An Introduction to Multicultural Education.* 5th ed. Upper Saddle River, N.J.: Pearson Education.

Bell, L. A. 2007. "Theoretical Foundations for Social Justice Education." In *Teaching for Diversity and Social Justice,* 2nd ed., edited by M. Adams, L. A. Bell, and P. Griffin, 3–14. New York: Taylor and Francis.

Bonilla-Silva, E. 2014. *Racism without Racists: Color-Blind Racism and Racial Inequality in Contemporary America.* 4th ed. Lanham, Md.: Rowman and Littlefield.

Castagno, A. E. 2008. "'I Don't Want to Hear That!' Legitimating Whiteness through Silence in Schools." *Anthropology and Education Quarterly* 39, no. 3: 314–33.

Castagno, A. E. 2011. "What Makes Critical Ethnography 'Critical'?" In *Qualitative Research: An Introduction to Methods and Designs,* edited by S. D. Lapan, M. T. Quartaroli, and F. J. Riemer, 373–90. San Francisco: Jossey-Bass.

Castagno, A. E. 2014. *Educated in Whiteness: Good Intentions and Diversity in Schools.* Minneapolis: University of Minnesota Press.

Doane, W. 2003. "Rethinking Whiteness Studies." In *White Out: The Continuing Significance of Racism,* edited by A. W. Doane and E. Bonilla-Silva, 3–18. New York: Routledge.

Du Bois, W. E. B. 1935. *Black Reconstruction in America: 1860–1880.* New York: Free Press.

Ferguson, A. A. 2000. *Bad Boys: Public Schools in the Making of Black Masculinity.* Ann Arbor: University of Michigan Press.

Giroux, H. A. 1997. "Rewriting the Discourse of Racial Identity: Towards a Pedagogy and Politics of Whiteness." *Harvard Educational Review* 67, no. 2: 285–320.

Gonzales, R. G. 2016. *Lives in Limbo: Undocumented and Coming of Age in America.* Berkeley: University of California Press.

Haviland, V. S. 2008. "'Things Get Glossed Over': Rearticulating the Silencing Power of Whiteness in Education." *Journal of Teacher Education* 59, no. 1: 40–54.

Hess, D. E., and P. McAvoy. 2015. *The Political Classroom: Evidence and Ethics in Democratic Education.* New York: Routledge.

Hytten, K., and J. Warren. 2003. "Engaging Whiteness: How Racial Power Gets Reified in Education." *International Journal of Qualitative Studies in Education* 16, no. 1: 65–89.

King, J. E. 1991. "Dysconscious Racism: Ideology, Identity, and the Miseducation of Teachers." *Journal of Negro Education* 60, no. 2: 133–46.

Ladson-Billings, G. 1995. "Toward a Theory of Culturally Relevant Pedagogy." *American Educational Research Journal* 32, no. 3: 465–491.

Leonardo, Z. 2009. *Race, Whiteness, and Education.* New York: Routledge.

Leonardo, Z., and R. K. Porter. 2010. "Pedagogy of Fear: Toward a Fanonian Theory of 'Safety' in Race Dialogue." *Race, Ethnicity, and Education* 13, no. 2: 139–57.

Lewis, A. E. 2003. *Race in the Schoolyard: Negotiating the Color Line in Classrooms and Communities.* New Brunswick, N.J.: Rutgers University Press.

Lewis, A. E., and J. B. Diamond. 2015. *Despite the Best Intentions: How Racial Inequality Thrives in Good Schools.* New York: Oxford University Press.

Lipsitz, G. 2006. *The Possessive Investment in Whiteness: How White People Profit from Identity Politics.* Revised and Expanded Ed. Philadelphia: Temple University Press.

Loutzenheiser, L. W. 2001. "'If I Teach about These Issues They Will Burn Down My House': The Possibilities and Tensions of Queered, Antiracist Pedagogy." In *Troubling Intersections of Race and Sexuality: Queer Students of*

Color and Anti-oppressive Education, edited by K. K. Kumashiro, 195–214. Lanham, Md.: Rowman and Littlefield.

Madison, D. S. 2005. *Critical Ethnography: Methods, Ethics, and Performance.* Thousand Oaks, Calif.: Sage.

Marx, S. 2006. *Revealing the Invisible: Confronting Passive Racism in Teacher Education.* New York: Routledge.

May, S., and C. E. Sleeter. 2010. "Introduction." In *Critical Multiculturalism: Theory and Praxis,* edited by S. May and C. E. Sleeter, 1–16. New York: Routledge.

McIntosh, P. 1990. "White Privilege: Unpacking the Invisible Knapsack." *Independent School* 49, no. 2: 31–36.

McIntyre, A. 1997. *Making Meaning of Whiteness: Exploring Racial Identity with White Teachers.* Albany: State University of New York Press.

McLaren, P. 1995. "White Terror and Oppositional Agency: Towards a Critical Multiculturalism." In *Multicultural Education, Critical Pedagogy, and the Politics of Difference,* edited by C. E. Sleeter and P. L. McLaren, 33–70. Albany: State University of New York Press.

Miles, M. B., and A. M. Huberman. 1994. *Qualitative Data Analysis: An Expanded Sourcebook.* 2nd ed. Thousand Oaks, Calif.: Sage.

Mills, C. W. 1997. *The Racial Contract.* Ithaca, N.Y.: Cornell University Press.

Morrison, T. 1970. *The Bluest Eye.* New York: Vintage.

Nieto, S., and P. Bode. 2012. *Affirming Diversity: The Sociopolitical Context of Education.* 6th ed. Boston: Pearson Education.

Orfield, G., and E. Frankenberg. 2014. *Brown at 60: Great Progress, a Long Retreat and an Uncertain Future.* Los Angeles: Civil Rights Project/Proyecto Derechos Civiles.

Paris, D., & H. S. Alim. 2014. "What Are We Seeking to Sustain through Culturally Sustaining Pedagogy? A Loving Critique Forward." *Harvard Educational Review* 84, no. 1: 85–100.

Pascoe, C. J. 2007. *Dude, You're a Fag: Masculinity and Sexuality in High School.* Berkeley: University of California Press.

Pollock, M. 2004. *Colormute: Race Talk Dilemmas in an American School.* Princeton, N.J.: Princeton University Press.

Sleeter, C. E., and C. A. Grant. 2008. *Making Choices for Multicultural Education: Five Approaches to Race, Class, and Gender.* 5th ed. New York: Wiley.

Sleeter, C. E., and P. McLaren. 1995. "Introduction: Exploring Connections to Build a Critical Multiculturalism." In *Multicultural Education, Critical Pedagogy, and the Politics of Difference*, edited by C. E. Sleeter and P. L. McLaren, 5–32. Albany: State University of New York Press.

Tuck, E. 2011. "Humiliating Ironies and Dangerous Dignities: A Dialectic of School Pushout." *International Journal of Qualitative Studies in Education* 24, no. 7: 817–27.

Valenzuela, A. 1999. *Subtractive Schooling: U.S.–Mexican Youth and the Politics of Caring*. Albany: State University of New York Press.

Willis, P. 1977. *Learning to Labor: How Working Class Kids Get Working Class Jobs*. New York: Columbia University Press.

Being Nice to the Elephant in the (Class)Room

Whiteness in New Latino Diaspora Nebraska

JESSICA SIERK

> Everyone's going to be nice to each other and everyone's going
> to respect each other, but no one's going to step on any toes
> and say anything about it. Part of the problem is that if people
> do ask about it, they're scared the other person is going to
> automatically be offended. I feel like if you're going to ask
> someone, like, "Did you immigrate here?" you'd have to really
> word it carefully to not seem like you're breaking them down
> for coming here.
> —Grace, interview, November 24, 2015

Grace, a White student at Springvale High School, called race "the elephant in the room." The unwritten rules of Niceness encourage students like Grace to ignore issues of race and ethnicity in favor of a false sense of positive human relations. Yet Niceness oversimplifies the complex dynamics of Whiteness, racism, and oppression. Niceness, an individual attribute, feeds into the idea that racism is abnormal when, in reality, racism is perpetuated systemically, institutionally, culturally, and societally. In this chapter, I examine how Niceness intersects with demographic change by looking at how students and school personnel from two New Latino Diaspora (NLD) high schools enacted Niceness in their daily interactions, and as a result, perpetuated inequity.

Niceness is a manifestation of Whiteness. I define Whiteness as "a socially constructed ideology that systematically privileges those identified as White, while oppressing those not identified as White" (Sierk 2016, 79). Similar to Niceness, Whiteness is often assumed to be about individuals—White *people* who identify and are identified as racially White. Yet Whiteness is more complicated than how people see themselves and others; it's a system of rules (some explicitly written in legal jargon, others implicitly understood by all and enforced by the dominant group) that are used (both intentionally and unintentionally) to maintain the status quo of White supremacy. Like Niceness, Whiteness is an "equal opportunity employer" (Lipsitz 1998, viii). As Leonardo (2007) states, "Blacks, Latinos, and Asians participate in Whiteness, although it benefits Whites in absolute terms" (272). The same can be said for Niceness; to maintain polite interactions, everyone is capable of and encouraged to turn a blind eye to inequity.

Demographic Change and Niceness

Specifically of interest to this chapter's examination of Niceness is how it overlaps with instantiations of demographic change. Gibson (1988) examined interactions between Valleysiders (White community members) and Punjabis (Sikh immigrants) in rural California, and asserts that the Valleysiders generally liked the individual Punjabis they associated with on a regular basis. Furthermore, the Punjabis were "quick to point out, only a small minority of Valleysiders were openly hostile" (77). This assertion that only some Valleysiders were openly hostile presents racism as individual manifestations of overt prejudice. Furthermore, Niceness was emphasized in this community's response to diversity. For example, "some [teachers] reported that they tried to 'shield' Punjabis from rude remarks and called offending students aside to tell them their behavior was unacceptable. . . . Some said they 'simply insisted on respect.' Others said they 'ignored' the cracks, unless they got really out of hand" (149–50). These responses placed blame for "occasional" infractions on individual students rather than on a broader societal and institutional environment that tolerates and perpetuates the behavior in question; furthermore, these responses accentuated Niceness as a way of combatting prejudice.

Valdés (2001) has critiqued the social isolation of English learners in California schools, and expounds on the taken-for-granted nature of racism by pointing out, "Individuals of goodwill are not aware that they have become instruments of dominant interests. . . . [I]n many cases, people 'consent' to preserving the status quo and to maintaining existing power relationships simply by accepting established practices without question" (155). Thus, while it might not seem "nice" to question the status quo, the Niceness associated with accepting established practices often facilitates the continuation of practices that are implicitly racist.

Bejarano (2005) also describes Niceness in her study of urban youth culture and border identity in a metropolitan Southwestern high school. As she notes, "At least two Chicanas explained their White friends were not 'mean' to them and mostly did not speak to Mexicans because of language barriers" (156). Thus, rather than being hostile or "mean" to their Mexican classmates, White, monolingual students convinced their Mexican peers that their seclusion was due to a language barrier. Monolingualism gave the White students an excuse for not interacting with the Mexican students, while simultaneously preserving positive human relations. As a result, the White students could comfortably seclude themselves from their Mexican counterparts without this segregation being questioned. Lest this sound like "blaming the White students," it is the systemic critique (e.g., the structural preeminence of unproblematized English monolingualism) here that matters, with the advantaged White students as the perhaps unwitting, but still self-advantaging, agents.

The New Latino Diaspora

The aforementioned studies took place in areas where one might expect Latinxs to be present, especially since much of California and the southwestern United States were formerly Mexican territory. In contrast, this chapter focuses on the *New* Latino Diaspora, defined by Murillo and Villenas (1997, cited in Hamann, Wortham, and Murillo 2002) as the temporary and permanent settlement of increasing numbers of Latinxs in areas that had not traditionally been home to them. In terms of this distinction's impact on how Niceness operates, there are important continuities and similarities with the previous studies; yet, as Frankenberg (1997) asserts, "In times and places when Whiteness and White dominance are being built or reconfigured, they are highly visible, named, and asserted, rather than invisible or simply 'normative'" (5). Therefore, the fast-changing and improvisational nature of multiethnic interactions in the NLD (Hamann, Wortham, and Murillo 2002) more intensely highlight (or make explicit) the practice and tensions of Niceness, adding to our understanding of how communities appeal to Niceness while at the same time "othering" newcomer populations in line with White supremacy and racist nativism that occurs across contexts.

Orfield (2009) explains how the NLD impacts K–12 education: "In a single generation, we have vast migrations transforming major areas of the region, creating multiracial schools and communities, and bringing linguistic and cultural diversity into many regions" (11). The ways in which NLD communities respond to this vary widely (Hamann, Eckerson, and Gray 2012); some of these responses rely heavily on the norms of Niceness. For example, in their analysis of media coverage of U.S. Immigration and Customs Enforcement raids that occurred synchronously at six meatpacking plants in December 2006, and at a seventh plant in May 2008, Hamann and Reeves illustrate how NLD communities react to Latinx newcomers (at least as captured in the mainstream print media). These reactions involve story lines related to local educational institutions. One such story line is "a narrative of children as innocent victims applied to detainees' children, with an accompanying storyline of schools as sites of refuge and teachers and administrators as step-in family for children" (Hamann and Reeves 2012, 29). Such story lines demonstrate explicit tolerance, even acceptance, of newcomer children while simultaneously ignoring some of the larger systemic barriers faced by newcomer families (e.g., difficulty in attaining citizenship, unsafe work environments, stress and isolation associated with undocumented status); all of this is consistent with the norms of Niceness.

Research Site and Methods

Nebraska is a state in which the NLD has contributed to drastic demographic changes. Ceballos and Yakushko (2014) cite U.S. Census data stating, "Although Nebraska and other Great Plains and Midwestern states do not have the same large numbers of recent immigrants and refugees as US border states, the rate of immigration to this region is significantly higher than those states" (183). Yet this demographic change is not impacting *all* communities in the state of Nebraska. As Gibson (2002) states, "Even in states with a limited immigrant presence, we find individual communities undergoing rapid transformation" (242).

This is especially true when the school-age population in these communities is considered. According to Stacy, Hamann, and Murillo (2015), 16 percent of the Latinx population in Nebraska is under the age of 18 (336). Putting these two points together—that the demographic change is not equally distributed geographically and that the Latinx population is younger with a higher portion of children—schools' responses to demographic change associated with the NLD are of the utmost importance.

Compared to the approximately 11 percent of the Nebraska population and the 18.1 percent of the U.S. population that identifies as Hispanic (U.S. Census Bureau 2018), several Nebraska school districts are serving significantly larger Hispanic populations. Two of these school districts are the research sites for the study presented in this chapter. These two nonurban NLD high schools will be referred to as Stockbridge High School (approximately two-thirds Hispanic) and Springvale High School (approximately one-half Hispanic).[1] Both communities have experienced significant demographic change in the last ten to twenty years.

This chapter stems from a larger ethnographic research project (Sierk 2016) that described the coming-of-age experiences of youth from these two communities, with particular focus on how race, and more specifically Whiteness, was constructed and understood by individuals in these particular NLD contexts. As such, it sought to answer the following central research question: "How do students view themselves, their home communities, and their aspirations as they transition from high school to their postsecondary plans?"

Given the study's focus on racialization and its societal and educational implications, Critical Race Theory was used as a theoretical framework. In particular, tenets of Critical Race Theory related to the endemic nature of racism

(Ladson-Billings 2013; Leonardo 2009), interest convergence (Bell 1995), and intersectionality (Crenshaw 1991) were used when collecting and analyzing data. In terms of Niceness, racism is not seen as an integral component of the fabric of everyday life. Instead, it comprises "abnormal, unusual, and irrational" acts that violate the norms of Niceness; it is understood as rare and lamentable. The fact that racism inhabits the very pieces of our daily life in the form of "ideologies and practices in a variety of sites in the social formation that reproduce racial inequality and domination" (Omi 2001, 279) gets both obscured and denied under the rules of Niceness. Interest convergence elicits questions about how diverse populations are included in previously majority White communities, and in whose interest particular responses to diversity are pursued in reality versus perception. Intersectionality is central to the present study in that Niceness manifests itself differently as it interacts with various combinations of social identities (e.g., race, ethnicity, gender, class, citizenship, and language).

As a White researcher, it is important that I acknowledge my own positionality in this work. I grew up in a community that, while I was living and attending school there, transitioned from being a majority White community to one that is majority Latinx. Therefore, I was somewhat familiar with the context within which I was conducting research. In the last five to ten years, however, NLD communities like Stockbridge High have begun to attract refugee populations from places like Somalia and Sudan—cultures and contexts with which I am less familiar. Likewise, although Springvale High students and I share the common experience of coming of age in a NLD community that was roughly 50 percent Latinx, my graduating class was over two hundred students—almost six times the size of Springvale's. Although I had my own experience with this topic, it was important for me to remain as objective as possible, to allow my participants' stories to come through unadulterated by any "insider" knowledge.

This chapter draws on ethnographic data I collected at Stockbridge and Springvale High Schools between February and December 2015. Data collection included twenty-seven days of participant observations (Spradley 1980) on various days of the week and in different settings (e.g., assemblies, school hallways, homeroom periods, and classrooms). I also conducted ethnographic interviews (Spradley 1979) with thirty-one school personnel and twenty-one students in the spring of 2015, and follow-up interviews with thirteen students in the fall of 2015. I utilized Fasching-Varner's (2014) twofold approach to data analysis when analyzing field notes, interview transcripts, and other artifacts by first coding individual participant data sets and then refining codes based on cross-case comparisons. Vignettes that privilege participant language are used throughout my findings in an effort to create an "on-record body of narratives that serve to develop meaningful research findings" (Fasching-Varner 2014, 165). This approach allowed me to see the interconnectivity of my participants' narratives, thereby locating Niceness within the lenses of the lived experiences of students and school personnel from these two high schools.

Polite, Tolerant Niceness

Students and school personnel at both schools stressed tolerance, which was seen as proof that racial and ethnic conflict related to the changing demographics of these two high schools was not an issue. But the weight and celebration of tolerance acted to defuse and deny such issues existed, leaving the underlying causes of conflict unresolved. Eddie, a Guatemalan student at Springvale High, described the school's social climate by contrasting polite, respectful interactions with underlying jealousy, hatred, and overall mixed feelings: "I would've preferred the honesty . . . to break all the tensions. Lots of times in [Springvale], it was mostly a Christian community so people were just afraid of getting a bad name. That's why they were polite and afraid to be honest." He gave as an example how his classmates treated Sergio, one of Springvale High's Mexican students: "Lots of kids would talk a lot of trash behind his back, but when he was around they'd be nice to him and everything, and lots of them asked me why I was friends with him because obviously I was one of the honors students as a senior, and an athlete and everything, and he wasn't, so they called him a loser, basically, and what are you doing with a loser? But what none of them knew is what he's going through in his life." The emphasis placed on Niceness at Springvale High made a substantive resolution of group differences impossible (Jackman 1994). Eddie's example of how his peers treated Sergio to his face versus behind his back highlights the contrast between Niceness and honesty. In this instance students acted polite, following the norms of Niceness, in order to preserve positive, albeit shallow, human relations.

White students and school personnel saw acceptance and "getting along" as proof that racism was not a problem at Springvale High. When asked what he would tell someone coming to Springvale High for the first time, Michael, a White student, stated, "I'd tell them to be ready for a language barrier at certain points, but also just to be accepting of everyone because you can see in our school, new people are coming in and they're accepted right away. They automatically say, 'Wow, [Springvale] is so nice.' Everybody's so accepting. We really aren't judgmental because I feel like with all those different races, different cultures, you have to accept everybody." Relatively speaking, Springvale High was seen as a more accepting school than some of the other schools in the vicinity; time and time again, I heard from students and school personnel that students from one neighboring school in particular would transfer to Springvale High for this reason. Implicit in Michael's statement, however, is the assumption that acceptance automatically follows diversity.

Michael's reference to language barriers functions similar to Bejarano's (2005) findings. White, monolingual students (as well as some bilingual English–Spanish speakers) at Springvale High were able to avoid interactions with the school's more recent Guatemalan students on the basis of language.[2] For example, Javier, a Mexican bilingual English–Spanish speaker, identified language as an indexical marker that distinguished newcomers from established Guatemalan students, stating, "I think they should be able to communicate with us . . . with Hispanics. I think it's a good thing that they're coming here, because they get the education that [Eddie] got and now he knows how to speak English."[3] Similarly, Chloe contrasted Eddie with the recent Guatemalan newcomers: "He came here and he wanted to conform, he wanted to learn English, he wanted to get into sports. And they're just like, no, you have to learn our language. And we're just like, this is America. Yeah, there's different languages, but learn English, we're an English-speaking school." As Bejarano (2005) has noted, "The lack of knowledge in either language restrained them from attempting to cross group borders and thus share their commonalities" (134). The emphasis of a language "barrier" further solidified the boundaries between "mainstream" and English as a second language (ESL) students, creating a social structure that rationalized what could potentially be seen as "not nice" behavior.

Similar to those at Springvale High, school personnel at Stockbridge High emphasized that the school was "making it work," which they attributed to mutual respect, tolerance, and open-mindedness. As Mr. Hughes, a guidance counselor, stated, "I think the kids feel like they're treated respectfully and the kids that I talk to really feel like their teachers care about them. We're able to, for the most part, have a very open mind and are very tolerant of each other. That's not to say that kids don't get frustrated with teachers, and teachers don't get frustrated with kids because we know that happens. But when you really look at the overall picture, we're able to make it work." Mr. Mercer, a science teacher, also emphasized how polite Stockbridge High students are, crediting their Niceness to a certain Midwest mind-set: "The kids amaze me because it's just that Midwest mentality to where they're very polite. They're very respectful. It cracks me up because every time I have to hand back papers, they're saying thank you, thank you, thank you, thank you. I get twenty-five thank-yous, and so every time I was saying you're welcome, you're welcome, you're welcome, you're welcome. It's funny because I think to myself, 'Gosh, I'm getting tired of saying you're welcome,' but then I think that's pretty cool that kids can do that." What Mr. Mercer refers to as "that Midwest mentality" draws on the stereotypical notion that people in the Midwest are raised to be courteous, friendly, and easygoing. The well-known concept of "Minnesota nice" has recently been commandeered by other Midwestern states—including Nebraska, which adopted "Nebraska Nice" as an official slogan for a time. Some contested this rebranding because they thought it made the state seem "plain and boring" (KETV 2014), while others pointed out the hypocrisy of the new mantra. Much like the saying, "Bless your heart," in the South, "Nebraska Nice" acts as a facade, concealing underlying racial tensions while perpetuating Whiteness and preserving positive human relations.

Intentional, Individual Niceness

Related to the aforementioned arrival of Guatemalan newcomers at Springvale High, being Mexican is seen as more acceptable than being Guatemalan. For example, Eddie alluded to anti-Guatemalan sentiment as he self-identified racially and ethnically: "I am Hispanic. I am Guatemalan, and for some reason at school it's kind of like they see us lower and joke around, so I'd rather be called a Hispanic. It's more of an equal thing." Olivia related her own experiences with anti-Guatemalan sentiment at Springvale High:

> Sometimes they make jokes about Guatemalans, and I'm like, what?
> There's this one kid who's totally against them, and I'm like, what
> the heck? Yeah it's weird. I was like, does this happen in other
> schools? Because it always happens here. And they can tell how
> you're Guatemalan and how you're Mexican, and I was like, no you
> can't! People are always like, oh you're Mexican. And I'm like, no, I'm
> Guatemalan. Because they're just like, all the kids who come here
> from Guatemala are in the ESL program and stuff. And they point
> it out, and I was like, what's the big deal they come from there?
> That's not affecting you, they're not even talking to you.

Since Olivia didn't fit the Guatemalan stereotype (she was not in the ESL program, had light skin, and did not speak an Indigenous language or dialect), her classmates assumed she was Mexican. In the hierarchy of the school, where Guatemalans are on the bottom, Olivia "passed" as Mexican but was nonetheless impacted by her classmates' discriminatory jokes and remarks about Guatemalans.

Impact versus intention play a major role in what is perceived to constitute racism within the confines of the school. Olivia, for example, singled out one of her classmates in particular who was "totally" against Guatemalans. The comments he made were seen as overtly and intentionally racist. On the other hand, Chloe, a White student, admitted to making "racist jokes" around Eddie but contended that her intention was to be funny (a benign, and possibly even *nice*, intent, as the two were friends), therefore attempting to nullify the racist impact of her jokes.

Students weren't the only ones who participated in excusing racism based on intentionality. At Stockbridge High, Ms. Anderson, an English teacher, acknowledged the role of race in teacher-student conflicts when discussing an incident between a White teacher and a Somali student, but discredited the student's allegations of racial discord under the guise of intentionality:

> I've had one student that has told me that she wrote a paper for
> English 2 that the Somali African Americans are all being—I don't
> want to say *abused*, but being cornered—and they just are treated

terrible by the teachers, and a lot of racism is going on. I looked at
her and I said, "What are you talking about?" Honestly, I think
because of the attitude that she has towards the teachers . . . I mean,
she'll walk in when we're walking out or when I had a line of ten
people she'd move to the front. And I'd tell her, "You have to go back
of the line," and she would get very angry. I know she's in another
class now . . . she came in just as that teacher was going to lunch
yesterday, and sometimes you just have to have your lunch. You just
can't do anything else. And she got mad at the teacher because she
said, "No I'm not going to help you. It was due yesterday. I'm going
to lunch." "Well can't you just look this over now?" And that teacher
said, "No I'm sorry. I'm going to lunch today." And she got really
huffy with the teacher. So I think her perception is not what
happens, but I think that she thinks it is. She thinks it's like that. I
personally think it's probably because after you've had her for a term,
you're so tired of trying to make her realize that she's not the most
important in the room, and she thinks she should be.

Rather than acknowledging in her assessment of this student that cultural differences and misunderstandings may be a factor, Ms. Anderson silenced the student's concerns, delegitimizing her grievances and leaving the issue unresolved. Ms. Anderson saw the other teacher's actions—going to lunch instead of addressing the student's concerns about a late assignment—as well intentioned. Thus, the student's contention that she was being treated unfairly due to her race (i.e., the impact of the teacher's action) was null and void in the allegation of racism. While Ms. Anderson's words and actions may seem "not nice," they are important to the perpetuation of Niceness as a whole. Allegations of racism directly challenge Niceness and are easily discredited along the lines of intentionality.

Niceness stands in direct contrast to what usually comes to mind when the topic of racism arises. As a society, we still cling to the more overt definition of racism, reminiscing about the "bad old days" of Jim Crow segregation and lynching the "other" in the town square. But racism has evolved, as color blindness has become the rule of our more "tolerant" society. Jackman (1994) elucidates this contrast, stating, "The ideological pressures created by dominant groups are more likely to be subtle and insidious than blatant or hostile" (2). She goes on to explain, "The concept of tolerance implicitly neutralizes the issue of social inequality. By directing attention to the defusing of conflict without regard to its underlying causes, it places more weight on societal stability than on the substantive resolution of group differences" (46). Thus, while tolerance and Niceness may seem like a solution to the problem of racism, they are actually contributing factors in the perpetuation of this modern, covert instantiation of racism.

As such, when students of color allege racism, White students and teachers interpret this as an accusation that they are "not nice." After all, they maintain that they do not treat people differently based on race (color blindness); rather, their behaviors are driven by people's personalities and other individual characteristics. Thus, racism goes uninvestigated and remains unchallenged in favor of White students' and teachers' defense of their own Niceness and egalitarianism. This perpetuates the status quo, preventing equity from being realized.

Similarly, Ms. Ferguson, an English teacher at Springvale High, maintained Niceness in the way of the myth of positive human relations while simultaneously disbelieving students' charges of racism: "I think that it speaks volumes that the kids get along. Every once in a while . . . you've been in here when we had the one student who always goes off about being Brown and that's just part of who he is. I just let it go, because that's just the way he is. There might be some resentments or racism that goes on that we don't know about, but I think for the most part the kids truly do get along and accept each other for the way they are." Ms. Ferguson ascribes the student's comments about being treated differently because he's "Brown," which I observed firsthand (field notes, March 26 and April 22, 2015), to a personal trait (i.e., "that's just part of who he is") rather than an institutional bias. Ms. Ferguson also states that if there is racism going on, she and her fellow teachers are unaware of it. By claiming ignorance, Ms. Ferguson upholds the rules of Niceness and is freed from any responsibility to act.

Niceness requires that racism is acknowledged only in acts that intentionally seek to discriminate against individuals. To be nice is to be well intentioned; yet, as Castagno states, "Whether the outcome was intended or not is a distraction. When we focus on the intent, we generally lose sight of the real, material outcome. . . . Good intentions mean very little if we do not take responsibility and cannot be held accountable" (2014, 43–44). This focus on individual, intentional attitudes and actions serves as a convenient excuse that leaves racism's damage unaddressed. Aal describes this as "the difference between impact and intention" (2001, 306). If the impact of an action, ideology, or policy is discriminatory, from a consequence standpoint it does not matter whether said action, ideology, or policy was carried out or enacted with "good intentions." In terms of Ms. Ferguson's claim of ignorance, her own and her students' good intentions (i.e., "the kids truly do get along and accept each other for the way they are") are more heavily weighted in her view than "some resentments or racism that goes on that we don't know about." Digging into these resentments would require acknowledging her own role in a system that disadvantages roughly half of her students. It is much easier to focus on one's own ability to be nice than to go up against the status quo, which has taken centuries to form and is bigger than any one individual, school, or community.

Uncritical, Silent Niceness

Out of fear, White students and school personnel avoided the topic of race, not sure how to broach these conversations without offending someone. In the realm of Niceness, it is viewed as better to have ignored the elephant in the room than to have stepped out of one's comfort zone and caused offense. Niceness prevents the act of ignoring uncomfortable topics from being viewed negatively, as it is well intentioned; but offending someone, especially when it comes to racial matters, puts one at risk of being deemed racist. It's better to be safe than sorry.

As previously mentioned, however, students of color (like Eddie) longed for something deeper than these polite interactions. I also observed this as several of the school's Hispanic students voluntarily brought up topics related to race and ethnicity. For instance, a student selected racial bias as the topic for his research paper and briefly engaged in a conversation with me about the Michael Brown shooting (field notes, April 22, 2015). Earlier in the semester I also observed Sergio and a classmate working on a project in Mr. Benson's government class, for which they had selected immigration and *la raza* (the race) as the central issue for their imagined third political party's platform (field notes, February 18, 2015). Hispanic students' choices in these open-ended assignments presented their White counterparts (both students and teachers) with opportunities to engage in conversations about race; yet more often than not, these opportunities for rich, meaningful discussions fell short of their full potential.

White school personnel and students called upon their performative "tools of Whiteness" (Picower 2009), opting to remain silent rather than take the risk associated with engaging in potentially contentious conversations about race. Castagno (2008) asserts that teacher silence around issues of race teaches students to "avoid such talk in the future," reducing "the likelihood of systemic change" (326). Mazzei (2008) uses similar themes in her study, and suggests that educators must "provide the milieu where the masks of racially inhabited silence can be removed in safety" (1133). Thus, while acceptance may have been an implicit goal launched in response to the diversified student population, the lack of explicit attention left White students and school personnel without the knowledge of how to push for something more than acceptance, thereby leaving Hispanic students' concerns unaddressed and their experiences underappreciated. This form of color blindness placed White teachers' and students' illusion of Niceness and egalitarianism above the genuine inclusion of students of color.

Furthermore, White students and school personnel saw their diverse high school as training grounds for future acceptance of difference. For example, Ms. Falk stated,

> I think it's a good thing for the students. If they go to a job or they
> go to a college, it is going to be diverse, and I don't think they'll

> think anything of it. That's just the way they grew up, and that's just
> the way it is. Looking at my [own] kids, they don't think anything of
> it when we're talking about people, or they're talking about friends.
> It's never whether they're White or Hispanic. I don't really think
> they feel it's a real issue on a big scale. In my eyes, it could just be a
> plus, getting them ready for the world because everywhere they go is
> going to be diverse now.

While the exposure Springvale High provides to its White students does make them potentially better prepared for other diverse environments, it does not facilitate much in the way of solidarity (see Nieto 2010) between the school's White and Hispanic students. By seeing exposure to and acceptance of difference as sufficient, students leave their high school's contact zone (Pratt 1991) without critically encountering it.

Ms. Falk stating "that's just the way it is" promotes an uncritical view of why Springvale is nearly majority Hispanic when other towns less than ten miles away have Hispanic populations of less than 5 percent. While students are aware that the local food processing plant is largely responsible for the town's relatively recent diversification, they are not encouraged to question why that is the case. In this way, White students and school personnel unconsciously act as "instruments of dominant interests" (Valdés 2001) in their efforts to protect and promote Niceness. While this exposure to "diversity" is advantageous as students apply to colleges and market themselves for job opportunities, it disproportionately benefits White students at the expense of students of color.

In an alternate, more equitable scenario, this exposure would be a means to an end rather than the end itself. Rather than seeing exposure as the desired result, if solidarity was the goal, all students would prosper. Yet this scenario requires that Niceness is abandoned and that potential conflicts, which often arise when we acknowledge our nation's complicated history and present with racism, are faced head-on. As long as we continue to favor Niceness, we will settle for exposure and continue to bolster White students' résumés at the expense of the educational experiences of students of color. If one of the aims of schooling is to prepare students to better the world around them and be productive citizens in a democratic society, then students should be given the tools and opportunities to "actively use their advantages responsibly to create an alternative racial arrangement that is less oppressive" (Leonardo 2009, 98).

Conclusion: Moving away from Niceness and toward Justice

The emphasis on Niceness, and the associated avoidance of challenging racism, at these two high schools (and schools like them) points to a lack of teacher preparation, and an ensuing lack of student skills, related to engaging in productive race talk. Students (and school personnel) must be taught how to critically reflect on their experiences to truly understand how they've been unconsciously influenced by Whiteness as an ingrained societal ideology. NLD schools like Springvale and Stockbridge High Schools present unique contexts in which students can not only encounter their own White privilege but also to learn how to leverage that privilege to further the aims of social justice. But this is not something that can occur under laissez-faire racial leadership and policies implicitly focused on maintaining a "nice" school climate; rather, such preparation must be explicit and carefully planned, enacted, and monitored, and conflict must be accepted as a necessary (albeit sometimes uncomfortable) part of the process.

Tackling the silence surrounding race is potentially the most important thing to be done in support of building critical solidarity. A lot of the silence in the present study's two high schools was due to fear. For instance, when Grace described the elephant in the room, she mentioned that White students were scared of offending their Hispanic peers by asking them questions about their backgrounds that were specifically related to immigration. Thus, one of the tasks of teacher preparation is to ensure that educators are prepared to have these conversations, even when they seem "not nice."

Teacher preparation can no longer promote an agenda focused on a "heroes and holidays" approach to multicultural education (Menkart 1998); rather, teacher preparation must transition from liberal to critical multiculturalism (Vavrus 2015). Teacher educators must be prepared to engage in dialogue about oppression and privilege in an effort to redistribute the rights and advantages associated with educational opportunity. This engagement must go beyond pedagogy (see Thompson 2003); it must include questioning the hegemony at all levels of education, as well as in surrounding social contexts (e.g., health care, law enforcement, and government).

In turn, school personnel must engage their students in critical conversations about oppressive power dynamics in their communities. For example, school personnel and students at Springvale High widely accepted that the local food processing plant was the main catalyst for the community's demographic change. Yet no one questioned the power structure in place that created the correlation between that type of work and the Hispanic population that was largely tasked with doing it. This correlation was accepted as natural, as if Hispanic workers are innately talented at tasks associated with food processing. This is, of course, not true. In questioning such issues that are often taken for granted, teachers can foster their students' abilities as allies and change agents. While this may result in a "less nice" schooling environment and will likely be uncomfortable for many White teachers and students, abandoning Niceness is the only way for justice to prevail.

Notes

1. I use the word *Hispanic* throughout this chapter to remain true to my participants' own words. In their self-identifications, my participants of Mexican and Guatemalan descent used this term instead of *Latinx*.

2. During the 2014–15 school year, Springvale High's population of English learners more than doubled. Most of this increase was due to the arrival of new students from Guatemala. I rarely encountered these newcomers in my observations, with the exceptions of passing a homogeneous group in the hallway near the main entrance on my way into the school before the first bell, and while observing the Construction and Automotive Technology classes where, even there, they remained separate from the other students in the class (field notes, March 31, 2015).

3. Many of Springvale High's Guatemalan students—including Eddie, a fluent Q'anjob'al speaker—spoke dialects and indigenous languages that were different from those of the school's Mexican students. Eddie moved to Springvale from Guatemala in the fifth grade, speaking little to no English.

References

Aal, W. 2001. "Moving from Guilt to Action: Antiracist Organizing and the Concept of 'Whiteness' for Activism and the Academy." In *The Making and Unmaking of Whiteness*, edited by B. B. Rasmussen, E. Klinenberg, I. J. Nexica, and M. Wray, 294–310. Durham, N.C.: Duke University Press.

Bejarano, C. L. 2005. *¿Qué onda? Urban Youth Culture and Border Identity.* Tucson: University of Arizona Press.

Bell, D. A. 1995. "*Brown v. Board of Education* and the Interest Convergence Dilemma." In *Critical Race Theory: The Key Writings That Formed the Movement*, edited by K. Crenshaw, N. Gotanda, G. Peller, and K. Thomas, 20–28. New York: New Press.

Castagno, A. E. 2008. "'I Don't Want to Hear That!': Legitimating Whiteness through Silence in Schools." *Anthropology and Education Quarterly* 39, no. 3: 314–33.

Castagno, A. E. 2014. *Educated in Whiteness: Good Intentions and Diversity in Schools.* Minneapolis: University of Minnesota Press.

Ceballos, M., and O. Yakushko. 2014. "Attitudes toward Immigrants in Nebraska." *Great Plains Research* 24, no. 2: 181–95.

Crenshaw, K. 1991. "Mapping the Margins: Intersectionality, Identity Politics, and Violence against Women of Color." *Stanford Law Review* 43, no. 6: 1241–99.

Fasching-Varner, K. J. 2014. "(Re)searching Whiteness: New Considerations in Studying and Researching Whiteness." In *Researching Race in Education: Policy, Practice, and Qualitative Research*, edited by A. D. Dixson, 153–68. Charlotte, N.C.: Information Age.

Frankenberg, R. 1997. "Introduction: Local Whitenesses, Localizing Whiteness." In *Displacing Whiteness: Essays in Social and Cultural Criticism*, edited by R. Frankenberg, 1–34. Durham, N.C.: Duke University Press.

Gibson, M. A. 1988. *Accommodation without Assimilation: Sikh Immigrants in an American High School*. Ithaca, N.Y.: Cornell University Press.

Gibson, M. A. 2002. "The New Latino Diaspora and Educational Policy." In *Education in the New Latino Diaspora: Policy and the Politics of Identity*, edited by S. Wortham, E. G. Murillo Jr., and E. T. Hamann, 241–52. Westport, Conn.: Ablex.

Hamann, E. T., J. Eckerson, and T. Gray. 2012. "Xenophobia, Disquiet, or Welcome? Community Sense-Making and Related Educational Environments in the New Latino Diaspora." Paper presented at the annual meeting of the American Anthropological Association, San Francisco.

Hamann, E. T., and J. Reeves. 2012. "ICE Raids, Children, Media, and Making Sense of Latino Newcomers in Flyover Country." *Anthropology and Education Quarterly* 43, no. 1: 24–40.

Hamann, E. T., S. Wortham, and E. G. Murillo Jr. 2002. "Education and Policy in the New Latino Diaspora." In *Education in the New Latino Diaspora: Policy and the Politics of Identity*, edited by S. Wortham, E. G. Murillo Jr., and E. T. Hamann, 1–16. Westport, Conn.: Ablex.

Jackman, M. R. 1994. *The Velvet Glove: Paternalism and Conflict in Gender, Class, and Race Relations*. Berkeley: University of California Press.

KETV. 2014, May 8. "'Nebraska Nice' New State Slogan." http://www.ketv.com /news/nebraska-nice-new-state-slogan/25880756.

Ladson-Billings, G. 2013. "Critical Race Theory—What It Is Not!" In *Handbook of Critical Race Theory in Education*, edited by M. Lynn and A. D. Dixson, 34–47. New York: Routledge.

Leonardo, Z. 2007. "The War on Schools: NCLB, Nation Creation and the Educational Construction of Whiteness." *Race Ethnicity and Education* 10, no. 3: 261–78.

Leonardo, Z. 2009. *Race, Whiteness, and Education*. New York: Routledge.

Lipsitz, G. 1998. *The Possessive Investment in Whiteness: How White People Profit from Identity Politics*. Philadelphia: Temple University Press.

Mazzei, L. A. 2008. "Silence Speaks: Whiteness Revealed in the Absence of Voice." *Teaching and Teacher Education* 24, no. 5: 1125–36.

Menkart, D. 1998. "Heritage Months and Celebrations: Some Considerations." In *Beyond Heroes and Holidays: A Practical Guide to K–12 Anti-racist, Multicultural Education and Staff Development*, edited by E. Lee, D. Menkart, and M. Okazawa-Rey, 376–78. Washington, D.C.: Network of Educators on the Americas.

Nieto, S. 2010. "Affirmation, Solidarity, and Critique: Moving beyond Tolerance in Multicultural Education." In *Language, Culture, and Teaching: Critical Perspectives*, 2nd ed., 247–63. New York: Routledge.

Omi, M. 2001. "(E)racism: Emerging Practices of Antiracist Organizations." In *The Making and Unmaking of Whiteness*, edited by B. B. Rasmussen, E. Klinenberg, I. J. Nexica, and M. Wray, 266–93. Durham, N.C.: Duke University Press.

Orfield, G. 2009. *Reviving the Goal of an Integrated Society: A 21st Century Challenge*. Los Angeles: Civil Rights Project/Proyecto Derechos Civiles.

Picower, B. 2009. "The Unexamined Whiteness of Teaching: How White Teachers Maintain and Enact Dominant Racial Ideologies." *Race Ethnicity and Education* 12, no. 2: 197–215.

Pratt, M. L. 1991. "Arts of the Contact Zone." *Profession*, 33–40.

Sierk, J. L. 2016. "*Coming of Age in the New Latino Diaspora: An Ethnographic Study of High School Seniors in Nebraska*." PhD diss., University of Nebraska.

Spradley, J. P. 1979. *The Ethnographic Interview*. Belmont, CA: Wadsworth.

Spradley, J. P. 1980. *Participant Observation*. New York: Holt, Rinehart and Winston.

Stacy, J., E. T. Hamann, and E. G. Murillo Jr. 2015. "Education Policy Implementation in the New Latino Diaspora." In *Revisiting Education in the New Latino Diaspora*, edited by E. T. Hamann, S. Wortham, and E. G. Murillo Jr., 335–47. Charlotte, N.C.: Information Age.

Thompson, A. 2003. "Tiffany, Friend of People of Color: White Investments in Antiracism." *International Journal of Qualitative Studies in Education* 16, no. 1: 7–29.

U.S. Census Bureau. 2018. "Nebraska QuickFacts." https://www.census.gov/quick
facts/ne.

Valdés, G. 2001. *Learning and Not Learning English: Latino Students in American
Schools*. New York: Teachers College Press.

Vavrus, M. 2015. *Diversity and Education: A Critical Multicultural Approach*.
New York: Teachers College Press.

4

Niceness in Special Education

An Ethnographic Case Study of Benevolence, Goodness, and Paternalism at Colina Cedro Charter High School

Sylvia Mac

Compared to the common school championed by Horace Mann in the 1800s—which provided free universal education to children—special education is a relatively new institution in the United States, having only been mandated by federal law in 1975 with the passage of the Education for All Handicapped Children Act of 1975. While some schools and institutions existed in the 1900s for disabled students, states historically repeatedly upheld the exclusion of these children despite compulsory education laws (Yell, Rogers, and Rogers 1998). The right for disabled students to attend public school grew out of the civil rights movement, spurred on by key legislation such as *Brown v. Board of Education* in 1954, to provide disabled students with an equal opportunity to attend public schools. More recently, advocates have pushed for inclusion in schools, where disabled students are fully included in the general education setting alongside their nondisabled peers. As a result, special and inclusive education has long been framed as a kind, benevolent public service that provides opportunities to those for whom they had been traditionally denied.

Charter schools have a similar stated "nice" goal of serving underserved communities. Originally, progressive educators in the 1980s developed charter schools in order to create educational alternatives in poor communities of color. Charter schools were guided by social justice principles with hopes to improve access to quality schools, as well as academic performance. In return for autonomy in teaching and curriculum, charter schools were willing to offer increased accountability, presumably through student test scores. Today's charter schools no longer represent the original ones that were rooted in the community and mainly run by educators, because it was not long before "the social justice motor was appropriated and reengineered by philanthropic, corporate, hedge-fund and real estate interests" (Fabricant and Fine 2012, 2). Nevertheless, charter schools are seen by many as a noble and socially just endeavor.

This chapter focuses on how Niceness operates to maintain educational inequity through special education at a small charter school in Southern California. It seeks to understand how class, race, and ability intersected to produce material consequences that maintain educational inequity for special education students at Colina Cedro Charter High School. I argue that in the same way that uncritical multicultural education has been unsuccessful because of its failure to engage in issues of power and distribution of resources (Castagno 2014), inclusive education has also failed to significantly change the landscape for disabled students as a whole because it has relied on simply being a nice and noble pursuit without interrogating how social constructions of race, class, and ability have led to low expectations and reified educational inequality.

I define Niceness as acts that are socially acceptable, virtuous, and respectable. Niceness, or doing the "right" thing, is at the heart of both special education and charter schools. Both have the stated purpose of providing quality education for marginalized students and of ensuring that all students have access to excellent education. Despite their good intentions, however, special education and charter schools have not been able to ameliorate long-standing inequalities. Artiles (2011) notes, for example, an "interesting paradox" in which the "civil rights response for one group of individuals (i.e., learners with disabilities) has become a potential source of inequities for another group (i.e., racial minority students), despite their shared histories of struggle for equity" (431). That is to say, while special education has afforded educational opportunities for some, it has not been without consequence for others, as demonstrated by the historical and persistent overrepresentation of students of color in special education (Artiles 2011; Beratan 2008; Blanchett, Klingner, and Harry 2009; Fergus 2016; Harry and Klingner 2006). Similarly, despite their positioning as an engine for social justice, charter schools have actually exacerbated racial segregation (Frankenberg et al. 2012; Miron et al. 2010; Whitehurst, Reeves, and Rodrigue 2016) and have a history of underenrollment of disabled students (Dudley-Marling and Baker 2012; Waitoller, Maggin and Trzaska 2017).

This chapter begins with an overview of the conceptual framework that provides the foundation for analysis and a description of the context in which the critical ethnographic case study was performed. Next, I outline how Niceness informs special education at Colina Cedro Charter High School, and I focus on three primary iterations of Niceness in this context: benevolence, constructions of goodness, and paternalism. In the end, special education functions to maintain educational inequity, as measured by access to quality education and the lack of support for struggling students, both of which lead to material consequences during and after K–12 schooling for poor, disabled students.

Conceptual Framework and Methodology

Scholars have noted the need for an interdisciplinary approach that considers the ways that "race and dis/ability are co-constructed" (Annamma, Connor, and Ferri 2013, 6) in a framework that combines Disability Studies and Critical Race Theory (DisCrit). Accordingly, disability is understood as "a political identity, socially constructed in tandem with race and class, rather than an objective medical condition" (Annamma, Ferri, and Connor 2018, 48). This chapter utilizes the DisCrit framework to understand how special education may serve to reproduce social inequality in poor, disabled students of color. A central tenet of DisCrit holds that "gains for people labeled with dis/abilities have largely been made as the result of interest convergence of White, middle-class citizens" (Annamma, Connor, and Ferri 2013, 11). Thus, while special education has been characterized by Niceness or "benevolent humanitarianism," it has always been a "social categorisation of weaker social groups" (Tomlinson 1982, 5).

This critical ethnographic case study took place over the course of one school year in a small, urban charter school that I call Colina Cedro Charter High School, which serves students in grades nine through twelve in a working-class neighborhood ("Eastwick") in a large city in California ("Colfax"). Participants included three students enrolled in special education, the special education teacher, the special education teaching assistant, a regular education algebra teacher, the school principal, and the two founders and charter writers of Colina Cedro. I used a variety of methods, including participant observation, interviews, and document analysis. I spent time at the school as a volunteer three days per week in the special education classroom, and assisted students in both the regular and special education classrooms. I made observations in the special education classroom, as well as the regular education classrooms where students with individualized education programs (IEPs) were present. I observed classes in a variety of subjects, including algebra, biology, chemistry, English, government, U.S. history, and world history. I conducted semistructured interviews with each of the participants that lasted thirty minutes to an hour, and were followed by a thirty-minute "member check," whereby the participant and I had an opportunity to read through the interview transcript to ask for clarification, modification, or deletion within a month of the interview. I analyzed documents and artifacts, such as assignments, tests, and quizzes used in the regular and special education classrooms, school- and district-level data regarding disability enrollment and diagnoses, standardized testing data, student work, student IEPs, the school charter, and the school employee handbook.

Context and Setting: Colina Cedro Charter High School

The staff at Colina Cedro seemed to be driven by nice and virtuous acts; two of the ten teachers had previously served in the Peace Corps. Dr. James stated that prior to joining Colina Cedro, he came from a much more affluent district and also taught at a local university. He worked in the local university's master's degree program for educational administrators, and he felt his students just "wanted to move on the salary scale." So he felt that a change was necessary because he didn't feel he was "really helping anyone with anything really, except to make more money." The school founders seemed to share the desire to perform Niceness: they told me they purposefully looked for "the neediest population in Colfax." After they established a successful charter in a suburban area of Colfax, they were looking for "a bigger challenge" and thus started Colina Cedro in the inner city.

Special education at Colina Cedro was also characterized by the desire to do the "right" thing. The principal, Dr. James, was a parent of two students with disabilities. He pushed for the inclusion of his own children at the school and believed strongly that Colina Cedro should provide the same opportunities to all children. Previous to his tenure at Colina Cedro, special education at the school ran very traditionally, where students with IEPs were pulled out of the general education classroom for special education services. When he became principal, Dr. James decided to move the school to a completely inclusive program, where all special education students were fully included in (or "pushed in") general education classrooms. He was proud of the push-in model and told me he "loved" it.

The staff did create a class called Study Skills, which students with IEPs took as an elective study hall–type class, but students were otherwise enrolled in all general education classes. Of the twenty-five or so students receiving special education support (the number fluctuated throughout the year, as a result of late additions or withdrawals), the majority were labeled with a specific learning disability, with two students labeled as other health impaired and only one student labeled as having an emotional disorder. Given that the school's population comprised 81 percent Latinx students, they also represented the majority of those enrolled in special education at Colina Cedro. Black students made up the rest.

Benevolence: Niceness without Expertise, Experience, or Resources

The staff at Colina Cedro was driven to implement inclusion because it was the nice, or socially acceptable, thing to do. These benevolent intentions, however, could not compensate for the special education staff's lack of experience or training in successful inclusive education. Neither Ms. Rutherford, the special education teacher, nor Ms. Castillo, the special education teaching assistant, had experience with inclusion. In fact, Ms. Rutherford previously worked in a private school setting where every student was a student with a disability. Additionally, as the only two special education staff members, Ms. Rutherford and Ms. Castillo were often overwhelmed and did not have the resources to properly implement inclusive education. Without expertise, experience, or resources, benevolent intentions led to negative educational experiences for the students at Colina Cedro.

While the staff always referred to the model at Colina Cedro as "inclusive" or "cotaught," the actual model I saw each day did not resemble an inclusive or cotaught setting. This seemed to stem from the fact that no one had experience with inclusion or had a clear definition for it, despite their benevolent intentions to give their students access to the general education curriculum. Coteaching is essential to inclusion and is defined as "a specific service delivery option that relies on collaboration" (Cook and Friend 2010, 4) between special and general education to provide services to disabled students in the general education classroom. When I described coteaching to Ms. Castillo, she said, "I never thought about that. That's, uh . . . that would be a good idea, maybe?" It seemed she had not ever be told what coteaching is, despite being responsible for doing it. Ms. Nowak, a general education algebra teacher, seemed to also be unclear on how she was supposed to be supporting students with disabilities in her class: "I just wish I would have, like, more suggestions—what exactly to do, and . . . what I can do to help them." Neither Ms. Rutherford nor Ms. Castillo ever cotaught but were there primarily in the background in general education classrooms for support (circulating to ensure students were on task, keeping track of assignments, noting who was failing or missing assignments, answering questions, etc.). Equipped only with benevolence, the staff at Colina Cedro was ill prepared to implement coteaching models that would lead to successful inclusive education.

The scheduling did not permit Ms. Rutherford or Ms. Castillo to be in the general education classroom more, even though the school sought to provide inclusive education. Out of the six class periods, three were Study Skills classes, and one was Ms. Rutherford's planning period. This meant she only had two class periods per day designated to provide inclusion services in the regular education classrooms. An inclusive education program cannot be successful if the two special education representatives spend more time inside the special education classroom than outside it.

Lacking more resources and staff, Ms. Rutherford tried to bring students together in groups in general education classes so that she could attend one or two classes and see several students at once. Unfortunately, this meant that if one student's schedule did not work out that way and he or she happened to end up in a class with few other special education students, that student would likely not be receiving special education services at all. Regarding the following school year's plan, Ms. Castillo said, "Pretty much we're, like, where the most kids are—that's where we have to go. And then there's other classes, and it depends on the, on the kid, you know, like the student. Um, but pretty much, other classes, it's like, there's gonna be a world history class, there's only two students there so I'm gonna go there, like, once a week, maybe? And just ask the teacher what they're doing, but I'm not gonna sit there." In the upcoming school year, Ms. Castillo would only attend a world history class with only two special education students once a week, and she would not even have any interaction with the students, just the teacher. The contact with the teacher would consist solely of knowing what the assignments were. If these students did not come to Study Skills, they would receive no help at all.

It was impossible for Ms. Castillo and Ms. Rutherford to provide push-in support to nearly thirty special education students spread across four grade levels without really sitting down to make a plan with Dr. James and the general education teachers. It seems there was very little conversation at all, much less taking time to make a plan, about the initial decision to move to full inclusion. Ms. Nowak, believing that inclusion was not working, asked Ms. Rutherford about the possibility of doing some pull-out. "Basically, she [Ms. Rutherford] said she can't," Ms. Nowak told me. "Because the principal doesn't want that—yeah. I think he's really pushing for, like, the in . . . the in-class [work]. Ah, so, yeah. So that was, that was the end." This poor execution driven only by benevolence led to unequal educational access for the students with disabilities at Colina Cedro. Sheer will and benevolence did not work, however, and Ms. Rutherford said that in the following year, they would be providing pull-out support rather than inclusive push-in support. After trying for just one year, motivated by good intentions but without expertise, experience, or resources, Colina Cedro was prepared to return to a traditional pull-out model. This is unfortunate given that when inclusion is approached correctly, *all* students can benefit from it (Cosier, Causton-Theoharis, and Theoharis 2013; Hehir et al. 2016; Rujis, Van der Veen, and Peetsma 2010).

Constructions of Goodness: "Nice Kids" and "Bad Boys"

DisCrit "focuses on the ways that the forces of racism and ableism circulate interdependently, often in neutralized and invisible ways, to uphold notions of normalcy" (Annamma, Connor and Ferri 2013, 11). At Colina Cedro, notions of normalcy (and thus deviancy) were indeed reified in invisible ways. Fergus (2016) argues that schools promote "an ideology of achievement based on individual effort and cognitive prowess" that "absolves schools from any responsibility to promote access and opportunity for all students" (122). As a result, racism and ableism circulate through the hidden curriculum (i.e., things taught implicitly, not explicitly) at schools. I saw this through the ways that the staff members expected students to embody Niceness, or characteristics that are virtuous and respectable. Staff celebrated meritocracy, with the underlying message that "nice" people get "nice" things. While it is no doubt nice to praise students' hard work and students who overcome hardships to succeed, it places the focus on the individual rather than on systemic inequities.

Meritocracy was sometimes used to determine which students would receive more help. Rather than receiving help as needed, I saw both Ms. Rutherford and Ms. Castillo use effort as a factor for determining which students were "nice" or "good," and therefore who received help. Santiago, a Colina Cedro senior diagnosed with a specific learning disability who was characterized by his teachers as "lazy," was enrolled in chemistry, but he never received any push-in help from either Ms. Rutherford or Ms. Castillo. When they found out that Santiago failed a multiple-choice quiz in chemistry because he failed to mark even one answer on the quiz (he turned it in blank), neither Ms. Rutherford nor Ms. Castillo appeared shocked, asked him why he did that, or admonished him to ask for help the next time. Instead they just laughed it off as another story of how lazy Santiago was. When I asked him why he did not mark any answers, he told me he was so lost, he didn't see any point in trying. When I asked why he didn't ask Ms. Rutherford or Ms. Castillo for help, he responded, "There's no point." The teachers frequently allowed him to nap or talk with friends during Study Skills classes, despite the fact that he was failing chemistry. In order to at least get *some* points, I watched Santiago copy another student's correct answers—"correcting" his quiz for half credit. In fact, Ms. Rutherford told Santiago to focus on raising his grade in English because he was going to fail chemistry anyway. His failure did not appear to bother his teachers, presumably, because he was not a "good" kid.

By contrast, a student named Alejandro, who was also diagnosed with a specific learning disability, received much more help than Santiago did because he was seen as a "nice kid" who worked hard. I observed that Ms. Castillo frequently sat next to him during an Algebra Extended class to help him with assignments and homework. In an interview, Ms. Castillo stated, "Some kids, I'm like, ugh, why . . . I don't want to be mean, but you know it's, they, they don't want to pass. But for Alejandro's case, I mean, he's such a nice kid and I really wish him well, and I feel bad, you know, when he's struggling. And he really doesn't get it, so yes, I, you know, for those kids, I kind of go out of my way to help them because I think they deserve that help." Alejandro was a well-mannered, well-liked student who was not perceived as having a behavioral problem. He struggled as much as some of the other students in Algebra Extended, and maybe more, but since he was seen as a "nice kid" he had the benefit of the doubt that his struggles were "real," while other students' struggles were self-made by their perceived laziness and poor behavior. I never observed Ms. Rutherford and Ms. Castillo helping Santiago with his chemistry assignments (or even the math that would allow him to do the calculations) either in Study Skills or the general education class, even though he frequently complained of not understanding chemistry. Alejandro, on the other hand, "deserved" extra support from his teachers because they believed he individually tried hard and behaved in ways that they appreciated.

Niceness in Special Education 61

These interactions demonstrate what Broderick and Leonardo (2016) call "goodness as ideological property." They argue that "our identities as 'smart' (or not) and 'good' (or not) are actively constituted . . . and that cultural institutions of schooling play central roles in shaping our identities within the boundaries of these ideological systems" (55). For example, Santiago seemed to react to the teachers' preference for helping other students instead of him by frequently referring to himself and another student in Study Skills as "bad boys." He seemed to internalize this label and tried to live up to it and encouraged another student to join them in being "bad." He often napped, joked and talked with friends, or generally goofed off during Study Skills. Broderick and Leonardo (2016) further contend that notions of smartness and goodness result in material consequences; for Santiago, this meant far less support and guidance than were given to "good" or "nice" students like Alejandro.

For other disabled students at Colina Cedro, the opportunity to remain in the general education classroom all day, without having to sacrifice an elective to come to Study Skills, was also dependent on constructions of smartness and goodness: those who were seen as "smart" or "good" were enrolled in Study Skills, while others (not "good" and/or "smart") remained in general education for the full day. Even a general education class such as Algebra Extended (remedial Algebra I) served as a way to track all low-level (not "smart") students and students with behavioral problems (not "good"), whether the students had IEPs or not. Ms. Nowak, the algebra teacher, was adamant that Algebra Extended was "not working." When I asked what she meant, she said,

> Basically, in Algebra Extended, you have the lowest kids, usually with very poor behavior, so even if you have a student who came right away and was very low, but tried, by looking what's around that student, like, nobody tries, no motivation, they feed off each other and they become the same. So this year I suggested that instead of putting those lower students all in one class, spread them [out]. Let them work with someone who is more motivated. Because when they see this, if they see, oh, Johnny takes notes, I think I have to do the same, so it's like a better influence on them.

Ms. Nowak saw how grouping these students together led to students learning to be the "bad" and "low" students. She suggested that they did not have the motivation to become "good" students because they were in a class known for the lowest and worst students, so there really wasn't any expectation to become better or different.

Ms. Castillo spoke to how "good" and "bad" identities affected students' confidence to become a self-fulfilling prophecy:

> They're just wasting—like, I don't want to sound like . . . it's just, it's just wasted time. I don't, I don't know because they're sitting there

> and they're so lost. And they . . . I mean their confidence, also, I
> think affects them because they, they feel like, I don't know, like a
> failure because they can't understand anything. And it's not like they
> *can't*; it's that they were lost somewhere along the line and they're
> just totally lost. And now they act as if they don't care. And then
> they just start playing around and, whatever, wasting time, and I
> think it's sad.

Ms. Castillo felt the students' time was wasted because they "feel . . . like a failure," and as a result, they disengage from class and "start playing around and, whatever."

Through these interactions, teachers at Colina Cedro demonstrated the ways students were taught and held to concepts of normalcy implicitly through the processes of special education: a celebration of hard work and meriting more help or a different classroom placement by being a "nice" student. These examples also revealed the material benefits afforded or denied based on constructions of "good" or "smart" identities and how educational inequality was maintained for already marginalized students. The staff expected the students to exemplify Niceness in the form of socially acceptable and respected behavioral traits such as hard work and good behavior; students who did not conform to this idea of Niceness received little help or were segregated in Study Skills or Algebra Extended, despite a stated inclusive education program.

When the school staff members perpetuate this myth of bad, lazy students and families as a contributing factor in low academic achievement, it doesn't matter how kind or nice their intentions may be. This deficit thinking is dangerous because it reveals unacknowledged classism (Gorski 2005) as well as ableism (Apple 2001) and racism (Fergus 2016). Liasidou (2012) argues that "the gaze is squarely placed on students' presumed 'deficits' and common practice is to silence the ways in which disability is, to a significant extent, an ideologically and socially mediated phenomenon that emanates from and rests upon wider sociopolitical and cultural contextual factors" (171). Presumed deficits were either attributed to a student's disability as a biological truth, rather than a socially constructed one or, alternately, a deficit in the student's personality, race, or class. Similar to the debunked culture of poverty theory, which paints poor students of color as lazy and morally deficient (Gorski 2005), students in this study were seen as "bad" students whose families didn't care about their education. These students were expected to "overcome," and those who were unable to do so failed. Moreover, when these students did fail, they were perceived as not trying hard enough. The narrative of overcoming is popular when speaking about both poor students of color and disabled students. Poor, disabled students of color are expected to overcome both their poverty and the academic problems related to their disabilities. They are expected to be successful in a school system that is primarily built to serve the needs of students who fit within "normal" development parameters. Rather than complain about the special education program at Colina Cedro, these students were expected to work extra hard to succeed. Their failure in these classes meant they were not trying hard enough. A strong work ethic is undoubtedly important to student success, but it ignores the fact that systemic inequalities cause some students to start out much farther behind than others.

Paternalism: Deficit Thinking Disguised as Niceness

Ms. Rutherford and Ms. Castillo appeared to subscribe to negative stereotypes regarding their students, but these stereotypes were covered by seemingly nice attitudes. This paternalistic ableism is frequently a problem in special education (Kirby 2017). Hahn (1986) argues that this paternalism "enables the dominant elements of a society to express profound and sincere sympathy for the members of a minority group while, at the same time, keeping them in a position of social and economic subordination" (130). While real sympathy and concern may come from a desire to be nice, they can have negative effects.

When asked to describe her role as a teaching assistant, Ms. Castillo stated that she took notes for students and had to "babysit." She did not say this disparagingly; on the contrary, she thought she was being nice and was happy to help. But treating the students in this way fed into the stereotype that disabled students need others to save them or to do it for them. Ms. Castillo often spoke of the special education students as wholly dependent and incapable on their own. When speaking of her role in the regular education classroom, she said, "I'm the one listening for the kids, I guess. So I take all the notes and I help them, you know, like, I write the notes in such a way so that when were back in the classroom, they can understand better . . . because sometimes these kids can't understand, like, the questions and they just, they have a hard time." In this statement she appeared to infantilize the students. She took the notes for them as an act of Niceness because she felt it would help them to understand it better. With her help, however, students did not learn to be self-sufficient or successful, meaning that the students' marginalized position remained unchanged.

Others in the school also displayed paternalistic attitudes under the guise of Niceness. The intersection of poverty, race, and disability created, for this school, a population in need of rescue, revealing some dangerous stereotypes. In this case Niceness opened the door for paternalistic benevolence. During interviews, I felt a sense that the teachers and principal pitied the students and their families, and they felt that working at *this* school with *these* students was valuable, meaningful work that made a difference. It seemed that the staff felt this was meaningful and important work because the students' circumstances were "sad." Consider, for example, Ms. Castillo's feelings regarding working at Colina Cedro: "It's kind of sad because they [the students] have other issues and stories. And I used to work for, just a normal school, and not, you know, and here's their backgrounds, their upbringings, there's a lot of *things*. You know, personal things going on with them. And that, to me, makes it, like, they're special kids. You know, I just feel so bad, you know, I'm reading their IEPs and whatever, and it's just sad. The other kids, they just had learning disabilities or whatever, but they weren't, like, homeless—they didn't have issues like that." Ms. Castillo distinguished her former school as "normal," thus making this school with its high-needs population "abnormal." As a "nice" person, she felt that the students' poverty and extreme circumstances made them "special," and it made her "feel so bad." Part of Ms. Castillo's engagement with Niceness lay in the fact that she seemed to pity the students and positioned them as needing to be rescued.

The school and the teachers served as this rescue. Despite her nice intentions about starting Colina Cedro in the Eastwick neighborhood, one of the founders, Ms. Fanning, said some shocking things about the students. She explained to me how her Entrepreneur class worked in the on-campus café the class operated. She allowed the students to run all aspects of the café, including collecting and counting the money. She said, "And I would sit there with them whenever they handled money, you know because this was, these were poor kids—the temptation would have been huge. Um, and I didn't want to even tempt them, you know, they were good kids; I liked all of them. But you know, they're poor." She offered the explanation that "they're poor" as a completely reasonable explanation for not trusting them to count the money on their own; she assumed their temptation to steal would be "huge" since the kids were poor students of color. She attempted to claim that she wasn't disparaging the students, because they were "good" and she liked them, but she ultimately made demeaning statements about her students that revealed the negative stereotypes she held about poor students.

When Ms. Fanning was telling me about the café, she told me about one student who did extremely well in that setting. She told me how great he was at calculating costs and called him an "incredibly bright kid," but then she began talking about him going to jail, "and someday he'll run his own restaurant, if he ever gets out of jail. I mean, he'll probably be in and out of jail for a while and then he'll run his own restaurant." It did not appear that the student had actually ever gone to jail, but she just assumed it to be a part of his career trajectory. She thought he'd "probably" go to jail before owning a restaurant. This was all pure speculation on her part, her assumption of where a kid from Eastwick would go. In another instance, she lamented that "these kids" would "end up on the street as drug users because they don't have *any* skills." While she made these statements with sentiments of caring for the students and why she wanted to "reach" them, they revealed some dangerous negative stereotypes. But the situation also provided the impetus for her Niceness; without a group of students needing her help, there would be no need for Colina Cedro.

These paternalistic views demonstrate another way that DisCrit can be helpful in recognizing how racism and ableism operate in conjunction. DisCrit "emphasizes the social constructions of race and ability and yet recognizes the material and psychological impacts of being labeled as raced or dis/abled, which sets one outside of the western cultural norms" (Annamma, Connor, and Ferri 2013, 11). While the staff members wanted to help the students for whom they felt bad, their focus on the students' poverty, race, and ability as individual deficits meant they were able to ignore the systemic inequalities that affect poor urban schools. Colina Cedro, although positioned as the heroic savior, provided very few opportunities for the students; and despite being opened as a charter focused on science, technology, engineering, and math, the school did not have a computer lab or media center, science lab, library, or even a cafeteria. Instead, it operated behind another school's property, renting out its extra outdoor classrooms. For students of Colina Cedro, there were very real material impacts of being marked as poor, disabled students of color. Additionally, the negative stereotypes were perpetuated because they were covered with an altruistic and nice (if paternalistic) goal of serving and helping needy children. While Colina Cedro used nice language and had good intentions, the underlying deficit thinking remain unchanged, and thus was unable to fully address class-, race- and ability-based inequities and instead maintained the status quo.

The Maintenance of Inequality in Poor, Disabled Students of Color

DisCrit argues that "racism and ableism are normalizing processes that are interconnected and collusive. In other words, racism and ableism often work in ways that are unspoken, yet racism validates and reinforces ableism, and ableism validates and reinforces racism" (Annamma, Connor, and Ferri 2013, 6). At Colina Cedro, race, class, and ability intersected and interacted to reproduce social inequality for poor, disabled students of color. Teachers were able to ignore the systemic inequities because they focused instead on what they determined to be individual deficits. If teachers perceived students to be "bad boys" rather than "nice kids," then they would be allowed to fail because failure was in these instances a natural consequence of poor effort. This is especially true for disabled students because "once in special education, the processes will stress, explicitly or implicitly, the negative aspects bound up with handicap or needs—the *incapacity*, the *inability*, or *disability*" (Tomlinson 1982, 121). This is further complicated by race, as scholars have pointed out the racial biases that result in more students of color being referred, and ultimately placed, in special education (Connor 2017; Harry and Klingner 2006; Skiba et al. 2006). On their IEPs, students at Colina Cedro were almost exclusively defined by their deficits and inabilities, so low academic achievement was expected; success was a delightful surprise. Despite the school's good intentions and desire to serve a marginalized population out of Niceness, I never got the feeling that anyone actually expected Santiago or any of the other "bad boys" to succeed. Similarly, no one seemed to be surprised or upset about them failing their courses.

Disabled students, especially Black and Brown disabled students, have particularly poor transition outcomes, including high dropout rates and difficulty transitioning to postschool life, and these lead to high unemployment and high incarceration rates (Altman 2005; Harris, Owen and Gould 2012; Smith and Routel 2010). The dismal outcome for students with disabilities has become even more dire given the emergence of the global knowledge economy. Tomlinson (2013) states that knowledge economy refers to "advances in information and communication technologies, especially the speed with which information can be processed and passed around, and increased digitalization of information" (18), which ultimately leads to an "increased demand for higher-level skills and diminished demand for lower-level work" (21). Employment in these higher-level skills areas requires increasingly more higher education and various credentials and certifications. With such a large number of disabled students dropping out of high school or not pursuing higher education, "low attainers," as Tomlinson (2013) calls them, are increasingly marginalized as they are unable to participate in the knowledge economy. Of course, not being able to participate in higher-skilled areas means either unemployment or working in low-skilled areas. Using this understanding of both general and special education as a stratifying tool in a global knowledge economy, I have argued that the push for inclusion solely because it is "nice" or the "right" thing to do has failed to adequately address the needs of disabled students or to significantly improve educational inequity overall. As a result, special education remains a way to "separate out young people on the basis of ability or disability and the resulting separation by social class and ethnicity" (Tomlinson 2017, 11).

References

Altman, B. M. 2005. "The Labor Market Experience for People with Disabilities: The Conundrum." *Work and Occupations* 32, no. 3: 360–64.

Annamma, S. A., D. J. Connor, and B. A. Ferri. 2013. "Dis/ability Critical Race Studies (DisCrit): Theorizing at the Intersections of Race and Dis/ability." *Race Ethnicity and Education* 16, no. 1: 1–31.

Annamma, S. A., B. A. Ferri, and D. J. Connor. 2018. "Disability Critical Race Theory: Exploring the Intersectional Lineage, Emergence, and Potential Futures of DisCrit in Education." *Review of Research in Education* 42, no. 1: 46–71.

Apple, M. 2001. "Comparing Neo-liberal Projects and Inequality in Education." *Comparative Education* 37, no. 4: 409–23.

Artiles, A. J. 2011. "Toward an Interdisciplinary Understanding of Educational Equity and Difference: The Case of the Racialization of Ability." *Educational Researcher* 40, no. 9: 431–45.

Beratan, G. 2008. "The Song Remains the Same: Transposition and the Disproportionate Representation of Minority Students in Special Education." *Journal of Race, Ethnicity, and Education* 11, no. 4: 337–54.

Blanchett, W. J., J. K. Klingner, and B. Harry. 2009. "The Intersection of Race, Culture, Language, and Disability: Implications for Urban Education." *Urban Education* 44, no. 4: 389–409.

Broderick, A. A., and Z. Leonardo. 2016. "What a Good Boy: The Deployment and Distribution of 'Goodness' as Ideological Property in Schools." In *DisCrit: Disability Studies and Critical Race Theory in Education*, edited by D. J. Connor, B. A. Ferri, and S. A. Annamma, 55–67. New York: Teachers College Press.

Castagno, A. E. 2014. *Educated in Whiteness: Good Intentions and Diversity in Schools*. Minneapolis: University of Minnesota Press.

Connor, D. J. 2017. "Who Is Responsible for the Racialized Practices Evident within (Special) Education and What Can Be Done to Change Them?" *Theory into Practice* 56, no. 3: 226–33.

Cook, L., and Friend, M. 2010. "The State of the Art of Collaboration on Behalf of Students with Disabilities." *Journal of Educational and Psychological Consultation* 20, no. 1:1–8.

Cosier, M., J. Causton-Theoharis, and G. Theoharis. 2013. "Does Access Matter? Time in General Education and Achievement for Students with Disabilities." *Remedial and Special Education* 34, no. 6: 323–32.

Dudley-Marling, C., and D. Baker. 2012. "The Effects of Market-Based School Reforms on Students with Disabilities." *Disability Studies Quarterly* 32, no. 2. http://dsq-sds.org/article/view/3187/3072.

Fabricant, M., and M. Fine. 2012. *Charter Schools and the Corporate Makeover of Public Education: What's at Stake?* New York: Teachers College Press.

Fergus, E. 2016. "Social Reproduction Ideologies: Teacher Beliefs about Race and Culture." In *DisCrit: Disability Studies and Critical Race Theory in Education*, ed. D. J. Connor, B. A. Ferri, and S. A. Annamma, 117–27. New York: Teachers College Press.

Frankenberg, E., G. Siegel-Hawley, J. Wang, and G. Orfield. 2012. *Choice without Equity: Charter School Segregation and the Need for Civil Rights Standards*. Los Angeles: Civil Rights Project/Proyecto Derechos Civiles. https://escholarship.org/uc/item/4r07q8kg#page-5.

Gorski, P. 2005, September 23. "Savage Unrealities: Uncovering Classism in Ruby Payne's Framework." http://www.edchange.org/publications/Savage_Unrealities.pdf.

Hahn, H. 1986. "Public Support for Rehabilitation Programs: The Analysis of U.S. Disability Policy." *Disability, Handicap, and Society* 1, no. 2: 121–37.

Harris, S. P., R. Owen, and R. Gould. 2012. "Parity of Participation in Liberal Welfare States: Human Rights, Neoliberalism, Disability and Employment." *Disability and Society* 27, no. 6: 823–36.

Harry, B., and J. Klingner. 2006. *Why Are So Many Minority Students in Special Education?* New York: Teachers College Press.

Hehir, T., T. Grindal, B. Freeman, R. Lamoreau, Y. Borquaye, and S. Burke. 2016. *A Summary of the Evidence on Inclusive Education*. São Paulo: Instituto Alana. http://alana.org.br/wp-content/uploads/2016/12/A_Summary_of_the_evidence_on_inclusive_education.pdf.

Kirby, M. 2017. "Implicit Assumptions in Special Education Policy: Promoting Full Inclusion for Students with Learning Disabilities." *Child Youth Care Forum* 46, no. 2: 175–91.

Liasidou, A. 2012. "Inclusive Education and Critical Pedagogies at the Intersections of Disability, Race, Gender, and Class." *Journal for Critical Educational Policy Studies* 10, no. 1: 168–84.

Miron, G., J. Urschel, W. J. Mathis, and E. Tornquist. 2010. *Schools without Diversity: Educational Management Organizations, Charter Schools, and the Demographic Stratification of the American School System*. Boulder, Colo.: National Education Policy Center. http://nepc.colorado.edu/publication/schools-without-diversity.

Rujis, N. M., I. Van der Veen, and T. T. Peetsma. 2010. "Inclusive Education and Students without Special Educational Needs." *Educational Research* 52, no. 4: 351–90.

Skiba, R., A. Simmons, S. Ritter, K. Kohler, M. Henderson, and T. Wu. 2006. "The Context of Minority Disproportionality: Practitioner Perspectives on Special Education Referral." *Teachers College Record* 108, no. 7: 1424–59.

Smith, P., and C. Routel. 2010. "Transition Failure: The Cultural Bias of Self-Determination and the Journey to Adulthood for People with Disabilities." *Disability Studies Quarterly* 30, no. 1. http://dsq-sds.org/article/view/1012.

Tomlinson, S. 1982. *A Sociology of Special Education*. London: Routledge and Kegan Paul.

Tomlinson, S. 2013. *Ignorant Yobs? Low Attainers in a Global Knowledge Economy*. London: Routledge.

Tomlinson, S. 2017. *A Sociology of Special and Inclusive Education: Exploring the Manufacture of Inability*. New York: Routledge.

Waitoller, F. R., D. M. Maggin, and A. Trzaska. 2017. "A Longitudinal Comparison of Enrollment Patterns of Students Receiving Special Education in Urban Neighborhood and Charter Schools." *Journal of Disability Policy Studies* 28, no. 1: 3–12.

Whitehurst, G. J., R. R. Reeves, and E. Rodrigue. 2016. *Segregation, Race, and Charter Schools: What Do We Know?* Washington, D.C.: Center on Children and Families, Brookings Institution. https://www.brookings.edu/wp-content /uploads/2016/10/ccf_20161021segregation_version-10_211.pdf.

Yell, M. L., D. Rogers, and E. L. Rogers. 1998. "The Legal History of Special Education: What a Long, Strange Trip It's Been!" *Remedial and Special Education* 19, no. 4: 219–28.

5

Nice Work

*Young White Women, Near Enemies,
and Teaching inside the Magic Circle*

SALLY CAMPBELL GALMAN

> This lady—the future elementary teacher—has always loved
> children. Her mother, her husband or boyfriend (even strang-
> ers in the streets) have remarked upon her natural aptitude
> with children and small animals. She is gracious, nurturing,
> often soft-spoken, and is usually married (or engaged). The
> words money, career, union, labor, or even job are rarely
> mentioned—leaving listeners with the impression that she
> does not need to rely solely on her income as a teacher to
> survive.
> —Erica R. Meiners, "Disengaging from the Legacy of Lady Bountiful
> in Teacher Education Classrooms"

As U.S. public elementary school students become more diverse, the new teacher cadre has become more homogeneously young, White, and female (Ingersoll and Merrill 2010; King, McIntosh, and Bell-Ellwanger 2016; Zumwalt and Craig 2005). Teacher education programs, despite attempts to recruit more diverse preservice teachers, have nonetheless also remained mostly White and female. And despite more and better conversations about race in those programs, gender and its entanglement with critical perspectives on race remain largely uninterrogated except to note, without comment, that elementary education continues to be a feminized sphere (Acker 1999; Galman and Mallozzi 2012).

Such practices fall short for several reasons. *Feminization* as a term has a prickly history harking back to the need for reliable, malleable, and plentiful cheap labor at the dawn of compulsory schooling. Similarly, its reification is built upon mythologies about female biological aptitude, folklore then (as now) used to justify poor wages and frame teaching as semiprofessional work suitable only for women (Galman 2012). The term *feminization* is further problematic in its tendency to treat gender as isolated, rigidly dichotomous, and biological instead of intersectional, cultural, and performative (Renold and Allan 2006). And, finally, the whole picture is theoretically chancy because, at the end of the day, it isn't really about women: this argument frames female presence in terms of "axial" male absence and positions masculinity as a corrective (Mallozzi and Galman 2015; Martino 2008). This is especially true in early schooling contexts, where the numerical dominance of women, and the feminization hypothesis result in accusations of "inappropriate femininity of culture within schools" (Griffiths 2006, 401).

This chapter explores how gender and work come together for young, White, middle-class preservice teachers themselves. The analyses here are born out of, yet not framed by, the "feminization" discourse and its concomitant axial maleness. Instead, I look at how idealized femininity and ideas of feminine work create the problem of "nice" in the context of teachers' aspirations and imagined trajectories. This conceptualization of "nice" includes performances of idealized femininity and the specific cultural expectations that shape White middle-class girlhood and, later, women's experiences at work across contexts but especially in teaching. This chapter thus asks two key questions: How does work become a performance of idealized White middle-class femininity? And how does being "nice" create potentially negative outcomes for teachers and students alike?

Via analyses of data from an ethnographic study of one cohort of young, White women in an elementary preservice teacher preparation program in 2004–2006, this chapter focuses on participant perceptions of their aptitude for, experiences with, and understandings of their work as gendered, affective labor and their construction of the teacher as an expression of ideal femininity. Finally I suggest that young, middle-class, White women's obsession with appearing "nice" is ultimately deleterious to them and potentially damaging to the students in their future care.

Nice White Girls

When I was working as an elementary school teacher, one of my wise senior colleagues had a saying that has stayed with me: "When trying to find out where some behavior or idea comes from, you don't need to look far. Remember that kids never lick it off the wall. The source is usually much more deliberate." Thus with young women, the source for their ideas about identity and work are usually fed to them with great intentionality—in the media. Ideal womanhood, as a form of femininity, is laid seductively before them throughout girlhood (Mazzarella and Pecora 2002).

Images of female teachers in American popular media paint an exhaustive picture. As McWilliam (1996) writes, these include exaggerated teacher tropes ranging from the Rockwellian and grandmotherly spinster schoolmarm to the hackneyed, sexually transgressive seductress for whom one might be, literally (as in the Van Halen song) "hot for teacher." Young White women coming of age in the mid- to late 1990s also engaged with a different archetype situated firmly in the middle: the "schoolmistress," who is the original nice White girl next door. She is loving without the stigma of old age and sexually desirable without being sexually knowledgeable. She is young, pretty and nice, almost certainly White, and focused on nurturing children as the work of love and as marriage and motherhood's antechamber. Said work of love is certainly poorly paid, as it would be unfair to ask for adequate financial remuneration for something that comes naturally and is inherently rewarding.[1] Her beauty directly reflects her good character, as only the ugly are unkind, like so many toothless fairy-tale witches or hook-nosed, swarthy Disney villainesses. She waits in the classroom for a man, marriage, and family of her own, as compulsory heterosexuality and the primacy of male attention are key components of the feminine ideal.

These femininities are reflected in relevant media expressions. American women who were the age of participants in this study would have grown up with 1990s media and the powerful generational gender imagery communicated there. A few examples: The grade school teacher Miss Marquez played by Jennifer Lopez in the 1996 film *Jack* is attractive and kind, and rarely seen teaching; she spends the entire film ministering to the emotional needs of her students.[2] In the 1996 film adaptation of Roald Dahl's *Matilda*, the character performing the obvious valued feminine identity, Miss Honey, is kind and attractive, sexually unaware, with the innocence (and, one should note, the powerlessness) of a child. In this way she is ostensibly more able to minister to the needs of children, being herself basically a child. Again, the only "bad" teachers are the ugly ones (Dahl's Miss Trunchbull), the headstrong ones (Muriel Spark's titular character in *The Prime of Miss Jean Brodie*) or those not interested in heterosexual destinies (Lillian Hellman's protagonists in *The Children's Hour*). Meanwhile, a casual internet search for movies about teachers reveals multiple and varied portrayals of male teachers, but only one or two movies about female ones—and the majority of the men are secondary education teachers, while nearly every female teacher is working in the early grades. Notably, male teachers' transgressions are as deep and varied as their well-rounded characters, while female teachers' shallow character arcs nearly always hinge on sexual transgressions. Failure to be virginal, or heterosexual, or to appeal directly to the male heterosexual gaze seem to top the bill in this regard.[3]

This aligns with research on more than one generation of young women's beliefs about what constitutes a "good" teacher: As Weinstein (1989) found, when elementary preservice teachers are asked to describe a "good" teacher, they emphasize caring, understanding, warmth, friendliness, and an ability to relate to children. Criticality, intellectualism, pedagogical or content knowledge, and political acumen did not appear to be as relevant. Similarly, other studies have found that White women are invested in appearing to care and "love" children but markedly evasive of and resistant to critical explorations of privilege and injustice that might damage their performances of the feminine ideal and the benefits associated therewith (Frankenberg 1993; Gillespie, Ashbaugh, and DeFiore 2002). Certainly, White women in the United States (and in other contexts as well) undergo a gender socialization that emphasizes avoidance of interpersonal conflict (Coffe and Bolzendahl 2017; Tannen 1990), but there is a strategic and self-preserving element in play as well. As Tatum and Knaplund (1996) found, White women are eager to avoid stepping "outside the magic circle" of White privilege: they are keenly aware of the disruption to their aspirational futures that this unavoidably would entail.

And make no mistake: none of this is innocuous. Per Connell's (2005) hegemonic or "emphasized" femininity, it is all indicative of a woman who is so comfortable with the racist, sexist status quo and general patriarchal subjugation in which she participates, and she perpetuates these power structures despite the fact that doing so is in direct contradiction with her own well-being and that of those in her care (Mallozzi and Galman 2014). Such femininity is so comfortable with dominant culture and traditional North American gender roles—including the belief that men are superior to women—that winning male romantic attention becomes a primary goal and subscription to these roles and beliefs is desirable (Downing and Roush 1985; Galman 2006).

Methodology

This chapter presents analyses of data from an ethnographic study of nineteen young, White, middle-class women in a university elementary teacher preparation program in the western United States between 2002 and 2004.[4] These data constitute a subset of a larger corpus of data from a three-site comparative ethnographic study that included two other university teacher preparation contexts, but the patterns here are representative of a distinct trend found across all the young White women at all three study sites.[5] All participants in these analyses are White, heterosexual, middle-class, female preservice elementary teachers under the age of twenty-three, working at the undergraduate level at a public university with one of the highest tuition rates in the United States at the time. The women featured here were in their last phases of coursework, though they had not yet begun their student teaching semesters. As noted earlier, these participants would have been young adolescents in the mid- to late 1990s in the United States, which was an era of economic prosperity that created the conditions for a generation of postfeminist claims around the irrelevance of feminism and the achievement of supposed equality (Douglas 2010). Similarly, it is important to note that while university contexts are often assumed to be politically progressive and even left-leaning, the student body at this university was somewhat more conservative and generally affluent.

The data were collected between 2002 and 2004, with some postgraduate follow-up in later years. Data sources include multiple open-ended ethnographic interviews, artifact analyses, and participant observation across a range of study contexts, including classrooms and a diverse array of social settings. Analyses were recursive in nature, incorporating modified grounded theory–coding strategies from Strauss and Corbin (1998).

Working at Niceness

For study participants, being a good teacher meant being nice. According to study data, being nice entailed two specific tasks. The first was *performing the work of love*: not engaging politically or critically but instead focusing on affective tasks with individual children performing work as love. The second was *maintaining the appearance of nice*: avoiding conflict in relationships as well as maintaining a pleasing physical and behavioral appearance that appeals to the male heterosexual gaze.

Performing the Work of Love

Telling a story about work as a natural, affective, and largely effortless task was one important part of maintaining the appearance of nice. Among participants, it would have been considered inappropriate to say, instead, that one chose to become a teacher because of the summers off and good medical benefits.[6] The only acceptable reason for wanting to become a teacher was to partake in the work of love and the performance of the idealized feminine. As one participant, Mari, explained, "I just want to be that one teacher that everyone loves, who's really nice, and gentle and sweet, and the kids always remember her."

Not surprisingly, nearly all participants in this study professed their love of all children, their love for the classroom, and their desire to love and be loved, along with a biological aptitude for loving as their primary qualification for becoming elementary school teachers. "It just comes naturally to me" was something echoed in nearly every conversation about why individual participants decided to become teachers. As another participant, Megan, described her professional discernment trajectory, "It was just kind of natural for me to do it. When I was little [family members] all told me I was a mother type or I'd be a teacher. It just kind of felt like the natural profession for me; I always tried to take care of the little kids on the playground when I was playing when I was little. I would find a little three-year-old and help them down the slide or push them on the swings or something. So I've always been interested in kids since I was a kid myself." And another, Lindsey, explained,

> We all talk about how we are so lucky to have a job where we get to
> be with all the cute little kids, where we get hugs and kisses every

day, where we get to do a job we really, really love. I mean, you could never have these kinds of intrinsic rewards in a business firm. We all feel this way. We're so lucky. I love kids. *Loooove* them. I've always had a kind of nurturing thing—everyone says it is so natural for me—and I feel like I really want to reach out to kids. You don't get paid a lot of money, but in the end the reward is ten times better. I think it's also good if I want to have a family.

This was echoed in the statements of other participants, including Morgan, who went so far as to suggest that her professional destiny was literally inscribed in her body such that she was powerless to evade it: "Becoming a teacher was so natural. My mom was like, 'Ever since you were a little girl I knew you'd be a teacher. You were so good with little kids.' And she was right. It was totally in my blood. You can't deny it." The idea of teaching as "natural" and biologically destined was also a frequent theme in participants' stories of career discernment. Like Morgan, participants did not position themselves as agents in their own lives but rather as passengers of unavoidable destiny, void of free will, being moved by an unseen hand toward a "natural" career in teaching. As Lindsay noted,

When I was little I would, like, play teacher with my friends, with stuffed animals and pretend worksheets, and we even had a little chalkboard. I loved my teacher and wanted to be just like her. But then I got to high school and I wanted to be in real estate, like, to get an MBA, to be a businesswoman, and that's what I really focused on in college. But it really didn't feel natural, so I kept thinking, no, I won't be a teacher but it was like teaching was my calling. The [business degree] just felt like an uphill struggle, where I had to be so hard, so I quit the business major and went into teaching. It was like it always meant to be. I couldn't escape it.

Similarly, biology became destiny for Adrienne, whose aptitude took the form of being lovable and loved by children and baby animals: "My mom, my dad, my boyfriend—they all love that I'm going to be a teacher; they all said, 'Yeah, that's perfect for you.' My mom says that when I was growing up I was always so good with children, and our dogs when they were puppies, and all the neighborhood kids wanted me to babysit and they all loved me. So maybe I'm just supposed to do this, like destiny."

Professing and prioritizing love can also be a form of rhetorical distancing from interrogations of privilege and the political, and it is presented as the antithesis of university instruction and any other critical engagement with the work of the teacher. While love and Niceness are unavoidable and biological destinies, all else is undesirable and retrograde, not based in "reality"—which is to say, not aligned with these participants' particular experience and their own memories of schooling, which they saw as positive. Indeed, as many of them highlighted in their own stories of becoming teachers, and of frustration with teacher education, they disliked lesson preparation and coursework and would have preferred to focus on defining their work in the terms of the love and care that come "naturally" to them as women; it should be as effortless as love and as obvious as beauty, and nobody should ever see them sweat. As one participant, Sarah, explained,

> Our classes [are] a little political but I guess I expect that from [the university]. It's the ivory tower and all that. Reality is a little bit different. I mean, I really appreciate what they [teacher educators] are doing for us here, but it just isn't going to be practical in the real world. All the theory, it's great if you're going to be a professor, but I'm going to be a teacher of really, really little kids. I'm going to help little kids put their boots on and teach them ABC. The argument is that there [are] politics in everything, that we do politics when we teach, but we really don't. My teachers never did. They just loved us.

To further define the space between performing the work of love and criticality, more than once I asked individual participants about things they had seen in practicum placements, about teaching practices that weren't necessarily aligned with what they were learning about social justice in their university classrooms, or about low teacher salaries or contentious district policies—especially around issues like union membership, ethnic studies curricula, and parental leave for teachers, to name a few. In the words of one participant, "I'm not here for politics. I need to put the kids first. It's about the kids."[7] The implication that "politics" are self-interested, that one cannot be interested in children and social justice at the same time, or that one cannot pursue justice on behalf of "the kids" suggests that politics is not the issue as much as is the performance of emphasized and idealized femininity. It is also worth examining this as an avoidance not just of politics but of social justice and equity issues, and the privilege associated with the White, middle-class feminine ideal. While participants did not admit to feeling exempt from the issues that they lumped under politics, their privilege very much did exempt them. For example, in their narratives of future life and expected trajectories, most fully expected to marry men with income sufficient that they could "choose" to stay home rather than take advantage (or not) of parental leave policies. Similarly, they were not as concerned about salaries. Their Whiteness and associated White privilege, and the expectation among most of them that their student teaching experiences would be the last time they would be in a diverse school, made the question of an ethnic studies curriculum less interesting and compelling as well. Rhetorically skimming over these and other issues under the banner of "being here for the kids" is really little more than the White middle-class privilege As poster Kate notes at the blog *Black Feminist Thoughts*, "The only people who claim to be apolitical are the ones who experience unearned and unrecognized power from privileged identities (e.g., whiteness, maleness). These people are not forced to confront the politics of their identity because society mirrors the life they are living and the values they hold" (Kate, 2015).

Maintaining the Appearance of Nice

Doing nice work meant avoiding interpersonal conflict as well as maintaining a concordantly pleasing physical appearance and demeanor. Among study participants, the work of managing this took on the magnitude and depth of attention of a Jane Austen novel. Notably, during the period of data collection, there was discussion among the faculty about the established dress code for student teachers. This dress code was focused, rather predictably, on female students, and required a certain skirt length (below the knee), modest necklines, and the understated use of cosmetics, in addition to a rather nebulous—but certainly raced and classed—requirement for "professional dress."[8] I bristled more than once about this dress code, as there was no such specific exhortation directed at men, but most participants defended the dress code as a matter of smart strategy and self-preservation.[9] "I get it—the men don't have a dress code, but for girls, it *is* important that you look a certain way," said Katie, laughing at me, "You don't want girls out there looking like hookers, but you also don't want people in their jeans and sweats. You need to look professional, attractive, kept-up. Nobody will hire an ugly girl stomping around in combat boots." Yet nowhere in the dress code were women required to be pretty, because this was assumed; being pretty was a job requirement. As another participant explained, "All my friends who know me said I'd be perfect as a teacher—stuff like, I'm nice and young and pretty and the kids would love me."

Maintaining the appearance of nice also meant being submissive and pleasing in a variety of public contexts. Lindsay was placed in a school near the university, where she had little in common with her cooperating teacher, a middle-aged woman who frequently played the guitar in class and who created a whole social studies unit where she taught the children 1960s protest songs and took them on a faux peace march around the school grounds. I thought this was fantastic and interesting, but Lindsay was horrified, insisting that it was wildly inappropriate. When I asked her if she talked with the teacher to try to understand the thinking behind what she was doing, Lindsay explained that, for all her very unkind private grousing about this teacher with her fellow preservice teachers, she was not comfortable with what she thought was confrontational. "I'll sit there and watch and be polite, but—oh my *God*—I could never. She needs to like me."

Conflict avoidance was especially problematic in teacher education contexts, where participants were uncomfortable expressing dissent or appearing critical in the face of authority. All but one or two participants volunteered in interviews or university classrooms that they were "not feminist" and claimed a kind of political conservatism such that they found themselves in quiet disagreement with their largely progressive university faculty, whose views about the relevance of racism and the need for political engagement were dismissed as ivory tower nonsense. Again, like Lindsay's disapproval of the political content of her mentor teachers' lessons, these disagreements were exclusively the substance of conversation outside the classroom, and only then in social company, with eye-rolling, laughter, and furtive whispers. Notably, the need to avoid open, potential conflict headed off possible learning: divergent ideas were rarely aired during class discussions, such that I only gained access to them in the form of reflective journals, side conversations, or other private correspondence.

For example, following a reading assignment and class discussion on teaching about the civil rights movement, participants were required to complete a confidential reflective journal assignment (meaning they were to write, but had the choice to not share their writing with the instructor). In these journal entries participants thoughtfully acknowledged the presence of racism as a reality in U.S. culture and the necessity for teachers to teach about the civil rights movement. Yet they were also concerned about getting in trouble or appearing controversial by teaching this material. Here are some examples:

- Teaching Civil Rights is a controversial issue; as a teacher I will need to be careful and teach about Civil Rights in an unbiased way—that it's not right or wrong.
- How realistic is it [to teach about civil rights] in today's social climate and not lose your job?
- It is important for teachers to teach about racism, but it is not always that easy because the issues are very controversial . . . teachers need to address racism from all angles and different aspects to be fair.
- This is important, but I think elementary kids are too young to learn about it. I'm not sure it is age-appropriate.

Participant positioning of widely accepted and canonical American history content as somehow controversial and "age-inappropriate" was deeply informative and aligned with the performance of nice: Participant views were not based on the canon, per se, but rather on popular perceptions and hegemonic norms of nice behavior. In this universe, activism is not considered nice; it would indeed position participants very much "outside the magic circle" (Tatum and Knaplund 1996) and lock them out of the trajectory of emphasized femininity and its promised privilege. Similarly, that preservice teachers would opt out of teaching this content out of fear of being fired for failing to adhere to the tenets of Niceness (which is to say, to avoid difficult emotions, conversations, or conflict and by doing so to continue to cash in on White privilege, in particular) illustrates the stakes involved. Participants' belief in, subjugation to, and reification of a unidirectional hierarchical power structure in schools was evidenced by their fears of being precipitously fired for teaching or saying the wrong thing. That they were more comfortable with this reality than they were with any form of activism—for union protection or the like—speaks to the deep roots and familiarity of hegemony and hierarchy that defines these women's lives. As they say, better the devil you know.

Discussion: Nice Girls and Near Enemies

Cochran-Smith (1991) suggests that we can define good teaching as politically conscious and socially engaged, noting, "[Teachers] have to see beyond and through the conventional labels and practices that sustain the status quo by raising unanswerable and often uncomfortable questions. Perhaps most importantly, teachers who work against the grain must name and wrestle with their own doubts, must fend off the fatigue of reform and depend on the strength of their individual and collaborative convictions that their work ultimately makes a difference in the fabric of social responsibility" (284).

A *near enemy* is a philosophical construct describing two things that look the same but are not, as one of the two is actually a dangerous, damaging opposite. For example, mystery writer Louise Penny (2007) offers the illustrative case of compassion and pity, as "two emotions that look the same but are actually opposites. The one parades as the other, is mistaken for the other, but one is healthy and the other's sick, twisted" (198). For example, as Penny continues, "It looks like compassion, acts like compassion, but is actually the opposite of it. And as long as pity's in place there's not room for compassion. It destroys, squeezes out, the nobler emotion" (198). I would suggest that in the case of most of the young, White, female teachers in this study, *nice* is the near enemy of *good*, with the pursuit and maintenance of the appearance of Niceness driving out actual goodness as defined by Cochran-Smith (1991) and others—in this case, from the act of delivering high-quality instructions and seeking to improve children's lives by advocating for them. To do this kind of classroom good takes courage and often involves conflict, challenging both authority and the status quo; these stand in stark contrast to the goals of idealized femininity as embodied and defined by the study participants. Indeed, nice requires none of these. Instead, nice involves avoiding conflict, supporting existing power structures through obedience, and focusing on one's own appearances to such a degree that substance is easily forgotten.

As I have written elsewhere in similar and related analyses (Galman 2006, 2012), these participants demonstrated a marked need to please, to conform, and to be seen as "good girls"—often at the expense of valuable learning opportunities (Holland and Eisenhart 1992). This calls to mind Lindsay, who preferred to be nice rather than ask critical questions that might have helped her understand professional practice. Additionally, such good girls often avoided social and political engagement that would make them seem "unattractive" or compromise the performance of the "good girl" ideal (Galman 2006).

While a progressive, headstrong teacher who seeks to critique and disrupt racism in her school, join a union, or teach about the civil rights movement would not be seen as nice in the study context, she would certainly be behaving in ways that benefit her students. The nice teacher, meanwhile, does as she is told by the administration regardless of the effects of those actions. She fears stepping outside the magic circle. She guards her privilege and supposed neutrality and is potentially doing evil in the service of nice. As a post at the National Council of Teachers of English blog notes, "There is no apolitical classroom," and "no place for neutrality" (Standing Committee against Racism and Bias in the Teaching of English, 2017). Niceness—despite appearances—is not goodness, but it is obedience.

The Price of Nice

Nearly all participants told stories about teaching as destiny. More than once they described pursuing teaching careers after initial unsuccessful forays into other areas of work, notably in more historically male-dominated areas like business, medicine, and natural science. They were quick, however, to reframe abandoning these other paths and choosing teaching not as "settling" but rather as awakening to their natural abilities and destinies. As Lindsay explained in the paragraphs above, teaching was "natural" while business administration was "hard" and she "could not escape it."

It is clear that social and cultural reinforcement for girls and women choosing to work with children abounds, and women who choose to enter more historically masculine arenas experience alienation and burnout at much higher rates (Sadker and Sadker 1995; Taylor 2016). As Mari said, "I started out wanting to be a physical therapist, but in the end I went to education, where it wasn't all cutthroat and nasty." While none of the women said outright that they abandoned their first professional desires because they were isolated and alienated, or that they fled to the safety of teaching because it was practical, affirming, and familiar, they did, like Mari, talk about the more masculine work arenas as not feeling right, or somehow unnatural, or a bad "fit." Such is the established story of the nascent teaching career as a quasi-mystical calling that sought young persons out despite their attempts to do other things. In the developed narrative of professional trajectory, even their evasive attempts brought them closer to the inevitability of destiny.

The story of the "true calling" not only further reifies the idea of teaching as an affective, emotional calling rather than a job but also absolves the young woman of responsibility for her choices and failures: She can't help being pretty, nor can she outwit her powerful biological drives toward the "natural" work of care. She will fulfill her destiny as a blameless passenger of fate.

Nice work is costly, and not just to the young woman who succumbs to "destiny." The teacher who is most invested in appearances, and especially the appearance of being nice, is less likely to take on the difficult political work of speaking back to administration and standing up for children in the face of potentially damaging practices, relentless testing and accountability regimes, and racist everyday policies. They may be more likely to simply follow instructions, implementing policies and engaging in damaging practices without complaint in order to continue to be seen as nice girls; as noted earlier, that they do all of this with a smile is what makes Niceness the near enemy of goodness: Participants believed it was possible to love a child while also acting against his or her interests, as long as one did so in a nice way: more than one participant described implementing school disciplinary policies that would have disproportionately penalized boys of color.

The cost of putting Niceness—which is to say desirability—first could be particularly concerning when compared with the work of the teacher in a social justice and antiracist context. Teachers are often the first to unquestioningly enable racist policies in the name of behavior management or achievement rhetoric (Galman 2012; Leonardo 2002; Skiba et al. 2002).

Nice versus Nasty

In the universe of near enemies, nice can never do good, but "nasty" can. There were one or two "nasty" women among the study participants, all of whom were easily identifiable because they constructed the work of the teacher as political, transformative, and/or critical intellectual work and were uniformly disliked by their peers for venturing beyond the precarious boundaries of the "magic circle."

One such nasty woman was Anne; a White, middle-class twenty-two-year-old with tattoos and short hair, she consistently politicized her teacher education classroom experiences, critiquing the day-to-day operations of her student teaching placement and fellow preservice teachers' attitudes in light of her interest in teaching for social justice. She earned scowls and eye-rolling from most of the other young women in the cohort, who privately bemoaned Anne's "troublemaking" and suggested that her disruptive politicizing was a direct result of her physical appearance: Her short, masculine haircut, heavy lace-up boots, and tattoos made her stand out among the other women, all of whom sported nearly identical, feminine clothing, meticulous makeup, and long, blown-straight highlighted hair. "She really could just try," whispered another woman in the restroom one afternoon. "She could be almost pretty. Even if she gets a job, the parents will hate her." Others suggested that she was certainly lesbian.

Anne rightly guessed that she would be a poor fit in most public elementary schools, ultimately lasting only one year before going back to school to pursue a degree in library science. When asked about her poor fit, Anne described how being a "nasty" girl decreased both her comfortable fit as well as marketability: "I think that if I verbalized my beliefs [in school], however, people would be like, 'Watch out for this kid—she's going to test us, she's going to push us. Why do we want her when we could have so-and-so who has the same credentials as her and she's pretty and sweet and she'll do a good job? Let's hire her and let someone else deal with Ms. Political.' Men have a little bit more of an upper hand, because women are, 'What if this person doesn't like me? What can I do to please this person?'" Just as the young heroine of Michael Verhoeven's 1990 film *The Nasty Girl* is targeted for telling uncomfortable truths, and Hillary Rodham Clinton was called "that nasty woman" for bringing up Donald Trump's decades of tax evasion and deceitful business practices, nasty does the difficult good that nice impedes.[10] While Anne and the other not-so-nice girls are not the central focus of this chapter, their experiences highlight the larger pattern in place: Nice girls become teachers, whereas "nasty" ones do not.

So, what's the problem with being nice? It's not that the uninterrogated status quo is producing endless Dolores Umbridges, of recent Harry Potter fame, bent on evil with a smile, but rather that nice teachers are more likely to invest in appearances, and to obey and conform, because disobedience, intellectualism, and nonconformity are ugly. All manner of sins have been committed in the name of obedience and conformity. For example, participants believed that they were acting in the child's best interest when it seemed clear to observers that they were actively doing the opposite, as long as one did so in a "nice" way. In this way, the maintenance of nice vacates the ultimately powerful transformative and political possibilities of teacher's work—to a chilling effect.

Nice remains the near enemy of good. Young White women are ultimately more comfortable with patriarchy than they are with social justice; such is the relationship between the performance and maintenance of nice and the perpetuation of a racist, sexist status quo. Niceness sets one's value in terms of the heterosexual male gaze, as axial to maleness, and in terms of unchallenging acceptance and participation in hegemony. Further, this may help explain why over 50 percent of White women voted for Donald Trump in the 2016 presidential election, demonstrably against their own interests (Rogers 2016). White women effectively preferred to endorse an admitted sexual predator rather than vote for a woman who promised to enact policies that would increase their earning power, reproductive freedom, and access to improved health care, child care and maternity leave, to name a few (Hatch 2016; Kingston 2016). As Anderson (2016) writes, "White women bought into Trump's lies about immigrant rapists and decided they'd rather have the respect of their angry white fathers, brothers, and husbands than the respect of literally everyone else in the world" with "a head of state who

Nice Work   83

values them only insofar as he wants to fuck them." She continues, "Most white women don't want to be part of an intersectional feminist sisterhood. Most white women just want to be one of the guys. And we will all suffer for it." Being nice is more highly valued, easier, and more socially acceptable than is doing difficult good. While many of these participants have probably left teaching by now, the damage—to themselves, and to their students—has certainly already been done.[11]

Notes

1. A certainly apocryphal story making the rounds at the time featured a rude businessman intent on highlighting teachers' poor salaries who asked a young female teacher "what she made," to which she proudly answered, "I am a teacher. I make children happy every day. That is worth more than any amount of money." Variations on this story continue today.

2. Notably, Miss Marquez is not White. But she is featureless, Latinx in name only, washed and denuded of ethnic or racial identity in every other way. The vast majority of media schoolmistresses, from Miss Bliss to Teacher Barbie, absolutely are. This trend may be changing, but for the childhood identity formation and impressions of the participants in this study, the image of the young, White female ingenue was firmly ensconced.

3. There are certainly differences here in elementary and high school teachers, between whom popular media always draws a sharp distinction.

4. Participants were asked to identify their race, socioeconomic class, and sexuality.

5. Analyses and in-depth descriptions of the larger study can be found in Galman 2012.

6. Notably, when male preservice teachers openly admitted that they would only teach for the absolute minimum years required before becoming administrators, participants considered this acceptable, even praising the men for being "smart" and "strategic." Women who make similar statements are considered transgressive, failed women; see Galman and Mallozzi (2012).

7. I also heard similar sentiments from classroom teachers in the context of a push toward unionization for higher pay and better medical benefits.

8. For more on the problems with "professional" dress, see Rios (2015).

9. At the time of the data collection I was only slightly older than these participants, and they kindly cajoled and begged to be allowed to give me a "makeover" to help me on my own upcoming job search. They were genuinely worried that I would never get a job looking as I did, and I took their concern as a compliment, as indeed that was how it was intended in that particular cultural milieu.

10. The film depicts a true story about a young Bavarian woman whose unpopular investigations into her town's hidden cooperation with the Nazis resulted in harassment and death threats of such severity that she and her family were forced to flee to the United States.

11. Contemporary statistics suggested an attrition rate for this group hovering around 50 percent (Borman and Dowling 2008; Ingersoll 2001).

References

Acker, S. 1999. "Caring as Work for Women Educators." In *Challenging Professions: Historical and Contemporary Perspectives on Women's Professional Work*, edited by E. Smyth, S. Acker, P. Bourne, and A. Prentice, 277–95. Toronto: University of Toronto Press.

Anderson, L. V. 2016, November 9. "White Women Sold Out the Sisterhood and the World by Voting for Trump." *Slate.* http://www.slate.com/blogs/xx_factor/2016/11/09/white_women_sold_out_the_sisterhood_and_the_world_by_voting_for_trump.html.

Borman, G. D., and N. M. Dowling. 2008. "Teacher Attrition and Retention: A Meta-analytic and Narrative Review of the Research." *Review of Educational Research* 78, no. 3: 367–409.

Cochran-Smith, M. 1991. "Learning to Teach against the Grain." *Harvard Educational Review* 51, no. 3: 279–310.

Coffe, H., and C. Bolzendahl. 2017. "Avoiding the Subject? Gender Gaps in Interpersonal Political Conflict Avoidance and Its Consequences for Political Engagement." *British Politics* 12, no. 2: 135–56.

Connell, R. W. 2005. *Masculinities.* Berkeley: University of California Press.

Douglas, S. J. 2010. *Enlightened Sexism: The Seductive Message That Feminism's Work Is Done.* New York: Times Books.

Downing, N., and K. Roush. 1985. "From Passive Acceptance to Active Commitment: A Model of Feminist Identity Development for Women." *Counseling Psychologist* 13, no. 4: 695–709.

Frankenberg, R. 1993. *White Women, Race Matters: The Social Construction of Whiteness.* Minneapolis: University of Minnesota Press.

Galman, S. 2006. "Rich White Girls: Developing Critical Identities in Teacher Education and Novice Teaching Settings." *International Journal of Learning* 13, no. 3: 3–13.

Galman, S. C. 2012. *Wise and Foolish Virgins: White Women at Work in the Feminized World of Primary School Teaching*. Lanham, Md.: Rowman and Littlefield.

Galman, S. C., and C. A. Mallozzi. 2012. "She's Not There: Women and Gender in U.S. Research on the Elementary School Teacher, 1995–Present." *Review of Educational Research* 82, no. 3: 253–95.

Galman, S. C., C. Pica-Smith, and C. Rosenberger. 2010. "Aggressive and Tender Navigations: Teacher Educators Confront Whiteness in Their Practice." *Journal of Teacher Education* 61, no. 3: 225–36.

Gillespie, D., L. Ashbaugh, and J. DeFiore. 2002. "White Women Teaching White Women about White Privilege, Race Cognizance and Social Action: Toward a Pedagogical Pragmatics." *Race, Ethnicity and Education* 5, no. 3: 237–53.

Griffiths, M. 2006. "The Feminization of Teaching and the Practice of Teaching: Threat or Opportunity?" *Educational Theory* 56, no. 4: 387–405.

Hains, R. C. 2012. *Growing Up with Girl Power: Girlhood on Screen and in Everyday Life*. New York: Lang.

Hatch, Jenevieve. 2016, October 17. "Watch Trump Say 'True' When Called a Sexual Predator in 2006." *HuffPost*. https://www.huffingtonpost.com/entry /watch-trump-say-true-when-called-a-sexual-predator-in-2006_us_5804d258 e4b0162c043cd864.

Holland, D., and M. Eisenhart. 1992. *Educated in Romance: Women, Achievement and College Culture*. Chicago: University of Chicago Press.

Ingersoll, R. M. (2001). Teacher turnover and teacher shortages: An organizational analysis. *American Educational Research Journal*, 38(3), 499–534.

Ingersoll, R. M., and L. Merrill. 2010. "Who's Teaching Our Children?" *Educational Leadership* 67, no. 8: 14–20.

Kate. 2015, October 8. "Being Apolitical Is a Privilege." *Black Feminist Thoughts* (blog). https://blackfeministthoughts.wordpress.com/2015/10/08/being -apolitical-is-a-privilege/.

King, J. B., A. McIntosh, and J. Bell-Ellwanger. 2016. *The State of Racial Diversity in the Educator Workforce*. Washington, D.C.: U.S. Department of Education.

Kingston, A. 2016. "The Year of the 'Nasty Woman.'" *Maclean's* 129, nos. 48–49: 73.

Leonardo, Z. 2002. "The Souls of White Folk: Critical Pedagogy, Whiteness Studies, and Globalization Discourse." *Race Ethnicity and Education* 5, no. 1: 29–50.

Mallozzi, C. A., and S. C. Galman. 2015. "The Ballad of the Big Manly Guy: Male and Female Teachers Construct the Gendered Careworker in U.S. Early Education Contexts." In *Men, Masculinities and Teaching in Early Childhood Education: International Perspectives on Gender and Care*, edited by S. Brownhill, J. Warin, and I. Wernersson, 46–56. London: Routledge.

Mallozzi, C., and S. Galman. 2014. "Guys and 'the Rest of Us': Tales of Gendered Aptitude and Experience in Educational Carework." *Gender and Education* 26, no. 3: 262–79.

Martino, W. J. 2008. "Male Teachers as Role Models: Addressing Issues of Masculinity, Pedagogy and the Re-masculinization of Schooling." *Curriculum Inquiry* 38, no. 2: 189–223.

Mazzarella, S. R., and N. O. Pecora. 2002. *Growing Up Girls: Popular Culture and the Construction of Identity*. 3rd ed. New York: Lang.

McWilliam, E. 1996. "Seductress or Schoolmarm: On the Improbability of the Great Female Teacher." *Interchange* 27, no. 11: 1–11.

Meiners, E. R. 2002. "Disengaging from the Legacy of Lady Bountiful in Teacher Education Classrooms." *Gender and Education* 14, no. 1: 85–94.

Penny, L. 2007. *The Cruelest Month*. London: Headline.

Renold, E., and A. Allan. 2006. "Bright and Beautiful: High Achieving Girls, Ambivalent Femininities, and the Feminization of Success in the Primary School." *Discourse: Studies in the Cultural Politics of Education* 27, no. 4: 457–73. https://doi.org/10.1080/01596300600988606.

Rios, C. 2015, February 13. "You Call It Professionalism; I Call It Oppression in a Three-Piece Suit." Everyday Feminism. https://everydayfeminism.com /2015/02/professionalism-and-oppression/.

Rogers, K. 2016, November 9. "White Women Helped Elect Donald Trump." *New York Times*. https://www.nytimes.com/2016/12/01/us/politics/white -women-helped-elect-donald-trump.html.

Sadker, M., and D. Sadker. 1995. *Failing at Fairness: How Our Schools Cheat Girls*. New York: Touchstone.

Skiba, R. J., R. S. Michael, A. C. Nardo, and R. L. Peterson. 2002. "The Color of Discipline: Sources of Racial and Gender Disproportionality in School Punishment." *Urban Review* 34, no. 4: 317–42.

Southern Poverty Law Center. 2008. *School to Prison Pipeline Project.* http://www.splcenter.org/legal/schoolhouse.jsp.

Standing Committee against Racism and Bias in the Teaching of English. 2017, August 15. "There Is No Apolitical Classroom: Resources for Teaching in These Times." National Council of Teachers of English, blog post. http://www2.ncte.org/blog/2017/08/there-is-no-apolitical-classroom-resources-for-teaching-in-these-times/.

Strauss, A., and J. Corbin. 1998. *Basics of Qualitative Research: Techniques and Procedures for Developing Grounded Theory.* Thousand Oaks, Calif.: Sage.

Tannen, D. 1990. *You Just Don't Understand Me: Women and Men in Conversation.* New York: Morrow.

Tatum, B. D., and E. G. Knaplund. 1996. "Outside the Circle? The Relational Implications for White Women Working against Racism." Wellesley Centers for Women Working Paper Series 78, Wellesley College.

Taylor, C. J. 2016. "Relational by Nature? Men and Women Do Not Differ in Physiological Response to Social Stressors Faced by Token Women." *American Journal of Sociology* 12, no. 1: 49–89.

Weinstein, C. 1989. "Teacher Education Students' Perceptions of Teaching." *Journal of Teacher Education* 40, no. 2: 53–60.

Zumwalt, K., and E. Craig. 2005. "Teachers' Characteristics: Research on the Demographic Profile." In *Studying Teacher Education: The Report of the AERA Panel on Research and Teacher Education*, edited by M. Cochran-Smith and K. M. Zeichner, 111–56. Mahwah, N.J.: Erlbaum.

PART II

Niceness in Higher Education

6

The Perfect Storm of Whiteness, Middle-Classness, and Cis Femaleness in School Contexts

JOSEPH C. WEGWERT AND AIDAN/AMANDA J. CHARLES

The phenomenon of "Niceness" works to define the professional culture and ideological parameters of elementary education classrooms. Elementary teacher identities emerge largely from the intersections of Whiteness, cis femaleness, and middle-classness. These intersections pervade and shape the school cultures that exude Niceness. The same raced, classed, and gendered characteristics are reflected in colleges of education and offer a culture of Niceness in which young teachers begin in earnest their socialization into the profession and where professors of teacher education carry parallel identities. It is this characteristic of Niceness, we argue, that serves as a hospitable host for the neoliberal disease infecting both education and democracy. Insofar as Niceness functions to submerge conflict, avoid controversy, and mask difference, it also functions to elide critical analysis of social and economic inequities. As a result, school classrooms and colleges of education are complicit sites of anti-intellectual and authoritarian sensibilities (Bissonnette 2016).

The culturally dispersed hegemonic seeds of anti-intellectualism and authoritarianism are particularly potent in the fertile terrain of schooling. Schools operate institutionally to reproduce the historical and ideological narratives complicit in perpetuating hegemonic norms of capitalism, patriarchy, and White supremacy (Saltman 2014). Niceness provides a sanitizing and anesthetizing effect as it numbs difficult conversations, "neutralizes" issues of power and oppression, and smothers the resonances of difference against the normative heartbeat of sameness. As such, Niceness is characterized by avoidance of "disturbance, conflict, controversy, or discomfort" and a reframing of those conditions "in ways that are more soothing, pleasant, and comfortable" (Castagno 2014, 9). The disproportionate core identities of Whiteness, cis femaleness, and middle-classness represented in schools and teacher education programs serve to normalize the family contexts and educational experiences of most teachers and teacher candidates, privileging discourses of individualism, meritocracy, and neutrality. When children—and particularly children of color and children in poverty—are taught that success is almost exclusively a function of individual talents, initiative, and perseverance, they are offered the malignant narrative of meritocracy, of individualism without context (Anderson 2017). This is a narrative that ignores questions of power and thereby supports ideological and pedagogical false neutrality. In this circumstance curriculum aligns, supports, and is defined by instrumentality (Bissonnette 2016). Expunged of context, classroom spaces, curricular agendas, and the teaching act is framed around mechanistic skills, procedural knowledge, and dispositional compliance. These are the imperative forces and conditions of an increasingly authoritarian and anti-intellectual hegemony (Foley and Wegwert 2016).

In an effort to unpack Niceness and its curricular, pedagogical, and ideological implications, we examine public school and professional teacher education contexts. The boundaries between these two spheres are increasingly permeable as the neoliberal logic embedded in corporate school reform and corporate teacher education reform align to nurture a deepening cultural authoritarianism and anti-intellectualism (Giroux 2013; Saltman 2007). The testing regime, corporate curriculum, and consequent deskilling of teachers in school contexts parallel a market-driven, accreditation-based data fetish reframing university teacher education as training, complete with an instrumentalized curricula and school apprenticeship model largely devoid of sociopolitical contexts (Cochran-Smith, Piazza, and Power 2013; Saltman 2014).

Anti-intellectualism, embedded within the broader culture, finds its way into schools and teacher education programs. Already steeped in ideologies of individualism, meritocracy, and neutrality, teacher education candidates both demand and encounter curricula that emphasize proceduralism and common practice methods over research-based practice. This dynamic is further exacerbated as colleges of education maintain a skeletal level of tenure track positions and are staffed largely through yearly contracted clinical faculty. Coming from the ranks of practicing teachers, these clinical faculty are positioned politically and dispositionally to perpetuate proceduralism in lieu of critical inquiry (Foley and Wegwert 2016). When Niceness masks conflict, anti-intellectualism pervades colleges of education. Consequently, many students and faculty work to suppress ideas about teaching, learning, and the lives of students that conflict with their own experiences and understandings. As a result, too many teacher education classrooms are rife with dissonance and the avoidance behaviors it generates. Of course, in this feminized context, resistance is passive and subterranean; its ultimate effects serve to reproduce dominant relations of power, including patriarchy and White supremacy (Bissonnette 2016; Mazzei 2011).

Lortie's (1975) seminal sociological study of the teaching profession offers insight that helps to unpack the intellectual and political implications of this culture of Niceness and avoidance as it intersects with the development of teacher identity. Lortie notes that, unlike other professions, teachers enter their work lives carrying a long-standing "apprenticeship of observation" (61). Foley and Wegwert (2016) point to some of the implications, noting, "Since all teachers have been students and have had the opportunity to observe over 10,000 classroom hours, they enter the teaching profession with many preconceived notions about how they intend to teach. Their methods of teaching are biased by their lengthy observation experience. Also, evidenced by their choice to become teachers, these students are 'favorably disposed toward the existing system of schools'" (92–93). Hence, many teacher candidates come to understand teaching through the lens of their years of classroom experience—as students, but while thinking about becoming teachers. The sense of personal authority (authorship) regarding their teacher identity merges with their strong attachment to middle-class individualism and self-ownership of personal experience and opinion.

For the most part, it is White, middle-class, cis females who are *invited* into teaching. Their hegemonic performance of femininity allows their entry into the profession to not challenge the gender binary nor disrupt foundations of White supremacy. The young, White, middle-class, cis-female teacher candidates, themselves successfully schooled in anti-intellectualism and steeped in a culture that cripples critical sensibilities, are perfectly positioned to serve the intersecting hegemonic goals of capital, White supremacy, and patriarchy. Indeed, the gendered, raced, and economic locations of most teacher candidates, teachers, and teacher educators position them to avoid conflict, eschew controversy, proclaim neutrality and, consequently, reproduce dominant hierarchies and discourses of power. In this way, teachers bring their practiced patterns of anti-intellectualism and lack of criticality from teacher education programs into school classrooms, perpetuating rather than challenging social injustices (Wegwert and Foley 2017).

In the remainder of this chapter we briefly examine the linkages between Niceness, the constructs of White supremacy, middle-class social relations, and patriarchy. We then examine Niceness as a mechanism for silencing criticality and perpetuating capitalist patriarchy, looking specifically at how this dynamic plays out in school contexts. Finally, we look more directly at teacher education and how Niceness operates to suppress difference, normalize White middle-class notions of individualism and meritocracy, and submerge critical issues of power and oppression currently confronting the American polity.

Whiteness, Middle-Classness, and Cis Femaleness

Niceness and its constitutive elements of Whiteness, middle-classness, and cis femaleness combine to solidify, reproduce, and disseminate the oppressive linkages between White supremacy, capital, and patriarchy. These elements are intertwined as they each work to uphold the power of the others. Castagno (2014) extends the current literature on Whiteness to examine its linkages to Niceness and claims *"whiteness works through nice people"* (8; emphasis in the original). She argues that Whiteness operates as "a system of ideologies and material effects (privilege and oppression)" that serve as normative frameworks "against which others are judged and also a powerful, if sometimes, unconscious, justification for the status quo" (8). For their part, the vast proportion of teachers and teacher candidates are not only corrupted by the power of Whiteness and its sustaining mechanisms such as Niceness but they are also, quite literally, *produced* by them (Butler 1999; Castagno 2014).

As a mechanism of system maintenance, Niceness is also reflected in a middle-class "conservatism" designed to reify privilege. In many respects the middle class is a contradictory class, often failing to benefit directly from government policies and economic structures favoring corporate elites. Yet elements of social identity and the ideologies of individualism and meritocracy connect the middle class to hegemonic frameworks of capitalism (Brantlinger 2003). In schools, middle-class youth often encounter socialization into cultural systems of common sense (Geertz 1975) that naturalize middle-class attachments to autonomous individualism, meritocracy, and institutional neutrality (Agostinone-Wilson 2006; Wegwert 2008).

Socialized into a culturally constructed "womanhood" and the feminized culture in which it resides, cis females encounter strong pressures to avoid conflict and promote social harmony. Historical, cultural, and religious forces position cis females—particularly, those who are also White and from the middle class—into social and interpersonal roles that promote passivity. Brantlinger, Majd-Jabbri, and Guskin (1996) suggest that, from a marginalized position in society, "women's subjectivities must be seen as complex and divided into a variety of competing discourses" (589). Consequently, for educated middle-class cis females, the role of negotiating and maintaining family status within social institutions can create discursive and ideological contradictions between support for more inclusive educational structures and policies and those less inclusive structures and policies offering stratified advantage to their own children (Brantlinger, Majd-Jabbri, and Guskin 1996). In this way, class, patriarchy, and race are never far removed from one another. What we term a feminized culture, for example, is defined by patriarchy. Gender is an operational and ideological binary where the construct of "feminine" is hegemonically defined not only by the "masculine" but by a *toxic* masculinity that serves to marginalize, minimize, and ostracize the feminine. Hence, to speak of Niceness as an artifact of a "feminized" culture is to also locate it as a mechanism of hegemonic masculinity.

Silencing Criticality and Perpetuating Capitalist Patriarchy

In the current political and cultural contexts, teachers are faced with the difficult but necessary challenge of drawing their students into critique of an ever-hardening totalitarianism feeding on the dispossessed and marginalized in this country and across the globe (Giroux 2011, 2017). This is a powerful challenge. The contexts of teacher education and the teaching profession—immersed in a middle-class, feminized culture of "Niceness"—intersect with the anti-intellectualism of corporate school reform and its attendant attack on democratic life and the impoverishment of citizenship (Bissonnette 2016; Brown 2015; Duggan 2003). Notably, the resistance to criticality by teacher candidates sits in, and works to reproduce, a broader culture of cruelty (Giroux 2017). Ironically, Niceness sits at the center of this resistance to criticality and nurtures conditions of economic and political torture.

An exploration and analysis of Niceness requires an unpacking of patriarchy. Feminized Niceness is an artifact of patriarchy and is deployed on its behalf. The perpetuation of Niceness manifests in gender scripts in culture, in families, and in schools. That is, central to the prescribed gender performance of female-bodied children and adults is the Niceness characterized by submission and silence and deference to White, supremacist, capitalist patriarchy—"the interlocking systems of domination that reflect our reality" (Richardson 2015, 2). The rigid gender scripts embedded in the gender binary produce what bell hooks (2004) suggests is a "mutilated" but nonetheless hegemonic masculinity: "The first act of violence that patriarchy demands of males is not violence toward women. Instead patriarchy demands of all males that they engage in acts of psychic self-mutilation, that they kill off the emotional parts of themselves" (66). Those occupying the feminized end of the gender "equation" also reproduce a "toxic masculinity" (Hazen and Holloway 2017). As psychologist Terry Real notes, "It's important to remember that the feminine side of the equation can be man, woman, boy or girl. . . . Whoever is on the feminine side protects the masculine side from its own disowned fragility. You don't speak truth to power. You protect the perpetrator. You protect power" (quoted in Hazen and Holloway 2017). For public school teachers, who are over 80 percent female assigned and identified, the "feminine side of the equation" operates to protect toxic masculinity and the patriarchal system it perpetuates. This unwillingness or inability to "speak truth to power" undergirds anti-intellectualism, creating an impenetrable barrier to the skills of critical inquiry. Thus the knowledge and dispositions required for democratic citizenship seem ever foreign in school contexts.

The failure to "speak truth to power" has significant implications for all students, but especially for marginalized students. Recent research suggests that when teachers perpetuate the myths of autonomous individualism and meritocracy embodied in "the level playing field" narrative, marginalized students are not well served. Drawing on system justification theory in their study of diverse low-income students in Arizona, Godfrey, Santos, and Burson (2017) note that teaching a curricular narrative of societal fairness led to measures of increased self-esteem and classroom compliance / school compliance in elementary students, but these measures declined, especially for marginalized students, as they entered adolescence. They add, "We also uncover a surprising pattern of associations between early system justification and outcomes during this time: youth with greater system-justifying beliefs in sixth grade had better outcomes in sixth grade but worsening trajectories across sixth-to-eighth grade. . . . However, these same early beliefs about the fairness of the system may become a liability over time, as youth become increasingly cognizant of how the larger socioeconomic system puts them and their group at a disadvantage, and as their identity as a marginalized group member becomes more salient" (11). In short, when elementary teachers suppress difference, avoid controversy, and distort the dynamics and implications of power and oppression, they misrepresent the real world. For marginalized students, these unintentional but nonetheless potent distortions have lasting and negative impact (Anderson 2017; Godfrey Santos, and Burson 2017).

For middle-class White students this "avoidance" of social complexities is also miseducative and hegemonic as it naturalizes dominant understandings of meritocracy. For children, teachers, teacher candidates, and teacher educators, the construct of Niceness is often framed as "civility" and is commonly and hegemonically deployed to submerge conflict and neuter critique (Brantlinger 2004). As Mayo (2002) suggests, "The first problem with civility may be its almost necessary presumption that everything is fine. This is doubtless a familiar frame to anyone doing any kind of anti-bias education and is indicative usually of a dominant group's reluctance to acknowledge its dominance and, further, to acknowledge that its dominance negatively affects subordinate groups. In short, in an effort to minimize conflict, the discourse of civility ignores even the most blatant conflict" (83). Of course, the core issue in this collective delusion is that of "critical" education. Without the curricular imagination and professional courage to explore social or political realities, without reasonable personal thresholds for the inherent discordance of controversy, and without an academic grounding in the nature and significance of critical citizenship for democracy, teachers are ill disposed and ill equipped to come close to anything resembling classrooms engaged in critical education.

We explore here discursive frames educators use to maneuver Niceness as they develop and deploy their professional identities and avoid criticality. First, we find that classroom teachers often work to remind themselves and others to "be nice"—to avoid conflict and submerge difference. Aidan/Amanda Charles contributes to this analysis through personal narrative that dives down into the childhood memories and experiences where gender transgression and White supremacy collided with regulation of gender performance and Eurocentric Niceness. The result was an enforced passivity, in a context of false harmony, that nurtured a school culture of surveillance and aggression. Second, we widen our view to examine teacher candidates' deployment of "the golden rule" as a mechanism that normalizes the lives and conditions of White middle-class families and, simultaneously, abnormalizes those of marginalized students and communities. These manifestations of Niceness provide teachers and teacher candidates with discursive and ideological strategies that support their avoidance of complexity and conflict while maintaining their professional identities nested in frameworks of care and relational generosity (Houser 1996; James 2010; Mazzei 2011).

"Be Nice!" Submerging Criticality, Perpetuating Power

As part of the flight from the very real political and economic war on democracy, on schools, and on children, we find that educators are socialized to consider the classroom to be an environment that mediates these conditions and protects children. By sheer force of will, and Niceness, many seem to believe they can provide a classroom culture of acceptance, physical and ontological safety, and free inquiry. That is, despite a propensity to specifically and consistently resist and submerge curricular topics and classroom issues that introduce social, political, or cultural complexities, many teachers and teacher candidates embrace the belief that they can provide both safety and critical education. Yet the "caring and critical community" often *talked about* stands outside the material conditions that many students face. In so many classrooms—especially those with children and families of color, gender-nonconforming children, nontraditional families, and children from communities in poverty—the middle-class White identities and realities of educators contradict the lives of students and the communities in which they live:

- When a well-meaning elementary teacher insists to children of color that "the policeman is your friend," the disjuncture between that entirely unexamined claim and the realities of those children's lives serves to invalidate the seeming innocent generosity embedded in the goal of building a caring and critical classroom community.[1]
- When teachers deploy heteronormative language and curricula, children whose identities or families do not reflect these patterns are abnormalized and fail to experience recognition in the school and classroom context (Young 1990, 2000).
- So, too, when teachers (and teacher candidates) offer up lessons that attempt to draw children into middle-class narratives of meritocracy—such as, "hard work and sacrifice leads to success"—children who live in poverty are hearing that their parents and family members lack important personal qualities and deserve the hardships they face (Anderson 2017; Godfrey, Santos, and Burson 2017).

Teachers and teacher candidates are often ill prepared to see this disjuncture as they carry hegemonic ideologies of "individualism," "fairness," and "meritocracy" into their teacher education program and later their profession. The narratives of democracy and justice woven into the story of nation in America's schools—perhaps especially in America's middle-class schools—largely ignore conflict, be it racial, economic, cultural, or gendered. It turns out that conflict, historical or interpersonal, is not "nice"; it must be ignored and, if possible, hidden. Much of the historical narrative offered to children falls into "The Little Engine That Could" story line. This is a framework that memorializes competition, individual talent, and a level social/economic playing field and serves to justify the status quo.

So what of the belief that teachers can mitigate material conditions and can filter away injustice and offer a classroom space untainted by poverty, racism, and capitalist greed? They can't. They shouldn't. The mere belief that they can or should, however, is an artifact of the ideological delusion that infects our larger culture, teacher education, and schools themselves. At the core of this false belief lie strong cultural assumptions about the innocence of childhood and the need to protect children from harsh realities (truths) about their social world. In support of this belief, the field of educational psychology has provided an understanding of childhood framed by the assumptions of the "developmentally appropriate practice" model. This model is, however, rooted in a universalizing understanding of childhood. What is presumed to be universal is actually a reflection of Western, White, middle-class, individualistic, heteronormative beliefs about children and childhood—reifying the concept of the naturally developing child. "Postdevelopmentalism" calls us to question the culturally contingent modernist truth claims to universality and certainty (Blaise 2009; Kincheloe and Steinberg 1993; Lubeck 1998). At the core of critical education is the value and commitment to draw students into a deeper and more complex understanding of the world in which they live—both its social and natural elements. To the extent that the education offered to children masks these complexities in the name of comfort (of adults or students), as an artifact of Niceness, it is *miseducative* (Chomsky 2000).

Further, when "Niceness" becomes an exhortation—"Be nice!"—it individualizes and locates Niceness as a moral dictate without context. In this way, the absence or presence of Niceness is tied to a quality of personal character. As has been noted in the literature, character education as exhortation is often deployed as a mechanism of and justification for regimes of accountability—of children, but not of adults (Giroux and Purpel 1983; Kohn 1997; Liu 2014). In short, not only does the framework of individual accountability operate to absolve adults from *teaching* about collective responsibility and maintenance of the commons, but dictates around moral codes are also often grounded in dominant culture and thereby serve to disadvantage and penalize marginalized populations who have not been socialized into White middle-class Niceness (Brantlinger, Morton, and Washburn 1999). One of the attractions to teacher candidates and practicing teachers of such decontextualized demands for Niceness has to do with their own ideological attachment to neutrality and avoidance of conflict (Bissonnette 2016; Houser 1996).

One manifestation of this attachment to neutrality and avoidance occurs when there is conflict between students. All too often such conflict is addressed through adult dictates for children to "work it out" themselves. This hands-off Niceness demand creates a dangerous environment for some students. White middle-class students are more skilled at navigating Niceness in ways that entitle and privilege them at the expense of the marginalized racial, gender resistive, or cultural "others." Niceness works when it is attached to a principled commitment to the worth and dignity of all. Yet when it is deployed as a platitude and as an exhortation that calls children to negotiate bullying for themselves, simply through the force of courtesy, Niceness can produce tremendous harm and symbolic if not actual violence. In this way, Niceness manifests power, indirectly, as manipulation. That is, working outside the direct power mechanisms of patriarchy itself, Niceness services patriarchal power as an artifact of oppression. As a curriculum of gender, modeled by female teachers, female-bodied students are socialized and victimized by this process. Aidan/Amanda Charles offers this narrative[2] of such an experience:

> In September 2001, I was a new seventh-grade student at Talawanda Middle School, located in a small college community in the southwest region of Ohio. My seventh-grade peer group was composed of students from my small college community as well as from the surrounding rural areas and neighboring cities, which were predominantly White and largely impoverished. As an incoming student, I was new to the region and unfamiliar with the inner workings of the local culture. I am a White, gender-transgressive, female body, and just before I began my seventh-grade year I also began a negotiation process with the sexual/gendered expectations that I felt awaited my participation.
>
> Because I had no preexisting friendships among my peers, I took a seat at an empty table in the corner of my morning class on the first day of the fall semester 2001. An adjacent table was occupied by a group of five girls who immediately took issue with my hair and clothes, which were neither confrontational to the gendered expectations of my context nor in strict compliance. Although the teacher observed the bullying mechanisms that were employed by my peers (and that prevailed in the classroom's culture), they did nothing to demonstrate their witness to these events and, more significantly, did nothing to disrupt them.
>
> As the weeks neared the semester's end, the policing practices of my peers began to manifest in a way that actively disrupted the

classroom space and became increasingly impossible for my teacher to ignore. On one particular occasion, my peers arrived to our morning class with a paper bag full of dog feces and dumped the contents at the foot of the table where I sat alone. Despite the audible response of onlookers and the overwhelming smell, the class period came and went without comment, acknowledgment, or intervention from our teacher. The following day the teacher demonstrated initiative on behalf of the troubled space, for the first time. As class began, they announced that they had strategically arranged a seating chart and would be implementing an assigned-seating policy for the remainder of the school year. The new seating arrangement did not remove or displace any of the five girls who sat near me but instead added a sixth chair at their table, where I was to seat myself. Moments after I reluctantly joined the other students and took my seat, the teacher approached our table and firmly announced, "You have to learn to be nice to people you don't get along with."

By reframing the bullying behavior of my peers as interpersonal conflict, my teacher was able to justify the use of a laissez-faire mediation method in addressing a subject of difference (in this case, a female's lack of conformity to feminine norms). By strategically placing me beside these students who were enacting the policing mechanisms of patriarchy, they ensured that I would either incorporate these norms into my social presence or endure the stigma of refusing them as part of my educational experience. In this way, the teacher employed the regulation of stratification as an instructor in our classroom, infusing the politics of "nice" as a placating ambassador to the powers of a patriarchal condition.

During this period in my educational development I recall reducing and isolating my experiences to my own troubled relationship with public education. I have since come to understand the politics of those spaces and the performance of my teachers as a reproduction of the political period in which we all existed: an era defined by constrictive surveillance and an intensely regulated citizenship. In my post-9/11 adulthood I have witnessed this regulation produce a social ethic that complies with and endorses a hostile and ever-advancing imperial agenda. In our 2001 classroom context, this ethic was introduced and enforced through the Eurocentric politics of "nice" and its insidious corruption of "harmony."

Tied to the project of avoiding conflict and controversy, teachers and teacher candidates are also, ironically, pulled toward *not Niceness*. That is, while the discourse of Niceness is very powerful in educational contexts, many educators seem to readily embrace and employ *not nice* strategies of classroom "management" (Kohn 2005). The depth of the contradiction is breathtaking. Despite the rhetoric of community, of belonging, and of unconditional acceptance, the dominant framework for classroom "control" appears to be discipline by humiliation. Whether they employ "clip up, clip down" behavior management charts, public accountability for completed work, or supposedly coconstructed but largely unilateral behavior and consequence contracts, many classrooms are places of regular public examination and humiliation (Hurley 2016; Kohn 2014). It is amazing how nimbly and readily teacher education students step over and around their own claims to honor all children and their passionate statements about building community. As they talk about their own preferences regarding classroom management policies, and as they report on practices they observe in schools, many teacher education candidates readily embrace common practices of control over best practices of community (Kohn 2005).

Here, then, Niceness gives way to a countervailing discourse in education: individual accountability. Just as in the hands of middle-class, White, cis females, Niceness morphs into situational passivity, the *not nice* deployment of individual accountability also serves as an incarnation of individualist ideology that places consequence above context and submerges complexity. Culturally and institutionally, the war on children disproportionately victimizes non-White, nonheterosexual, and gender-nonconforming populations through discriminatory disciplinary structures (Epstein, Blake, and Gonzalez 2017; Gay, Lesbian, Straight Education Network 2016; Gilliam et al. 2016).

Aidan's/Amanda's story points to the deployment of Niceness that casts to the margins critique and complexity and the *not Niceness* patterned after dominant cultural assumptions—particularly regarding race and class. Aidan's/Amanda's experiences hold up for us how schools and educators are structurally and ideologically complicit in reproducing hegemonic systems of power.

The Golden Rule: Judging the Student "Other" against the Privileged Self

The Golden Rule—"Do unto others as you would have them do unto you"—is an ethical and relational dictate, and its variants cross religious divides and transcend time. On the surface, it appears philosophically unassailable—a pristine first principle beyond critique. In this sense, many might consider the Golden Rule as the "gold standard" for Niceness. Yet it is that apparent universality that marks it as potentially problematic—that is, in highly homogenous cultures, the simple and sleek ethic of the Golden Rule is readily held aloft for all to recognize and honor. Yet in heterogeneous, multicultural contexts this simplicity quickly complicates and erodes. Often, left in its place are the values, customs, and beliefs of the most dominant (not necessarily the most populous) cultural group. In a culturally diverse society like the United States, the dictate of the Golden Rule centers on the individual and naturalizes the privileges and preferences of dominant groups. This ethic calls upon us to think of our neighbors and their needs through the lens of our own individual experiences, preferences, and desires. In a field of capitalist social, economic, and political relations, some experiences, preferences, and desires are more privileged than others. Coming as they do from largely dominant racial and economic locations, it is no small coincidence that teacher education candidates are quick to cite the Golden Rule as an organizing principle of their educational philosophy and future classroom culture. For all intents and purposes, this ethic calls for a process of normalization. What becomes normalized, however, are the lives, families, experiences, and preferences of teachers and teacher education candidates; the Golden Rule places *them*, not their students, at the center of understanding.

Deployed in teaching and classroom contexts, Niceness elides difference; it calls adherents to focus on commonalities. This characteristic also underlies many institutional and cultural efforts toward "diversity" or "inclusion" initiatives (Castagno 2014; Houser 1996). The emphasis on common interests has the effect of broadening and diluting commonalities and entirely submerging any differences of consequence. Yet in considering the complexities of student learning, many elementary teacher candidates value the ideas of difference and choice—on the surface, at least. They often note that pedagogical and curricular choices are important because children are not all the same. While this recognition appears to be framed in an acknowledgment of "context"—meaningful differences, for example, of race, culture, and socioeconomic background—it actually is centered in the value of "preference," a close variant of "choice." Coming from a place of racial and often economic privilege, elementary teacher candidates appear to frame "difference" in a manner that reflects an individualist and consumerist mind-set in which difference connotes a justification of choices grounded in individual tastes or preferences rather than an understanding of systemic and material conditions that impact communities and individuals in very different ways.

For example, teacher education students frequently make reference to the notion that "every child is different and unique." This is a reasonable claim seemingly grounded in an appreciation for diversity. Yet these same students frequently connect this claim to another claim, one unsupported by cognitive research: "every child learns differently." This shift illustrates how potentially empty signifiers like "difference" serve as placeholders for ideas such as *individualism* and *choice* and, ultimately, provide the discursive and ideological scaffolding for *meritocracy*. At the same time, the claim that "every child learns differently" obscures the real complexities of cognitive science with a false complexity that suggests pedagogical strategies are useless amid this infinite variety of learning patterns. Paradoxically, this leads to a fundamental estrangement between the lessons offered by cognitive science and those individuals preparing to teach children.

The mistaken and miseducative notion that every child learns differently from every other child operates for many teacher education candidates as a convenient "escape" from curricular and pedagogical responsibilities. That is, the trope of difference allows teacher candidates to ignore questions of pedagogical strategy because their potential student population is unknowable. There is much in school contexts today that lures preservice teachers into this methodological nihilism. The prepackaged corporate curricula tied to testing regimes provide a useful end run for those who see teaching as information delivery as opposed to knowledge creation. In this way, pedagogy is reduced to the most procedural elements of *methods* as teacher candidates frequently claim that their great joy in teaching rests in being allowed to decide *how* to teach, even though prescribed curricula limits *what* teachers are allowed to teach. Teacher creativity manifests in practice, for example, in the latitude to plan whether math comes before or after lunch; student choice might rest in which of four consonant blends worksheets a child prefers working on first. The idea of learning differences morphs into individual choices, but it is always located within standardized curricula. Hence, we see *differences* without *distinctions*.

Herein rests an ironic contradiction: Like most middle-class Americans, teacher candidates are deeply attached to the ideology of individualism. As such, they reflect the embedded contradiction of individualism in a democratic society: embracing the liberal ideal of equality, treating individuals the same, while emphasizing the difference between individuals. In this dualism, however, sameness trumps difference. When we individualize difference we are left with sameness. This is a hegemonic strategy that evacuates difference of any meaning beyond mere preference. Teacher candidates frequently convey the belief that children are different from one another *and* should be treated the same. The result is a homogenization of difference: We all have differences (read: preferences), and that makes us the same. This notion, when joined with the normalizing dynamic of the Golden Rule, makes that sameness look very much like the identity, culture, and personal preferences of the teacher. Individualizing difference at best hides or at worst obliterates student differences based on gender, sexuality, race, and socioeconomic class, leaving the teacher's self in the vacuum of identity. The *normalizing* of middle-class Whiteness, as we have argued, includes a dysfunctional Niceness that masks difference and submerges conflict. It also produces a *deficit* ideology that pathologizes families and communities of color and children in poverty as structurally and morally deficient (Gorski 2011).

The effects of these normalizing functions are dramatic for students, and especially students from marginalized communities or identities. In addition to this process of normalizing—mapping dominant values, practices, and ways of encountering the world onto marginalized students and their families—there is a parallel dynamic of essentializing, especially for students and families in poverty.

It is no coincidence that novice teachers are very likely to encounter—from their teacher educators or from school district administration, or both—Payne's (2005) self-published (i.e., not peer reviewed) study, a heavily critiqued but widely disseminated example of deficit thinking in education (Castagno 2014; Gorski 2006, 2011; Ng and Rury 2006). "In the most basic terms," writes Gorski (2011), "deficit ideology can be thought of as a sort of 'blame the victim' mentality applied, not to an individual person, but systemically, to an entire group of people, often based on a single dimension of identity" (153–54). For teacher candidates already immersed in ideological assumptions that individualize, decontextualize, and normalize, the deficit worldview offers a welcome if not delusional framework for examining schools and families of difference. It serves as an ideological and pedagogical escape hatch, allowing teachers to essentialize non-White students and their families.

Whether engaged in normalizing or essentializing thinking and practices, teachers and teacher candidates work to deny material realities and systems of power. Whether confronted, challenged, or simply caught up in the dynamic of cognitive dissonance, this "magical" thinking often takes the discursive form of "good intentions." Yet, as Castagno (2014) reminds us, "Whiteness thrives on well-intentioned people, policies, and efforts. Part of being nice entails having good intentions toward other people. . . . When we focus on the intent, we generally lose sight of the real, material outcome. . . . Good intentions mean very little if we do not take responsibility and cannot be held accountable" (43–44). The practice of normalizing and essentializing, then, serve as convenient and satisfying mechanisms to center "good intentions" and push context and material conditions to the margins. This dynamic is one more way to allow teachers and teacher candidates to distance issues of injustice while "protecting" children from the harshness of the real world and to mask systems of power that operate to oppress, impoverish, criminalize, and ostracize those very children. At the root of these processes are increasingly visible cultural and political currents of anti-intellectualism and a seeping totalitarianism.

Niceness is a powerful factor in the socialization and professional identity of teachers. As a group, teachers are overwhelmingly White, middle-class, and cis female. The indoctrination into Niceness begins in childhood, is finely tuned in adolescence and young adulthood, and institutionally ingrained in teacher education programs and schools themselves through an emergent professional identity and a curriculum of instrumentality and compliance. Niceness serves as a hegemonic artifact and tool. The White, middle-class, cis females who disproportionately populate the teaching profession are overwhelmingly disposed to mask controversy, avoid conflict, and suppress difference. In this regard, they are complicit in reproducing White supremacy, social and economic inequities embedded in capitalist structures, and the oppressions of patriarchy. But complicity itself is not to be equated with control. The institutional structures of schools reflect and reproduce the dominant structures of power. The neoliberal forces of privatization and encroaching authoritarianism reach into the schoolhouse door and into the university halls. White supremacy, capitalism, and patriarchy are far more powerful, wide-ranging, and culturally embedded than the pedagogical reach or influence of teachers. Yet teachers play an important hegemonic role in perpetuating an encroaching anti-intellectual and authoritarian cultural regime.

Notes

1. This example was brought to my attention by Brandee Newkirk (B.A., University of Arizona, 2016) during a conversation about her experiences as the only African American child in her fourth-grade class in a predominantly White elementary school in Connecticut.

2. This narrative writing utilizes nonbinary pronouns and nonbinary language.

References

Agostinone-Wilson, F. 2006. "Downsized Discourse: Classroom Management, Neoliberalism, and the Shaping of Correct Workplace Attitude." *Journal for Critical Education Policy Studies* 4, no. 2: 129–58. http://www.jceps.com /archives/523.

Anderson, M. 2017, July 27. "Why the Myth of Meritocracy Hurts Kids of Color." *Atlantic Monthly.* https://www.theatlantic.com/education/archive /2017/07/internalizing-the-myth-of- meritocracy/535035/.

Bissonnette, J. D. 2016. "The Trouble with Niceness: How a Preference for Pleasantry Sabotages Culturally Responsive Teacher Preparation." *Journal of Language and Literacy Education* 12, no. 2: 9–32.

Blaise, M. 2009. "'What a Girl Wants, What a Girl Needs': Responding to Sex, Gender, and Sexuality in the Early Childhood Classroom." *Journal of Research in Childhood Education* 23, no. 4: 450–60.

Brantlinger, E. 2003. *Dividing Classes: How the Middle Class Negotiates and Rationalizes School Advantage.* New York: RoutledgeFalmer.

Brantlinger, E. 2004. "An Application of Gramsci's 'Who Benefits?' to High-Stakes Testing." *Workplace* 6, no. 1: 78–103.

Brantlinger, E., M. Majd-Jabbri, and S. L. Guskin. 1996. "Self-Interest and Liberal Educational Discourse: How Ideology Works for Middle-Class Mothers." *American Educational Research Journal* 33, no. 3: 571–97.

Brantlinger, E., M. L. Morton, and S. Washburn. 1999. "Teachers' Moral Authority in Classrooms: (Re)structuring Social Interactions and Gendered Power." *Elementary School Journal* 99, no 5: 491–504.

Brown, W. 2015. *Undoing the Demos: Neoliberalism's Stealth Revolution.* Brooklyn: Zone.

Butler, J. 1999. *Gender Trouble.* New York: Routledge.

Castagno, A. E. 2014. *Educated in Whiteness: Good Intentions and Diversity in Schools.* Minneapolis: University of Minnesota Press.

Chomsky, N. 2000. *Chomsky on Mis-education.* Lanham, Md.: Rowman and Littlefield.

Cochran-Smith, M., P. Piazza, and C. Power. 2013. "The Politics of Accountability: Assessing Teacher Education in the United States." *Educational Forum* 77:6–27.

Duggan, L. 2003. *The Twilight of Equality? Neoliberalism, Cultural Politics, and the Attack on Democracy.* Boston: Beacon.

Epstein, R., J. J. Blake, and T. Gonzalez. 2017. *Girlhood Interrupted: The Erasure of Black Girls' Childhood.* Washington, D.C.: Georgetown Center on Poverty and Inequality.

Foley, J. A., and J. C. Wegwert. 2016. "Dan Lortie, Schoolteacher: A Sociological Study (1975)." In *Popular Educational Classics: A Reader,* edited by J. L. Devitis, 91–100. New York: Lang.

Gay, Lesbian, Straight Education Network. 2016. *Educational Exclusion: Drop Out, Push Out, and the School-to-Prison Pipeline among LGBTQ Youth.* New York: Gay, Lesbian, Straight Education Network.

Geertz, C. 1975. "Common Sense as a Cultural System." *Antioch Review* 33, no. 1: 5–26.

Gilliam, W. S., A. N. Maupin, C. R. Reyes, M. Accavitti, and F. Shic. 2016, September 28. *A Research Study Brief: Do Early Educators' Implicit Biases Regarding Sex and Race Relate to Behavior Expectations and Recommendations of Preschool Expulsions and Suspensions?* New Haven, Conn.: Yale University Child Study Center.

Giroux, H. A. 2011. *Zombie Politics and Culture in the Age of Casino Capitalism.* New York: Lang.

Giroux, H. A. 2012, October 16. "Can Democratic Education Survive in a Neoliberal Society?" Truthout. http://www.truth-out.org/opinion/item /12126-can-democratic-education-survive-in-a-neoliberal-society.

Giroux, H. A. 2013. *America's Education Deficit and the War on Youth*. New York: Monthly Review Press.

Giroux, H. A. 2017, October 11. "The Vital Role of Education in Authoritarian Times." Truthout. http://www.truth-out.org/news/item/42217-the -vital-role-of-education-in-a-time-of-tyranny.

Giroux, H. A., and D. Purpel, eds. 1983. *The Hidden Curriculum and Moral Education*. Berkeley: McCutcheon.

Godfrey, E. B., C. E. Santos, and E. Burson. 2017. "For Better or Worse? System-Justifying Beliefs in Sixth-Grade Predict Trajectories of Self-Esteem and Behavior across Early Adolescence." *Child Development* 90, no. 1: 180–95. DOI:10.1111/cdev.12854.

Gorski, P. 2006, February 9. "The Classist Underpinnings of Ruby Payne's Framework." *Teachers College Record*. http://www.tcrecord.org/content .asp?contentid=12322.

Gorski, P. 2011. "Unlearning Deficit Ideology and the Scornful Gaze: Thoughts on Authenticating the Class Discourse in Education." In *Assault on Kids: How Hyper-accountability, Corporatization, Deficit Ideologies, and Ruby Payne Are Destroying Our Schools*, edited by R. Ahlquist, P. C. Gorski, and T. Montano, 152–73. New York: Lang.

Hazen, D., and K. Holloway. 2017, July 25. "Patriarchy and Toxic Masculinity Are Dominating America under Trump." AlterNet. https://www.alternet.org /trump-trauma/patriarchy-and-toxic-masculinity-are-dominating-america-under -trump.

hooks, b. (2004). *The Will to Change: Men, Masculinity, and Love*. New York: Atria.

Houser, N. O. 1996. "Negotiating Dissonance and Safety for the Common Good: Social Education in the Elementary Classroom." *Theory and Research in Social Education* 24, no. 3: 294–312.

Hurley, K. 2016, September 29. "The Dark Side of Behavior Management Charts." *Washington Post*. https://www.washingtonpost.com/news/parenting/wp /2016/09/29/the-darkside-of-classroom-behavior-management-charts/?utm_term =.6c4554626e32.

James, J. H. 2010. "Teachers as Mothers in the Elementary Classroom: Negotiating the Needs of Self and Others." *Gender and Education* 22, no. 5: 521–34.

Kincheloe, J., and S. R. Steinberg. 1993. "A Tentative Description of Post-formal Thinking: The Critical Confrontation with Cognitive Theory." *Harvard Educational Review* 63, no. 3: 296–320.

Kohn, A. 1997. "How Not to Teach Values: A Critical Look at Character Education." *Phi Delta Kappan* 78, no. 6: 428–39.

Kohn, A. 2005. "Unconditional Teaching." *Educational Leadership* 63, no. 1: 20–24.

Kohn, A. 2014. *The Myth of the Spoiled Child*. Boston: Da Capo.

Liu, X. 2014. "The Problem of Character Education and Kohlberg's Moral Education: Critique from Dewey's Moral Deliberation." *Philosophical Studies in Education* 45: 136–45.

Lortie, D. 1975. *Schoolteacher: A Sociological Study*. Chicago: University of Chicago Press.

Lubeck, S. 1998. "Is Developmentally Appropriate Practice for Everyone?" *Childhood Education* 74, no. 5: 283–92.

Mayo, C. 2002. "Education by Association: The Shortcomings of Discourses of Privacy and Civility in Anti-homophobic Education." In *Getting Ready for Benjamin: Preparing Teachers for Sexual Diversity in the Classroom*, edited by R. M. Kissen, 81–90. Lanham, Md.: Rowman and Littlefield.

Mazzei, L. A. 2011. "Desiring Silence: Gender, Race and Pedagogy in Education." *British Educational Research Journal* 37, no. 4: 657–69.

Ng, J. C., and J. L. Rury. 2006, July 18. "Poverty and Education: A Critical Analysis of the Ruby Payne Phenomenon." *Teachers College Record*. https://www.tcrecord.org/content.asp?contentid=12596.

Payne, R. K. 2005. *A Framework for Understanding Poverty*. Highlands, Tex.: aha! Process. First published 1996.

Richardson, S. 2015. *Gender Lessons: Patriarchy, Sextyping and Schools*. Rotterdam: Sense.

Saltman, K. J. 2007. "Schooling in Disaster Capitalism: How the Political Right Is Using Disaster to Privatize Public Schooling." *Teacher Education Quarterly* 34, no. 2: 131–56.

Saltman, K. J. 2014. *The Politics of Education: A Critical Introduction*. Boulder, Colo.: Paradigm.

Wegwert, J. C. 2008. "Democracy without Dialogue: A Civic Curriculum of 'the Middle Class Promise' for Citizens of the Corporation." PhD diss., Miami University.

Wegwert, J. C., and J. A. Foley. 2017. "Colleges of Education and the Making of the Neoliberal University." In *A Language of Freedom and Teacher's Authority: Case Comparisons from Turkey and the United States*, edited by F. Mizikaci and G. Senese, 53–65. Lanham, Md.: Lexington.

Young, I. M. 1990. *Justice and the Politics of Difference*. Princeton, N.J.: Princeton University Press.

Young, I. M. 2000. *Inclusion and Democracy*. Oxford: Oxford University Press.

Evaluating Niceness

*How Anonymous Student Feedback Forms Promote Gendered and
Flawed Value Systems in Academic Labor*

KRISTINE T. WEATHERSTON

Student feedback forms are anonymous, online reporting systems endorsed by most higher education institutions. Known by many names, such as Electronic Student Feedback Forms (e-SFFs), Student Evaluation of Instruction, Student Evaluation of Teaching (SET), and Student Evaluation of Teaching Instruments, these instruments utilize similar standards of design and sets of questions, and function similarly from institution to institution (Berk 2013). Such forms are intended to provide information to chairs, administration, and faculty about a professor's performance, pedagogy, and expertise (Ory 2000). They provide data about a professor over time and across different courses, are used in considerations for tenure and promotion and, in certain cases, provide professors with constructive criticism concerning their role in the classroom. Faculty of all rank are critical of their evaluation scores and feedback for a variety of reasons (Patton 2015), but contingent and tenure-track faculty tend to be more concerned than their tenured colleagues (Vasey and Carroll 2016) due to the arguably tenuous nature of their positions in the hierarchy of the academy. Consequently, students' perceptions — and biases — concerning their professors have increasing potential to affect professors' teaching evaluations and therefore a professor's ability to earn contract renewal, tenure, and promotion (Anderson 2010).

This chapter explores primarily the relationship among student evaluations, Niceness, gender bias, and equity within academia, blending personal anecdotal experience with broader academic trends. As Anderson (2010) notes, "White male professors may still be perceived as the 'typical' professor, the cultural norm against which women and ethnic minorities are compared" (470). Consequently, my experiences as a White woman shape my position in this exploration of Anderson's referent norms in the academic culture but do not preclude consideration of ethnic female identity in the spectrum of this discussion.

In 2015 a growing backlash emerged against e-SFFs, with reports and articles appearing within and outside academia—on, for instance, National Public Radio and in *Slate* and the *Washington Post, as well as recurring articles in the Chronicle of Higher Education*—that in summary, and not inaccurately, demonized anonymous evaluation systems as grossly flawed and worthless. Much of this new interest and reporting grew out of the comprehensive results from a 2014 survey conducted by the American Association of University Professionals (AAUP) in which over nine thousand faculty members participated and over five thousand submitted written comments. This study indicated sweeping patterns where faculty face negative and unfair assessment within e-SFFs. From the growing body of research conducted by educators, social scientists, psychologists, and data analysts, nuanced context emerges to support the AAUP's findings in terms of the quality and value of student evaluations. It's a complex and much-debated aspect of the education system. Several studies indicate that e-SFFs should not be used for decisions such as tenure and promotion *because they do not actually evaluate teaching* (Kogan, Schoenfeld-Tacher, and Hellyer 2010). Instead, they present opinions of students and their limited understanding of the many invisible or underlying dimensions of teaching. Often student evaluations of teachers tend to focus on delivery, style, personality traits (Boring 2017), and even appearance—all of which are intimately tied to gendered expectations and stereotypes. In short, female professors, unlike their male colleagues, are evaluated by their students according to expectations rooted in culturally spawned gender biases concerning the demeanor, behavior, and attitude of women in the academic environment.

With the shift in higher education toward a business economy emphasizing a return on investment, students are increasingly regarded as customers for whom teachers provide customer service. This adoption of corporate business models provides a system for quantifying teacher worth and educational value, and for leveraging employee accountability (Brooks 2001). The "global knowledge economy" dominates universities with neoliberal policies, managerial styles, and bloated administrations that impact universities as strategic sites of global processes (Brooks and Mackinnon 2001). Issues concerning the global information economy, the notion of knowledge work, and the roles of women within these systems intersect to reveal what Brooks and Mackinnon call "new and disturbing possibilities for gender regimes" (1).

Students can be astute and hold professors to high standards, but too often these standards boil down to a superficial discussion of whether professors are approachable and if they are perceived as nice (Laube et al. 2007). This reduction is problematic largely because approachability is relative and widely subjective; often Niceness is tacitly regarded as a performance aspect of gender, a "fuzzy concept" and social trait more associated with femininity than masculinity (Lippa 2002, 55). Given our current gender regimes, expectations of Niceness in the classroom present a false double standard and perpetuate gender bias onto the worldviews of our students' expectations of women. Niceness devalues our roles as educators,

Gender and the Cult of Grading

In part of the shift of education toward an emerging global knowledge economy (Brooks 2001), postsecondary teachers are evaluated and perceived not as members of sites of learning and producers of knowledge but as peddlers of the by-products of Niceness: grades. Knowing I must deliver information in a neoliberal marketplace, and under the capitalist structure of students as consumers, my job becomes equated with customer service. Pressure exists to package information like a fancy, expensive latte, served with a conciliatory smile, for an increasingly entitled customer base. This is not the job description of an educator, whose mission should be to equip students with tools, skills, and knowledge.

Grading is a veritable petri dish where the culture of Niceness grows. Further, grading provides a vast landscape on which the concepts of Niceness are negotiated and where feedback and critique must artfully be strategized to avoid being misconstrued by students as mean, thoughtless, or cold. Unlike an email or verbal comment, grades necessitate an exacting and final stamp on some aspect of student performance; if the recipient is resentful, that grade is frequently regarded as a personal affront, rendering the arguably dispassionate process of grading as an interpersonal interface between student and professor. Consequently, a good grade is "nice" and reflects nurture and caring; a bad grade suggests professorial apathy and a lack of compassion. This is true even when rubrics for grading protocols are crystal clear and widely disseminated.

To be nice in academia, faculty members adopt a variety of behavioral responses to course evaluations, including lowering standards, raising grades, grade manipulation, grading leniency, socializing with students outside class, and providing academic extras (Lindahl and Unger 2010). These activities, all of which could be considered a form of Niceness, devalue our roles as educators, and can provide a disservice to our students, who should expect to be challenged and pushed to earn their grades. The nice professor who brings in a snack may inadvertently offend a student. The nice professor who inflates grades for the chance at less evisceration in evaluations is doing his or her entire class a disservice (Stroebe 2016).

Still, many female professors feel compelled to consider the social impressions they are making whenever they interact with students, and especially when proffering assignment and course grades. Thus, in nearly every aspect of professional development and interaction, female professors are subject to scrutiny that might render unfavorable judgment when evaluations are submitted. This is true even when female professors establish reasonable boundaries concerning availability to students, response time to emails, and clarity of course expectations. Indeed, even minimal acts of self-care may represent acts against Niceness, negatively registered by students who need, on many levels, to learn and observe professional boundaries.

Gaming the Evaluation System

Faculty must protect themselves through syllabi, rubrics, and university policies. But fastidious documentation does not always protect the female professor from repercussions of opinion; when personal and professional priorities momentarily supersede professorial attention to individual students, chances are that we will hear about it in our evaluations in terms of being nice. Thus, women are bound to Niceness in a way that potentially hinders our growth as educators.

To compensate for this gendered interplay of time and space, Martin (2016) finds that women need to "lean in" and "game the system" in favor of perceived Niceness: "Women have reported engaging in tactics to show their sensitivity to student needs and illustrate their 'niceness.' Many also take steps to better project their authority and competence, such as by participating in acting workshops. They spend considerable time on course preparation and organization. Some of these steps increase actual teaching effectiveness. However, faculty members—male and female—acknowledge that e-SFFs can be gamed, and they offer advice on how to do so. Therefore, we are all encouraged to take the existing evaluation system as given and lean in" (7). The notion of Niceness is a construct—a performance as much as the construct of gender itself (Zevallos 2014). That some female faculty find it prudent to participate in acting workshops to hone a convincing demonstration of Niceness, to lean into the discomfort of a flawed and biased evaluation system in an effort to ensure favorable reviews, strikes me as a significantly preemptive measure, but not without justification. Women are burdened with seeming nice beyond what is expected of men (Bartlett 2005), and that may, to many, warrant an embellished classroom performance. The time spent building an illusion of Niceness would be better spent investing in meaningful experiences through which we are challenged and can grow in the realms of empathy, kindness, and compassion. Boring (2017) refers to this as an "opportunity cost" that reduces the time available for other activities academics need to build their tenure and promotion portfolios (35).

The more women lead or enforce, and the more masterful we become about our work and our disciplines, often the less "nice" we are perceived to be by the very students and administrations we benefit and support. Niceness is an assault on the genuine and organic camaraderie we aim to build, the professional equality we hope to achieve in the classroom, and the varying expectations of students taught by a male versus a female professor. The harder you make your students work, the less "nice" you are, and thus, the lower your evaluations and your own job security (Kamenetz 2014).

Social stereotypes hold that women are nicer and more nurturing than men (Lippa 2002); therefore, in terms of gender roles, women are expected to be nice, smiling, nurturing figures in the classroom regardless of the nature of our course content, the seriousness with which we take our studies and our students, and the passion of our intellectual delivery. Veering into the maternal is risky, but somehow, prescribed. As Bartlett (2005) states, "Perhaps, then, my expertise in being nice is a crucial factor in being seen to reasonably teach feminist material; perhaps it is important in alleviating the potential threat to belief and value systems such material can pose" (196). In other words, the interplay of gender and work, teaching from a feminist perspective, and teaching while female all resonate within my experiences in academia, my e-SFFs, and gender expectations of Niceness as a value system of labor.

Through thirteen years of teaching at the collegiate level, I've received a number of thoughtful evaluations praising my courses for content, structure, and my "tough love" approach. I get comments with some constructive feedback, but it's rare. Not long ago a student wrote, "Kristine is the TheBomb.com!" This comment provides absolutely no valuable data to me or to those who make decisions about my academic appointment. It reflects nothing of the time and energy I've invested, and utterly fails to support my pedagogy, nor does it give potential students reading my e-SFFs an accurate indication of my course content, or serve administration toward recognizing my commitment to higher education. It's funny, but useless.

Other comments, such as "Kristine is intimidating!" are similarly dubious in value. Am I intimidating but also *nice* about it? I balance my rigorous methods in the classroom with open door policy office hours, twenty-four-hour email turn-around, votes on class project topics, options for revisions, extra credit, and a fair attendance policy. These are my ways of "gaming the system," of "leaning in," of hacking my evaluations, perhaps at an "opportunity cost." Adopting flexible and open practices helps students manage their initial intimidation as a figure of authority through concepts of transparency and democracy. But none of my practices are constructed to present me as any nicer; they are not meant to be acts of Niceness. My goals are equity and fairness, though I recognize Castagno's (2014) point that sometimes well-intentioned policies and practices related to diversity actually maintain the status quo. There's real work to do in education; the majority of evaluations do not provide information to faculty on their weaknesses or strengths, nor do they identify areas of growth and efficacy.

Female Personality and Feminine Persona: Finding a "Nice" Balance

I joke that I'm the benevolent dictator in a faux democracy, and the truth is that I strive to build a space where learning happens for all students, all the time. I've invested in a tool kit of pedagogical strategies to reach different kinds of learners on multiple levels. I care about my students, but I'm not always nice. I remember vividly the student/professor dynamic of my own educational experiences. I connected with and learned the most from professors who cared—who intentionally designed courses and assignments with the goal of exciting and motivating me, and who concerned themselves with my experiences. I aim to repeat this practice, to lead by example. But I also understand this as manipulation of the gender play that my role as a female professor with an earned doctorate assumes: the "interpersonal variables such as 'warmth,' 'charisma,' and 'interest in students' have consistently been found to influence student evaluations" (Burns-Glover and Veith 1995, 70).

I favor passion and energy for my work over charm. As such, I strive to cultivate an authentic style as a professor and seek a harmonious balance between *who I am* and *what my job is.* Fernback (2015) discusses this balance as a process of constructing a teaching identity with sensitivity toward inspiring community participation and appreciating diversity of opinion. In doing so we give our students the potential to participate in John Dewey's "lived democracy" (Fernback 2015, 162). In my teaching practice, building a classroom based on ethical responsibility and egalitarian practices is paramount, and often leads to leaving Niceness behind, despite the risk of evaluation fallout.

Still, I am haunted by certain evaluations: nasty, stinging, crude comments about me, the woman, and not about my teaching; comments that undermine my efforts toward an equitable and egalitarian pedagogy; or responses from students who are blind to my efforts altogether. The most hurtful comments reinforce the notion that efforts toward Niceness in the classroom are akin to seeking perfection—and thus are impossible to achieve.

For women, Niceness creates a false double standard that echoes gender role expectations of the mid-twentieth century in a professional realm that typically boasts of enlightened and progressive standards. Growing evidence supports a strong gender bias in teaching evaluations, or "the negative female teacher effect" (Wagner, Reiger, and Voorvelt 2016), as real and with effects beyond the classroom. Boring (2017) believes that gender biases not only have a negative impact on female professors but also may be harmful to female students given the impact of a role model effect on student performance. Bartlett (2005) wonders when "seeming" and Niceness became important pedagogical markers (196).

Considering the wide range of research on how gender shapes assessment processes in all other areas of life, to think academia is an exception to gender bias is naive at best, dangerous to female professors at worst. Gender affects e-SFFs in a variety of ways, including a degree to which the professor's personality meets or escapes traditional notions of gender that makes a difference in the kinds of ratings students give (Laube et al. 2007). Studies show that while female professors are judged somewhat less harshly if they conform more to female stereotypes

(Simeone 1987; Voeten 2013), men still get bonus points for simply showing up male (Marcotte 2014).

Burns-Glover and Veith (1995) find that a paradox exists in the "feminine" and affectional variables that contrast with the perception of college teaching as a masculine, high-stress occupation and the existence of the university as a male-dominated, masculine-defined world. They stress the "expert versus mentor" dichotomy that often puts female professors in the double-bind of meeting student needs for a pseudocounselor and the professional expectations for competence and emotional distance.

To illustrate, after the 2016 election, returning to the classroom and facing twenty crestfallen, newly minted voters was challenging due to the complexity of the political landscape. The collision of affectional variables in the classroom and my own efforts toward political neutrality was unprecedented. Some students grieved, some cheered. I sought to demonstrate a balanced response while maintaining my personal commitments to equality and justice. My evaluations for that semester reflected appreciation for my outreach and response, though one student felt my extension of empathy was an indication of how "butt hurt" I was by the election results. It's no coincidence this is the same term used by bullies and trolls on the Internet.

Weaponizing Feedback: Vengeful Aspects of Student Evaluations

Though the reliability, validity, and potential uses of student evaluations of teaching have received a great deal of research and attention, the emotional impact on faculty has been largely ignored (Kogan, Schoenfeld-Tacher, and Hellyer 2010). The term *butt hurt* is crude; it implies anal rape. Those words devalue my concern for students, and they offend me personally. And that student's use of "butt hurt" is now part of my permanent evaluation record, visible to students. Lindahl and Unger (2010) explore the cruelty found in written responses, echoing Berk's (2013) assessment of student limitations, by looking into the anonymous comments students add to their numerical evaluations. Stroebe (2016) looks at how "revenge" plays a role in anonymous evaluations, noting the conscious strategy of students to punish a teacher for poor grades.

Students are aware that evaluations are used for high-stakes decision-making such as tenure, promotion, and contract renewal, so some students consciously make a decision to enact revenge upon a professor. Students choose whether or not to be "nice" in these evaluations, with no contextual requirements and no recourse for the targeted professor. Stroebe further states that revenge takes shape largely in the comments section, where students find a firm anchor to dole out punishment. In terms of cruelty, Lindahl and Unger (2010) recognize high levels of cruelty located in the comments section, citing the "deindividuation of anonymity as a mechanism of moral disengagement" and identifying not only a gender bias against women but also comments about women that are "obscene and unprintable" (72). Indeed, the student evaluation has the potential to become weaponized on both the personal and professional levels. In some cases, evaluation comments reflect characteristics of an arguably baseless, formal grievance that is never properly addressed yet remains indefinitely on record. This is further problematized by typically low percentages of evaluations completed in each class; thus, negative and vengeful comments are not sufficiently contextualized or tempered by a higher response rate that might reflect a broader spectrum of student opinions.

I've received obscene and unprintable comments, in addition to "butt hurt," ranging from how I look, to talk, to grade. That a professor would feel compelled to defend any aspect of her appearance or her accent against irrelevant student evaluation comments is absurd. That she should be similarly compelled to justify her grading rubrics, already articulated in her syllabi and demonstrated over time, is regressive and in all likelihood comes as the retaliatory result of a disgruntled, underperforming student who finds a convenient last word opportunity in the form of derogatory evaluation comments.

I turn to an anomaly I experienced in one particular semester. I was fifteen weeks pregnant at the start of the semester, and grew visibly more so over the duration. My e-SFFs reflected a puzzling increase in how students viewed me—kinder, gentler, nicer. I promise I was none of those things any more than usual; I was pregnant. I was exhausted, barely keeping up, and it was brutal. Bartlett (2005) notes of this anomaly in her own experiences teaching from a feminist perspective while pregnant, "Students were much more generous in their evaluations of my teaching for no apparent pedagogical reason . . . my appearance (so obviously) as a pregnant woman must have had the effect of 'softening' the material I was teaching. I was so obviously 'doing' femininity, I suppose, that the inflammable material I was espousing couldn't possibly be connected to me. Similarly as a pregnant body in academia, my unmasked embodiment must have superseded my 'passing' for an intellectual" (198). As physical entities navigating in a consumer-based space, our female bodies become a representation of Niceness and consumption, whether we want this or not. Students devoured my pregnancy with glee, taking photos of me and creating an Instagram account of my growing belly. Did my pregnancy and obvious human reproduction capabilities make me a nicer or more competent professor? No, but the evaluation anomaly exists, as does the Instagram account. It's too bad, in terms of e-SFFs, that I can't be pregnant every semester.

Whether women smile, are pregnant, look a certain way, or perform other acts of femininity, students judge them and their teaching in more punitive ways than their male counterparts. Boring (2017) finds that male and female students tend to give more favorable ratings to male professors on teaching dimensions associated with male stereotypes (of authoritativeness and "knowledgeability"), such as class leadership skills and the professor's ability to contribute to intellectual development (28). Though no studies have shown a correlation between beauty and teaching effectiveness (Deo 2015, sec. 1C), women are more closely judged on female stereotypes such as warmth, nurturing, Niceness, their personal styles, and physical attributes rather than the substance of the material taught (Anderson 2010; Deo 2015).

The 2014 AAUP survey results found "some women faculty members and faculty members of color report receiving negative comments on appearance and qualifications; it seems that anonymity may encourage such inappropriate and sometimes overtly discriminatory comments" (Vasey and Carroll 2016). Women are evaluated less favorably when they step outside traditionally feminine areas of knowledge (Simeone 1987, 64), adopt a feminist critical perspective (Bartlett 2005), or challenge hegemonic and racially constructed ideas that uphold the status quo (Castagno 2014). Ultimately, in academia and within the current evaluation system, women must prove themselves twice—first by demonstrating their own authority and competence, and second, by justifying the value of their work by being nice (Simeone 1987).

Rate My Professors: The Dangerously Unregulated Public Sphere of Evaluation Inequity

One need look no further than the website Rate My Professors (RMP) for data concerning Niceness, gender, and the moral disengagement of students in an anonymous, relatively unfiltered landscape.[1] Davison and Price (2009) provide a detailed analysis of RMP, calling into question the validity of the site rating system, noting rising issues in bias toward a number of groups: LGBTQIA instructors, older instructors, less experienced instructors, instructors who are anticipated to be more difficult or hold perceived values different from the student, and women instructors. Like institutional evaluation systems, the rating qualifications do little to predict actual learning outcomes, and by and large document rants or raves from students who value and want ease, Niceness, helpfulness, and entertainment.

Davison and Price found that one of the second most common themes in students' written comments involved instructor personality, mostly in a positive light, generally referring to a professor as "nice" or "cool" (58). In addition, RMP lends itself liberally to a factor of cruelty, fostered in an environment where moral disengagement operates unfettered and students engage in behavior that they would never engage in face-to-face (Lindahl and Unger 2010). Similar to e-SFFs, there's no recourse if a student is not nice in his or her RMP comments. At best, comments are superficially ego inflating and without academic context; at worst, they are akin to the cyberbullying rampant among teens in social media, and little better than an unvetted Amazon product review.

Evaluating Niceness 119

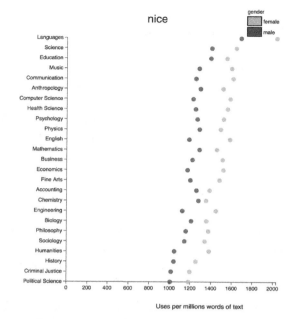

Schmidt's Data Map of "Nice" in Rate My Professors. Source: Reproduced from Schmidt (2015).

To expand upon how Niceness factors into RMP, Schmidt (2015) has compiled a data and visualization map of various key phrases to illustrate how different personality traits and personal characterizations fare in terms of gender. *Nice* is one of the terms analyzed in over fourteen million reviews at RMP. The visuals, utilizing the "All ratings" tab in the interface (combining positive and negative usage), reveal how female professors are discussed far more often in terms of "nice" than their male counterparts, across all twenty-five major academic disciplines. Variations on the term *nice*, including *kind* and *empathetic*, yielded similar but only slightly less gendered results, with male professors matching or moving past women in only one or two disciplines. The overwhelmingly gendered nature of "nice" in the RMP interactive chart is an indication of how the phrase is used to describe women more often than men in both positive and negative connotations. In contrast, the word *care* shows greater results for males in the "All ratings" tab than for women. In short, men can care, but at RMP, women must be nice.

What are the differences between Niceness, kindness, empathy, and caring? RMP doesn't differentiate. Niceness is a performance; it is not an authentic human characteristic, and comes saddled with virtue and social conventions. Niceness "seems like a weak substitute for more substantial virtues, like justice, charity, tolerance, and prudence" (Ward 2017, 118). Virtue is also gendered, inextricably tied to women and their sexuality, as noted in the optional red chili pepper icon that once existed at RMP to indicate a professor's "hotness."[2] The nice person is focused on him- or herself and the need to be perceived as nice. Kindness, empathy, and caring are ways of being, ways of focusing on others. Niceness comes with limitations in terms of rules, wrongdoing, and moral obligations (Goodman 2001). Niceness is an expectation, and if it is not complied with, that may result in offensive comments.

Gender theories reveal what we know: Women are expected to be nice, and men are expected to be leaders (Barnett and Rivers 2004). Men can care, but women must overtly demonstrate caring and Niceness. We have good reason to be suspicious of Niceness, particularly when what is being demanded is "civility-as-Niceness" (Ward 2017, 118). When gender roles are reversed, or expectations are not met, students will use the anonymous bullhorn of RMP to blast a professor, to seek revenge, and act in cruel, disembodied anonymity based on a moment when a grade negotiation didn't go in their favor or when a known attendance policy was enforced. This revenge on not-Niceness can be seen at websites like RMP, as well as at Facebook, Reddit, and Twitter. Stuber et al. (2009) suggest these popular sites "have the potential not only to reflect student opinion, but to create it" (387). The creation of information from unverifiable or false sources is dangerous; it reflects where we are today with "fake news" and core problems in society with information literacy. While e-SFFs are problematic in their own right, there is no escape on the Internet from the creation of opinion against one's failure to be nice.

While RMP forums are public, searchable by anyone, they exist in an uneven landscape and instead act on behalf of public shaming. Calls for Niceness in an academic context "de-legitimize the importance of attitudes, such as anger or indignation—that can be just and appropriate responses to relationships, practices, and institutions that are defective from a democratic point of view" (Ward 2017, 118). The reality—to teach material we've mastered, in equitable and accessible ways, with nuance and rigor—becomes moot. Our code of responsibility to our institutions is negated by our roles as jugglers of Niceness.

Nowhere in my union-backed contract does it say "Be nice," yet when it comes down to RMP, and the more formal university e-SFFs, my mastery of the subject, syllabi planning, countless hours of grading and preparation, service, and teaching tasks could boil down to a crucial moment interacting with a student when I wasn't nice. Realistically these were probably times I, or others, said *no*, or where we showed leadership or characteristics beyond what is expected of women. These not-nice moments seem to be what many students cling to and remember the most at RMP, and though it is not what we are required to deliver, we face vicious retribution when our Niceness doesn't meet an impossible standard. RMP serves as a container in which dissatisfied customers may leave their comments, a mostly unmoderated forum where cruelty and discrimination fester. While the site includes guidelines and terms of use for posts and content; the rigor of enforcement is questionable.[3] Davison and Price (2009) note their findings uphold the growing trend that students see themselves as customers purchasing a degree, where even positive comments at RMP adopt a consumerist point of view.

The ways gender bias plays out at RMP are complex, because students actively engage in posting about their instructors, performing a type of customer review task outside the university. RMP is a privately held, for-profit site. Students like the website (Davison and Price 2009; Stuber et al. 2009); it's outside the administration's purview and gives them a sense of rebellion. In contrast, I, like many of my colleagues, refuse to look at RMP. Recently a friend of mine, a nontraditional student earning a nursing and health care management degree online and at night while working full time, went to RMP to write a negative rating of a professor. Her concerns sounded legitimately based on poor teaching. Out of curiosity, she looked me up at RMP and was horrified at some of the negative ratings I've received. I wasn't surprised. I'll go out on a limb and say whatever is up there is not a real assessment of my teaching. I stopped looking at RMP years ago, and I refused to break my boycott of the site even while writing this chapter. The last time I looked, in 2010, I easily figured out who my hate raters were based on identifiable information they voluntarily posted. I was annoyed when a student wrote, "She's kind of cute. Kind of," not because my feelings were hurt, but because this comment is now part of my professional record. I hadn't earned any red chili peppers.

RMP is another platform for inequity, where Niceness, looks, easiness (a rating category in RMP), and nurturing are judged in a gendered, anonymous, cruelty-laced zone. "Easiness" is a specific category in RMP, though how this term is defined by the user cannot be confirmed. Davison and Price (2009) show that RMP presents gender-based standards under which female faculty are expected to perform. Fortunately, RMP ratings have yet to take a formal place in the tenure, promotion, hiring, and retention processes. Or have they? Stuber et al. (2009) address the rumored use of online evaluations like RMP as screening devices, in conjunction with an official teaching dossier, when looking at faculty candidates. Similarly, RMP could have negative impact on enrollment, which affects contingent faculty and hiring policies.

The Hard Sell: Disabusing Evaluation Identity Bias

Student feedback forms are a large part of the portfolios and packets used for contract renewal, tenure, and promotion. Smylie (2014) notes that evaluations are developed and implemented for nearly every step of the teaching occupation, "from admission to initial preparation programs, to licensure and certification, to on-the-job performance reviews, to tenure decisions, to retention and termination decisions" (97). Hearn (2001) notes that "the system is now more documented and, in that sense, more open, more accountable, yet still also open to abuse, not the least through greater job insecurity" (79).

As a non-tenure-track (NTT) full-time faculty member given the title assistant professor of instruction, I was hired in 2012 on a one-year contract. I submitted portfolios for contract renewal four times between 2012 and 2019 earning my first three-year contract in 2016 (the longest contract available for NTT faculty). Notably, as of my last contract renewal, I didn't have to submit the comments section of the e-SFFs. Maybe the university is only concerned with the quantitative results and less with feedback like "Kristine is TheBomb.com!" or how I was "butt hurt."

Perhaps the need for only the quantitative measures is cause for alarm; perhaps it puts out a fire. I'm of two minds about it. First, women are more harshly evaluated across the board in the observable statistical feedback than are their male counterparts (Wagner, Reiger, and Voorvelt 2016). Further, researchers who conducted statistical analysis of teaching evaluations concluded these evaluations don't measure teaching effectiveness, but measure student opinion and pretend it's the same thing (Deo 2015).

Second, while some comments are not helpful or contain cruel and discriminatory content, many contain information that wouldn't otherwise appear in the statistical data, reflecting meaningful interactions in and out of the classroom. I count numerous examples where students, presumably both male and female, provide some form of positive written comments. Due to anonymity, I have no way of knowing the gender of such students. Simultaneously, nearly every single class of every semester results in a handful of discriminatory or offensive comments, revealing nothing of my teaching practices, but speaking to Niceness and gendered social constructs.

Some comments reveal bonds between students and faculty or moments of clarity and insight concerning course content from a student's perspective; or they may reveal inconsistencies in the statistical data. Deo (2015) notes how female law faculty, particularly women of color, found positive information in their comments conflicting with harsh statistical data. She further discusses how women of color fare in evaluations in a large formal empirical study, the Diversity in Legal Academia Project (DLA): "Data from the DLA study indicate that women of color in legal academia confront ongoing challenges in the classroom and often vitriolic and biased teaching evaluations. Nevertheless, classroom success measured in part these biased and flawed student evaluations is used routinely for tenure and promotion purposes, with poor marks on student evaluations often cited for advancement and tenure denials for women of color faculty" (Deo 2015, 17). The DLA research reveals gender bias and discrimination in terms of race and ethnicity. As a result, Deo suggests that one option would be to eliminate evaluations altogether. Laube et al. (2007) find that "just as race and gender intersect in shaping most aspects of our lives, we suspect that race and other identity categories are likely to influence the ways in which students evaluate their teachers' performances of gender" (98). Wagner, Rieger, and Voorvelt (2016) question whether a fair measurement even exists.

For now, e-SFFs aren't going anywhere (Patton 2015), though they remain fraught with established difficulties concerning gender, race, age, sexual orientation, ethnicity, religion, and other locations of inequity. Andersen and Miller (1997) pointed out many years ago that department chairs and committees using e-SFFs for purposes of salary review, contract decisions, or promotion and tenure should keep in mind the ways students' reactions to male and female professors' teaching styles are judged differently. New data suggest problems in the design of evaluations, comments, and anonymity. Davison and Price (2009) urge institutions to create their own RMP-style websites, with well-designed evaluations focused on teaching and learning (62). There seems to be little meaningful benefit to e-SFFs (Smylie 2014) other than giving students the opportunity to do them, thereby allowing the consumer to comment on the product of education in often gendered and biased terms. As such, education is reduced to a commodity in the capitalist neoliberal global knowledge system and faculty are relegated to the role of sales reps. Are you good at selling your discipline in the appropriate manner, and do you do so with a smile? Are you nice enough to entice presumably intelligent twenty-year-olds into caring about their general education courses, or even their own major/foundations courses? You'd better cultivate those skills.

In terms of evaluations, Niceness should be ignored in lieu of civility, equity, democracy, and academic standards. Niceness is a "counterfeit virtue" (Ward 2017, 123). Many researchers argue that e-SFFs can be discarded altogether, as they do not actually evaluate teaching. Unintended consequences, such as leniency (Stroebe 2016, 814) and grade inflation (Kogan, Schoenfeld-Tacher, and Hellyer 2010), are a huge disservice to students. Researchers support a universal overhaul that eliminates or minimizes e-SFFs within the teaching portfolio. Academic institutions are encouraged to develop approaches to the evaluation of teaching where "effectiveness in promoting students' learning is the only determinant of the outcomes" (Laube et al. 2007, 99). Until then, gender-biased evaluations that discriminate against women in terms of style, approachability, and Niceness will continue to fail us—all of us.

Notes

1. See Rate My Professors, https://www.ratemyprofessors.com. At the time of the studies of RMP discussed herein, the website was named Rate My Professor.

2. Rate My Professor eliminated the chili pepper on or around June 2, 2018. https://www.insidehighered.com/news/2018/07/02/rate-my-professors -ditches-its-chili-pepper-hotness-quotient.

3. http://www.ratemyprofessors.com/TermsOfUse_us.jsp#guidelines.

References

Andersen, K., and E. D. Miller. 1997. "Gender and Student Evaluations of Teaching." *PS: Political Science and Politics* 30, no. 2: 216–19.

Anderson, K. J. 2010. "Students' Stereotypes of Professors: An Exploration of the Double Violations of Ethnicity and Gender." *Social Psychology of Education* 13, no. 4: 459–72.

Barnett, R., and C. Rivers. 2004. *Same Difference: How Gender Myths Are Hurting Our Relationships, Our Children, and Our Jobs*. New York: Basic Books.

Bartlett, A. 2005. "'She Seems Nice': Teaching Evaluations and Gender Trouble." *Feminist Teacher* 15, no. 3: 195–202.

Berk, R. A. 2013. *Top 10 Flashpoints in Student Ratings and the Evaluation of Teaching*. Sterling, Va.: Stylus.

Boring, A. 2017. "Gender Biases in Student Evaluations of Teaching." *Journal of Public Economics* 145, issue C: 27–41.

Brooks, A. 2001. "Restructuring Bodies of Knowledge." In *Gender and the Restructured University: Changing Management and Culture in Higher Education*, edited by A. Brooks and A. Mackinnon, 15–44. Buckingham, England: Open University Press.

Brooks, A., and A. Mackinnon. 2001. "Introduction: Globalization, Academia and Change." In *Gender and the Restructured University: Changing Management and Culture in Higher Education*, edited by A. Brooks and A. Mackinnon, 1–11. Buckingham, England: Open University Press.

Burns-Glover, A., and D. J. Veith. 1995. "Revisiting Gender and Teaching Evaluations: Sex Still Makes a Difference." *Journal of Social Behavior and Personality* 10, no. 4: 69–80.

Castagno, A. E. 2014. *Educated in Whiteness: Good Intentions and Diversity in Schools*. Minneapolis: University of Minnesota Press.

Davison, E., and J. Price. 2009. "How Do We Rate? An Evaluation of Online Student Evaluations." *Assessment and Evaluation in Higher Education* 34, no. 1: 51–65.

Deo, M. E. 2015. "A Better Tenure Battle: Fighting Bias in Teaching Evaluations." *Columbia Journal of Gender and Law* 31, no. 1: 7–43.

Fernback, J. 2015. *Teaching Communication and Media Studies: Pedagogy and Practice*. New York: Routledge.

Goodman, J. F. 2001. "Niceness and the Limits of Rules." *Journal of Moral Education* 30, no. 4: 349–60.

Hearn, J. 2001. "Academia, Management, and Men: Making Connections, Exploring the Implications." In *Gender and the Restructured University: Changing Management and Culture in Higher Education*, edited by A. Brooks and A. Mackinnon, 69–89. Buckingham, England: Open University Press.

Kamenetz, A. 2014, September 26. "Student Course Evaluations Get an 'F.'" National public Radio. http://www.npr.org/sections/ed/2014/09/26 /345515451/student-course-evaluations-get-an-f.

Kogan, L. R., R. Schoenfeld-Tacher, and P. W. Hellyer. 2010. "Student Evaluations of Teaching: Perceptions of Faculty Based on Gender, Position, and Rank." *Teaching in Higher Education* 15, no. 6: 623–36.

Laube, H., K. Massoni, J. Sprague, and A. L. Ferber. 2007. "The Impact of Gender on the Evaluation of Teaching: What We Know and What We Can Do." *NWSA Journal* 19, no. 3: 87–104.

Lindahl, M. W., and M. L. Unger. 2010. "Cruelty in Student Teaching Evaluations." *College Teaching* 58, no. 3: 71–76.

Lippa, R. A. 2002. *Gender, Nature, and Nurture*. Mahwah, N.J.: Erlbaum.

Marcotte, A. 2014, December 19. "Best Way for Professors to Get Good Student Evaluations? Be Male." *Slate*. http://www.slate.com/blogs/xx_factor /2014/12/09/gender_bias_in_student_evaluations_professors_of_online _courses_who_present.html.

Martin, L. L. 2016. "Gender, Teaching Evaluations, and Professional Success in Political Science." *PS: Political Science and Politics* 49, no. 2: 313–19.

Ory, J. 2000. "Teaching Evaluations: Past, Present, and Future." In *Evaluating Teaching in Higher Education: A Vision for the Future*, edited by K. E. Ryan, 13–18. New Directions for Teaching and Learning 83. San Francisco: Jossey-Bass.

Patton, S. 2015, May 19. "Student Evaluations: Feared, Loathed, and Not Going Anywhere." Chronicle Vitae. https://chroniclevitae.com/news/1011 -student-evaluations-feared-loathed-and-not-going-anywhere.

Schmidt, B. 2015. "Gendered Language in Teacher Reviews" (interactive chart). http://benschmidt.org/profGender.

Simeone, A. 1987. *Academic Women: Working towards Equality*. South Hadley, Mass.: Bergin and Harvey.

Smylie, M. A. 2014. "Teacher Evaluation and the Problem of Professional Development." Mid-Western Educational Researcher 26, no. 2: 97–111. http://www.mwera.org/MWER/volumes/v26/issue2/v26n2-Smylie-POLICY-BRIEFS.pdf.

Stroebe, W. 2016. "Why Good Teaching Evaluations May Reward Bad Teaching." *Perspectives on Psychological Science* 11, no. 6: 800–816.

Stuber, J. M., A. Watson, A. Carle, and K. Staggs. 2009. "Gender Expectations and On-Line Evaluations of Teaching: Evidence from RateMyProfessors.com." *Teaching in Higher Education* 14, no. 4: 387–99.

Vasey, C., and L. Carroll. 2016. "How Do We Evaluate Teaching? Findings from a Survey of Faculty Members." American Association of University Professors. https://www.aaup.org/article/how-do-we-evaluate-teaching#.WUKxbxPyvUp.

Voeten, E. 2013, October 2. "Student Evaluations of Teaching Are Probably Biased. Does It Matter? *Washington Post.* https://www.washingtonpost.com/news/monkey-cage/wp/2013/10/02/student-evaluations-of-teaching-are-probably-biased-does-it-matter/?utm_term=.d10109427799.

Wagner, N., M. Rieger, and K. Voorvelt. 2016. "Gender, Ethnicity and Teaching Evaluations: Evidence from Mixed Teaching Teams." *Economics of Education Review* 54: 79–94.

Ward, I. 2017. "Democratic Civility and the Dangers of Niceness." *Political Theology* 18, no. 2: 115–36.

Zevallos, Z. 2014, November 28. "Sociology of Gender." Other Sociologist. https://othersociologist.com/sociology-of-gender/.

8

The Role of Niceness in Silencing Racially Minoritized Faculty

CYNTHIA DIANA VILLARREAL, ROMÁN LIERA,
AND LINDSEY MALCOM-PIQUEUX

Racially minoritized faculty remain significantly underrepresented despite the growing representation of racially minoritized students in undergraduate and graduate programs (Jayakumar et al. 2009).[1] Although many university campuses are making efforts to increase the representation of diverse faculty, the revolving-door phenomenon that describes attrition of faculty from minoritized groups suggests that most campuses are not focused on sustaining diversity in the long term (Moreno et al. 2006). Without interrupting the usual conditions of culture, policy, and practice, campus diversity efforts will fall short (Moreno et al. 2006; Smith et al. 2004). Our curiosity to understand why campuses have difficulty disrupting the institutional structures (i.e., policies, practices, and culture) that disproportionately impact racially minoritized faculty led us to question the conversations taking place regarding racial equity in the professoriate. We question the extent to which the organizational culture informs which members of the professoriate can participate in such conversations. If campuses interested in a more diverse faculty are having conversations on racial inequity, are racially minoritized faculty able to fully participate and be heard in such conversations? If not, then what is keeping them from doing so?

Social and cultural pressures in the professoriate dictate how faculty are able to react to certain situations. For decades, racially minoritized faculty have described the presence of racism in predominantly White settings but have made conscious decisions to remain quiet due to the risks associated with speaking up (Tierney and Bensimon 1996). Though these decisions to be silent on issues of racism seem to come from an individual's own volition, they are wrapped up in social and cultural structures influenced by institutional and organizational histories and assumptions. It is imperative to examine how organizational culture and institutionalized norms contribute to silencing around issues of racial inequality. Studying the cultural elements of an organization helps to critically evaluate who or what is doing the silencing and who or what is being silenced. This chapter aims to contribute to the literature on organizations by interrogating the ways in which an organizational culture at a private, religiously affiliated liberal arts university engaged in dialogues around faculty diversity prevents racially minoritized faculty from fully participating. To guide this study, we asked the following research questions: (1) How do racially minoritized faculty perceive the organizational culture? (2) How do their perceptions of the culture shape their experiences? In our examination of these research questions, we found evidence that a culture of Niceness influenced most faculty decisions to keep silent on issues of racial discrimination and inequity. Ultimately, in this chapter, we argue that one campus's adherence to Niceness perpetuates cycles of marginalization within the academy by maintaining the status quo.

Racially Minoritized Faculty Experiences in the Literature

African Americans, Latinxs, and Native Americans remain underrepresented among higher education faculty (Finkelstein, Conley, and Schuster 2016; Integrated Postsecondary Education Data System 2016). The severity of this underrepresentation varies by academic discipline, institutional type, tenure status, and faculty rank. There is widespread recognition that colleges, universities, and community colleges must do more to ensure that their faculty both reflect and can effectively teach and mentor diverse student populations (Bensimon, Dowd, and Witham 2016; Gasman 2016; Taylor et al. 2010). The benefits of faculty diversity, particularly racial diversity, have been demonstrated consistently (e.g., Antonio 2002; Hurtado 2001; Hurtado et al. 2012; Ibarra 2001; Marin 2000; Milem 2001, 2003; Milem, Chang, and Antonio 2005; Smith 2015; Umbach 2006). Yet, many higher education institutions continue to struggle to achieve equity in the recruitment, retention, and promotion of racially minoritized faculty. Faculty search processes and hiring practices are often designed and implemented in ways that reproduce the status quo (i.e., an overwhelmingly White and male faculty) (Bensimon, Dowd, and Witham 2016; Gasman, Kim, and Nguyen 2011; Smith 2015). And when African Americans, Latinxs, and Native Americans do join the faculty ranks, they are usually among a few, and they often experience isolation, loneliness, marginalization, and racism in the classroom, among their colleagues, and within their home institutions (Essien 2003; Myers 2002; Stanley 2006; Smith 2002; Smith 2015; Sue et al. 2011; Turner 2002, 2003; Turner, Gonzales, and Wood 2008; Turner, Myers, and Creswell 1999). Though developing professional networks of support comprised of mentors and other scholars of color can mitigate some of these phenomena, many racially minoritized faculty feel they have little choice but to endure them in silence or leave academe altogether (Myers 2002; Smith 2002; Smith 2015; Turner et al. 2008).

Racism drives many of the interpersonal, departmental, and campus dynamics that act to marginalize and isolate African American, Latinx, and Native American faculty. Whether overt or subtle, racial bias and discrimination are highly detrimental to racially minoritized faculty professionally and personally (Smith 2002; Stanley 2006; Turner et al. 2008). For example, minoritized faculty, especially those who study issues related to race or use nondominant frameworks and critical methodologies, are more likely to have their expertise questioned and scholarship devalued by White faculty (Stanley 2006; Turner 2002). African American, Latinx, and Native American faculty members also tend to experience tokenism, wherein they are visible as representatives of their race but invisible as individuals, a burden not endured by their White colleagues (Turner et al. 2008). Racial bias also exists within the classroom, where White students more harshly evaluate racially minoritized faculty, particularly when teaching issues that pertain to diversity, race, and racism (Bower 2002; Delgado Bernal and Villalpando 2002; McGowan 2000; Mitchell and Rosiek 2006; Pittman 2010; Sampiao 2006; Stanley 2006; Stanley et al. 2003). Similarly, racially minoritized faculty, and particularly women, report being "presumed incompetent" in the classroom, often having their expertise and authority openly questioned by White students (Pittman 2010; Stanley 2006; Stanley et al. 2003). The effects of these racial microaggressions and biases experienced by minoritized faculty are very real, yet they remain largely invisible to their White colleagues.

In the absence of a critical mass of minoritized faculty within a given department or institution, scholars of color often report feeling unable to call out such instances of racism for fear that their White colleagues will question or invalidate their experiences (Smith 2015, Turner 2002, 2003). In an effort to maintain civility within their departments and institutions, many such faculty, especially those on predominantly White campuses, are often hesitant to confront those on campus who perpetuate racism (Smith 2015). African American, Latinx, and Native American faculty members commonly report that they "go along to get along" because they have witnessed the further alienation of racially minoritized faculty who break their silence and speak uncomfortable truths about race and racism to their White colleagues (Myers 2002).

This imposition of silence upon minoritized faculty—via normative pressures, threats from those with positional or de facto authority, or fear of retaliation—"ensure[s] the perpetuation of racism, sexism, and other forms of marginalization and exclusion in the university" (Ng 1997, 367). In this sense, silence has been used as a weapon (Ladson-Billings 1996) wielded against racially minoritized faculty to maintain the status quo.

Organizational Culture

Organizational culture is a framework useful in investigating the many nuances of an organization. In understanding an organization's culture, members can begin to explain behavior, norms, reactions, and beliefs, among other things (Bess and Dee 2008; Schein 1990). A number of scholars have contributed to the ways in which we study organizational culture in higher education (Bergquist 1992; Birnbaum 1988; Kezar and Eckel 2002; Marion and Gonzales 2013; Schein 1990, 1992; Tierney 1988); these scholars have provided myriad ways of defining and understanding the mechanisms that transmit culture and normalize behavior. Most often, definitions of culture include ways of understanding the physical space, structure, and symbols in conjunction with the rituals and routines of daily life (Bess and Dee 2008).

Organizational culture is defined as the patterns of basic underlying assumptions that an organization has created as a response to organizational problems; these assumptions have developed over time, are deeply embedded in the values and behaviors of an organization's members, and are held as truth (Schein 1992). Often scholars turn to formalized documents, philosophies, or mission statements to describe an organization; this approach, however, stays on the surface of a culture and how it is performed but does not get into how the history of the organization and its values have become taken for granted among its members. Missions indeed are mechanisms for understanding culture, but they are secondary (Schein 1992).

Our understanding of organizational culture, as informed primarily by Schein (1990, 1992) is a multilayered concept. At the core of an organization are the underlying taken-for-granted assumptions that dictate everything from how members are expected to behave to rewards, sanctions, and the layout of physical spaces. Assumptions are often hard to uncover because they reside at an unconscious level. The core assumptions of an organization influence the next layer, which manifests as an organization's espoused values. Espoused values inform what organization members determine to be good and bad. They are more public than underlying assumptions and are often prescribed in terms of a mission or values statement. Finally, at the outermost layer of organizational culture are artifacts; these usually manifest at a surface level in the form of language, symbols, and structure (Schein 1990).

Ultimately, organizational culture can provide clues about how individuals can feel safe in being their authentic selves (Reis, Trullen and Story 2015). Historically, White and male sociocultural values informed the construction of practices and policies at universities (Delgado Bernal and Villalpando 2002). The values and assumptions of the founders of higher education have institutionalized everything from faculty hiring practices to tenure and promotion reward systems (Tierney and Bensimon 1996). These institutions are inherently exclusionary to racially minoritized individuals.

Our Study

This study is situated at Valley Oaks University (VOU; the name is a pseudonym). In the fall of 2015, VOU partnered with the Center for Urban Education (CUE) to develop and implement strategies to diversify its faculty. In the years preceding the partnership, VOU's student body had become increasingly racially diverse; however, its faculty remained overwhelmingly White. VOU's leadership recognized the need to build its institutional capacity to recruit, hire, and retain racially minoritized faculty. Using a participatory action research approach (Bensimon and Malcom 2012; Kemmis and McTaggart 2008), CUE and VOU worked together to explore current institutional and departmental hiring practices with the goal of understanding how these practices worked to undermine VOU's stated aspirations for a more racially diverse faculty.

After reviewing faculty hiring and retention data, disaggregated by race and ethnicity, the Provost of VOU and two faculty leaders constructed an evidence team of eighteen faculty members drawn from departments across the institution. For ten months, the evidence team and researchers from CUE engaged in an in-depth collaborative inquiry process. Evidence team members participated in a series of seven three-hour working sessions in which they examined their own faculty search guidelines, reviewed and deconstructed artifacts of the hiring process (e.g., position announcements, interview questions, evaluation rubrics), considered the role of explicit and implicit racial biases in evaluating candidates, and sought to understand how institutional policies and practices affected the experiences of newly hired racially minoritized faculty at VOU. CUE researchers designed tools to aid in the inquiry process and facilitated the often "difficult" conversations that arose as evidence team members were challenged to consider how seemingly "race neutral" hiring practices produced racialized hiring outcomes. Over the course of this participatory action research process, evidence team members worked together to redesign their faculty search guidelines, put in place new procedures for search committee formation, and design and implement new requirements for future searches.

Though the initial focus of the work with VOU was the hiring process, several minoritized faculty on the evidence team raised concerns about retention, and more specifically, the harmful effects of institutional culture and departmental climate on the experiences of and, ultimately, the retention of current racially minoritized professors. Some racially minoritized evidence team members recounted personal experiences of isolation, humiliation, and marginalization at VOU. These frank conversations led the team to critically reflect on the ways in which the unspoken rules and norms of VOU may contribute to negative experiences of racially minoritized faculty. Following this meeting with VOU's evidence team, our team of CUE researchers felt it was important to the success of the larger action research process to conduct a more in-depth exploration of the experiences of racially minoritized faculty at VOU in order to understand equity challenges as they relate to faculty retention. The findings presented in this chapter resulted from this study of the experiences of VOU's racially minoritized faculty.

Methods

We used purposeful sampling to select and recruit informants to participate in our interviews (Merriam and Tisdell 2015). The university provost shared a spreadsheet with contact information for all VOU faculty who self-identified as Asian, Black, Latinx, or multiracial. To have a sufficient sample representation of race, gender, rank, and discipline, we emailed all thirty-four faculty on this list. Twenty-three accepted our invitation, and we conducted interviews during the fall of 2016. We made a conscious decision to not use data from three interviews because of their part-time status; this exclusion comes with the knowledge that part-time faculty have a vastly different experience with an organization's culture compared to their full-time counterparts. Our interview data included three Black women, two Black men, five Latinx women, three Latinx men, four Asian women, one Asian man, one Muslim woman, and one multiracial woman; however, we refrain from identifying participants with markers other than pseudonyms to preserve their anonymity. Since we were interested in their overall experiences as faculty members, we asked questions to understand their experience with hiring and recruitment, orientation to the university, and tenure and promotion. Each interview lasted from sixty to ninety minutes and was transcribed for analytical purposes.

To analyze our data, we used NVivo Pro 11 software to conduct two rounds of coding. We engaged in a first cycle of open coding to capture themes inductively, followed by a more targeted method of coding informed by our theory in the second round (Saldaña 2013). We created a codebook for the second round of coding and followed each round by memoing our analysis to sort our codes into broader themes.

Findings

Interviews with racially minoritized professors yielded the emergence of themes relating to participants' perceptions of the organizational culture and how their perceptions of that culture shaped their experiences. In this section we first describe how racially minoritized faculty perceived the organizational culture through their descriptions of VOU's organizational structures and processes (artifacts); strategies, goals, and philosophies (espoused values); and unconscious, taken-for-granted thoughts and feelings (assumptions) (Schein 1992). The three themes outlining the informants' perceptions of the organizational culture include Niceness, an emphasis on the church's religious tradition, and a public commitment to diversity.

VOU's Expectations of Niceness

Questioning unspoken norms and assumptions that perpetuated inequalities in experiences were challenging because at VOU being nice to each other was equated with not being confrontational. Several interview participants described VOU as having a culture of Niceness. Racially minoritized professors believed that VOU's culture required them to be polite, diplomatic, and nonconfrontational. The socialization process for these professors included an iterative cycle of learning the acceptable rules of engagement. Words like *polite* and *diplomatic* reinforced the espoused value of being nonconfrontational, which shaped and maintained individual thoughts and feelings about being nice. Although being nice in the workplace makes it feasible for professors to establish mutually respectful relationships, inequalities in professional experiences persist when the culture of Niceness curtails opportunities to address racism.

Through the socialization cycle, racially minoritized faculty also learned that there were consequences for those who challenged or held colleagues accountable for their racist behaviors. Ruby, who experienced racism in her department and felt overburdened with additional responsibilities that her White colleagues did not have, problematized how VOU's culture of Niceness negatively impacted her professional productivity and emotional well-being: "Yeah, it's like you're supposed to . . . I'm sorry. You're supposed to be . . . it's that culture of Niceness and service, but almost to the point of being a martyr. You always have to work. And the thing is, there cannot be conflict. If you raise an issue, you are seen as a troublemaker. Everybody has to get along." As seen in Ruby's response, the unspoken rule of avoiding conflict hides the realities of racially minoritized faculty. During the interviews, minoritized professors peeled back the layers of VOU's culture of Niceness to illustrate how it diverted attention away from racism. Miles stated that "things are going on behind closed doors," but on the surface, there is a culture of Niceness. He stated this when describing an incident where a colleague complained about experiencing discrimination "all the way up to the [university] president." This colleague, Miles explained, was met with a lot of smiles and Niceness, but nothing was done to prevent these types of discrimination from reoccurring.

VOU's Emphasis on Religious Tradition

When describing VOU's culture, several participants attributed Niceness to the religious tradition present at the institution. VOU's religious traditional values stemmed from the mainline Protestant denomination that professors perceived as being embedded in White European values. When we asked George to recollect his initial impressions of VOU, he said that the university's commitment to diversity and equity resembled the mainline Protestant Church's efforts on racial diversity: "I just had the sense that it was pretty stable . . . it didn't look like a diverse place . . . and they're really trying to diversify and move toward racial equity, and they were trying at the time, but it seemed to match up with my own experience of the [mainline Protestant] world, that it's White, sort of [that] European mentalities are central, and everything else is kind of marginal and peripheral." George's response outlined how efforts for racial diversity at VOU were peripheral to the university's culture. Similar to George and his insider knowledge about the mainline Protestant culture and values, Eric learned how to speak the mainline Protestant language. He believed that White faculty used coded words like *fit* to label people whom they perceived shared the same mainline Protestant, White European values: "So, the question of fit might matter. And it may be different now, but the fit was a big factor back then, and that's code for something. What does it mean to fit? If it means to fit into, like, a [European mainline Protestant] culture, that could mean you're not argumentative, it could mean nonconfrontational. And what is that code for?" From the perspective of racially minoritized faculty, VOU's religious, traditional values were encrypted within White European norms.

As a mainline Protestant university, VOU's mission was deeply rooted in the church's tradition to encourage varying opinions and to question, probe, and seek truth. Signs illuminating the diversity of the student body were visible through flyers that promoted VOU's value for inclusivity and the new designation as a Hispanic-Serving Institution. The university's value for diversity manifested through the language administrators, faculty, and staff used to construct the campus as a pluralistic environment. Yet racially minoritized faculty who were outsiders looking through a veil told a different story about VOU's inclusivity of diverse voices and perspectives. For example, Yveth distinguished the ideal of pluralism from the act of practicing pluralism in everyday interactions:

> Last spring there was an interfaith service, led by one of our [mainline Protestant] pastors. And they called it [an] interfaith service, and I went to it. But it felt to me like it was actually just a [mainline Protestant] service that was inclusive of other traditions. So it was [a mainline Protestant] style service, and they had students of, I don't know of what religion they were, but reading the Koran, and Hindu scriptures, and Buddhist scriptures. But they

weren't from the religions they were reading, so they were including scriptures from other religions, but it didn't feel pluralistic. Our mission on campus seems to be pluralistic, but there are some things, like it's theoretical instead of practical, at this moment. We haven't gotten to the actually pluralistic environment. We're still inclusive, which means that it's still a very [mainline Protestant] campus, and we're still allowed to hang out here and be here.

Although university staff created a space where students and faculty could learn about different religions, Yveth's response illustrates the ways racially minoritized faculty felt silenced when participating in activities where their experiences and perspectives were the learning outcomes. Minoritized professors at VOU believed that they were allowed to hang out and physically be on campus, but their ideas, perspectives, and values continued to be peripheral to the campus mainline Protestant values. The application of Schein's (1992) organizational culture theory untangles the ways unquestioned patterns of individual perceptions about pluralism benefit those in positions of power—in this case, the White majority population on campus.

VOU's Public Commitment to Diversity

The lack of symbolic cultural representation on campus was another reason why racially minoritized professors perceived VOU's commitment to diversity as a superficial initiative. In addition to the stratification of racial representation in the faculty and administrative bodies, the campus did not have murals, statues, and buildings reflective of the student body diversity. Notwithstanding the multicultural office, which resembled a travel agency for students interested in studying abroad, participants were critical about VOU's commitment to diversity because there were no designated spaces on campus for Latinx students in spite of the campus-wide efforts to define itself as a Hispanic-Serving Institution. For professors of color at VOU, the culture of Niceness manifested in the campus artifacts, often in the form of language, espoused values of diversity, and individual thoughts and behaviors that being nonconfrontational nurtured a pluralistic environment. As we outline in the following section, the way racially minoritized professors perceived the campus culture shaped their experiences.

Expectations of Niceness Shape Practices That Silence

As a way to discuss the influence of the organizational culture on racially minoritized faculty, informants shared stories of how administrators silenced them from disrupting the culture of Niceness. They described how administrators reified the culture of Niceness through perceived qualities of being a good fit. Traditionally, administrators have coveted professors who were nice and polite and who did not complain. Administrators granted access to leadership positions to professors who they perceived had qualities of being a good fit. Although Miles believed that racially minoritized professors were asked to serve on more committees than White faculty, he distinguished service work on issues of diversity from leadership roles: "It depends on the type of service you're talking about. If it's service having to do with some diversity issues, yes. If it's service that can cause maybe some type of wave—say, for instance, you're on a committee where they're giving out honorary degrees or something, and you wanted to bring in, say, a liberal black speaker to get an honorary degree—well, that might not work out. You might get dropped off that committee." Miles's description outlines how administrators silenced minoritized faculty by not appointing them to positions where they might make waves. The unchallenged belief of being a good fit stratified racially minoritized professors away from positions of power. Most tenured faculty in our sample perceived administrators as silencing them from addressing significant problems with racial inequity by not allowing them to serve in positions of power. A smaller number of informants explained how administrators silenced them for being vocal and outspoken about inequalities. According to Crystal, administrators stopped assigning her as a senior mentor for incoming racially minoritized faculty because of her reputation for disrupting the culture of Niceness by being outspoken about discrimination. When talking about how she would like to mentor new professors to negotiate and navigate the culture, she noted, "It's a hard acclamation [being a faculty member], but rarely do [administrators] let me actually see the new faculty of color coming in, 'cause I kind of have that reputation. They never ask me. They never asked me to come and talk to them. And I'm one of the few faculty that across the board has been able to negotiate the academy and get new faculty understanding and hook them up, but they . . . and I volunteer. I've written, but they never ask." Crystal's response highlights how administrators silence outspoken racially minoritized professors by not inviting them to mentor junior faculty. Since Crystal was resistant to VOU's culture of Niceness, she believed that administrators did not want her to empower junior racially minoritized faculty to resist the culture instead of navigating through polite and nonconfrontational language and behaviors. The consequences of administrators relying on socially constructed qualities of being a good fit in a campus shaped by a culture of Niceness erase the experiences of minoritized professors and silence them from addressing racial inequities through the university's formal processes.

Maintaining Niceness through Self-Silencing

Racially minoritized faculty described feeling the need to silence themselves as a way to fit in with the culture at VOU. Their conformity to the behavior and beliefs of the group allowed them to gain acceptance from their colleagues and member-

Niceness and Racially Minoritized Faculty   137

ship in the professoriate. By remaining silent they felt that they were preserving the harmonious work relationships with their colleagues as well as securing their chance at tenure and promotion. Participants expressed conforming to silence specifically around conversations of race and racism because they did not want to cause trouble or create discomfort among their colleagues. They tacitly avoided any negative repercussions by remaining silent; this allowed them to focus on acquiring tenure. In this sense, their conformity to silence was also seen as an individual-level coping mechanism of doing nothing, which came at the expense of protecting the status quo that emphasized and validated Niceness above all else.

Participants also described certain unspoken and unchallenged rules that dictated how faculty were allowed to respond to issues on campus. In describing these rules, racially minoritized faculty generally stated that "being nice" meant they were unable to ask critical questions or speak up about microaggressions and racist comments. Were they to speak up, they would be classified as troublemakers. Maria recalled having to speak in a manner that was consistent with the culture at VOU as way of maintaining Niceness and ensuring she was well liked before achieving tenure: "When you're pretenure you wanna be very careful in what you say. And make sure that everyone likes you and you keep that culture of Niceness. So, you don't want to be that minority person who's saying things and making a ruckus, and then people just see you as not nice. So you have to maintain that culture of Niceness, myself and others, even though we might be struggling with that." Maria's statement exemplifies self-silencing as an unspoken norm rooted in the organization's cultural element of Niceness. The emphasis on minority status was shared in other interviews as well. Racially minoritized faculty explained that their race complicated the expectation of Niceness because of implicit biases and stereotypes colleagues have of them. Edwin discussed the difficulties he's faced trying to advocate for diversity as a male abiding by the expectations of Niceness:

> We have advocated for diversity in a polite and civil manner, using the proper procedures of the university. Every year, for example, the president gets a report on the state of diversity on campus from the Office of Multicultural Programs. In that report, every year it says we need to address recruitment and retention [of racially minoritized faculty]. Every year that polite, appropriately delivered report is given to the president, and every year it's ignored. So, you know that what's coming next, the only time we get heard in that way, is when we make a big noise about it. But when we do that, what do we do? We fulfill their stereotypes of us, and then they use that as justification to ignore us. So we get caught in this trap, this self-fulfilling prophecy that they initiate; they make us into those kinds of people.

Edwin, who made noise around faculty diversity following the expectations around Niceness, told us later that his voice is no longer heard. His multiple attempts to be heard by the university president were ignored, albeit nicely, and now Edwin chooses to not speak up as a mechanism of self-preservation.

Participants also described feeling as though the organizational culture required them to silence elements of their racial or cultural identities. The campus-wide focus on increasing diversity created space for more representational diversity, but the organizational culture focused on Niceness excluded individuals on the margins of the White, European, mainline Protestant center. Cheryl described literally turning down the volume on her music in her car when she entered the parking lot on campus. Although no one directly insisted she do so, she did it so as not to draw direct attention to the fact that she is different from other faculty and students:

> I don't know, not to go too deep, but I just felt like when I'd come on campus I have to turn into this professor, I have to be a different person. Like today, pulling in I was listening to music that I won't name and just like . . . and then I was pulling into the parking lot and I noticed people were looking at me and then I notice it was because of my music, so I turned it down. There's a sense of not being able to be me type of thing. But this is not the first place that I felt that at, so I'm used to masking that a bit. But I knew that would be the case coming in because I knew what the demographics were from being a student here.

In Cheryl's attempt to not stand out or cause trouble, she made the decision to turn down the volume on her identity to secure membership among the faculty at VOU; ultimately, she wanted to fit in with what she thought was expected of a faculty member. This situation is not unlike what other participants described as leaving their identity at the door, or having to code-switch between their ethnic and professional identities.

Discussion

Overall, our findings illustrate that the organizational culture of VOU impacts the ways silence allows racial inequity in the professoriate to persist. Our study emphasizes an urgent need for more scholarship on organizational culture, expectations of Niceness within academia, and how both areas of scholarship should include an evaluation of silence as an impediment to achieving racial equity in the professoriate and beyond.

We found evidence that Niceness, in fact, permeated VOU's organizational culture. Niceness was present not only in how participants described the campus culture and practices but also in how they described the school's public commitment to diversity and the religious tradition. As a result, we argue that it was ultimately Niceness that influenced most faculty decisions to remain silent on issues of racial inequity. Contrary to what is implied by the term, Niceness at VOU put limitations on what racially minoritized faculty could say and on how they could engage in the culture. Though Niceness connotes something pleasant, in this case it prohibited racially minoritized faculty from speaking out about injustices, microaggressions, and institutionalized racism. Ultimately, we argue that adherence to the expectation of nice behavior perpetuates cycles of marginalization within the academy.

Beyond this claim, our findings also support the argument that Niceness is a mechanism of Whiteness (Castagno 2014). The fact that Niceness was so prevalent in these conversations allows us to suggest that Whiteness working through nice people (Castagno 2014) maintains a barrier for racially minoritized faculty operating within the professoriate. Until higher education can dismantle the norms and values placed on Niceness and the culture of collegiality (Bergquist and Pawlak 2007), racially minoritized faculty will never feel welcome in a culture operating under White values and norms. Our findings illustrate that Niceness influenced not only the way faculty interacted with one another but also their ability to participate in the organizational culture through self-silencing.

A culture of Niceness that tends to result in silence has an unintended trickle-down effect for students. It is possible for students to learn these behaviors in their interactions with faculty and administrators and, in turn, act in ways that are safe, nice, and uncritical, resulting in maintenance of the status quo. Additionally, the Niceness that maintained silence on the issue of faculty diversity and equity at VOU resulted in absolutely no policy changes for over a decade. Niceness therefore makes it possible for policies to remain uncontested for sustained periods of time and, as a result, to maintain exclusions toward racially minoritized individuals.

In our efforts to interrogate VOU's organizational culture, we investigated the impacts that organizational culture has on organizational silence and implicitly on change. In our findings we see that an expectation of Niceness works to reinforce a culture that is compliant, collegial, and silent on important issues regarding racial equity. Using a critical lens to investigate Niceness in higher education administration, we provide a critique of Niceness that is necessary to continue the conversation on equity. We find that in understanding how Niceness maintains silence and inequity our contribution will be to create administrator awareness on the direct impacts of their Niceness in maintaining a White status quo.

Note

1. We use the term *minoritized* instead of *minority* as conceptualized by Harper (2012) to illustrate "the social construction of underrepresentation and subordination in U.S. social institutions, including colleges and universities." Individuals are considered racially minoritized when they are treated in ways that render them inferior because of their race under particular circumstances that work to maintain Whiteness.

References

Antonio, A. L. 2002. "Faculty of Color Reconsidered: Reassessing Contributions to Scholarship." *Journal of Higher Education* 73, no. 5: 582–602.

Bensimon, E. M., A. C. Dowd, and K. Witham. 2016. "Five Principles for Enacting Equity by Design." *Diversity and Democracy* 19, no. 1. http://www.aacu.org/diversitydemocracy/2016/winter/bensimon.

Bensimon, E. M., and L. E. Malcom. 2012. *Confronting Equity Issues on Campus.* Sterling, Va.: Stylus.

Bess, J. I., and J. R. Dee. 2008. *Understanding College and University Organization: Theories for Effective Policy and Practice.* Sterling, Va.: Stylus.

Bergquist, W. H. 1992. *The Four Cultures of the Academy.* San Francisco: Jossey-Bass.

Bergquist, W. H., and K. Pawlak. 2007. *Engaging the Six Cultures of the Academy: Revised and Expanded Edition of the Four Cultures of the Academy.* San Francisco: Jossey-Bass.

Birnbaum, R. 1988. *How Colleges Work: The Cybernetics of Academic Organization and Leadership.* San Francisco: Jossey-Bass.

Bower, B. L. 2002. "Campus Life for Faculty of Color: Still Strangers after All These Years?" *New Directions for Community Colleges* 2002, no. 118: 79–88.

Castagno, A. E. 2014. *Educated in Whiteness: Good Intentions and Diversity in Schools.* Minneapolis: University of Minnesota Press.

Delgado Bernal, D., and O. Villalpando. 2002. "The Apartheid of Knowledge in the Academy: The Struggle over 'Legitimate' Knowledge for Faculty of Color." *Equity and Excellence in Education* 35, no. 2: 169–80.

Essien, V. 2003. "Visible and Invisible Barriers to the Incorporation of Faculty of Color in Predominantly White Law Schools." *Journal of Black Studies* 34, no. 1: 63–71. DOI: 10.1177/0021934703253687.

Finkelstein, M. J., V. M. Conley, and J. H. Schuster. 2016. *Taking the Measure of Faculty Diversity*. New York: TIAA Institute.

Gasman, M. 2016. "The Five Things No One Will Tell You about Why Colleges Don't Hire More Faculty of Color." *Hechinger Report*. http://hechingerreport.org/five-things-no-one-will-tell-colleges-dont-hire-faculty-color/.

Gasman, M., J. Kim, and T.-H. Nguyen. 2011. "Effectively Recruiting Faculty of Color at Highly Selective Institutions: A School of Education Case Study." *Journal of Diversity in Higher Education* 4, no. 4: 212–22.

Harper, S. R. 2012. "Race without Racism: How Higher Education Researchers Minimize Racist Institutional Norms." *Review of Higher Education* 36, no. 1: 9–29.

Hurtado, S. 2001. "Linking Diversity and Educational Purpose: How Diversity Affects the Classroom Environment and Student Development." In *Diversity Challenged: Evidence on the Impact of Affirmative Action*, edited by G. Orfield, 187–203. Cambridge, Mass.: Harvard Education Publishing Group.

Hurtado, S., C. L. Alvarez, C. Guillermo-Wann, M. Cuellar, and L. Arellano. 2012. "A Model for Diverse Learning Environments: The Scholarship on Creating and Assessing Conditions for Student Success." In *Higher Education: Handbook of Theory and Research*, vol. 27, edited by J. C. Smart and M. B. Paulsen, 41–122.

Ibarra, R. A. 2001. *Beyond Affirmative Action: Reframing the Context of Higher Education*. Madison: University of Wisconsin Press.

Integrated Postsecondary Education Data System. 2016. *Biennial Fall Staff Survey, 2015–16*. Washington, D.C.: National Center for Education Statistics.

Jayakumar, U. M., T. C. Howard, W. R. Allen, and J. C. Han. 2009. "Racial Privilege in the Professoriate: An Exploration of Campus Climate, Retention, and Satisfaction." *Journal of Higher Education* 80, no. 5: 538–63.

Kemmis, S., and R. McTaggart. 2008. "Participatory Action Research: Communicative Action and the Public Sphere." In *Strategies of Qualitative Inquiry*, edited by N. K. Denzin and Y.S. Lincoln, 271–330. Thousand Oaks, Calif.: Sage.

Kezar, A., and P. D. Eckel. 2002. "The Effect of Institutional Culture on Change Strategies in Higher Education: Universal Principles or Culturally Responsive Concepts?" *Journal of Higher Education* 73, no. 4: 435–60.

Ladson-Billings, G. 1996. "Silences as Weapons: Challenges of a Black Professor Teaching White Students." *Theory into Practice* 35, no. 2: 79–85.

Marin, P. 2000. "The Educational Possibility of Multi-racial/Multi-ethnic College Classrooms." In *Does Diversity Make a Difference? Three Research Studies on Diversity in College Classrooms,* 61–83. Washington, D.C.: American Council on Education/American Association of University Professors.

Marion, R., and L. D. Gonzales. 2013. *Leadership in Education: Organizational Theory for the Practitioner.* Long Grove, Ill.: Waveland.

McGowan, J. M. 2000. "African-American Faculty Classroom Teaching Experiences in Predominantly White Colleges and Universities." *Multicultural Education* 8, no. 2: 19–22.

Merriam, S. B., and E. J. Tisdell. 2015. *Qualitative Research: A Guide to Design and Implementation.* San Francisco: Jossey-Bass.

Milem, J. F. 2001. "Increasing Diversity Benefits: How Campus Climate and Teaching Methods Affect Student Outcomes." In *Diversity Challenged: Evidence on the Impact of Affirmative Action,* edited by G. Orfield and M. Kurlaender, 233–49. Cambridge, Mass.: Harvard Education Publishing Group.

Milem, J. F. 2003. "The Educational Benefits of Diversity: Evidence from Multiple Sectors." In *Compelling Interest: Examining the Evidence on Racial Dynamics in Colleges and Universities,* edited by M. Chang, D. Witt, J. Jones, and K. Hakuta, 126–69. Stanford, Calif.: Stanford University Press.

Milem, J. F., M. J. Chang, and A. L. Antonio. 2005. *Making Diversity Work on Campus: A Research-Based Perspective.* Washington, D.C.: Association American Colleges and Universities.

Mitchell, R., and J. Rosiek. 2006. "Professor as Embodied Racial Signifier: A Case Study of the Significance of Race in a University Classroom." *Review of Education, Pedagogy and Cultural Studies* 28, nos. 3–4: 395–409.

Moreno, J. F., D. G. Smith, A. R. Clayton-Pedersen, S. Parker, and D. H. Teraguchi. 2006. *The Revolving Door for Underrepresented Minority Faculty in Higher Education.* San Francisco: James Irvine Foundation.

Myers, L. W. 2002. *A Broken Silence: Voices of African American Women in the Academy.* Westport, Conn.: Bergin and Garvey.

Ng, R. 1997. "A Woman out of Control: Deconstructing Sexism and Racism in the University." In *Women in Higher Education: A Feminist Perspective,* edited by J. Glazer-Raymo, B. Townsend, and B. Ropers-Huilman, 360–70. Boston: Pearson Custom.

Pittman, C. T. 2010. "Race and Gender Oppression in the Classroom: The Experiences of Women Faculty of Color with White Male Students." *Teaching Sociology* 38, no. 3: 183–96.

Reis, G., J. Trullen, and J. Story. 2015. "Perceived Organizational Culture and Engagement: The Mediating Role of Authenticity." *Journal of Managerial Psychology* 31, no. 6: 1091–1105.

Saldaña, J. 2013. *The Coding Manual for Qualitative Researchers.* Thousand Oaks, Calif.: Sage.

Sampaio, A. 2006. "Women of Color Teaching Political Science: Examining the Intersections of Race, Gender, and Course Material in the Classroom." *Political Science and Politics* 39, no. 4: 917–22.

Schein, E. H. 1990. "Organizational Culture." *American Psychologist* 45, no. 2: 109–19.

Schein, E. H. 1992. *Organizational Culture and Leadership.* San Francisco: Jossey-Bass.

Smith, D. G. 2015. *Diversity's Promise for Higher Education: Making It Work.* Baltimore: Johns Hopkins University Press.

Smith, D. G., C. S. V. Turner, N. Osei-Kofi, and S. Richards. 2004. Interrupting the Usual: Successful Strategies for Hiring Diverse Faculty. *Journal of Higher Education* 75, no. 2: 133–60.

Smith, P. J. 2000. "The Tyrannies of Silence of the Untenured Professors of Color." *UC Davis Law Review* 33, no. 4: 1105–33.

Stanley, C. A. 2006. "Coloring the Academic Landscape: Faculty of Color Breaking the Silence in Predominantly White Colleges and Universities." *American Educational Research Journal* 43, no. 4: 701–36.

Stanley, C. A., M. E. Porter, N. J. Simpson, and M. L. Ouellett. 2003. "A Case Study of the Teaching Experiences of African American Faculty at Two Predominantly White Research Universities." *Journal on Excellence in College Teaching* 14, no. 1: 151–78.

Sue, D. W., D. P. Rivera, N. L. Watkins, R. H. Kim, S. Kim, and C. D. Williams. 2011. "Racial Dialogues: Challenges Faculty of Color Face in the Classroom." *Cultural Diversity and Ethnic Minority Psychology* 17, no. 3: 331–40.

Taylor, O., C. B. Apprey, G. Hill, L. McGrann, and J. Wang. 2010. "Diversifying the Faculty." *Peer Review* 12, no. 3: 15–18. https://www.aacu.org/publications-research/periodicals/diversifying-faculty.

Tierney, W. G. 1988. "Organizational Culture in Higher Education: Defining the Essentials." *Journal of Higher Education* 59, no. 1: 2–21.

Tierney, W. G., and E. M. Bensimon. 1996. *Promotion and Tenure: Community and Socialization in Academe*. Albany: State University of New York Press.

Turner, C. S. V. 2002. "Women of Color in Academe: Living with Multiple Marginality." *Journal of Higher Education* 73, no. 1: 74–93.

Turner, C. S. 2003. "Incorporation and Marginalization in the Academy: From Border toward Center for Faculty of Color?" *Journal of Black Studies* 34, no. 1: 112–25.

Turner, C. S. V., J. C. González, and J. L. Wood. 2008. "Faculty of Color in Academe: What 20 Years of Literature Tells Us." *Journal of Diversity in Higher Education* 1, no. 3: 139–68.

Turner, C. S. V., S. L. Myers Jr., and J. W. Creswell. 1999. "Exploring Underrepresentation: The Case of Faculty of Color in the Midwest." *Journal of Higher Education* 70, no. 1: 27–59.

Umbach, P. D. 2006. "The Contribution of Faculty of Color to Undergraduate Education." *Research in Higher Education* 47, no. 3: 317–45.

9

The Self-Contained Scholar

The Racialized Burdens of Being Nice in Higher Education

COLIN BEN, AMBER POLEVIYUMA, JEREMIAH CHIN,
ALEXUS RICHMOND, MEGAN TOM, AND SARAH ABUWANDI

Niceness in discussions of race, gender, or any issue relating to identity creates a common conflict for marginalized peoples: to speak out and risk potential further marginalization or to remain silent and contain oneself. In institutions of higher education (IHEs), students of color are expected to "act nice" in the name of civil dialogue. In practice, this means neutralizing conversations on race, gender, and/or class inequalities that might create difficulty for White people. Niceness frames Whiteness as polite neutrality, with White comfort as the foremost concern and without addressing racism or accountability.[1] Niceness, however well intentioned, reinforces White supremacy (Arrington, Hall, and Stevenson 2003; Castagno 2014). Niceness limits, ignores, and avoids discussions on racism, sexism, and other forms of systemic discrimination. Niceness is a shield, protecting the status quo by subverting and sublimating the voices, presence, needs, history, and experiences of marginalized peoples. Yet Niceness is also strategically used by students of color (SOC) as a method of navigating predominantly White institutions (PWIs) to manage assaults on well-being and succeed academically and professionally.

In this chapter we explore how SOC in predominantly White colleges and universities are forced to perform Niceness, what harms Niceness creates, and how students strategically navigate Niceness. Failure to perform Niceness leads SOC to be labeled as "mean," "unprofessional," or "difficult," impeding current success and future advancement. We explore the performance and consequences of Niceness through counterstorytelling, a narrative tool of Critical Race Theory (CRT), which uses fiction and lived experiences to examine racial power from the perspective of marginalized peoples (Delgado 1989). To create this counterstory, we developed questions influenced by literature on Niceness and Whiteness and conducted a story sharing circle with students on their undergraduate experiences.

Niceness is a White racial discourse, which coerces SOC to silence or restrain themselves for the sake of propriety and self-preservation. This reinforces the White status quo and has serious emotional, physical, and academic consequences for SOC. However, students of color cleverly navigate the academy; finding academic and social enclaves while code-switching—strategically appealing to the discourse of Niceness. Niceness for survival highlights the toxicity of Niceness—not to be confused for the kindness and respect that students of color deserve at IHEs. The remainder of this chapter is divided into three sections, starting with a review of literature on Niceness, campus climate, counterstorytelling, and our methods. In the second section, we present the counterstory of our composite character Lily to illustrate the effects of Niceness on the educational, personal, and social relationships of students of color. We conclude with recommendations after considering the consequences of participating in Niceness in higher education.

The Story behind the Story

Being "nice" is generally understood as behavior that is pleasing, agreeable, or socially acceptable. In the United States, Niceness is a social construct of Whiteness and privilege that "shape[s] the rules concerning what is appropriate behavior, which attributes are more valued than others, and how people are supposed to interact with one another" (Arrington, Hall, and Stevenson 2003, 3). In predominantly White settings, Niceness avoids discussions of race, gender, and class inequality to promote gender- and color-blind worldviews, thereby maintaining Whiteness by avoiding racial friction, reinforcing oppression, and excluding SOC (Castagno 2014). Niceness through Whiteness wrongly reduces racism to individualized acts of meanness while downplaying casual, covert racism as unintentional missteps of an innocent individual with the expectation of forgiveness (Castagno 2014). This obfuscates systemic and structural implications of racism and microaggressions (Haviland 2008), forcing people of color to moderate or internalize their behavior (Stearns 1994). Niceness creates negative educational and schooling experiences for SOC, who cannot interrogate inequities without violating norms of Niceness.

In the classroom, instructors may use Niceness to temper or shut down conversations on race to avoid perceived controversy and sustain comfort or positivity for White students. Haviland (2008) describes this as "White educational discourse," reinforced by a "constellation of ways of speaking, interacting, and thinking, in which White teachers gloss over issues of race, racism, and White supremacy" (41). When SOC are exposed to racist, sexist, or homophobic discourse they are expected to temper their anger and calmly educate White peers or White faculty—if they are asked. Niceness allows Whites to avoid discomfort and appear innocent and educable. When White students make racist comments, this gives an opportunity to backtrack and defend statements as not racist; SOC are expected to give the benefit of the doubt and retract statements that may alter White students' self-perception. Niceness puts the onus on SOC to politely educate or be silent altogether, burdening SOC with additional labor that should be taken on by the institution and professors, creating unceasing self-awareness in educational settings because SOC must continuously alter their behavior and speech to ensure White comfort.

Niceness is pervasive at IHEs, and particularly at institutions attempting to project an image of racial diversity, or institutions that ignore or overlook campus climate—"institutional characteristics such as size, type, control, selectivity, and racial composition of the college" (Hurtado 1992, 546). Factors influencing campus climate include experiences with discrimination, prejudice, racial conflict, negative stereotypes, perceptions, harassment, and institutions ignoring underrepresented students' needs (Cabrera et al. 1999; Rankin and Reason 2005). These factors influence "the quality of life on campus," which "includes both the campus racial climate and the environment of support for students" (Hurtado 1992, 561). SOC experience more harassment, damaging stereotypes, and overall negative experiences than White students (Cabrera et. al. 1999). Even for IHEs that conduct campus surveys, Pewewardy and Frey (2004) suggest that "a 'hostile' learning environment and racial prejudice are seldom mentioned in university reports on ethnic minority student issues" (48). IHEs need to focus on the needs and experiences of SOC to foster an inclusive learning community on campus, especially at PWIs (Hurtado and Carter 1997). Of all student populations, Native American students' experiences are the least examined (Shotton, Lowe, and Waterman 2013) and reported in campus climate literature. Campus climate factors that are unique to Native American students need to be explored, especially by Native American students and scholars themselves (Brayboy et al. 2012; Pewewardy and Frey 2004). To turn the authors' experiences with the toxic climate of Niceness at PWIs into scholarly insight, we therefore turn to counterstorytelling.

CRT originates in legal scholarship using storytelling, legal analysis, and social theory to argue that racism is normal, not aberrant and permanent (Crenshaw et al. 1995). Race is a social construct that defines, affects, and influences the lived experiences of people of color. Similarly, Tribal Critical Race Theory (TribalCrit) adds that colonization is endemic to society, particularly for Indigenous peoples in the United States (Brayboy 2005). Together, CRT and TribalCrit reframe these social narratives through stories from personal experiences, histories, and even fiction by and about people of color to highlight structural and ideological power relationships. Stories are pedagogical and methodological tools for interrogating race; stories from the experiences and perspectives of people of color become counterstorytelling by subverting dominant narratives (Delgado 1989;

148 COLIN BEN ET AL.

Harper 2009). Counterstories relate ideas in ways that conventional scholarly analysis often cannot, synthesizing lived realities with fiction for relatable critical reflection. From Bell's (1992) science fiction tale "The Space Traders" as a metaphor for the ways the United States sacrifices the lives and labor of Black people for White benefits to Harper's (2009) use of qualitative interviews to create a composite counterstory to describe the experiences of Black male faculty through a unified narrative, counterstorytelling combines lived experiences and literary flare to examine experiences with racial power.

To build our counternarrative, the authors engaged in a story sharing circle. Three of the authors self-identify as Native American, one as mixed-race Black and White, one as Jordanian and Palestinian, and the last as Black and Asian. All authors are cisgender, with four female students of color and two male graduate students of color, ranging in age from twenty to thirty-nine. The goal was to share our experiences as racialized peoples at a PWI in open conversation, guided by a series of open-ended questions focusing on feelings of discomfort and visibility on campus, classroom conversations on race and the consequences, and recommendations for institutions to address concerns. Across three days we spoke for a total of three hours and thirty-seven minutes; we recorded the conversations, and transcribed and coded them to identify themes, shared experiences, and key examples, which were then used to create a composite character and counterstory that would relay our lived experiences with being silenced or our feelings of not belonging on campus. Because of our experiences as students of color, we placed CRT and TribalCrit at the center to understand intersections of racism and colonization from firsthand experiences with White supremacy in academia to assimilate SOC into Niceness and Whiteness. But, in the tradition of Bell (1992), we added a fictional twist to illustrate the systematic and structural effects. We blended the real experiences of students becoming disenfranchised by Niceness at a university with the blended story of Violet Beauregard in the classic film *Willy Wonka and the Chocolate Factory* (1971) to represent the effects of repression or self-containment in the face of Niceness.

The Self-Contained Scholar: Lily's Undergraduate Inflation

The Freshman Fifteen

Lily could feel the eyes of the entire class staring at her. She did not need eyes in the back of her head to know everyone in the auditorium was looking at her, waiting for her to speak. She was used to glances: people trying to place who she was or where she was from. Her light brown skin and wavy hair made her a racial Rorschach test; everyone saw what they wanted to see, and people were always

The Self-Contained Scholar   149

trying to put her in a box: "Oh, I love your hair, it's pretty and curly, but not too curly! Where are you from, you look so exotic!" Awkward racist questions were one thing, but the surprised reactions when people found out she was Black and Native American were even better: "How did that happen?" Now, in college in a bigger, more diverse city, things would be different. She would finally get to speak up. She would use all the new ideas and new people as opportunities to change everything. That was the plan, until curious glances became hardened stares in class today.

In her Introduction to Education class Lily sat up front. Having devoured her readings, she often arrived eager to engage. For the most part she liked the other students. Everyone was awkward, but friendly, as they got to know each other in the first month. But the friendly banter stopped once her class focused on race. The assigned readings stressed the importance of diversity in education, but a distant voice from the back of the class disagreed: "Diversity is good, but all this affirmative action brings in people who don't deserve to be here and lets them go to school for free. It's too much. There are a lot of diversity people who deserve to get in, but I didn't get any help, so why should they? I would have gone to Harvard if they didn't have to save seats for diversity students. Why do Black people need extra help to go to school anyway? It should just be about class." Lily's eyes nearly rolled out of her head. *Who is this White man, and why does he think he is better than everyone?* she wondered. While Lily's eyes were rolling, the rest of the class turned their eyes on her. She was one of the handful of students of color in this hundred-person class, and she just so happened to be the only student of color to show up today. Someone had to respond to the ignorance, and the eyes of the class just made her the spokesperson for every student of color ever. The pressure made her frustration boil even more.

As she raised her hand and turned her body so she could return her classmates' gaze, her classmates awkwardly found somewhere else to look. The class was silent. So Lily took the podium the eyes gave her. "You know that's not true," she said calmly but firmly. "Affirmative action doesn't mean free money or free admission. Racism has stopped way too many people from making their lives better through school. And if a few entitled-ass White men don't get to go to their first-choice school, that's something I think we can all live with." After scattered chuckles and a few *ooohhs*, some of the eyes staring back at her now seemed confused—except for one set of angry eyes near the back. Lily was ready to say more, but the professor jumped in: "Well, just focusing on race is probably too narrow. Let's think about the important point we just heard, what about class and economics for affirmative action? Everyone deserves to go to college. Thinking it's only about race is ignorant. Let's turn back to the chapter we read. What do you think it's trying to say about diversity?" As Lily turned back around, her confusion over the professor's comments only grew. *What does he mean, "ignorant"?* Lily thought she had made a valid point. After everyone looked at her for her opinion, it felt like she shouldn't have said anything. Lily felt more sideways glances behind her, less curious and more hostile. Suddenly she was under a gigantic magnifying glass. It felt like she took up the entire auditorium.

When class ended, Lily's desk seemed tighter, but she was more focused on leaving. She quickly packed up her things, put on her headphones, and tried to slip out of the lecture hall as quickly as possible. *Ignorant? What did he even mean by that?* On her walk home, Lily's music was interrupted by an email notification on her phone. It was from her professor. Her heart sank; she must have forgotten her discussion board this week. She tapped the screen instantly, worried she had lost ten easy points just a few weeks into class.

> Dear Lily,
>
> Thank you for your comments in class today, I appreciate that you always come to class having read the materials and submit your assignments on time. I understand you have strong opinions on the topic, for obvious reasons, but I want to make sure that we all play nice. I received some comments from other students after class, and frankly I'm concerned that even though you are well informed, the way you express yourself can be mean. Think about reining in your big personality, just a little bit. I think you have a very bright future, and as a class it will be better for all of us to get along and think about walking a mile in each other's moccasins. Please take this as a helpful suggestion; if you have any questions . . .

Lily stopped reading, vexed and perplexed. She thought, *Did he send an email to that asshole too? Was I mean? No way. I don't think so.* She replayed the memory again in her mind. Doubt crept in; Lily began to worry about her future. Maybe she did need to hold back. She had no words to respond to the email, so it was best just to keep it to herself. She wanted to make sure she could do something for her community, to give back in some meaningful way with her college experience. That was not going to happen if the professors thought she was mean. How would she get letters of recommendation? Maybe it was time to contain herself, just for now.

Weeks went on and Lily held herself in. She smiled in class, greeted everyone, and said only as much as she needed to. Short answers only, no responses to opinions, even if they were racist. As she kept her thoughts to herself she noticed her clothes starting to fit tighter. Keeping to herself was exhausting. Her mother always said she was full of hot air, but now she felt like a balloon. She told herself it was just the freshman fifteen she had been warned about.[2] She kept a healthy diet and exercise. Even though the scale didn't change, every week she felt a little bigger. It was like the magnifying glass stayed on her all the time. Nobody said anything, so why should she? She decided to keep it to herself.

The Self-Contained Scholar   151

Sophomore Slump

Lily made her way across campus toward the student union. It was game day, and she loved to show off her school spirit—even if the school's colors made her look like a blueberry. She could hear students chanting along her entire walk, and as she got closer she noticed a gaggle of White students chanting along with a man who was standing on a stage. At first, Lily did not care. Still, she pulled out one of her earbuds to listen. The man was shouting, "We need to deport illegal students! They don't belong!" She was not surprised by the sentiment, as she had actually heard worse in class—but hearing blatant racism spewed in public froze her in place.

The hateful stream of racist propaganda against Mexican Americans continued from the newly formed Men for American Rights club. Inside herself, Lily screamed louder than any of them: *Shut up, you ignorant Nazi idiots!* But her mouth never moved. She stood frozen, suppressing her frustration as her mouth curled to a deep frown. She didn't have to say anything; anger was written all over her face. Every second she stood to listen, the crowd felt more tightly packed, even though it looked like everyone was moving on to lunch. Suddenly she heard a shout from the sidelines, "Build that wall!" She snapped out of her stare. *What the hell is going on?* As she looked around, she noticed she was the only person of color near the stage. Lily felt everyone's eyes on her, staring. She was the elephant in the room, only everyone was looking right at her. When she met eyes with them, most quickly pretended to be looking at something else nearby, but some kept the uncomfortable stare and waited for her to look away.

Lily turned back toward the stage and made eye contact with a White student in a polo shirt and khakis walking toward her. "So, what do you think?" he asked. It was a rhetorical question; he was just trying to troll her now that he had finally stopped staring. As he stepped into the sun his baseball cap, on backward, did little to block the sun blazing into his eyes. "Everyone has the right to an opinion," Lily mumbled dismissively, but inside she screamed, *You racist asshole!* His beeline approach and condescending tone put Lily on the defensive. Nobody would speak up with her or for her—not in this crowd. Why should she have to be the voice of reason? The other student turned back toward the stage, seemingly satisfied with his intimidation tactics. Quickly but calmly Lily made her way out of the crowd and into the student union, finding it harder to slip between people in the crowd.

Lily went to the Office of Student Organizations office and asked the student worker there if she could speak to a supervisor about the club's racist chants. With a too-big smile, the female White student worker feigned sincerity: "Oh gosh. I'll tell my supervisor right away." Lily wanted to be direct. *Why don't I tell the supervisor, and we try to get something done?* She hesitated. *Anything more, and she'll think I'm being mean; then nothing will get done.* Lily waited patiently as the student worker casually disappeared into the office. After five minutes, Lily could tell she was being ignored, so Lily left. *This door seems narrower than before,* she thought as she squeezed through it. She started to walk toward the main student services desk, but knew that since it was the free speech area, she was likely to get the same useless excuse: Everyone has a right to an opinion—*especially if you're White,* she thought to herself.

Lily made her way outside to her favorite spot near the student union. Trees shaded her from the sun, and the nearby buildings did not have windows. Finally alone, she sat down. The bench seemed smaller today as she felt the frustration ballooning within her. She started to feel nauseous, her stomach twisting as she thought back on what had just happened. *Did I do the right thing? Of course,* she reasoned, *it wasn't safe to say anything. Not there. But wouldn't that be a perfect teaching moment? I still want to be a teacher, and students can be ignorant.* Lily mulled over her future: *It might be my job someday, but it sure isn't today. I'm here to go to class and earn my degree, like everybody else.* Reflection did little for her throbbing headache and stomach pains. She reached into her bag for Tylenol and Tums for a little relief before she rushed to meet her best friend, Nizhoni, for lunch. Lily wasn't hungry, but at least she could talk to someone who would actually listen. Even though they were not from the same community, Nizhoni always understood her, or tried her hardest to. Lily spotted the back of Nizhoni's head from across the room; her long dark hair always stood out against the sea of blonds.

As Lily slid into the booth, she tried her best not to push the table into Nizhoni's space. *They must keep moving these benches closer and closer, packing us in like sardines.* "This booth gets smaller every time we sit here, maybe the food is just too good," Nizhoni said with a laugh. Lily smiled. "Girl, food is the last thing on my mind right now. Did you hear that White power rally by the union?" Lily recounted what had happened as Nizhoni's face shifted from shock to frustration to recognition. "He really stared you down like that?" Nizhoni asked.

Lily nodded. "Do I look like I'm lying?"

Nizhoni knew Lily's looks well, and chuckled. "You know these . . ." Nizhoni glanced around and lowered her voice ". . . White people." Lily snorted and let out a laugh through her drinking straw. Nizhoni never said "White people" too loud; it made every conversation feel like they were starting their own revolution. "They get to say what they want, with no consequences, and nobody cares how much it hurts us. That's why I went to student health for counseling," Nizhoni added confidently.

Lily stared at Nizhoni like she had just announced she had the plague. "What? But you're so happy all the time!"

"Sure, with friends," Nizhoni replied, running her french fries through the ketchup on her plate. "We both live in the same racist world. I knew I couldn't do it alone; I had to tell someone. You know how they say, 'Choose your battles wisely?' It doesn't apply to us, you can't avoid it, you just have to minimize damage. Especially on campus. You have to be safe."

The Self-Contained Scholar   153

Lily was shocked. Counseling had never crossed her mind; she was not crazy, but then again, neither was Nizhoni. The longer she talked to Nizhoni, the more her appetite came back. After a long lunch they got up to leave, and Lily slid out of the booth easily and thought, *It must have been the people behind us pushing it in; that's why the booth was so cramped.*

Senioritis

Lily sat at a desk in the Multicultural Student Services Office, staring at her to-do list. She reflected on how she got here—a place she could not imagine being when she had graduated high school four years earlier. In subtle and loving ways her family had always pushed her to continue: her nephew and nieces drew pictures for her dorm room, and elders provided her a meal and a lesson when they visited. After family visits, she would rush to her room and let out the tears that she held back. She wanted to go back with them to a place that did not make her prove herself, not only academically or professionally, but as a multiracial person of color from a rural community. She was ready to flee the endless encounters with micro-aggressions and overt racism on campus. Luckily, her mentor helped Lily navigate difficult interactions at school, with internships, scholarships, and advice about life. Overall, university life was daunting, and she had been exhausted too many times to count, but support from family, friends, and mentors helped. Now, nearly done, she was so ready to graduate.

Lily was lost in her thoughts until her laptop blipped. It was her professor, responding to her request to write her essay on current issues on Indigenous lands. Lily opened the email and felt her stomach drop. As she read, her heart beat so fast it made her hands shake. Why was this happening again? This was her capstone, an upper-division class far from the Intro to Education that had shut her down years ago. She reread the email in disbelief: "Thank you for running your idea by me prior to completing your essay. Unfortunately, this topic and population are unfit to write about for your essay, as it does not have adequate research behind it and may encourage bias, as has been seen by other students of color when writing about these topics. It may serve you to broaden your focus on American society rather than keep it to one population in this essay."

Lily looked around, wishing someone in the room could help her understand and figure out what to do. Her professor seemed so open-minded in class, welcomed multiple perspectives, and sometimes even quoted the university charter's commitment to "diversity, excellence, and equality." Well, at least on paper he encouraged it. Lily thought back on the handful of times she shared her experiences with her professor and peers. *Do they think that I am overreacting, or selfish?* She had come all this way; sometimes her passion, sparked by the experiences of her family and community, was all that pulled her through. Lily never turned in assignments just for the sake of finishing them; she truly wanted to utilize them to learn and understand so that she could give back.

She was dumbfounded. *What did I do wrong?* At least her professor acknowledged that every population has struggles, but why did this mean she couldn't highlight her community? *We're always left out of the conversation: Black and Native. And don't even get me started on Black Natives. Does the professor even know our issues?* She thought about collecting research to show to her professor that her experience was addressed in academia. She clicked on her Google Scholar bookmark to start a literature review to prove him wrong. She wondered, *Will it even make a difference if I call the professor out?* Lily had dealt with backlash before; she was not ready to go back to being the mean girl. *What if he gets the university involved?* Again, she thought about choosing her battles. She tried to play out every scenario in her head. *Best case, I have to write my paper, proving the professor wrong and getting credit. Worst case, I do all this work for nothing, and start over on something I don't care about, and it won't help my community.*

Lily closed the tab and went back to her email. She began to type, tears rolling down her face and hands trembling. She forgot about the crowded room; everything faded away as she focused on her laptop, leaning in:

> Dear Professor,
>
> I appreciate your response and I understand your concern for bias in my essay, as I do have close ties with this community and its issues. However, I feel that this essay is an opportunity for me to present a perspective that is left out of mainstream media and to connect existing research on other communities. I discussed this topic previously with our college dean, who is also my mentor. Dean Sampson was eager for me to write, add to the literature, and help my community. I plan to continue with this topic as I believe it has potential to provide a meaningful approach, reflective of the values in the university charter and mission. Please let me know if you have any questions.
>
> Sincerest regards, Lily

She looked over it two more times and then pressed Send. Lily felt like she had launched a nuclear attack, had pressed a button that could end her academic career. As regret crept in, she felt confident that she had not backed down from the truth. *Even if the professor tries to say I was mean, so what? It's all there in the writing, nice as could be. I've already been accepted into my master's of public health program anyway. If my community and others face these issues daily, then how can my professor end the conversation? The topic follows the rubric, and it was only a courtesy to let him know.* Lily thought it best to double-check, and forwarded the email thread to her mentor.

Surprisingly, Dean Sampson replied quickly. She wished Lily had talked to her first, but it was not the end of the world: "Finish this essay, graduate, and let me look into ways that our staff can appropriately address these situations in the future." Lily was relieved to have someone who listened, especially a woman of color with power at the university. *If only there were more of you!* she thought. Lily sent back a quick "Thank you!!! I feel like I always have to explain everything a million times in a million ways just to be heard a bit; thank you for listening." Dean Sampson must be on one of her locked-in-the-office, email-only days, because as soon as Lily hit Send, her mentor replied again: "There does need to be more understanding and encouragement of different perspectives, especially from professors who always talk about open dialogue. Thank you for letting me know what's really happening in class. Now, go finish your essay so we can celebrate!"

Lily was elated. *Finally, someone who agrees with me! This isn't the end. I am going to go to graduate school, and I'm going to help my community. With Dean Sampson around, maybe the university really will change.* Lily calmly closed her laptop and packed her bag. She started outlining her paper in her head as she walked to the library. Nothing else around her mattered now. She slid through the packed sidewalk effortlessly, like she was floating above the crowd. She was ready to say what needed to be said and, best of all, to graduate.

Discussion

Drawn from the experiences of the coauthors in our story sharing circle, these vignettes are composited from our undergraduate student experiences based on common feelings and aspirations. The three vignettes in our counterstory pull together the author's experiences, interactions, and encounters with Niceness and White supremacy at PWIs. Storytelling through CRT and TribalCrit synthesizes our story as a way of understanding and communicating how these negative experiences can be used to reshape institutions of higher education. As Brayboy (2005) emphasizes, "Stories are not separate from theories; they make up theory and are, therefore, real and legitimate sources of data and ways of being" (430), validating students' lived experience. Central to this analysis are the understandings from CRT and TribalCrit that racism (particularly White supremacy) and colonization are endemic to society, shown through Lily's experiences in the three vignettes in classrooms, on campus, and in communications with professors.

In "The Freshmen Fifteen," Lily started out optimistically, wanting to learn and make a positive impact until classroom encounters shut her down. The combination of her classmate's racist comment and her professor using his position of authority to devalue Lily's opinion and positionality created a racially hostile environment that required Lily to conform to norms of Niceness and Whiteness or be shut down. In class, the professor strategically diverted a conversation that he deemed uncomfortable, demonstrating "White educational discourse," which leaves students feeling disregarded and unsupported at PWIs (Haviland 2008, 41). The professor's email further accused Lily of uncivil discourse—targeting her tone without acknowledging the veracity of the content of what she had said in class. His desire for a "safe space for all students" meant Lily's "well-informed" stance was dismissed, accompanied by warnings that her academic or professional success might be at stake. The professor effectively sacrificed Lily's own well-being in service of institutional racism.

Lily's story emphasizes how Niceness causes self-containment through simultaneous isolation and hypervisibility for SOC (Brayboy 2003; Cabrera et al. 1999). In our conversations, we found common negative experiences with Niceness we had not shared with each other, bonding over experiences that felt like isolated incidents, without the need for self-censorship. Discovering shared experiences in a space of respect and validation initiates an important path of healing for SOC, allowing us to validate each other and laugh about the absurdity of those experiences. Just as Lily found support from her friends, family, and mentor, sharing with people who can genuinely understand combats stress that SOC endure. Safe spaces or enclaves on campus are necessary places where SOC can share their concerns and experiences with trusted allies and peers (Hurtado and Carter 1997; Solórzano, Ceja, and Yosso 2002). This puts the onus on IHEs to hire more faculty and staff of color to facilitate support for students. As Lily's story emphasizes, students often lack the resources or ability to question or contradict a professor's hostility without intervention from allied administrators. Simultaneously, IHEs should facilitate training for White professors in every academic discipline to reveal how professors' well-intentioned or nice behaviors are harmful to students of color. IHEs must diagnose their problems with annual campus-wide and departmental climate assessments to gauge experiences of their student body and to maintain accountability (Hurtado 1992; Pewewardy and Frey 2004; Solórzano, Ceja, and Yosso 2002). Student assessment is vital; as Lily's conversation with Nizhoni has shown, students speak and act in different ways with peers, and peer sharing opens up new stories that are not ordinarily shared in formal assessments. Lily's story is part of our TribalCrit and CRT frameworks to push for practical changes on campus, since storytelling is theory making and "theory and practice are connected in deep and explicit ways such that scholars must work toward social change" (Brayboy 2005, 430).

Our counterstory emphasizes different manifestations of White educational discourse, either in changing topics in the classroom, emails calling for collegiality and decorum, or diverting student research agendas that would be relevant and useful for students' home communities. Suggesting that Lily's background would create bias to compromise validity because it is based on her experiences and other students covertly suggests Lily's incompetence or lack of rigor in research (Gutiérrez y Muhs et al. 2012). Self-censorship can stem from students' need for survival and can be critical for avoiding hostility, but feeling unsafe to speak out enhanced Lily's self-doubt and stress: she froze, holding in her anger, even when unfruitfully seeking on-campus resources designed to help campus climate. Forced and strategic self-censorship has physical consequences, however. Racial hostility has multilayered effects, including "racial battle fatigue" (Smith, Yosso, and Solórzano 2011). In each of our three counterstory vignettes, Lily's self-censorship and self-silencing lead to bottled-up emotions, feelings, and stresses that cause her to inflate like Violet Beauregard in *Willy Wonka and the Chocolate Factory*. Lily's self-perceived ballooning is a manifestation of feelings of hypervisibilty and the many emotional and physical tolls of racial battle fatigue.[3]

Furthermore, IHEs must recognize racialized historical contexts of education, such as forced assimilation of Native American students (Lomawaima and McCarty 2006) or how IHEs and PWIs benefit from slavery (Wilder 2013). With these institutions entrenched in that history of oppression, TribalCrit and CRT remind us that these conditions may have changed shape, but not disappeared; the underlying racism and colonization remain strong. Our counterstory provides context that broadens and complicates existing dialogue about Niceness and Whiteness in the academy by centering discussion from the perspectives of students of color. Lily's story emphasizes the importance for faculty of all fields to educate themselves in the experiences of SOC and how faculty may affect student experiences. If institutions or faculty are truly invested in student well-being, resistance to Niceness starts by naming and recognizing oppressions students face on campus.

For undergraduate students of color, Niceness is a harmful silencing technique that frames them as problems; as Du Bois eloquently illustrates, "Between me and the other world there is ever an unasked question: unasked by some through feelings of delicacy, by others through the difficulty of rightly framing it. To the real question, How does it feel to be a problem? I answer seldom a word" (Du Bois 1903, 5). Niceness and Whiteness are embedded in educational experiences, policing behaviors, and fostering White supremacy. Institutions that tout or value academic freedom use Niceness to suppress the voices of students of color while providing a guise of innocence for White supremacy. Lily's story illustrates how "it feels to be a problem," as Niceness silences and suffocates. Niceness has few consequences for those who perpetrate it (i.e., Lily's White professors and peers), but for students of color it can cause an introversion, with deleterious physical, social, and physical effects summarized in racial battle fatigue. Not all students of color will contain themselves, and most will not balloon up like Lily did. But the consequences of Niceness are negative and severe, especially for students who have not become proficient in code-switching or found supportive and understanding peers and mentors.

Our counterstory illustrates how PWI administrators, faculty, staff, and students must create, foster, and enrich communities of support. Institutional policies may declare the importance of diversity, but for a student trying to figure out life, school, and a future, those words are hollow without actual support. Our past experiences informed the counterstory at the core of this chapter, but our current experiences in school, and even in the writing of the chapter, are informed by our relationships to mentors like Dr. Jessica Solyom or Dr. Bryan McKinley Jones Brayboy, whose feedback and mentoring informed and guided our collective writing. Mentorship and community are keys to retention (Brayboy 2003), but these must be supplemented with reflexivity, accountability, and commitment from White faculty, staff, and administrators. As our protagonist Lily found out, well-intentioned advice can be demoralizing and silencing. Niceness becomes suffocating through Whiteness because it is inflexibly hostile for students of color; implicating White students or faculty in racism is considered "not nice," even when true. Meanwhile, racially hostile sentiments are coddled in the name of free expression, so long as they use a nice tone. We ask that instructors and administrators continuously educate themselves on how to respectfully intervene in these situations in ways that are helpful to SOC, and to understand that student responses to racism that are not nice, like outrage or frustration, are reasonable, normal, and even admirable qualities that are essential foundations to antiracism.

Notes

1. Throughout this chapter we use Castagno's (2014) definition of Whiteness as the "structural arrangements and ideologies of race dominance" (5). According to Castagno, "Racial power and inequities are at the core of whiteness, but all forms of power and inequity create and perpetuate whiteness" (5).

2. The term *freshman fifteen* is a common expression used to denote the weight (arbitrarily set at fifteen pounds) that a student supposedly gains in the first year of college.

3. Racial battle fatigue highlights the deleterious effects of racism through the litany of symptoms manifested physically (weight gain, hypertension, tension headaches, extreme fatigue, loss of appetite), psychologically (anxiety, worrying, insomnia, loss of self-confidence), socially (strained relationships or professional success), or through any combination of the three (Solórzano and Yosso 2000; Smith, Yosso, and Solórzano 2011).

References

Arrington, E. G., D. M. Hall, and H. C. Stevenson. 2003. "The Success of African American Students in Independent Schools." *Independent School* 62, no. 4: 10–19.

Bell, D. A. 1992. "The Space Traders." In *Faces at the Bottom of the Well: The Permanence of Racism*, 158–194. New York: Basic Books.

Brayboy, B. M. J. 2003. "The Implementation of Diversity in Predominantly White Colleges and Universities." *Journal of Black Studies* 34, no. 1: 72–86.

Brayboy, B. M. J. 2005. "Toward a Tribal Critical Race Theory in Education." *Urban Review* 37, no. 5: 425–46.

Brayboy, B. M. J., A. J. Fann, A. E. Castagno, and J. A. Solyom. 2012. *Postsecondary Education for American Indian and Alaska Natives: Higher Education for Nation Building and Self-Determination: ASHE Higher Education Report 37*, no. 5. Hoboken: John Wiley & Sons.

Cabrera, A., A. Nora, P. Terenzini, E. Pascarella, and L. Hagedorn. 1999. "Campus Racial Climate and the Adjustment of Students to College: A Comparison between White Students and African-American Students." *Journal of Higher Education* 70, no. 2: 134–60.

Castagno, A. E. 2014. *Educated in Whiteness: Good Intentions and Diversity in Schools*. Minneapolis: University of Minnesota Press.

Crenshaw, K., N. Gotanda, G. Peller, and K. Thomas. 1995. *Critical Race Theory: The Key Writings That Formed the Movement*. New York: New Press.

Delgado, R. 1989. "Storytelling for Oppositionists and Others: A Plea for Narrative." *Michigan Law Review* 87, no. 8: 2411–41.

Du Bois, W. E. 1903. *The Souls of Black Folk*. Chicago: A. C. McClurg.

Gutiérrez y Muhs, G., Y. F. Niemann, C. G. González, and A. P. Harris. 2012. *Presumed Incompetent: The Intersections of Race and Class for Women in Academia*. Logan: Utah State University Press.

Harper, S. R. 2009. "Niggers No More: A Critical Race Counternarrative on Black Male Student Achievement at Predominantly White Colleges and Universities." *International Journal of Qualitative Studies in Education* 22, no. 6: 697–712.

Haviland, V. S. 2008. "Things Get Glossed Over: Rearticulating the Silencing Power of Whiteness in Education." *Journal of Teacher Education* 59, no. 1: 40–54.

Hurtado, S. 1992. "The Campus Racial Climate: Contexts of Conflict." *Journal of Higher Education* 63, no. 5: 539–69.

Hurtado, S., and D. F. Carter. 1997. "Effects of College Transition and Perceptions of the Campus Racial Climate on Latino College Students' Sense of Belonging." *Sociology of Education* 70, no. 4: 324–45.

Lomawaima, K. T., and T. L. McCarty. 2006. *"To Remain an Indian": Lessons in Democracy from a Century of Native American Education*. New York: Teachers College Press.

Pewewardy, C., and B. Frey. 2004. "American Indian Students' Perceptions of Racial Climate, Multicultural Support Services, and Ethnic Fraud at a Predominantly White University." *Journal of American Indian Education* 43, no. 1: 32–60.

Rankin, S. R., and R. D. Reason. 2005. "Differing Perceptions: How Students of Color and White Students Perceive Campus Climate for Underrepresented Groups." *Journal of College Student Development* 46, no. 1: 43–61.

Shotton, H. J., S. C. Lowe, and S. J. Waterman. 2013. *Beyond the Asterisk: Understanding Native Students in Higher Education*. Sterling, Va.: Stylus.

Smith, W. A., T. J. Yosso, and D. G. Solórzano. 2011. "Challenging Racial Battle Fatigue on Historically White Campuses: A Critical Race Examination of Race-Related Stress." In *Covert Racism: Theories, Institutions, and Experiences*, edited by R. D. Coates, 211–37. Vol. 32 of *Studies in Critical Social Sciences*. Leiden, Netherlands: Brill.

Solórzano, D., M. Ceja, and T. J. Yosso. 2002. "Critical Race Theory, Racial Microaggressions, and Campus Racial Climate: The Experiences of African American College Students." *Journal of Negro Education* 69, nos. 1–2: 60–73.

Solórzano, D. G., and T. J. Yosso. 2002. "Critical Race Methodology: Counter-storytelling as an Analytical Framework for Education Research." *Qualitative Inquiry* 8, no. 1: 23–44.

Stearns, P. N. 1994. *American Cool: Constructing a Twentieth-Century Emotional Style*. New York: New York University Press.

Wilder, C. 2013. *Ebony and Ivy: Race, Slavery, and the Troubled History of America's Universities*. New York: Bloomsbury.

10

Performative Niceness and Student Erasure

Historical Implications

NICHOLAS BUSTAMANTE AND JESSICA SOLYOM

Although efforts to increase a representation in academic settings had been ongoing, the civil rights movement ushered in a decade of enhanced education reform and proposals that paved the way for culturally responsive curriculum and education delivery. In the 1960s, Chicanos/as in the Southwest and California came together to coordinate and outline education services that would meet the needs of local communities and make education relevant to students who had historically been excluded from postsecondary opportunities. *El Plan De Santa Bárbara: A Chicano Plan for Higher Education* (Chicano Coordinating Council on Higher Education 1969) was one such manifesto. Written and advocated by the Chicano Coordinating Council on Higher Education, the plan lobbied for implementation of culturally relevant curriculum for Chicano/a students in the University of California system and eventually lead to the establishment of a Chicano/a studies program at the University of California–Santa Barbara in 1969.

The document set a precedent for how an academic institution could resituate itself to meet the needs and concerns of a specific community within its metropolitan proximity and advocated for the "strategic use of education" through the implementation of a college curriculum that was culturally and pedagogically responsive to the needs of the state's diverse residents. Although the University of California–Santa Barbara responded to the plan by developing curriculum that prepared a network of scholar advocates dedicated to community development and responding to existing community needs, many institutions have failed to follow in their footsteps.

This chapter focuses on the experiences of three Latino law students attending a public law school in the Southwest. We present the findings of a study that explored the pressures faced by the students, who reported feeling like they were "alone" or only "one of less than a handful" of Latinos in law school. Out of fear of being (mis)labeled as combative, antagonistic, or disagreeable and losing valuable opportunities to research and network with legal practitioners, these students adopted behavior that allowed them to achieve self-preservation and avoid becoming the target of racial micro- and macroaggressions but ultimately reproduced Whiteness and educational inequity.[1] Their stories present implications of the social pressure to be "nice" in higher education settings. Drawing from Latino Critical Race Theory, we present a counterstory informed by in-depth interviews with the students and describe the behavior they had to enact to be considered desirable and successful, including selectively choosing to refrain from debates on controversial and difficult topics such as race, gender, and/or class inequalities. These students described their behavior as based on Euro-Western standards of politeness; such behavior presents important considerations for the historical struggles for representation and knowledge production of people of color in higher education settings. We conclude by offering a discussion on epistemic justice by examining how stifling speech and muting the perspectives of those who traditionally have been excluded from academia affects outcomes in creating a holistic learning environment.

Latinos in Law

Although Latinos represent the fastest growing ethnic group in the United States, making up 18 percent of the total population (Flores 2017), they are underrepresented in the legal field at all levels. For Arizona, the state in which this study took place, Latinos make up a large portion of the total state population, at 31 percent (Pew Hispanic 2016). Students described their law school as belonging to a university that prides itself on being rooted in the local community, and noted that Latinos accounted for just over 10 percent of their law class. This number is higher when compared to the national average; from 1993 to 2008, national matriculation for Latino law students rose just two points, from 3.1 percent to 5.1 percent (Lewin 2010). At first glance, the enrollment at this particular law school is impressive and even suggestive of advancements in higher education and democratic access to the legal profession. Yet when it is examined more deeply, we see this is not the case.

Milem et al. (2013) reported that the number of total law degrees awarded by the state's legal institutions increased by more than 100 percent from 281 in 1995 to 630 in 2013, yet the proportion of law degrees awarded to Latinos decreased, from 15 percent to 9 percent. The diminished rate of degrees awarded may contribute to low numbers of Latino law practitioners in the state. Nationally, Latinos make up only 4 percent of attorneys (Flores 2017). When the statistics are disaggregated by gender, we see that Latinas account for less than 2 percent of American lawyers. Lastly, Latinos remain underrepresented not only in practice but also in the professoriate. As of 2011, Latinos accounted for only 3.1 percent of total tenured law professors in the United States (Mertz et al. 2011). Although it is tempting to discuss the systemic reasons why Latinos remain underrepresented in law programs, we have chosen to focus on the experiences of the few who are successfully admitted, the pressures they face as being only "one of a few," and strategies used to survive what can feel like lonely and hostile education environments.

A law school education plays an important role in developing a sense of civility and leadership and prepares students for their future work as citizens and professional law practitioners. Eberly (1998) posits that civil society prioritizes the common good over self-interest. For students of color who come from historically underrepresented backgrounds, perceptions of the "common good" may differ from those of their peers. Communication, collegiality, autonomy, and accountability are believed to combine to produce civil environments in social interactions (Shanta and Eliason 2014), yet students who appear too passionate about actions or events may be perceived to engage in uncivil behavior. It is important for educators to examine the tacit ways students are prepared (or not) to address controversial subjects. The students in this study reported having to consider whether to bring attention to the fact that although immigration and human rights cases proliferate court cases reviewed by border states, their class discussions may not focus on understanding the experiences of Latino communities as they relate to the legal topics discussed. Many chose to engage in behaviors considered to be socially acceptable, but that did not allow them to share the histories, life experiences, and values of diverse communities in their classrooms.

Their experiences align with research on campus climate for students of color. In order to avoid being branded as uncivil or disruptive, students of color may feel it is important to learn early on how to make sense of the academy, including its values and expectations, and various "conceptions and definitions of success, and the models of professional and personal life that it offers to those aspiring to join [professional] ranks" (Austin 2002, 103). Since students of color are especially sensitive to the fact that incivility can arise in an oppressive or authoritarian system when students and faculty members react to a perceived power struggle, they may choose to alter the way they engage in class discussion—if they choose to engage at all (Shanta and Eliason 2014).

Niceness is defined as the pressure or compulsion to perform agreeably and may manifest in the use of positive, "politically correct" language and behaviors. In short, students of color may strategically deploy Niceness, even subconsciously, as a method of navigating lonely or hostile environments. This may be more common in predominantly White institutions and used to achieve academic, social, and professional goals. An unintended consequence of Niceness is that it may allow White interlocutors to avoid controversial discussions of race, gender, and sexuality and insulate them from feeling uncomfortable or assuming responsibility for social change. In order to ascertain the experiences of students of color in law school our study asked some key questions: What are the day-to-day experiences of Latino law students? What pressures do they face when topics related to race arise in the classroom? And, how do students view their educational experience? In the style of Latino Critical Race Theory, their individual *testimonios* are foregrounded and combined into a counterstory featuring an amalgam known as Guillermo who is in his first year of law school.[2]

Latino Critical Race Theory (LatCrit) is an offshoot of Critical Race Theory (CRT). Arising in the mid-1970s, CRT is predicated upon three main principles: (1) race is and has always been significant in U.S. society; (2) the United States was established with the colonial intention of promoting and protecting the property interests of Whites; and (3) the intersection of race and property is important because it serves as the primary foundation in securing important rights for certain groups over others (Bell 1995; Ladson-Billings and Tate 2017). Not only is racism perceived to be endemic to society, but its intercentricity with other forms of subordination, including gender, sexuality, and class, may require specific attention to the ways in which race and these other intersecting identities create distinctive forms of oppression for unique groups (Crenshaw 2018). LatCrit honors the principles of CRT and adds that the context facing Latinos in the United States may present additional considerations for the ways in which intersecting attributes such oppression based on gender, class, sexuality, immigration status, surname, phenotype, heritage language, accent, and culture influence the social, education, and justice outcomes of Latinos (Pérez Huber 2010; Valdes 1997).

LatCrit scholars place value on experiential knowledge and posit that reality is situational and socially constructed. Its practitioners solicit and incorporate *testimonios*, storytelling, and narratives as valid approaches through which to examine race and racism in education, law, and policy (Fernández 2002; Pérez Huber 2009; Urrieta and Villenas 2013). The focus on what is referred to as "voice scholarship" is intended to provide a counterstory as a way to counteract or challenge the dominant story. By collecting stories of marginalized peoples, LatCrit scholarship creates an opportunity for oppressed communities to disrupt majoritarian narratives and learn to trust their own senses, feelings, and experiences, giving them authority in the face of dominant accounts of social reality that claim universality (Pérez Huber 2010). We use LatCrit and the research technique of soliciting *testimonios* to engage the intersection of race, identity, class, and power relations in institutions of higher education and to guide our analysis.

Guillermo's (Counter)Story

As one of only a handful of students of color in his law class, Guillermo began the fall semester of 2017 feeling apprehensive. His family was proud that he had been accepted to law school, but knowing they were proud did not quell his feelings of uneasiness as he walked into the building. The first day of class began with one of his professors taking a roll call.

> "Gill-er-moh?" he called out.
>
> Guillermo, who had been too self-conscious to speak, raised his hand and nodded to confirm his presence.
>
> "Is that right?" the professor asked.
>
> "It's Gee-*yair*-moh," he stated. Taking care to slow his pronunciation, knowing that sometimes non-Spanish speakers had a difficult time understanding the Spanish pronunciation of his name.
>
> "That's William, right?"
>
> "Yes." He paused and, noticing the professor's furrowed brow, mumbled, "You can just call me Will."
>
> "Okay." The professor nodded and continued calling names from the student roster. From that day forward his classmates and professor referred to him as Will.

Guillermo learned throughout the first weeks the importance of blending in and not drawing attention to himself. He also learned to be prepared to answer difficult questions during cold calls.

Another valuable lesson was learned a month later when the topic of warrantless police searches and seizures came up. The class discussion had been focused on reasonable suspicion of criminal activity. With knowledge of how warrantless searches impacted people in his community, he was reminded of a piece of legislation that had recently been enacted to allow police officials to pull over anyone they suspected of being in the United States illegally. He had heard his cousins and neighbors share stories of being pulled over for no apparent reason. "Maybe we're too Brown. Too Mexican." They had laughed, but the laughter was tinged with a hint of sadness as those listening to the story nodded, all too familiar with the irony of police officers suspecting people of Mexican ancestry of not belonging to their ancestral homelands.

He was deep in thought when his professor continued. "What does reasonable suspicion of criminal activity look like, Will?"

Guillermo paused to think and responded in his deep voice, "This question reminds me of another question: *Who* does reasonable suspicion look like? If you think about it in terms of the recently enacted legislative bill, it would seem the public thinks anyone with a permanent tan fits the bill." He then shared an example of a local community member who had recently been detained, but Guillermo quickly ended his story when he realized he did not have a legal case example to draw from, which is what the professor was looking for. Embarrassed, Guillermo looked around the classroom and realized he was the target of several impatient glares from his classmates. From then on, the professor called on him less and less and, when he did, rushed to ask follow-up questions to another student as soon as Guillermo uttered his last word. After this experience, Guillermo decided it would be best to avoid points of conflict in the classroom and discussions that might further single him out. He would not share personal stories. As the only Mexican American in class, he didn't want his White peers to further frown upon him and his examples. He felt like he was wasting class time presenting examples that fell outside the scope of the assigned reading material.

For a time Guillermo was successful, and the semester progressed with few hiccups. Toward the middle of the semester Guillermo was attending his U.S. Constitutional Law class when a debate on the fundamentals of free speech, and whether a local city has the power to prohibit a group from protesting, caught his attention. The professor began by sharing an example of a recent civil rights protest:

> On August 12, 2017, a group of protestors gathered in Charlottes-
> ville, Virginia, for a Take-Back Lee Park rally. The crowd was
> protesting the removal of General Robert E. Lee's statue. Protestors
> described their efforts as a defense of American history and a
> promotion of free speech. They wanted to protect what they
> believed were key historical representations of American history.
> Soon after, chants began to surface declaring "White lives matter"
> and "Jews will not replace us!"

As Guillermo listened, he thought about how their calls exposed ideological underpinnings that extended beyond the loss of relics of the Civil War. These relics also represented whether the United States would become a nation that recognized the collective humanity and rights of all peoples, or whether those with concentrated melanin, descendants of those who had been forcibly removed from their African ancestral homelands, should remain chattel.

Feeling a rising sense in anxiety, Guillermo looked around at his classmates. Some were discreetly checking their email, while others riffled through previous class notes. Few appeared to be listening, and for those who were there was only lukewarm interest. He decided not to get involved in the discussion. One classmate raised his hand.

> "So how did things end?"
> "The rally ended in the death of three people, including a
> thirty-two-year-old woman, Heather Heyer, who was struck when a
> demonstrator used his car to drive into a gathering crowd of

counterprotestors. What does this case teach us about civil rights and constitutional law, if anything?" asked the professor.

Hands shot up around him. Although he did not speak, Guillermo noticed that as the semester progressed, class discussions became increasingly politicized and heated, yet few students directly talked about the role of race relations and its effect on law.

Later, in the safety of his apartment, Guillermo read through stories posted on his social media accounts. He had somehow missed news of the riots because he had been studying for his midterm exams. First, he read stories published by popular national media outlets. Next, he read stories by independent and locally owned media that targeted a young and diverse readership. It was clear the nation had been left appalled, hindered, and divided as the result of the deadly rally. How could one describe and comprehend the turn of events? Some, like his White liberal classmates, called it a racist riot and referred to the protestors as White supremacists intent on inciting racial division and promoting race-based violence.

The majority defended the protestors, blaming the deadly turn of events on liberal counterprotestors who had shown up to assert, among other things, that Black lives matter. The group had called for an extended look at the structural and societal effects of racial inequity. The most emblematic public reaction appeared to be one of confusion and ineptitude about how to reply to the accusations of structural and racial inequity and the senseless loss of Heather Heyer's life. This ineptitude was cemented over the next few days as the Executive Office, and President Donald Trump, avoided acknowledging the ongoing accusations of systemic White supremacy.

Almost a week later, the president issued a formal statement asserting that his administration "condemn[s] in the strongest possible terms this egregious display of hatred, bigotry, and violence on many sides, on many sides." What remained apparent to Guillermo from Trump's response was the United States' inability to articulate structural inequity and comprehend the particularized impacts of a history of racism. In short, the United States as a society and at its highest levels of leadership appeared to lack the capacity to acknowledge the ongoing role of race and racism in social division—much less take action to correct it. Perhaps, like Guillermo, the president and mainstream media simply wanted to avoid a discussion of structural inequity and the role of history in contributing to why people of color might be angry. The fact that the president felt compelled to lay blame on both sides, disregarding the violent manifestations of racism demonstrated by the so-called Alt-Right protestors seemed indicative of a larger compulsion to avoid discussions of race and power for the sake of maintaining a veneer of civility.

Unlike Guillermo, the president and his cabinet, including his highest advisers, had the advantage of benefiting from decades of access to higher education and positions of social power. Such individuals have historically had access to leadership and policy making that could redress the social and racial inequity being protested, yet they seemed to lack awareness of the issues plaguing historically marginalized peoples. Guillermo recalled reading a Pew Research Center study that indicated that "relatively few adults say they have a lot in common with those who don't share their own racial background. . . . Among those who are single-race white, 62% say they have a lot in common with people in the U.S. who are white, while about one-in-ten or fewer say they have a lot in common with people who are black, Asian or American Indian" (Parker et al. 2015). Maybe their lack of exposure to those from diverse and historically oppressed backgrounds made it difficult for them to understand inequity. How could people in elite spaces know what it's like to walk or drive down the street and have to keep your hands visible at all times? How could they avoid the need to avoid being seen in dark neighborhoods late at night for fear of being pulled over, accused of committing a crime, or—worse—shot and killed if they had never interacted with people who did? How could they understand how racial fears and stereotypes contribute to the use of "stand your ground" laws as a way to justify the disproportionate killing of people of color? The apparent inability of the president and his team, which did not include one person of color, to serve as insightful leaders suggested to Guillermo a larger need for diversity in leadership and increased access for people of color to positions of power and institutions that expose leaders and policy makers to diverse perspectives.

People of Color in Higher Education: Reconciling Law, Justice, and Niceness

The trajectory of rights for people of color in the United States has historically been articulated along an arc of race, class, ethnicity, gender, and exclusion. The rights and experiences of students of color within the American education system is no different. The maintenance of socioeconomic inequity for marginalized communities has largely hinged on a lack of access to elite spaces of education in addition to acute articulations of racial inferiority and a lack of acknowledgment of the collective struggles faced by people of color.

Presently, two conceptions of antiequity and race exist. At one end lies the discourse of color blindness—that is, the belief that race no longer matters. Such arguments rely on meritocratic beliefs of fairness and justice. In other words, those who work hard are rewarded for their efforts, and any misgivings or shortcomings are blamed on personal choice and individual lack of effort. Ultimately, proponents of this view believe racism no longer exercises the power to structurally disenfranchise individuals. At the opposite end of the spectrum are those who promote the discourse of reverse racism—the growing conception that majority groups are subject to systemic discrimination from historically marginalized groups in society. In other words, dominant groups believe they are now being disenfranchised in the same ways historically marginalized peoples have been.

The latter critique can broadly be understood as either an attack on White entitlement or the dissolution of a meritocratic system. For believers of reverse racism, institutional support for policies like affirmative action exemplify and affirm the nexus of anti-Whiteness and minority privilege. Generally, for students of color, institutional support of affirmative action has paved access into elite spaces of education traditionally withheld from them. Though beneficial, the boons of affirmative action for students of color, including access to spaces of education, have not come without cost or contestation.

Currently, access to higher education for students of color hangs in a precarious state as the future of affirmative action, or race-conscious admissions policies, remain under attack and a lightning rod for larger discussions of structural inequity and discrimination. The Trump administration, via former attorney general Jeff Sessions, reportedly took aim at race-conscious admissions, vowing to investigate supposed discriminatory admissions practices at institutions of higher education. This, along with lawsuits brought on by Students for Fair Admissions that take aim at the University of North Carolina–Chapel Hill and Harvard University for their race-conscious admissions policies, argue that civil rights laws protect everyone against discrimination.[3] Their complaint suggests that current admission policies discriminate against dominant populations in the same manner that previous policies discriminated against students of color. Such sentiments rely on the argument that race-conscious admissions privilege minority applicants to the detriment of well-qualified White and Asian applicants.

Absent from this focus are the perspectives and experiences of students of color whose inclusion and capacity to produce diversity of thought within the classroom is the very purpose race-conscious factors exist in admissions policies. The intended outcome—diversity of thought, presented in diverse classrooms, as defined by the institution—is not addressed. In effect, these lawsuits brought on by Students for Fair Admissions only address the supposedly less scrutinized admission of less-dominant subgroups of racialized students and not whether diverse and challenging experiences are occurring in the classroom.

In *Grutter v. Bollinger* (2003), the U.S. Supreme Court upheld the use of race as a factor in school admissions as constitutional and not in contradiction to the Fourteenth Amendment's equal protection clause.[4] Specifically, the court held that use of race was narrowly tailored to meet the University of Michigan Law School's intended goal of attaining a *critical mass* of underrepresented students.[5] The school's "laudable" goal of creating critical mass was intended to expand a "cross-racial understanding and the breaking down of racial stereotypes" for the purposes of fulfilling its educational mission and in preparing students to become capable leaders in both a future diverse society and within the legal profession.[6]

Critical mass, as stated by the school's dean of admissions and later rearticulated by the Supreme Court, is a body of underrepresented students sufficient to constitute a meaningful representation and "encourage underrepresented minority students to participate in the classroom and not feel isolated."[7] In *Fisher v. University of Texas at Austin* (2013) and its follow-up, known as *Fisher II* (2016), the Supreme Court again upheld the constitutionality of race-conscious admissions.[8] In *Fisher II* the Supreme Court held that universities must prove that race is considered only as necessary to meet the permissible goals of affirmative action. The permissible goal of affirmative action in higher education settings is defined as allowing academic institutions to "pursue the educational benefits that flow from student body diversity." *Fisher II* further provided that diversity in a student pool would result in a "robust exchange of ideas [and] exposure to differing cultures."[9] The university's rationale was that encouragement of such a direct exchange in the classroom would result in more diverse learning outcomes.

In their totality, these cases provide the legal criteria necessary for evaluating the necessity of diversity in education and expose a fissure in a popular understanding of who has the right to be educated. The respective plaintiffs in these cases demonstrate that education in the United States is fundamentally linked to an interest in Whiteness.[10] In that sense, access to education is a property interest that—much like *real property*—is policed and safeguarded.

Education and knowledge production are fundamentally rooted in relations of power. As Foucault (2003) stipulated, "The genealogy of knowledges is located on a different axis, namely the discourse–power axis" (178). Western modernism and the institutions underpinning its progeny, including law and institutions of higher education, maintain racialized and classed aspects of how those relations of power were initially promulgated (Medina 2011). Fundamental to interrogating the role of inequity and the law is questioning the impact of so-called race-neutral laws. For decades scholars have suggested that an appropriate mechanism for identifying and articulating the pitfalls of race-neutral laws is to place at the forefront alternative perspectives. As such, they have advocated for the recognition and valuing of epistemologies and pedagogies that emerge from a socioeconomic, sociocultural, and political history distinct from the vantage point of dominant cultures (Anzaldúa 1987; Brayboy 2005; Collins 1986; Delgado Bernal 1998; Ladson-Billings 2017). The purpose of this valuation is the contestation of dominant assumptions and sources of knowledge that have functioned to marginalize vulnerable populations.

The experiences of marginalized people, particularly those of color, was predicated on the subjectivity of how knowledge came to be recognized. Eurocentricity and White Supremacy as global ideologies for establishing relations of power were perpetuated precisely because they "concentrated all forms of the control of subjectivity, culture, and especially knowledge and the production of knowledge under its hegemony" (Quijano 2000, 540). The subjectivity of whose knowledge

Performative Niceness and Student Erasure   171

is characterized as genuine and what perspectives are legitimated within the academy is part of a history of racialized relations of power.

Crucial to a disruption of power is decentering who are considered valid producers of knowledge, highlighting the experiences of racialized persons, and recognizing those latter accounts as legitimate sources of knowledge. This is particularly relevant to academic spaces that are believed to be racially neutral. A natural extension of recognizing the accounts of historically oppressed or any non-dominant group's people is an inquiry into how their perspectives are received when voiced. If Niceness is the pressure to not talk about race or the compulsion to gloss over the impacts of structural discrimination, then any legitimate engagement of that from people who have been systemically subjugated necessitates an abrupt departure from the terms and conditions of engaging in nonconfrontational or "nice" terms. To effectively talk about justice or oppression we must have blunt and honest dialogue.

Guillermo's First Semester, Continued

Guillermo awoke in the late-fall semester and proceeded through his morning routine. He began by shaving. As he looked into the mirror he was startled to see or rather to *not* see that facing him, where his reflection ought to be, was a clear image of the wall behind him. Frantically, he rubbed his eyes and looked again. No reflection. With rising panic he shouted:

"*¿Que chingado esta pasando aqui?*" (What the fuck is going on here?)

Guillermo admonished himself and continued rubbing his eyes. Slowly he began to notice the room fading around him and wondered if, after so many late nights reading the small text in his law casebooks, he was finally losing his eyesight. *It's too soon for that,* he thought, and took a deep breath. After a few moments his surroundings dissipated entirely, leaving him surrounded by darkness. Nothingness. Finally, he heard a familiar voice, one he hadn't heard since childhood. It was the voice of his now-deceased grandmother:

"*¿Que? ¿No puedes ver?*" (What? Can't you see?)

The question was followed by a discernible, glowing outline. Within a few moments Guillermo was shocked to have his vision restored, only to find himself staring at the spirit of his grandmother walking toward him.

Bewildered and frightened, he asked, "*¿Abuela?*"

"*Si, mijo, soy yo. No te sorprendas y cuentame—¿que pasó?* (Yes, my son. It's me. Don't be surprised, and tell me—what's going on?) Did you lose yourself?"

Sadly, Guillermo responded, "¡No sé! I don't know what is happening. I can't see myself!"

As she approached, her worn face just as he remembered, she responded, "We need to talk. I'm here to help you." After a brief pause, she continued. *"Te amo, pero estoy tan enojada contigo."* (I adore you, but I am very upset with you.)

"¿Porqué? ¿Que hice?" (Why? What can I do?)

"You forgot about us. Why don't you talk about us?"

"Us? What do you mean? Who is *us?"*

"Us. *Tus seres queridos.* (Your loved ones.) You let our stories, the stories of our family, our *gente* (people), go untold. You went to school to help us but you don't talk about our struggles. *Y eso no puede ser.* (It cannot be this way.) *¡Tienen que saber! ¡Tienes que hablar! ¿Si no les cuentas, qué cambiara?"* (They need to know! You must speak! If you don't share our stories, how will things change?) Firmly squeezing his hands, she continued: "Just talk to me, tell me why you have lost your voice."

Guillermo, sensing her care, responded, "You won't understand, it's difficult."

"Then why did you go to school?"

"Like you said. For our family. They raised me to know it's important to have the title of lawyer. Law school is helping me learn how to think about inequality and how to help the families. They wanted me to go to school and increase representation porque our community is so numerous and yet so underrepresented. We are still unequal in law. There aren't many Latino lawyers, and so many academic and professional spaces keep us out. *No nos escuchan ni nos incluyen, pero I still try.* (They don't listen or include us but . . .) I go to school and I am the only one from our background. It's lonely. *Y a nadie le interesa de donde vengo or que nos pasa."* (And nobody is interested in where I come from nor what happens to us.)

Looking at him sadly, his grandmother responded, "Entiendo, because you went to school and did what you wanted to do. What I don't understand is why you don't talk about your own experiences or ours if they are important to you, if we inspired you. Remember why you went to school in the first place."

"It's been jarring. It's very different for me. The classes are a lot bigger. There are a lot of gringos. A lot of people don't look like me. Some stare. I hate that. I just want to be seen as a student doing my work, and don't want other people who don't have the same experiences to be coming after me. I don't want to have to educate them all. I don't want to start anything. Honestly, I just keep to myself, even outside the classroom. I don't want to interact with anyone. In larger classes, I have been afraid of speaking up. The makeup of the classes impacts my experiences. It's a feeling of loneliness. I feel like I'm in a professional environment that the school wants us to have but at the same time I get the impression I am not welcome."

"Mijo, do you feel pressured to be quiet?"

"Sí. They don't like disruption from the topic area. We're there to focus on the law. If you do bring those issues up, you get these looks. They look at me like I'm being the Brown man in the classroom, so of course I would. The other Brown students read between the lines and get the gist of what I'm saying, but they look at me like, 'be quiet and be glad you're here. Don't be *that* guy. Enjoy your stay. Just keep quiet.'"

"Sé que es difícil. Entiendo. It's hard. But you have to speak up, especially because you are the morenito in the classroom. There are others like you who cannot be in class to tell their story. You cannot be afraid. No one is telling you to be mean to anyone or to take away from anyone's learning. Just speak up a little. You come from a long line of people who have fought to survive. You were born out of love. We have put you there. We are with you. No te agüites. I will check on you in a year."

Deconstructing Abuela's Advice

We began this chapter by stating that in order to not be (mis)labeled as disruptive, difficult, or irrational by classmates or faculty, students of color in predominantly White institutions may strategically employ particular performances of politeness and civility in the classroom. Surviving campus spaces that feel lonely or hostile can depend on students' ability to avoid confrontation and be "nice" to those around them. Yet by marginalizing and muting the perspectives and life experiences of people who fall outside the norm of their White peers, the experiences of diverse groups become subverted, out of fear of reprisal, and ultimately erased from institutions of higher education. Abuela's response to Guillermo raises important points about the necessity of challenging dominant perspectives. Her words suggest that it is important, if epistemic justice is to be achieved, to create a space where marginalized peoples can challenge dominant perspectives. She validates Guillermo's wariness with racial battle fatigue, yet points to the urgency of pushing back and challenging behaviors associated with Niceness that fail to expose his peers to the realities faced by people of color.[11] In short, she reminds him that his voice and his presence matters not only because of his family and his community but also because it can change the climate of elite spaces of higher education.

Testimonial justice refers to the concentrated effort to neutralize individual prejudices. It requires an orientation "rooted in one's 'testimonial sensibility' or second-nature perception of others' credibility effects of prejudicial stereotypes that would otherwise influence one's credibility judgments" (Anderson 2012). Addressing testimonial injustice requires reconceptualizing and reorganizing conditions in which marginalized perspectives are recognized for their "capacity as knowers" and issued "ready-corrected judgments of credibility" (Fricker 2007, 97). Due to the skewed nature regarding whose perspectives are valued in conditions that promote testimonial injustice, a dominant group's social imaginary produces and promotes "active ignorance by circulating distorted scripts" (Medina 2013, 68) that render the accounts of students of color as incredible and unbelievable. It is this distortion of scripts that provides the conditions for the promulgation of testimonial injustice. Fundamental to this process of legitimization are counterstories, *testimonios*, and narratives that validate and represent diverse perspectives that otherwise go unheard. In short, Abuela's statements are a call for hearers to actively participate in creating conditions that facilitate open-mindedness and grant a level of credulity to the lived experiences of nondominant subgroups.

Abuela's advice and determined resolution seek to disrupt the relations of power that lead to the incredulity of perspectives that exist outside dominant narratives. Niceness is fundamental in the reproduction of testimonial injustice because it actively reproduces the conditions necessary for circulating social imaginaries that overlook and obfuscate the perspectives and lived realities of people of color. Guillermo's story illustrates the conditions that discredit the level of credulity given to students of color by dominant members of society, including professors, and the students balance their capacity to belong against the backdrop of merit, entitlement, and agreeability. Pressured adherence to amicable behavior, no matter the topic, normalizes the terms of discourse that are incompatible with serious inquiries and engagements of inequity.

Castagno (2014), in explaining the pernicious effect of Niceness suggests, "Politeness, like niceness, is a mechanism of whiteness. By defining the terms of engagement, politeness and niceness naturalize a particular sort of interaction, communication, and perspective that is void of any context, history, or knowledge of race and power" (83). This is fraught, and irreconcilable with the purposes of higher education and, more specifically, with what the Supreme Court rearticulated as the compelling interests of institutions of higher education to educate students through the diverse perspectives of their classmates.

A Year Later

When Guillermo awoke to his lack of reflection once again, he was not surprised. Somehow he knew that this time his lack of visibility was not due to anything he had done wrong but rather to the promised journey of his grandmother. He was not surprised to see her standing before him a few moments later.

"Mijo, how are things?"

"Todo bien. It's been better. I feel like I learned a lot, and I think I did well for myself. Things in the classroom got better as the year progressed, and I was able to challenge students who had other views."

"Are you speaking up?" She smiled at him, her eyes twinkling with a look of love he remembered fondly.

"Sí, I am talking. I got cold-called on a discussion of affirmative action and there was one other Latino student in the class. I felt totally empowered. I felt like I did not have to go it alone. I spoke my truth; knowing that someone had my back, someone who knew where I was coming from who shared my background, made me feel stronger to talk about it. Also, in another class, the students were welcoming. In Indian Law, where most of the students were Native American or other diverse peoples, I felt really comfortable talking about race and social issues. Even though it was about Native American issues, some of the issues applied to Latinos and Blacks. It felt right, and it felt comfortable. I think a part of it was that there were students of color."

"¿Que se te olvidó el nopal que tienes en la cabeza? (Did you forget your roots?) Did you forget that you're Indigenous too?" She laughed. "Do you think it was better that you said something?"

"Sí, if I had kept quiet, something would have been lost down the road. Maybe decades go by where you lose pride in your perspective and principles you have been aligned with forever. We're fifty years removed from the Chicano movement. We may lose the sense of need to fight for our rights and our sense of urgency for justice in the moment. What are we going to be like in fifty more years? Are we going to lose our sense of justice? That's what I fear. We, as future lawyers, as students, as people, need to be at the forefront of those discussions. Gracias Abue, for reminding me to speak. To not be invisible."

This chapter has explored the concept of Niceness, defined as the pressure or compulsion to perform agreeably. We suggest that Niceness manifests in the use of positive, "politically correct" language, silence, and/or behaviors that ultimately insulate White interlocutors from feeling uncomfortable or assuming responsibility for social change. Niceness allows controversial discussions of race, gender, and sexuality to be avoided and ignored. The students in this study, as represented in the composite character Guillermo, suggest that Niceness is strategically used, even subconsciously, as a method of navigating lonely or hostile predominantly White institutions to achieve academic, social, and professional goals. For them, Niceness manifests as the pressure to conform oneself in a constantly amenable fashion. By failing to interrogate how Whiteness and power affect social outcomes for non-White groups, and "through the ignoring of race and power within schools, educators contribute to the hegemony of deficit thinking and meritocracy" (Castagno 2014, 88). The silencing of students of color, whether publicly or tacitly promoted, is an invariable product of Niceness. Regardless of whether the silence is self-imposed or driven by pedagogical practices, Niceness suggests that the sense to conform and behave in an undisruptive manner is preferential and of more value than the desire to disrupt racist narratives.

We have advanced the proposition that the pressures of Niceness may function as a way to avoid becoming the target of microaggression. But it also serves as a coercive tactic. Coerced Niceness, resulting from fear of reprisal or ostracization, contributes to the stresses associated with students of color in education and underpins historic racialized power relations rampant in academia (Yosso et al. 2009). Guillermo's counterstory draws on the notion of testimonial injustice to make sense of how the act of performing Niceness silences the accounts and knowledge of students of color by stifling any serious conversations on institutional inequity. More specifically, testimonial injustice occurs when "a speaker receives a deficit of credibility owing to the operation of prejudice in the hearer's judgement" (Fricker 2013, 1319). The effect is a pernicious and subtle erosion of the diversity of thought from a pool of students who are well suited to provide alternative understandings of contemporary societal shortcomings.

The collective accounts that inform Guillermo's testimony and historical experiences express pressures to perform nicely. Yet comfort and amenability are traded at the expense of critical dialogue. This ill-balanced exchange contributes to pedagogical and curricular choices that encourage students to "stop talking about race and ethnicity because it's making [them or others] upset"; difficult and necessary dialogue is replaced with "a nice environment where everyone feels welcome," one that avoids serious interrogation in which "other people can hear it and . . . get offended" (Castagno 2014, 91). The focus on amenability and civility, though necessary in any coherent legal dialogue, potentially avoid discussions that can influence the perspectives of future legal practitioners and lawmakers.

Niceness stifles the speech of students of color and further isolates their knowledge and perspectives. In short, it impacts the capacity of students to critically engage in the classroom and perpetuates an uneven distribution of power through its emphasis on value-neutral perspectives. It mechanizes a color-blind perspective that obfuscates the particularities of disparity. In this sense Niceness "maintains power and privilege by perpetuating and legitimating the status quo while simultaneously maintaining a veneer of neutrality, equality and compassion"

(Castagno 2014, 149). Guillermo's experiences highlight how the pressures to conform and act amicably add to the burdens of being a person of color in higher education. The angst of being branded as a disruptive person or a token limits the possibility of his perspective being heard. This, compounded with the demographics of the classroom, results in a sense of loneliness and disengagement from classroom discussions—and particularly those relating to race.

We conclude by stating that the expectations felt by students of color to perform amicably in class and draw away from engaging structural inequities like racism and White supremacy work against not only the intentions advanced by *Grutter*, *Fisher*, and *Fisher II* but also perpetuate broader historical inequities related to epistemic justice. Their disengagement and shying away from discussions on race, power, and history allows distorted scripts and reductionist narratives that remain in circulation to further reproduce hegemony. Future articulations and comprehensions of justice will necessitate the views, histories, and perspectives of those from whom positions of influence have traditionally been withheld. Their potential for causing disruption or uneasiness are incidental to fashioning more acute understandings of power inequity.

Notes

1. Microaggressions are subtle insults that can manifest as "automatic acts of disregard" directed toward people of color, often automatically or unconsciously, that stem from "unconscious attitudes of white superiority and constitute a verification of [racial] inferiority" (Davis 1989, 157). In Guillermo's story, ignoring the stories of his community or failing to engage in discussions of racial injustice and law becomes a microaggression. Unlike microaggressions, they are neither directed at nor designed to offend a specific person but rather reinforce stereotypes of racialized groups as "either criminals, illiterates, or intellectual inferiors" (Russell-Brown 1998, 140).

2. *Testimonios* refer to narratives or life stories that highlight a larger truth experienced by those who have experienced oppression. They can relay accounts of injustice, of pain, and of struggle experienced by members of a particular group. In Latino Critical Race Theory, *testimonios* are a form of storytelling solicited from historically marginalized peoples in order to highlight previously ignored, hidden, subverted, silenced, and/or marginalized truths. Such accounts allow us to understand how social, political, legal, and institutional practices influence the quotidian affairs of oppressed communities to maintain an overall state of inequity. To learn more about *testimonios*, intersectionality, and the power of storytelling, see Fernández (2002), Pérez Huber (2009, 2010), and Urrieta and Villenas (2013).

3. By claiming that a school's admissions practices preference minority students by considering race and ethnicity as a partial element of a holistic assessment of an applicant's ability to add diverse experiences to the education of their peers, this group argued that these admissions practices are detrimental to the equal protection of White students in their application process.

4. Grutter v. Bollinger, 539 U.S. 306, 123 S. Ct. 2325, 156 L. Ed. 2d 304 (2003) held that when race-based action is necessary to further a state's compelling governmental interest—namely, in receiving the educational benefits of diversity—the action does not violate the constitutional guarantee of equal protection so long as the narrow-tailoring requirement is also satisfied.

5. Narrowly tailored is the requirement that a law be written to fulfill only the intended goals stated in the law and not have a collateral effect of impacting laws or groups outside the law's intended purpose.

6. Grutter v. Bollinger, 233. The court noted how accounting for race for the purposes of establishing a diverse educational experience was markedly different from merely admitting students of color the purposes of meeting a predetermined requisite pool of minority students or a fixed quota. The court stated that admitting minority students "simply to assure some specified percentage of a particular group merely because of its race or ethnic origin would be *patently unconstitutional*" (emphasis added).

7. Grutter v. Bollinger, 218.

8. Fisher v. University of Texas at Austin, 133 S.Ct. 2411, 570 U.S., 186 L. Ed. 2d 474 (2013); Fisher v. University of Texas at Austin, 136 S. Ct. 2198, 579 U.S., 195 L. Ed. 2d 511 (2016).

9. Fisher v. University of Texas at Austin (2016), 2211.

10. Both *Grutter* and *Fisher II* highlight a fear over race conscious admissions processes—namely, the fear that White students are being dispossessed of equal protection under the law.

11. Racial battle fatigue occurs when people of color are forced to contend with race based micro- or macroaggressions. This type of fatigue is distinguished by physiological symptoms such as increased tension headaches and backaches, rapid breathing and/or heart rate, extreme fatigue, gastric distress, loss of appetite, and elevated blood pressure (Pierce 1995). Individuals may also experience psychological discomfort such as a heightened or constant state of anxiety and worrying, increased swearing and complaining, inability to sleep or sleep broken by haunting conflict-specific dreams, intrusive thoughts and images, loss of self-confidence / feelings of hopelessness, difficulty in thinking coherently or being able to speak articulately under racially stressful conditions, hypervigilance, frustration, denial, emotional and social withdrawal, anger, anger suppression, verbal or nonverbal expressions of anger, withdrawing oneself and/ or keeping quiet in social situations, and resentment (Pierce 1995; Smith,

Hung and Franklin 2011; Solórzano and Yosso 2000). Lastly, effects of micro- and macroaggressions can cause more than just bodily and psychological harm to the individual person; they can cause strain on their social and personal relationships jeopardizing their professional, academic, and personal success (Solyom, Chin, and Ryujin 2007).

References

Anderson, E. 2012. "Feminist Epistemology and Philosophy of Science." In *The Stanford Encyclopedia of Philosophy,* edited by E. N. Zalta. http://plato.stanford .edu/archives/fall2012/entries/feminism-epistemology.

Anzaldúa, G. 1987. *Borderlands: La Frontera.* San Francisco: Aunt Lute.

Austin, A. E. 2002. "Preparing the Next Generation of Faculty: Graduate School as Socialization to the Academic Career." *Journal of Higher Education* 73, no. 1: 94–122.

Bell, D. 1995. "Who's Afraid of Critical Race Theory?" *University of Illinois Law Review* 1995: 893–910.

Brayboy, B. M. J. 2005. "Toward a Tribal Critical Race Theory in Education." *Urban Review* 37, no. 5: 425–46.

Castagno, A. E. 2014. *Educated in Whiteness: Good Intentions and Diversity in Schools.* Minneapolis: University of Minnesota Press.

Chicano Coordinating Council on Higher Education. 1969. *El Plan de Santa Bárbara: A Chicano Plan for Higher Education.* Oakland, Calif.: La Causa.

Collins, P. H. 1986. "Learning from the Outsider within: The Sociological Significance of Black Feminist Thought." *Social Problems* 33, no. 6: 14–32.

Crenshaw, K. 2018. "Demarginalizing the Intersection of Race and Sex: A Black Feminist Critique of Antidiscrimination Doctrine, Feminist Theory, and Antiracist Politics." In *Feminist Legal Theory,* edited by K. Bartlett, 57–80. New York: Routledge.

Davis, P. C. 1989. "Law as Microaggression." *Yale Law Journal* 98, no. 8: 1559–77.

Delgado Bernal, D. 1998. "Using a Chicana Feminist Epistemology in Educational Research." *Harvard Educational Review* 68, no. 4: 555–83.

Eberly, D. E. 1998. *America's Promise: Civil Society and the Renewal of American Culture.* Lanham, Md.: Rowman and Littlefield.

Fernández, L. 2002. "Telling Stories about School: Using Critical Race and Latino Critical Theories to Document Latina/Latino Education and Resistance." *Qualitative Inquiry* 8, no. 1: 45–65.

Flores, A. 2017, September 18. "How the U.S. Hispanic Population Is Changing." Pew Research Center. http://www.pewresearch.org/fact-tank/2017/09/18/how-the-u-s-hispanic-population-is-changing/.

Foucault, M. (2003). *Society Must Be Defended: Lectures at the Collège de France, 1975–1976*. Edited by M. Bertani and A. Fontana. Translated by D. Macey. New York: Picador.

Fricker, M. 2007. *Epistemic Injustice: Power and the Ethics of Knowing*. New York: Oxford University Press.

Fricker, M. 2013. "Epistemic Justice as a Condition of Political Freedom?" *Synthese* 190, no. 7: 1317–32.

Ladson-Billings, G., and W. F. Tate IV. 2017. "Toward a Critical Race Theory of Education." In *Critical Race Theory in Education: All God's Children Got a Song*, 2nd ed., edited by A. D. Dixson, C. K. Rousseau Anderson, and J. K. Donnor, 21–41. New York: Routledge.

Lewin, T. 2010, January 6. "Law School Admissions Lag among Minorities." *New York Times*.

Medina, J. 2011. "Toward a Foucaultian Epistemology of Resistance: Counter-memory, Epistemic Friction, and Guerrilla Pluralism." *Foucault Studies* 12: 9–35.

Medina, J. 2013. *The Epistemology of Resistance: Gender and Racial Oppression, Epistemic Injustice, and the Social Imagination*. New York: Oxford University Press.

Mertz, E., F. Tung, K. Barnes, W. Njogu, M. Heiler, and J. Martin. 2011. LSAC Grants Report Series. Newtown, Penn.: Law School Admission Council.

Milem, J. F., W. P. Bryan, D. B. Sesate, and S. Montaño. (2013). *Arizona Minority Student Progress Report, 2013*. Phoenix: Arizona Minority Education Policy Analysis Center.

Parker, K., J. M. Horowitz, R. Morin, and M. H. Lopez. 2015. "Race and Social Connections—Friends, Family and Neighborhoods." In *Multiracial in America: Proud, Diverse and Growing in Numbers*. Washington, D.C.: Pew Research Center. http://www.pewsocialtrends.org/2015/06/11/chapter-5-race-and-social-connections-friends-family-and-neighborhoods/.

Parker, L., D. Deyhle, S. Villenas, and K. C. Nebeker. 1998. "Guest Editors' Introduction: Critical Race Theory and Qualitative Studies in Education." *Qualitative Studies in Education* 11, no. 1: 5–6.

Pérez Huber, L. 2009. "Disrupting Apartheid of Knowledge: Testimonio as Methodology in Latina/o Critical Race Research in Education." *International Journal of Qualitative Studies in Education* 22, no. 6: 639–54.

Pérez Huber, L. 2010. "Using Latina/o Critical Race Theory (LatCrit) and Racist Nativism to Explore Intersectionality in the Educational Experiences of Undocumented Chicana College Students." *Journal of Educational Foundations* 24, nos. 1–2: 77–96.

Pew Hispanic. 2016, April 19. "2014, Hispanics in the United States Statistical Portrait." Pew Research Center. https://www.pewhispanic.org/2016/04/19/2014-statistical-information-on-hispanics-in-united-states/.

Pierce, C. M. 1995. "Stress Analogs of Racism and Sexism: Terrorism, Torture, and Disaster." In *Mental Health, Racism and Sexism,* edited by C. Willie, P. Rieker, B. Kramer, and B. Brown, 277–93. Pittsburgh: University of Pittsburgh Press.

Quijano, A. 2000. "Coloniality of Power, Eurocentrism, and Latin America." *Nepantla: Views from South* 1, no. 3: 533–80.

Russell-Brown, K. 1998. *The Color of Crime: Racial Hoaxes, White Fear, Black Protectionism, Police Harassment, and Other Macroaggressions.* New York: New York University Press.

Shanta, L. L., and A. R. Eliason. 2014. "Application of an Empowerment Model to Improve Civility in Nursing Education." *Nurse Education in Practice* 14, no. 1: 82–86.

Smith, W. A., M. Hung, and J. D. Franklin. 2011. "Racial Battle Fatigue and the Miseducation of Black Men: Racial Microaggressions, Societal Problems, and Environmental Stress." *Journal of Negro Education* 80, no. 1: 63–82.

Solórzano, D., and T. J. Yosso. 2000. "Critical Race Methodology: Counter-storytelling as an Analytical Framework for Education Research." *Qualitative Inquiry* 8, no. 1: 23–44.

Solyom, J., J. Chin, and K. Ryuijin. 2007. "Be Careful What You Ask For: *Educación para Todas/os,* the Perils and the Power." *Nevada Law Journal* 7:862–82.

Urrieta L., Jr., and S. A. Villenas. 2013. "The Legacy of Derrick Bell and Latino/a Education: A Critical Race Testimonio." *Race Ethnicity and Education* 16, no. 4: 514–35.

Valdes, F. 1997. "Poised at the Cusp: LatCrit Theory, Outsider Jurisprudence, and Latina/o Self-Empowerment." *Harvard Latino Law Review* 2, no. 1: 1–59.

Yosso, T., W. Smith, M. Ceja, and D. Solórzano. 2009. "Critical Race Theory, Racial Microaggressions, and Campus Racial Climate for Latina/o Undergraduates." *Harvard Educational Review* 79, no. 4: 659–91.

PART III

Niceness across Schools and Society

11

Community Resistance to In-School Inequities

Disrupting Niceness in Out-of-School Spaces

KATIE A. LAZDOWSKI

Racism is not enacted by malicious acts alone, but is commonly carried out through covert actions or even in well-intentioned or nice ways. In examining issues of racial inequity, various scholars describe how incompetence and lack of knowledge about Whiteness and racism perpetuate inequitable practices. As Bush (2004) notes, well-intentioned people who perform Whiteness cause more harm than good, often without a sense of where things went wrong. Leonardo (2004) states that "Whites today did not participate in slavery but they surely recreate White supremacy on a daily basis" (141), in part because of the lack of realization that White people often have to the privilege that comes with the color of their skin (McIntosh 1992). Said differently, "the unearned advantages that Whites, by virtue of their race, have over people of color . . . is symptomatic of the utter sense of *oblivion* that many Whites engender toward their privilege" (Leonardo 2004, 138; emphasis added).

More recent research based in high-performing school districts illustrates how the constructs of Whiteness inform the same "good intentions" that end up being detrimental to students of color. In her ethnographic study set in an urban school district, Castagno (2014) examines how well-intentioned policies and practices surrounding issues of diversity are actually taken up and implemented. Her findings show that the implementation of such policies actually reifies Whiteness and sustains racial inequities. Lewis and Diamond (2015) shift our gaze from the urban setting to a suburban one and uncover the racial inequities that exist in a high-performing, well-resourced district, attributing such inequities to people's racial ideologies and cultural belief systems. They conclude that because of the race neutrality of stated policies and how they are actually practiced, racial inequality is reproduced, and many of the practices that disadvantage students of color (specifically Black and Latinx students) in reality help White students. The authors find that "even those operating with the best intentions can contribute to negative consequences, particularly if they are operating *without full awareness* of and information about the ways that racial dynamics are part of daily life and beyond" (Lewis and Diamond 2015, 169; emphasis added). Important to note is the difference between intent and impact. While White people may not intend to be malicious, the impact of their words and actions can be harmful to people of color. It is this disconnect—a lack of knowledge—that works to sustain systemic racism. Informed by Critical Race Theory, and drawing on the construct of racial literacy, findings from this chapter suggest that individuals' racial literacy plays a vital role in upholding or dismantling the factors that sustain racism.

In this this chapter, which is based on twenty months of ethnographic research, I analyze data from my role as a participant observer and parent-activist in four different community groups.[1] I present discursive acts that demonstrate how Cartfield community members uphold a "strong schools" image by way of "nice narratives," whereas others practice their racial literacy and call into question not only the nice narratives, but often the speakers of such narratives.[2] Such interrogation counters the definition of the term *nice*, as it is often disruptive and uncomfortable acts that are not nice. Taken together these examples demonstrate that interrupting Niceness—an act that runs risk of being perceived as not nice—is an effective approach to disrupting Whiteness in public spaces. In the case of Cartfield, data show that exhibiting racial literacy and interrupting Niceness allow the calling into question of the same "strong schools" narrative that served to cover up the existing racial disparities in the racially diverse, high-performing district.

Theoretical Framework: The Intersection of Niceness and Racial Literacy

Delgado and Stefanic (2012) note that Critical Race Theory (CRT) is a lens not only to identify but to *transform* the relationship between race, racism, and power. One of the numerous tenets to which CRT subscribes is the fact that race and racism are socially constructed. Race is not a biological entity, but rather a result of social thought, discourse, and relations. Therefore, a particular group's status is fluid, and each may be redefined and possess more or less power at any particular moment in history. Another tenet of CRT relevant to this discussion is that racism is an omnipresent structure in the United States. Dominant discourse or "grand narratives" such as false conceptions of equality, color blindness, and meritocracy sustain racism's existence through a lack of acknowledgment. If people lack the racial literacy to critically examine and question these narratives and other factors that perpetuate and sustain racism, they run the risk of dismissing their role in dismantling systemic racism. Racial literacy shows potential to disrupt the ongoing trend of well-intentioned actors who sustain racial inequities through a lack of awareness; this lack of awareness sustains "racism without racists" (Bonilla-Silva 2009). In this way, racial literacy is reflective of CRT's emphasis on transformation: Actors' increased knowledge can shift the relationship between race, racism, and power.

Racial Literacy

Guinier (2004) first introduced the construct of racial literacy in her seminal piece "From Racial Liberalism to Racial Literacy: *Brown v. Board of Education* and the Interest-Divergence Dilemma." In her commentary Guinier discusses the flaws of the *Brown* decision, noting that in its aftermath the "tactic of desegregation became the ultimate goal, rather than the means to secure educational equity" (95). She describes the historic ideologies that would not be changed with a single court ruling; the segregation that existed prior to *Brown* was based in a larger issue that wouldn't be changed by a court decision: White supremacy. She posits that to counter the ideologies that sustain White supremacy there must be an awakening, "a paradigm shift from racial liberalism to racial literacy" (100).

Since the publication of Guinier's piece, scholars from various fields have defined and applied racial literacy differently. Within the field of education, Horsford (2011) defines it as "the ability to understand what race is, why it is, and how it is used to reproduce inequality and oppression" (95). From Whiteness studies, Twine (2004) places more focus on White parents and the "resources," "patterns of practice," (882) and "racial vocabularies" (884) they use to "actively train their children to resist racism" (882). Twine suggests that while the work of White parents is often hidden, it still serves as a form of antiracist work at a macrolevel. As Rogers and Mosley (2008) state, an important aspect of Twine's work is the focus she places on teaching and learning of racial literacy, a subject Rogers and Mosley take up in their teacher education research. For purposes of this chapter, I align with Winans's (2010) definition of racial literacy as an ability to "critically examine and continually question how race and racism inform beliefs, interpretive frameworks, practices, cultures, and institutions" (477).

Racial literacy emphasizes an individual's role in maintaining systemic racism rather than dismissing individuals as powerless in the larger system—a stance that is in itself a way of maintaining the status quo. Winans (2010), for example, describes how this has happened with the construct of color blindness. We accept racism by noting, "Oh, they're just color-blind" as code for "They don't know any better," instead of confronting the perpetuator of color blindness and holding them accountable by way of further education and racial literacy development. (For their description of color-blind racism, see also Bonilla-Silva [2009] and Rodriguez [2008]). Racial literacy counters this laissez-faire approach by highlighting each actor's role, thus placing the onus on individuals to take ownership and develop and practice a sense of racial literacy. Yet as the cases in this chapter will illustrate, the challenge lies in the act of confrontation. Exhibiting one's racial literacy and calling attention to constructs that sustain racism often demands that an individual go up against the Niceness trends that society tends to value.

Methods

The data presented in this chapter are from a larger, twenty-month ethnographic study based in the town of Cartfield. To date, the majority of research that draws on or examines racial literacy is based in in-school settings (e.g., K–12 settings, higher education settings, and teacher education). Seldom have scholars examined racial literacy in out-of-school spaces (Lazdowski 2017). My work contributes to this conversation by examining the *out-of-school* factors that sustain or resist *in-school* racial inequities.

Data featured in this chapter are predominately transcriptions from public meetings, given the focus on how community members' discursive acts and actions serve to uphold or resist the "strong schools" narrative many use to describe the racially diverse, high-performing district. My analysis of participants' language is informed by critical discourse analysis (Fairclough 1991; Van Dijk 1987). Van Dijk (1987) has posited that racism is perpetuated through everyday text and talk (newspapers, conversations, television, textbooks, etc.). Critical discourse analysis allows us to unpack participants' discursive practices and notice Niceness in action.

Positionality

I am a White, cisgender, heterosexual woman. I came to this work as a Cartfield community member myself, which afforded me an insider status in my research. As someone who had (quite literally) bought into the "strong school" narrative and purchased a home in Cartfield, I was curious to see how the school administration would address the racist attacks I had heard about that targeted a high school teacher of color. I attended peaceful protests, spoke during the public comment portion of school committee meetings, and joined various equity-oriented groups (many of which I am still an active member in). When I began researching and formalizing my role as a participant observer, I made a conscious decision not to let my researcher role compromise my role as a (vocal) White parent activist.

I would be remiss if in writing about racial literacy I did not acknowledge my own racial literacy development process. It is ongoing and the result of years of self-exploration, attendance at workshops geared toward Whites, and reading a plethora of literature. I am especially grateful for the relationships I have formed and deepened with people of color both as a result of and apart from our activism work together. It is a result of my conversations with friends of color that I have learned the most and have been challenged to examine and alter my practices of Whiteness.

Research Setting: Cartfield's "Strong Schools"

Located in the U.S. Northeast, the Cartfield Regional School District exhibits all of the characteristics Oakes and Rogers (2006) outline in defining high-performing districts: those with "above-average educational spending in the state, highly qualified teachers, ample instructional materials, a well-stocked library, plentiful college preparatory classes" (22). This suburban school district spends five thousand dollars more per pupil than the state average. In the nearby urban district less than twenty-five miles away, the per-pupil spending is one thousand dollars less than the state average. Furthermore, Cartfield's students of color population is representative of national averages. In the 2014–15 school year, students of color represented 39 percent of the total enrollment.[3] This is in keeping with the 41 percent students of color enrolled in schools in the U.S. Northeast (National Center for Education Statistics 2012). Students in the district perform well, as is evidenced by high-stakes test score results, graduation rates, and college acceptance rates. Many people choose to live in Cartfield because of the reputable "strong schools." Yet a closer examination of student performance data unveils a discrepancy between White students' scores and those of students of color (e.g., Black and Latinx students) (Lazdowski 2017). Essentially, students of color perform well enough—at average rates—yet their White peers are excelling at rates well above the state average. This existing *disguised* achievement gap (Lazdowski 2017, 98) goes unnoticed, thus allowing White students to continue to outperform their peers of color, rather than addressing the inequities that sustain the discrepancy.

When something happens that compromises the district's reputation, such as the racist attacks toward high school teacher Diane Sherry, many community actors respond with efforts to reclaim the strong schools narrative that is under threat.[4] The examples contained herein show how *out-of-school* actors' nice discourse runs risks of dismissing the severity of the situation at the cost of the students, teachers, and staff *in schools* and, at the same time, what happens when people who are aware of the underlying constructs captured in the comments call them into question, in perceivably not-nice ways. We begin with Loretta's example.

"I Will Name You by Name!" Challenging Power in the Name of Democracy

The public comment portion of each school committee meeting provides the space for individuals to pose questions, voice their opinions, and express their concerns or support about a particular topic. At the school committee meeting on June 24, 2014, many residents were in attendance to comment about the recent racist attacks on Diane Sherry yet were denied the opportunity to speak by the chair of the school committee.

Mr. Kelly, a White man, noted the record number of people in attendance to show their support for the teacher of color and then preemptively changed the protocol of public comment at that particular meeting. He did so in a polite, civilized fashion, one that would make someone who went up against him look rude and uncivilized. He began the school committee in a nonchalant fashion, stating, "In the district I work in, something last week inspired me to look at our public comment policy. When I looked it over, I realized that we haven't been following it for the last year. Everybody have it? [*Referring to a piece of paper.*] So it's really important to me as a public body that we follow our policies and the public comment policy." The chair went on to reference the U.S. government curriculum he teaches in his role as a history teacher in a nearby district, likening the public comment portion of a school committee meeting to the constant struggle of balancing liberty with order.

Yet in response to Mr. Kelly, a White woman, Loretta, unannounced and uninvited, approached the microphone and the following exchange took place:

> LORETTA: I protest! You should be ashamed of yourself for trying to shut us down. You have a room full of people in here that are trying to speak and practice democracy . . . (applause from audience)
>
> MR. KELLY [*trying to interject*]: This is democracy.
>
> LORETTA: You should be ashamed of yourself, Mr. Kelly. You should be ashamed of yourself, and I will name you by name.[5]

Loretta takes a strong stance against Mr. Kelly in response to his limitation of public comments at the meeting. She calls him out on his decision to change the protocol at *this* particular meeting, and she is backed by various audience members. While the chair had tried to limit the comments portion of the meeting to five speakers at three minutes each (for a total of fifteen minutes), Loretta and others' protests result in the comments portion lasting thirty minutes, which includes comments from seven people. Loretta's strong stance, which could be perceived as rude given the volume of her voice and assertive nature, has shifted the power structure in this particular moment. By way of her assertiveness, Loretta reclaims the public comment portion of the school committee meeting, which directly results in narratives of support for the teacher of color and inevitably brings to the surface the fact that racism endures in both overt and covert forms in a school district that advocates for and proclaims equity in its mission statement.

"Thank You for Your Public Service": The Dangerous Effects of Niceness

The June 24, 2014, school committee meeting was particularly charged given the large audience (over one hundred people) and what brought them there.[6] Many spoke in support of Diane Sherry, and in doing so drew attention to the racial discrepancies in the school district. Yet among the supportive comments, there was the occasional testament from White parents about the positive experience of their (White) children in the schools. Such a statement came from Janet Miller:

> I'm Janet Miller. I'm a resident of Cartfield. I have three children who've gone through the schools. [*Turning to direct her comments to the school committee members.*] I want to take a minute and just thank all of you for your public service. [*Murmurs from audience members indicating disapproval. Janet turns to the audience members and asks them if they are okay before speaking over them and continuing.*] I appreciate what you do and the time you take away from your families and your personal lives and the dedication and thought that you give to our schools and our community and the policies.

Janet Miller opens her comment by politely acknowledging and thanking the school committee members for their time and effort as public volunteers. In expressing her gratitude she embodies politeness, an attribute that runs counter to the passionate—perceivably angry—tone many speakers before her have exhibited. Her thank-you is presumably a welcome change for school committee members, who have previously listened to a series of negative comments, and it undoubtedly serves to win their respect. At the same time, her polite tone is in juxtaposition to that of the previous speakers, and it thus devalues the comments from those speakers by positioning them as rude, angry, or uncivilized—that is, anything but nice.

The mumbles from the audience indicate that audience members are aware of the agenda behind Janet's comments—one that runs contrary to the reason many of them are in attendance. Yet when Janet hears the audience members she acknowledges them, and in doing so dismisses them in order to reclaim the public space as her own. Instead of simply ignoring the mumbles from the audience, her acknowledgment of them draws attention to the fact that she has been interrupted—an act society views as rude, and it thus positions them as such, discrediting their presence in that space. By positioning them as rude, Janet is better able to disregard their protest about what she is saying and position herself as the one who holds power in that moment. In a society that values politeness, this small interaction with audience members inevitably serves to discredit audience members and in doing so adds value to the content of Janet's message. She continued,

> I don't think our schools are perfect, I think they're far from that.
> My own experience has been that faculty and the administration
> have always been responsive. That path has not always been clear,
> but I've always felt that I've been heard and there's always been good
> and steady attempts to deal with the issues my children have had. I
> recognize that my experience is not everyone's, and I know that
> there's a lot more work to be done, but I just wanted to come tonight
> and give voice to my own experience and also thank you and the
> administration and the faculty.

What is dangerous is the fact that Janet's comments are "drenched in Whiteness" (Johnson 2017). While Janet starts by acknowledging that the schools aren't perfect, she quickly counters this position by sharing the positive experience of her children. And while she recognizes that her "experience is not everyone's," she does not openly identify herself as White. Her color-blind approach (Bonilla-Silva 2009) pushes race aside and allows her to (re)claim the strong school system by way of telling how well served her (White) children are.

Her statement "I recognize that my experience is not everyone's, and I know that there's a lot more work to be done" is a nice gesture—one that displays she has considered others' experiences and thus is *adequately* aware. Yet her lack of mention of her skin color reifies her Whiteness, and displays a lack of racial literacy, as she does not draw attention to how the skin color of her children has influenced their experience in the schools. She further exhibits this lack of awareness when she states, "I just wanted to come tonight and give voice to my own experience." As a White woman, she positions herself as someone who lacks power in Cartfield's current climate when stating she needs to "give voice" to her experience (and, presumably, the experience of others like her). She is either unaware or, if aware, she is abusing her White privilege (McIntosh 1992) by situating herself as part of an oppressed group—those who actually need "to give voice" to their experiences.

In closing, Janet describes the difficult year it has been (which we are to assume she believes is a result of Diane Sherry's situation): "I think the time of the embattleness [sic] of what we've been experiencing needs to end, and this year has been a very challenging year for all members of the community, and the schools, and so I will cede my last minute. I will say I hope we have a good summer and a productive and a thoughtful one. Thank you again." Her final comment, "I will say I hope we have a good summer and a productive and a thoughtful one," suggests that people move on from the uncomfortable tension this year's embattlement has caused. The idea of "let's all move on and come together in the fall" is a pleasant one, yet the nice undertones of the "this too shall pass" approach positions racism as episodic, something that can be solved through reflective practice and the distance July and August may offer. It positions Diane Sherry as the reason for the embattle-

Community Resistance to In-School Inequities   193

ment rather than acknowledging the need to examine the contributing factors that led to and allowed for repeated racist attacks. By adopting this "let's move on" approach, Janet Miller distances herself from the issue. She excuses herself—and White people in general—from playing any part of the same systemic racism she ironically serves to uphold by way of the nice narrative she displays during her two-minute public comment. This separation of self from systemic racism is demonstrative of a lack of racial literacy (Twine 2004), or what might be labeled as racial *illiteracy*; and the speaker following Janet Miller directly called her on it.

"As One White Woman to Another": Drawing Attention to Racial Illiteracy

Upon hearing Janet's comments, and realizing she still had one minute left, Erin Lenten quickly approached the microphone, despite the fact that she had not been assigned a number by the chair of the school committee meeting. She was polite, first asking, "If I may, could I use her last minute with permission?" The chair granted her permission, and she started the way others before her had, stating and spelling her name for the record. She then began her statement:

> ERIN: I just wanted to jump in here to respond as one White
> woman *[looking directly at Janet Miller]* to another. I have prepared
> something, so I'm gonna read that. *[She unfolds a piece of paper and
> begins to read.]* As we travel through Cartfield center we see those
> signs *[referring to the banners that hang in the center of town]* that say,
> "Cartfield is the perfect place to live, the perfect place to work, the
> perfect place to learn." But I would be remiss, and I would be
> abusing my White privilege, if I did not stop and ask, *Who* is
> benefiting? Who, in these schools? For which children is this the
> perfect place to learn? *[Members of the audience applaud.]* As this
> school year draws to an end, it's time to reflect on our performance.
> And yes, there are some good things that go on *[looking up from the
> paper, and gesturing to Janet Miller, who is again sitting in the audience]*,
> but do we really deserve the A-plus *[again referring to the banners]*
> that we so freely flaunt as a town? Or is this just propaganda, a
> facade we display to deter us from digging too deep and
> discover[ing] the institutional racism that exists in our town and in
> our schools? A year in review: In October [2013] graffiti containing
> the N-word is found in a bathroom and on Diane Sherry's class-
> room door. Did we improve throughout this year? Earlier this year
> [2014] a note with the N-word and the word *gun* in the same
> sentence is deemed *nonthreatening*. As the school year closes, Diane

Sherry is no longer in her classroom. Her students no longer benefit from her intellect and her excellent teaching practice. Under the leadership, where do we find ourselves? Have we succeeded? Far from it. Not only have we been unsuccessful, it's been a pitiful performance. And what message are we sending our students as a result of the lethargic nature with which we've dealt with these issues?

MR. KELLY [INTERRUPTING]: Thank you. That's time, that's it.

ERIN [SPEAKING FREELY, NOT READING]: Excellent, thank you. I just hope that when my daughter goes to school she knows how to understand her White privilege and that she's not going to a school that models how to *abuse* White privilege.

In having composed her statement ahead of time, Erin Lenten shows she has reflected about the content of her public statement prior to its delivery. Her statement about the banners and her questioning of how their content reflects or fails to reflect various people's experiences is a public display of her racial literacy. Her message shows evidence of how she "critically examine[s] and continually question[s] how race and racism inform beliefs, interpretive frameworks, practices, cultures, and institutions" (Winans 2010, 477). Erin unapologetically questions, or rather demands to know (based on the volume and assertive tone in her voice), "For which children is this the perfect place to learn?" She questions whether the banners that hang on lampposts in Cartfield center "deter us from digging too deep and discover[ing] the institutional racism that exists in our town and in our schools" and, further, "what message are we sending our students as a result of the lethargic nature with which we've dealt with these issues?" Erin is pointing to the administration's response to overt racist attacks in the district; asking questions is a subtle yet effective way to call out district leaders on their inability to effectively address the racist attacks on Diane Sherry.

Yet Erin doesn't stop there. Her questions quickly change to a factual recount as she provides "a year in review." Here she describes the time line of the past year, outwardly, *publicly*, displaying the district's repeated mistakes. Her act of airing the district leaders' dirty laundry is uncomfortable, quite different from the warm nature of Janet's thanks and praise. Erin's words are remarkably powerful in this sense, as they discredit Janet's words by calling into question the leadership's worthiness of such thanks and praise.

Thus, aside from its content, what makes Erin's message more powerful is the timing and the delivery of her statement. She capitalizes on Janet's unused minute and inserts her narrative in these final sixty seconds. Erin resists Niceness in the act, even going beyond her minute, in order to call attention to the color-blind undertones of Janet's comment. The juxtaposing content of their narratives—yet their shared identity as two White women, two White mothers, no less—makes

Erin's statement even more powerful as it draws attention to Janet's racial illiteracy and thus devalues the statement Janet had previously made. By openly acknowledging not only her white skin but the privilege associated with it, Erin overtly calls out Janet on her own failure to do so. She draws attention to the color-blind undertones of Janet's narrative by openly owning her own Whiteness when she says she would like to respond "as one White woman to another."

Furthermore, by drawing attention to her White privilege, Erin exhibits not only her awareness of being White but also the responsibility that comes with it, stating it would be irresponsible—an *abuse* of White privilege—not to question the content and the impact of the banners hanging in town: "I would be remiss, and I would be abusing my White privilege if I did not stop and ask, *Who* is benefiting?"

Near the end of Erin's statement Mr. Kelly cuts her off, indicating her time is up. While she is at a clear stopping point, Erin continues anyway. She departs from her scripted statement and personalizes her message by referencing her own child—"I just hope that when my daughter goes to school . . . she's not going to a school that models how to abuse White privilege"—angrily suggesting that the current leadership's racial literacy is lacking. As she has previously alluded, racial illiteracy is an abuse of White privilege.

"White People Always Ask Us for Proof": The Detrimental Impact of Good Intentions

Like Erin Lenten, Marie Abekam is another example of someone who disrupts Whiteness by calling attention to nice narratives in not-so-nice ways. Just a few weeks after the June 24 school committee meeting, a local radio station hosted a live radio forum on the Cartfield town common. The radio station, which holds monthly forums in various local communities, invites community member panelists and the general public to explore a relevant topic. Everyone present is invited to ask questions and make comments. This particular forum intended to explore the presence of racism in Cartfield, and in the Cartfield schools, given the racial attacks and resulting tensions that took place during the prior school year. On August 21, 2014, one of the two White radio announcers hosting the event began with the following introductory statement:

> It's been said that we live in a postracial society, and there are
> moments, like this one, right here in the middle of Cartfield on a
> very nice August morning, when you might think it true. But events
> not far away suggest otherwise. We talk mostly [about] the racial
> divide coast to coast, but in Cartfield? A series of racial incidents at
> Cartfield Regional High School and the way they were handled has

created divisions in town. While there is passionate support for the school's administration, there are others who speak of institutional racism, and that the events of the past year point to a pattern. A community that has long prided itself on tolerance, inclusion, and social justice has been forced to look inward.

The host introduces the difficult, often perceived as taboo, topic of racism in a delicate, unassuming, and safe fashion, all of which are characteristics that exhibit Niceness. The host's use of "coast to coast" serves to distance Cartfield from the racial divide by way of presenting the divide as a national issue, not a local one. Additionally, he questions the actual existence of racism in Cartfield, asking, "but in Cartfield?" Furthermore, the manner in which he presents people's perspectives about the topic insinuates there are right and wrong sides. His description of those who passionately support the administration, and the "others" who speak of racism, sets up one group as well-intentioned, passionate supporters and the other as troublemakers. In addition, his opening lines about a postracial society and his use of "you might think it true" imply that postracial America *could* exist, despite the falsity of this idea (Wise 2012). The introductory narrative exhibits the racism embedded in such an event: The act of debating whether racism exists or not—no matter what the context or location—undermines the experiences of people of color who experience it daily.

Marie, a woman of color, takes the opportunity to draw attention to the troublesome nature of the forum. Intending to explore the existence of racism in Cartfield, Marie points out the preposterousness of such a mission: "Whenever we get into a discussion about race, White people always ask us for proof that racism exists. I would like for the discussion to begin at a place where we acknowledge that racism exists and take it from there. It *does* exist. We live in a racist, unequal society. Cartfield is not different." Marie's encouragement to acknowledge racism's existence, and to begin the conversation with this understanding, is in direct contrast with the purpose the radio forum served: to educate by providing "proof" (to use Marie's words). Thus, in a few phrases she not only undermines the intended goal of the forum but also highlights the absurdity of its participants' taking the time to *contemplate* racism's existence. The content of her message in combination with her boisterous delivery might have caused many to deem Marie's words as inappropriate and uncalled for, characteristics that are not nice. In hosting a public forum and talking about racism and *not* practicing color muteness (Pollock 2004), the Cartfield community is able to take pride in its attempt, but Marie's words serve as the pin that pops their self-declared progressive bubble. As Marie points out, positioning people of color as needing to prove their experiences with racism is racist in itself. By naming this issue she demonstrates how Whiteness is further perpetuated through such an event despite its nice, well-intentioned attempt to draw attention to inequities.

Thus, by speaking out, Marie educates listeners (both those physically present and those listening to the radio). Her words highlight two trends in antiracism initiatives: First, conversations often contemplate the existence of racism by way of enlisting people of color to share their experiences as a form of proof that racism is prominent (see Akom 2008 and Guillermo-Wann 2010, which exemplify this notion). The radio forum is no different, and by labeling this fact, Marie unveils where Cartfield community members are in their racism-related conversations: There is still the need to prove racism exists, rather than placing efforts toward dismantling it. Second, Marie's act of explicitly addressing White people highlights the fact that Whites' lack of racial literacy is a large contributing factor to sustaining racism's existence. This stresses the need to focus less on people of color and their experiences with racism, and more on those who—perhaps unintentionally, and even unknowingly—perpetuate it.

As the examples in this chapter show, Niceness is often uncovered in perceivably not-nice ways. Those who exhibit a sense of racial literacy do so in fashions that might be viewed as rude, uncomfortable, or overtly direct. Yet it is actors' racial literacy that allows them to call into question the nice narratives that, when left unquestioned, help maintain the inequitable structures. Through their words, community members demonstrate that noticing and confronting discursive acts of Niceness, or *nice narratives*, provide opportunities to foster racial literacy by unveiling the not-so-nice narratives such as White privilege (McIntosh 1992), color blindness (Bonilla-Silva 2009), and color muteness (Pollock 2004) that are embedded in their comments. In essence, this nice / not-nice discursive combination calls attention to how Niceness, and *best intentions*, are sustained through a lack of awareness—a lack of racial literacy (Winans 2010). The discourse from school committee meetings and other community-wide events uncovers that community members don't frequently "critically examine and continually question how race and racism inform beliefs, interpretive frameworks, practices, cultures, and institutions" (Winans 2010, 477). This deficit sustains not only "nice" narratives but also the existing racial inequities in our society.

In using a racial literacy lens to look at Niceness, we uncover the hidden potential that racial literacy can bring in shifting our gaze from those who experience racial inequities toward those who sustain them. This suggests that the existing racial inequities might be altered through explicit education and practice of racial literacy. This chapter illustrates the impact of what happens when people practice racial literacy and act on their knowledge, often disrupting Niceness through uncomfortable, perhaps not-so-nice ways. If we are to make progress toward equity, we must not brush the tension under the rug, back down, or turn our heads the other way in the name of Niceness but rather embrace the tension and treat the uncomfortable space as a teachable moment for the sake of racial literacy development. As Loretta,

Erin, and Marie have illustrated, behaviors that might be perceived as boisterous, rude, and direct are needed to counter the not-so-nice effects of Niceness.

Notes

1. The four groups included school committee meetings; an equity and excellence subcommittee of the school committee; a group focused on community, culture, and climate; and a community-wide group called Undoing Racism. In this chapter, the examples included are from school committee meetings and a public radio forum.

2. The name of the community, and the names of participants, are pseudonyms.

3. Statistics are from the state's Department of Education website, not cited here so as to protect anonymity.

4. In the fall of 2013 and into the winter of 2014, Diane Sherry, a Cartfield Regional High School teacher of color, was subjected to multiple racist attacks including slashed tires, hate speech graffiti, and threatening notes. Though she tried for months to work with the school district to address these issues, little effort was made by the district. At the March 25, 2014, school committee meeting, Sherry described the "anemic response" she had experienced from the district.

5. All transcriptions from the meeting are taken from the local media station's broadcast of the June 24, 2014, Regional School Committee.

6. A month earlier, at the March 25, 2014, school committee meeting, Diane Sherry shared her testimony before the committee members during the public comment portion of the meeting. The meeting was well attended—standing room only, with perhaps 150 people present, many of whom were Sherry supporters—by both people of color and White people. When Sherry got to the microphone a dozen people stood behind her in solidarity as she read a ten-minute statement to the school committee members and administrators, in front of local television station cameras. The atmosphere was charged. People applauded and stood at the end of Sherry's statement.

References

Akom, A. A. 2008. "Ameritocracy and Infra-racial Racism: Racializing Social and Cultural Reproduction Theory in the Twenty-First Century." *Race Ethnicity and Education* 11, no. 3: 205–30.

Bonilla-Silva, E. 2009. *Racism without Racists: Color-Blind Racism and Racial Inequality in Contemporary America.* Lanham, Md.: Rowman and Littlefield.

Bush, M. E. 2004. *Breaking the Code of Good Intentions: Everyday Forms of Whiteness.* Lanham, Md.: Rowman and Littlefield.

Castagno, A. E. 2014. *Educated in Whiteness: Good Intentions and Diversity in Schools.* Minneapolis: University of Minnesota Press.

Delgado, R., and Stefanic, J., eds. 2012. *Critical Race Theory: The Cutting Edge.* Philadelphia: Temple University Press.

Fairclough, N. 1991. *Discourse and Social Change.* Malden, Mass.: Polity.

Guillermo-Wann, C. 2010, November 19. "A Post-racial Era? The Campus Racial Climate for Multiracial Undergraduates." Paper presented at the Annual Meeting of the Associate for the Study of Higher Education, Indianapolis. https://eric-ed-gov.silk.library.umass.edu/?id=ED530896.

Guinier, L. 2004. "From Racial Liberalism to Racial Literacy: *Brown v. Board of Education* and the Interest-Divergence Dilemma." *Journal of American History* 91, no. 1: 92–118.

Horsford, S. D. 2011. *Learning in a Burning House: Educational Inequality, Ideology, and (Dis)integration.* New York: Teachers College Press.

Johnson, M. E. 2017. "The Paradox of Black Patriotism: Double Consciousness." *Ethnic and Racial Studies* 41, no. 11: 1971–89. http://www.tand fonline.com/doi/full/10.1080/01419870.2017.1332378#aHR0cDovL3d 3dy50YW5kZm9ubGluZS5jb20vZG9pL3BkZi8xMC4xMDgwLz AxNDE5ODcwLjIwMTcuMTMzMjM3OD9uZWVkQWNjZXNzPX RydWVAQEAw.

Lazdowski, K. A. 2017. "Countering the 'Strong Schools' Narrative: Community Response to Racial Inequity in a High-Performing District." PhD diss., University of Massachusetts–Amherst.

Leonardo, Z. 2004. "The Color of Supremacy: Beyond the Discourse of 'White Privilege.'" *Educational Philosophy and Theory* 36, no. 2: 137–52.

Lewis, A. E., and J. B. Diamond. 2015. *Despite the Best Intentions: How Racial Inequality Thrives in Good Schools.* New York: Oxford University Press.

McIntosh, P. 1992. "White Privilege and Male Privilege: A Personal Account of Coming to See Correspondences through Work in Women's Studies." Unpublished manuscript. http://www.collegeart.org/pdf/diversity/white-privilege-and -male-privilege.pdf.

National Center for Education Statistics. 2012. *The Condition of Education 2012* (NCES 2012-045). U.S. Department of Education, National Center for Education Statistics: Washington, DC. http://nces.ed.gov/pubsearch.

Oakes, J., and J. Rogers. 2006. *Learning Power: Organizing for Education and Justice*. New York: Teachers College Press.

Pollock, M. 2004. *Colormute: Race Talk Dilemmas in an American School*. Princeton, N.J.: Princeton University Press.

Rodriguez, D. 2008. "Investing in White Innocence: Colorblind Racism, White Privilege, and the New White Racist Fantasy." In *Teaching Race in the Twenty-First Century*, edited by L. Guerro, 123–34. New York: Palgrave Macmillan.

Rogers, R., and M. Mosley. 2008. "A Critical Discourse Analysis of Racial Literacy in Teacher Education." *Linguistics and Education: An International Research Journal* 19, no. 2: 107–31.

Twine, F. W. 2004. "A White Side of Black Britain: The Concept of Racial Literacy." *Ethnic and Racial Studies* 27, no. 6: 878–907.

Van Dijk, T. 1987. *Communicating Racism: Ethnic Prejudice in Thought and Talk*. Newbury Park, Calif.: Sage.

Winans, A. E. 2010. "Cultivating Racial Literacy in White, Segregated Settings: Emotions as Site of Ethical Engagement and Inquiry." *Curriculum Inquiry* 40, no. 3: 475–91.

Wise, T. 2012. "What Is Post-racial? Reflections on Denial and Reality." *In America* (blog), CNN. http://inamerica.blogs.cnn.com/2012/01/31/opinion-tim-wise-what-is-post-racial-reflections-on-denial-and-reality/.

12

"I Want to Celebrate That"

How Niceness in School Administrators' Talk Elides Discussions of Racialized School Discipline in an Urban School District

MARGUERITE ANNE FILLION WILSON AND DENISE GRAY YULL

How, despite policy reforms aimed at increasing educational equity, do racial inequities persist? Specifically, in an upstate New York urban school district we will call Rivertown, how do blatant racial disparities in exclusionary discipline persist despite educators' good intentions for the success of "all children"? The framework of Critical Race Theory (CRT) in education (Howard and Navarro 2016; Ladson-Billings and Tate 1995; Leonardo 2009) helps explain the persistence of inequity. CRT assumes that racism and White privilege are the foundation of U.S. society rather than being exceptions to otherwise equitable institutions (Bell 1992; Delgado and Stefancic 2001). Schools, Spring (2016) argues, have always functioned on the dual purpose of (1) destroying the cultures and peoples of Native North America in a "civilizing" mission; and (2) denying the right to education to people of color, particularly Black communities. In this chapter we draw upon the framework of CRT to examine the discourse of Rivertown school administrators, pinpointing when and how the dynamics of Niceness (Castagno 2014) are deployed to gloss over the blatant racialized disproportionality in school discipline.

While most educators are well intentioned, persistent and damaging racial ideologies of colorblindness and White superiority paired with deficit perceptions of families of color thwart progress toward racial equity (Castagno 2014; Pollock 2001, 2004). For example, in her study of a California high school, Pollock (2001) demonstrates that rather than discussing race openly, teachers and administrators practice colormuteness, whereby "people in schools and districts across the country routinely resist talking about even the most blatant racial achievement disparities" (9). One dynamic that explains the prevalence of colormuteness is White fragility—the tendency for White people to resist discussions of race because of low tolerance for race-based stress (DiAngelo 2011). White teachers who have not had exposure to teacher education programs that require them to examine their internalized racial ideologies (such as colorblindness) worry that merely talking about race automatically makes them racist (Vaught and Castagno 2008). Many White teacher candidates come to schools of education never having thought about their own Whiteness and having developed resistance strategies that serve to protect White supremacy (Levine-Rasky 2000; Picower 2009). Teachers are socialized into a "culture of nice" (Castagno 2014) in public schools where adults implicitly agree to focus on the positive, the good, and the pleasant, preventing discussion of issues that are "not nice"—such as institutional racism, sexism, classism, and heteronormativity. Therefore, Niceness, as Castagno argues, firmly holds educational inequities in place by refusing to acknowledge them.

This chapter is derived from our larger critical ethnographic study of a race-conscious approach to parent engagement in Rivertown, a school district in upstate New York undergoing rapid demographic shifts as Black families migrate there from New York City. A primary focus of our research and activism over the past four years has been the disproportionate disciplining (suspending, expelling, and arresting) of students of color, particularly Black students, in the district. In 2014, for example, 14 percent of Black high school students in Rivertown received a suspension, versus only 4 percent of White high school students. This pattern in Rivertown mirrors the disproportionate suspending of students of color nationwide, and racial disproportionality remains even when controlling for poverty (Skiba et al. 2011; Wilson, Yull, and Massey 2018). In 2002, nationwide, Black students were *three times* more likely than White students to receive suspensions (Wald and Losen 2003). Skiba et al.'s (2011) analyses indicate that "students from African American families are 2.19 (elementary) to 3.78 (middle) times as likely to be referred to the office for problem behavior as their White peers" when the behavior is the same or similar (85).

In this chapter we shift our focus from the school setting to an out-of-school context: the Rivertown Board of Education and its administrators. Based on a critical discourse analysis (CDA) of audio-recorded school board meetings, we analyze how school administrators and board members approach (or resist) discussions of this issue. While some research has explored teachers' perceptions of students, discipline, and their implicit biases against students of color (Gibson et al. 2014; Gilliam et al. 2016; Gregory and Mosely 2004), less attention has been placed on how administrators and school board members, at the district level, make sense of such disparities. Based on Pollock's (2001) findings that "district adults . . . typically revealed their racialized analyses only in locations far away from schools" (5), such as district offices, we would expect more open discussions of racialized achievement and discipline patterns in school board meetings. Yet we would also expect that, at any level, the dynamics of Niceness keep inequities firmly in place (Castagno 2014) and may override the possibility of racialized analyses. In this chapter we trace when, how, and to what ends board members and administrators deploy Niceness, and when they do not.

The Community and Schools of Rivertown

Rivertown has a population of almost fifty thousand, and including the surrounding metropolitan area has a population of approximately 250,000.[1] The racial demographics of Rivertown, according to U.S. Census categories as of 2010, are: 81.5 percent White, 14.4 percent Black or African American, 6.4 percent Hispanic or Latino, 1.2 percent American Indian or Alaska Native, 4.9 percent Asian, 0.2 percent Native Hawaiian or Other Pacific Islander, and 2.6 percent Some Other Race. More than one-third of the population lives below the poverty level. As a typical upstate New York postindustrial city, Rivertown's population has decreased (from over eighty thousand people in the mid-1950s) due to the departure of certain big-name industries. In comparison, the school-age population in Rivertown is 48 percent White, 27 percent Black, 13 percent Latinx, 9 percent multiracial, and 3 percent Asian or Pacific Islander, illustrating the demographic shift. Mirroring the city demographics, school administrators in the Rivertown City School District are overwhelmingly White (out of nine principals, eight are White and one is Black; out of eight assistant principals, seven are White and one is Hispanic), as are school board members (only one is Black), and teachers (full-time teachers are 95.5 percent White). The superintendent and assistant superintendent, both currently White women, sit on the school board, as does a rotating student member who acts as a liaison between the board and the high school student body.

In the past decade, the district has been cited by New York State for its disproportionate disciplining of students of color, especially Black students. Despite this, the district has maintained a race-neutral perspective on the problem, focusing on reducing the number of suspensions overall rather than racialized disproportionality specifically. This context led to a series of events that we witnessed during our ethnographic study: first, a new superintendent—a White woman—was hired from out of state to ostensibly fix the school climate and equity issues. This superintendent—who focused her attention on race-conscious programs—was, however, perceived by the dominant White majority as unfriendly (to Whites), hostile, and favoring the needs of the Black community at the expense of the White majority. This "aggrieved entitlement" (Kimmel 2017, 18), experienced by the White majority as it perceived that resources and privileges to which it felt entitled had been taken away, resulted in rising hostility against the superintendent and, eventually, led the school board to fire her. At the same time, parents of color began to organize through a newly formed community organization we will call Parent Advocates, collectively attending board meetings and speaking on behalf of the programs and policies that prioritized racial equity. After the firing of the superintendent, an interim superintendent, a White man, was hired, followed several months later by a second interim superintendent, a White woman, who was then hired as the permanent superintendent after a nationwide search. This permanent hiring occurred during the time of data collection for the present chapter.

Methods

The larger study that this chapter draws upon is a critical ethnography exploring the nexus of theory and practice in a parent engagement program in the context of the school district's policy-making practices. The data include four years of ethnographic field notes, audio recordings of focus group meetings with parent participants in Parent Advocates and the parent engagement program, participant observation in school board meetings and meetings with administrators, and analysis of documents from the district and school levels, including the district's code of conduct, PowerPoint presentations, and student and parent handbooks.

The corpus of data for this chapter are audio recordings of four public school board meetings, alongside associated documents, from January 2017 to June 2017. Although we had been attending board meetings prior to this and draw upon these prior observations to inform the present analysis, we focus here on a microlevel CDA of those four meetings for which we have audio recordings. Among the traditions of discourse analysis, CDA is unique in placing power relationships and the discursive reproduction (and contestation) of ideology at the center of analysis, emphasizing "the role of discourse in the (re)production and challenge of dominance" (Van Dijk 1993, 249). CDA employs close textual analysis (of both spoken and written discourse) to elucidate the power relations and historically constituted ideologies at work both within and outside the text (Fairclough and Wodak 1997). Furthermore, in an analysis of racial discourse, paying attention to silence is especially important. In a context where colormuteness is the norm, one must pay attention not only to what is said (explicitly and implicitly) about race but also to what is not said.

In this chapter we focus our analysis specifically on two types of agenda items: school building reports, and reports on special programs. During the time of data collection, we heard building reports from two of the elementary schools and one of the middle schools. These presentations, given by the principal, typically included the following components: the features that make the school "unique"; the school's mission statement; discipline data broken down by grade level and compared to previous years; achievement data with an emphasis on progress throughout the year; and plans for the future. The reports on special programs during this time period included the restorative practices pilot; the school resource officer (SRO) program; the superintendent's disciplinary hearing process; and the revision of the district's code of conduct.

The meeting transcripts were coded for salient themes, guided by the following focal questions:

- What are the strategies of Niceness that participants (administrators, teachers, board members) use, and in what ways, if any, do these strategies gloss over inequities?
- When do participants talk in race-conscious language? When do they talk in racially coded language? When do they talk in race-neutral language?
- Where do participants locate the "problem"? Is it a matter of student behavior, school culture, adult decisions, or something else?
- How do administrators represent students, teachers, and parents? How do they represent school culture and norms?
- In what ways are the foregoing discursive moves and silences "nice" or "not nice"? For whom and to what ends is Niceness maintained in these moments?

In addition to qualitative coding, transcripts were analyzed for word frequency counts to identify the words most frequently used by participants. While word frequency counts do not in and of themselves tell much about how language is used *in context*, they can point to further avenues for analysis. After coding and analyzing for word frequencies, codes were indexed and counted for frequency. In the next section we describe the themes that emerged most frequently in participants' talk.

Niceness in School Administrators' Talk: Reinforcing Color-Blind Ideology

Through applying CDA to school board meetings in Rivertown, we find that school administrators elide discussion of existing racial inequities around both achievement and discipline by deploying the following discursive moves: (1) reporting findings to the board in color-blind terms, without disaggregating the data by race, thus perpetuating a "nice" silence around race and a focus on changing student behavior; (2) thanking and praising the teaching staff for their good intentions, dedication, and sacrifice in choosing to work in an "urban" school, thus implicitly perpetuating a White savior complex; (3) reframing negative portrayals as positives by reinforcing commonsense discourses of "respect" and "safety"; and (4) categorizing students in contrasting ways, by recounting "heartwarming stories" about successful students and those who have been saved in contrast to students who are criminalized and constructed as inherently dangerous. All of these discursive moves are "nice" on the surface, emphasizing the pleasant and the heartwarming, while

Race-Neutral Reports on Achievement and Discipline

Throughout the school board meetings, race is ever present yet never mentioned. This is particularly important when we consider that rates of discipline referrals and suspensions are reported from each building yet never disaggregated by race, even though the district has been repeatedly cited by New York State for its racially disproportionate disciplinary practices. In Middle School A in 2014, for example, 37 percent of Black students received out-of-school suspensions, while only 7 percent of White students received the same suspensions. In contrast, in presenting data on Middle School A at one school board meeting, the principal, Mr. Howard, presented the number of referrals *only* by grade level and year. While the sixth and eighth grades have seen a reduction in referrals and suspensions since 2014, the graph he presented demonstrated that the seventh grade has shown a slight increase in suspensions. Mr. Howard glosses over this problem by explaining, in race-neutral language, that seventh grade is a "difficult year" due to puberty: "The seventh grade in terms of in-school suspension and out-of-school suspension has . . . has kind of maintained that, we've . . . seventh grade, as [name] can tell you back there, seventh grade is a very difficult year in a child's life *[laughter]*, a lot of biology going on in the seventh grade *[laughter]*." Here, by focusing on the "biology" that is assumed to happen for all children in seventh grade, the principal normalizes the increase in suspensions and elides a discussion of the other factors—such as teacher decision-making processes—that could be contributing to this increase. As he makes this discursive move, the audience laughs politely. Then, while showing the next slide, he makes a similarly evasive move by instructing the board to ignore a piece of data that appears problematic:

> One of the things, for the days of ISC [In-School Suspension] or the out-of-school suspensions, um, it does show a 10 percent increase, um, but don't for one second, don't focus on that 10 percent increase. But if you look at the bottom, the bottom line, you will see the number of students suspended decreased by 46 percent, so we've really worked hard to decrease those out-of-school suspensions. So while the 10 percent increase, um, is obviously not something we are happy to see, balancing it with the amount of kids that are actually staying with us in school and getting their work and having contact with their teachers during the day is more important, obviously, than um, putting them out of school.

Here Mr. Howard deploys Niceness by attempting to focus the board members' attention on the positive, insisting that the 10 percent increase "is obviously not something we are happy to see," but that its problematic nature can be simply ignored and "balanced" by comparing it to a better number—the overall number of students suspended, which decreased. Yet what these data imply is that while the number of students suspended decreased, the number of *days* of suspension increased, revealing that a smaller number of students are the recipients of greater punitive consequences. Mr. Howard does not guide the board toward this kind of analysis, and throughout the presentation, race is never mentioned.

In addition to being race neutral, participant talk about student discipline consistently locates the problem in the students themselves. Repeatedly, participants return to the goal of improving student behavior rather than discussing other factors such as teachers' decision-making processes, implicit biases, or the overarching frame of zero tolerance that persists despite the district's changes to the code of conduct to emphasize restorative practices. The assumption here is that students are solely responsible for the number of referrals and suspensions that are doled out. For example, in a presentation to the school board about the changes in the code of conduct, one of the presenters explains, "I wanna really hone [*sic*] in on [the idea] that the discipline is not punishment; discipline is, is an overall approach and it's, uh, the root of the word is *to teach*, so we're really looking not only at when students, um, act out or do any inappropriate behavior is to correct the behavior, but to replace it as well, because [that] really is the goal of discipline, and so that they become more civil and self-aware." While on the surface level this appears to be a move away from punitive discipline and toward a restorative approach, the focus is still entirely on modifying student behavior. The phrases "act out," "inappropriate behavior," "correct the behavior," and "become more civil and self-aware" reflect a behaviorist model that assumes that identifying behavior, stopping it, and replacing it is sufficient to tackling disciplinary problems. It assumes that the only problem is students' decision-making, or, in the words of many administrators, their "ability to self-regulate." The complex sociocultural problem of understanding students' behavior, perceiving what is problematic and what is not (and why), and responding to that behavior in a culturally appropriate manner is reduced to an individualistic model of understanding students' maturing brains and modifying their behavior. Such an approach misses the mark of the restorative model and ensures that the district never has to discuss structural problems.

While these are not necessarily nice representations of students (they are, after all, based in deficit models), in locating the problem in students, the presenter behaves "nicely" toward the teachers (some of whom are in attendance), whose intentions are assumed to be good, kind, and pure and who are not held responsible for the inequitable disciplinary decisions. In a blatantly evasive moment, for example, Mr. Howard instructs the school board to refocus its attention away from the negative statistics and toward the positive ones, all the while speaking in race-neutral language to gloss over the racialized disparities in discipline hiding just below the surface of the data presented. It is to the praising of teachers' intentions—and

Praising Teachers' Labor, Sacrifice, and Good Intentions

how this functions to uphold inequities through nice discursive moves—that we now turn.

Another way that Niceness operates in participants' talk is through the praising of teachers for their hard work, dedication, and sacrifice. The words *recognize, celebrate, thank, proud, passion,* and *dedication* permeate the transcript as building administrators and board members praise the teachers for their efforts, elevating intent over impact. For example, in reporting on achievement data for Elementary School A, the principal, Ms. Watson, congratulates the teachers for doing the work that makes children successful: "We are pretty proud of it, and what it tells me is that our teachers are doing their job. Their job is to move a child from September to June and have them earn a year's worth of growth, minimally." What stands out here is, first, Ms. Watson's insistence that the teachers are responsible for the students' growth and, second, that a teacher's job is merely to move children from one level to the next. This technistic approach (Kincheloe and Steinberg 1998) to defining teachers' work overlooks the important role that teachers must also play beyond academic skills—in building relationships, creating community, developing culturally responsive teaching strategies, and welcoming parents by treating them as equal partners in their children's education. The technistic approach reduces teachers' jobs to something that is easily measurable, and leaves out the rest. Ms. Watson later returns to commenting on the teachers' determination, hard work, and sacrifice, adding, "So, I think it's absolutely the determination of the teachers to get this right, and keep working and getting it right, and engaging in that professional development, and taking it on so that they can look at a child—and you know we talk about IEPs [individualized education programs] for individual kids—they have in essence created that for every single child in their classroom, they differentiate." Here Ms. Watson represents teachers as not only being determined and hard-working, but also as going above and beyond what is expected of them to individualize instruction to the level that is typically expected only of special education teachers. While this discursive move functions to minimize the importance of the specific needs of students with disabilities, it also serves to construct teachers as heroic, as doing everything they possibly can to meet the needs of their students. It is a very nice, glowing representation of teachers and their work.

Such polite moves toward applauding and celebrating teachers occurs in a context specific to this district: In 2016, the superintendent at the time was under scrutiny from the teachers' union for several labor complaints. Because the teacher's union succeeded in convincing the school board to oust the former superintendent, we speculate that the current context of praising teachers arises from this history, especially given that a smattering of teachers usually attends each board meeting.

The pressure to please and protect the teachers' feelings is strong, as their collective power could at any moment oust yet another superintendent or other administrator, including the building principals.

Across all of the discourse in the board meetings, what emerges from these first two themes is an interpretive frame in which the adults (teaching staff, administrators, and so forth) are given credit for having created success through their own hard work and sacrifice, while the students are held responsible for the negative school climate, conflict, and perceived lack of safety. Furthermore, the "nice" focus on teachers' labor absolves them of responsibility for their disciplinary decisions. If students are solely responsible for their bad behavior and teachers come to work with good intentions, sacrifice, and a desire to "save" the "bad" students, then the students are left to blame for the punitive consequences to which they are subjected. Such representations of the problem as residing in students' behavior, and the complete absence of race from the conversation, protects teachers from experiencing the discomfort associated with White fragility (DiAngelo 2011) and elevates intent over impact. Being nice to the teachers takes priority over scrutinizing the root causes of disciplinary issues.

Leveraging Commonsense Discourses: Respect and Safety

> I BELIEVE
> if I am respectful, safe and responsible
> for my own actions and words,
> and if I work hard everyday,
> I will achieve success.
> IF I BELIEVE IT, I WILL ACHIEVE!
> (Elementary School A pledge)

A third way in which Niceness operates is through "commonsense" discourses: those that are difficult to refute because they rely on values so taken for granted that they are challenging to articulate clearly. As a result, these commonsense discourses—in this case, repeated references to the collocated concepts of respect and safety, as exemplified in the pledge quoted above—remain ambiguous and undefined. The word *respect*, for example, can take on very different meanings based on context; it can mean honoring a person's humanity and inherent dignity, or it can mean obedience to authority. And *safety* can mean the right to be free from violence, intimidation, and disrespect (*the right to safety*), or it can mean heightened security and surveillance (*technologies of safety*). Through examining how these discourses are deployed, we find that the latter meanings—respect as obedience to authority, and safety as security and surveillance—are those privileged by participants.

Respect, for example, is a discourse that often remains undefined. As Ms. Price, principal of Elementary School B, reports, "For every week, we have a focus. Last week was how to be respectful." She assumes that the definition of "respectful" is obvious to the adults hearing the presentation, but *not* obvious to elementary school children, who must be explicitly taught because they have presumably not learned what respect means in their home environments. Tellingly, respect is also mentioned in the presentation to the school board on the role of the SROs: "And to foster educational programs and activities that will increase student knowledge and respect, uh, for the law and the functions of the law enforcement services." Here, "respect" in the context of "respect for the law" takes on the connotation of obedience to authority. Likewise, in the discussion on the new code of conduct, which has removed zero-tolerance language and replaced it with restorative practices, the presenters implicitly link respect with success and the modification of student behavior through modeling and intervening: "And so we've really looked at that restorative language and about that respect. In fact, um, *[laughs]*, [name] called me earlier and she has a bunch of slides and she was just gonna break out in song, R-E-S-P-E-C-T *[laughter]* and flip through all of the slides, because really, that really is at the heart of this, if you want, um, an environment where everyone respects one another . . . and when they're not finding success, we work with them to respond appropriately and redirect and intervene in a way that models positive behavior." Here the presenter makes a joke about reducing their entire presentation to a performance of the song "Respect" (written in 1965 by Otis Redding and popularized by Aretha Franklin), to which the audience responds with laughter. In doing so, the presenter refers to an existing cultural script expressed through a song, glossing over the details of the presentation and the need to define exactly what "respect" means when discussing student behavior and disciplinary consequences. This flippant gloss is significant when we consider that it is the vague categories of "disrespect" and "insubordination" that are particularly vulnerable to racially biased decision-making among educators (Annamma, Morrison, and Jackson 2014). Because cultural scripts for respect diverge sharply, the omission of a specific definition of "respect" leaves the behavioral norm of Whiteness unexposed and unchallenged. And an additional irony exists: White administrators' appropriation of the contributions of Black rhythm and blues icons to reinforce White behavioral norms for children in schools, far removed from the original meaning of the song.

Respect, furthermore, is often discursively collocated with notions of safety, which further reinforces the definition of respect as obedience to authority and rigid behavioral norms. In the discussion of the code of conduct, one presenter states, "For all school staff, we are looking for a welcoming school community, a community that's safe and respectful." And later, in discussing the role of the SRO, the presenter states, "We would expect our SRO to create a safe and orderly environment, maintain and encourage a climate of mutual respect." In both of these statements it is the adults who create the standards of respect and safety, which are assumed to operate hand in hand. Furthermore, safety is discursively linked to the threat of school violence, which is used to justify the presence of police in schools: "[The SROs] are to establish a close partnership with school administration to provide a safe school environment. We know from, um, all the school shootings that, um, have happened in the past ten years, only one school, um, that was targeted had an armed officer. No other buildings, um, that were targeted had such a resource because, they are the first responders." In discursively linking safety with school shootings, this speaker invokes images of school-based violence and represents police as a deterrent to school shootings. And in one dramatic example, a school board member—in responding to the district's move away from zero tolerance—uses fear of guns and drugs to argue against restorative practices:

> So I'm asking, when you take that [zero-tolerance] language out, is
> that sort of part of that same idea of trying to phrase things
> differently, or is it literally like, well, you know, somebody could
> come and sell heroin at the high school, or put a gun to somebody's
> head, but that's okay, you get to do it more than once 'cause we don't
> have a zero tolerance? That's—I'm trying to understand, is it a
> language issue, or is it actually our decision about the response that
> gets made, and I guess I have that same question about, you're
> saying the idea of progressive, so if a student, let's say, leaps to a level
> four thing, do you still try to say, "Let's do a quiet time out with you
> and your gun?"

Here the board member makes an absurd, red herring argument—hinged upon the performance of White ignorance—that uses fear of drugs and guns to discredit restorative justice, and implicitly argues for returning to zero tolerance. Here is a discourse that may sound "nice" and innocent on the surface level but threatens to undermine the already fragile commitment to developing restorative practices in the district.

The above examples show that by repeatedly linking respect with safety, and safety with the threat of school-based violence, Rivertown administrators rely on commonsense discourses to justify an increase in policing (through the use of SROs) and punishment (through the use of suspensions). *Respect*, a nice-sounding word that seems to connote respect for students' humanity and rights, in this context takes on the decidedly less nice meaning of obedience to authority and the threat of punishment. Through the use of nice discursive moves such as flippant humor (the singing of the song "Respect") and the performance of White ignorance and innocence (the board member's catastrophic scenario of guns and drugs), attention is shifted away from disproportionate disciplinary practices and toward mitigating the threat of school-based violence.

Constructing "Good" and "Bad" Students

While teachers are often present in the school board meeting space and therefore are the recipients of many of the acts of Niceness, the students, unsurprisingly, are often absent. When students are present at board meetings, it is primarily for the purpose of being put "on display" for the board, to highlight the achievements of a select group of "successful" students. For example, in one board meeting, three White high school boys who were enrolled in Odyssey of the Mind, an enrichment program for students deemed "gifted," presented at length on their project. This presentation was followed immediately by a report by the high school science club, in which the two teachers in charge of the club enumerated the achievements of the girls from the club who were present—two White girls and one girl of color. Board members were very receptive to these presentations, smiling, clapping, and effusively praising these successful college-prep students. These "heartwarming stories" of individual students' successes serve to highlight the experiences of a select group of students, but they also gloss over the inequities buried in the silences of those who are not present.

In contrast, there are the students not typically present at these board meetings—those deemed "bad," or, in the terminology used by board members and administrators alike, "high flyers" or "repeat offenders." This carceral language is applied to students who are repeatedly the recipients of punitive discipline. For example, when discussing Middle School A's youth development team, Mr. Howard represents a specific group of seventh graders in the following way: "We have one and a half youth development team members now who are working with our kids, we are providing yet another outlet for kids to somebody to talk to, another person to help kids, you know, calm them down when they need that, make connections with those kids, and they've targeted a group of seventh-grade kids who are high flyers, as we call them, they're the kids who really need that, you know, to have another extra pair of eyes on them, and they're working with them to try to help them, um, be successful in school." What is salient here, in addition to the overtly negative labeling of a group of seventh-grade students, is that, in Mr. Howard's logic, being "bad" is a justification in itself for greater surveillance by youth development workers, who are one step away from SROs. The change in tone is also significant; the principal begins by stressing the positive ("working with," "help kids," "make connections"), then abruptly shifts into a discourse of surveillance and carcerality ("target," "another extra pair of eyes on them"), and back into positivity ("working with them," "try to help them"). This embedding of carceral language within discourses of helping students shows that the principal may sincerely see surveillance and authoritarian control as part of "helping" the students labeled as "high flyers." The discourse of helping also serves to soften the impact of the punitive, carceral language.

In addition to the "bad kids" who are identified and labeled by administrators, there are additional deficit conceptions of other groups of students that are likewise taken for granted by board members and administrators. Ms. Watson explained that her teachers were surprised by students' academic performance and, specifically, their linguistic skills: "I heard one teacher say, 'I have never heard our kids talk, use vocabulary, like they are now, I never thought, I never thought of even using some of those words and yet the kids are just expressing, using those words.' So, I think it's absolutely the determination of the teachers to get this right, and keep working and getting it right." Here not only does the credit go to the teachers for providing the appropriate language input for students who are assumed to have deficient language input at home, a misconception that literacy scholars have critiqued (Heath 1983), but the expression of surprise also reveals generally low expectations of students' academic and linguistic abilities.

Finally, discourses of saving children who are assumed to be damaged by trauma permeate the administrators' discourses as well. Ms. Price told a heartwarming story about Max, the therapy dog at Elementary School B:

> Max is also there for, I will give an example. This weekend a parent called. They have some very stressful things that happened in their home over the weekend and let us know ahead of time. The boy came to school, told his teacher right away everything that happened. [Name] said, "Send him down." Max was there. And this is a boy who does exhibit anxiety at times. He went and found Max, and after about ten minutes with Max it was reported out to me at the end of the day that that triggered a shift in that boy.

The board members immediately jumped onto this heartwarming story. When Ms. Price added, addressing the board, "You're welcome to come see Max anytime," one board member animatedly said, "Really?" and Ms. Price proceeded to give details on when to visit Max. This story—of a little boy plagued by anxiety because of trauma at home being saved by an adorable dog—became the highlight of that school report. While helping children who are having problems at home is an important part of the work that schools do, there is a way in which this story serves to reinforce the predominant "culture of poverty" frame that blames parents and families for the problems their children face. This elides any discussion of the trauma that children may also be facing when they enter a school building that has already labeled them as problems.

In the foregoing examples, the contrast between representations of good, successful students (the high achievers put on display for the school board) and bad, criminalized students (those who are in need of increased surveillance) functions to uphold Niceness by once again locating the problematic behavior in individual students rather than in the structural conditions in which they find themselves.

This reinforcement of discourses of meritocracy protects the feelings of the teachers, who are praised for their "determination" and for "saving" children. This representation reinforces a White savior trope that emphasizes the teachers' good intentions and elevates their actions as heroic, all the while representing families (understood, in racially coded terms, as families of color) in ways that are decidedly *not* nice—as traumatizing and neglectful of their children.

In this chapter we have demonstrated through CDA that school administrators, in their reports to the school board, cover up the existing racial inequities around both achievement and discipline through four interrelated discursive moves: (1) engaging in color-blind reports about achievement and discipline; (2) praising teachers for their good intentions; (3) using commonsense discourses of safety and respect to justify policing and punishment; and (4) constructing contrasting "good" and "bad" labels for students that rely on deficit assumptions about communities of color. Each of these discursive moves functions to soften the impact of potentially bad news and elevates good intentions over inequitable impacts, providing further evidence that Niceness functions to keep Whiteness firmly in place (Castagno 2014). We have traced how educational administrators deploy these discursive tactics of Niceness to carefully talk around and smooth over the existing racial inequities, as well as the ways in which their discourse frequently represents students, parents, and communities of color in deficit terms. In representing the school culture—particularly the labor of teachers—in "nice" ways and students and families of color in "not nice" ways (especially students labeled "high flyers"), school administrators perpetuate the inequitable status quo by refusing to name it.

Contributing to existing work that has examined silences in race talk in the school system (Castagno 2008, 2014; Pollock 2001, 2004) and the dynamics of White fragility (DiAngelo 2011) that prevent honest discussion about structural racism, this chapter has demonstrated the importance of examining moment-to-moment discourse in school board meetings, where considerable power is wielded and problems are represented according to prevailing ideologies in schools and society. Examining discursive features such as word choice, collocation, joking, laughter, tone, and positioning enables the discourse analyst to uncover ideologies that speakers implicitly draw upon. The ideologies expressed by adults in the Rivertown school system are unsurprising given decades of educational research that has shown the same belief systems to be prevalent: a staunch allegiance to meritocratic thinking that emphasizes regulating student behavior, deficit constructs and criminalization of students who do not align to the school's rigid behavioral expectations, colorblindness, carceral culture, the elevation of good intentions and sacrifice over impact, and a technistic approach to teaching and learning that singularly focuses on improving test scores. These ideologies, which are decidedly *not nice* in terms of their impacts on students and families of color, are made to *sound nice* through deploying commonsense discourses of "safety" and "respect." As such, they are difficult to pinpoint and disrupt until uncovered through a systematic analysis of moment-to-moment talk.

The problem of undoing Whiteness in the school system is multilayered and complex, and will certainly not be solved based on one critical ethnographic study. But several implications for policy and practice emerge from the specific example of Rivertown. First, given the discursive tendency toward colormuteness, the district would benefit from requiring building principals to report achievement and discipline data broken down by race, sex, economic disadvantage, and disability. This would require more robust data-tracking systems, especially when tracking disciplinary events that occur within the confines of the school, such as referrals and in-school suspensions. (Schools already report out-of-school suspensions by race and sex to the state.) The Rivertown district would benefit from electing and hiring more board members, teachers, and administrators of color who come from the communities about which many adults still hold deficit ideologies. There is a clear need in Rivertown for critical teacher education and professional development that develops White teachers' and administrators' ability to navigate the discomfort brought on by conversations about race, with the aim of developing a school culture that moves toward directly naming inequity even though doing so undermines the alluring veneer of Niceness. A critical conversation around the role of police in schools, beyond the commonsense discourse of "safety," must take place. And finally, the district would benefit from a stronger commitment to restorative justice practices and a move away from zero tolerance, not only in the *language* of its policies but also in its belief systems and daily practices. These changes would move toward conversations that are decidedly *not* nice yet necessary for accurately naming and addressing the multilayered problem of racially disproportionate disciplining in Rivertown.

Note

1. To protect the anonymity of the city, citations are not given for the various statistics herein.

References

Annamma, S., D. Morrison, and D. Jackson. 2014. "Disproportionality Fills In the Gaps: Connections between Achievement, Discipline, and Special Education in the School-to-Prison Pipeline." *Berkeley Review of Education* 5, no. 1: 53–87.

Bell, D. A. 1992. *Faces at the Bottom of the Well: The Permanence of Racism.* New York: Basic Books.

Castagno, A. E. 2008. "'I Don't Want To Hear That!' Legitimating Whiteness through Silence in Schools." *Anthropology and Education Quarterly* 39, no. 3: 314–33.

Castagno, A. E. 2014. *Educated in Whiteness: Good Intentions and Diversity in Schools*. Minneapolis: University of Minnesota Press.

Delgado, R., and J. Stefancic. 2001. *Critical Race Theory: An Introduction*. New York: New York University Press.

DiAngelo, R. 2011. "White Fragility." *International Journal of Critical Pedagogy* 3, no. 3: 54–70.

Fairclough, N., and R. Wodak. 1997. "Critical Discourse Analysis." In *Discourse as Social Interaction*, vol. 2, edited by T. A. van Dijk, 258–84. London: Sage.

Gibson, P. A., R. Wilson, W. Haight, M. Kayama, and J. M. Marshall. 2014. "The Role of Race in the Out-of-School Suspensions of Black Students: The Perspectives of Students with Suspensions, Their Parents and Educators." *Children and Youth Services Review* 47: 274–82.

Gilliam, W. S., A. N. Maupin, C. R. Reyes, M. Accavitti, and F. Shic. 2016, September 28. "Do Early Educators' Implicit Biases Regarding Sex and Race Relate to Behavior Expectations and Recommendations of Preschool Expulsions and Suspensions?" Research Brief, Yale University Child Study Center, New Haven, Conn.

Gregory, A., and P. M. Mosely. 2004. "The Discipline Gap: Teachers' Views on the Overrepresentation of African American Students in the Discipline System." *Equity and Excellence in Education* 37, no. 1: 18–30.

Heath, S. B. 1983. *Ways with Words: Language, Life, and Work in Communities and Classrooms*. Cambridge: Cambridge University Press.

Howard, T. C., and O. Navarro. 2016. "Critical Race Theory 20 Years Later: Where Do We Go from Here?" *Urban Education* 51, no. 3: 253–73.

Kimmel, M. 2017. *Angry White Men: American Masculinity at the End of an Era*. New York: Nation Books.

Kincheloe, J., and S. Steinberg. 1998. *Unauthorized Methods: Strategies for Critical Teaching*. New York: Routledge.

Ladson-Billings, G., and W. F. Tate IV. 1995. "Toward a Critical Race Theory of Education." *Teachers College Record* 97, no. 1: 47–68.

Leonardo, Z. 2009. *Race, Whiteness, and Education*. New York: Routledge.

Levine-Rasky, C. 2000. "The Practice of Whiteness among Teacher Candidates." *International Studies in Sociology of Education* 10, no. 3: 263–84.

Picower, B. 2009. "The Unexamined Whiteness of Teaching: How White Teachers Maintain and Enact Dominant Racial Ideologies." *Race Ethnicity and Education* 12, no. 2: 197–215.

Pollock, M. 2001. "How the Question We Ask Most about Race in Education Is the Very Question We Most Suppress." *Educational Researcher* 30, no. 9: 2–12.

Pollock, M. 2004. *Colormute: Race Talk Dilemmas in an American School.* Princeton, N.J.: Princeton University Press.

Skiba, R. J., R. H. Horner, C. Chung, M. K. Rausch, S. L. May, and T. Tobin. 2011. "Race Is Not Neutral: A National Investigation of African American and Latino Disproportionality in School Discipline." *School Psychology Review* 40, no. 1: 85–107.

Spring, J. 2016. *Deculturalization and the Struggle for Equality: A Brief History of the Education of Dominated Cultures in the United States.* 8th ed. New York: Routledge.

Van Dijk, T. A. 1993. "Principles of Critical Discourse Analysis." *Discourse and Society* 4, no. 2: 249–83.

Vaught, S., and A. E. Castagno. 2008. "'I Don't Think I'm a Racist': Critical Race Theory, Teacher Attitudes, and Structural Racism." *Race, Ethnicity, and Education* 11, no. 2: 95–113.

Wald, J., and D. J. Losen. 2003. "Defining and Redirecting a School-to-Prison Pipeline." *New Directions for Youth Development* 99: 9–16.

Wilson, M. A. F., D. G. Yull, and S. G. Massey. 2018. "Race and the Politics of Educational Exclusion: Explaining the Persistence of Disproportionate Disciplinary Practices in an Urban School District." *Race Ethnicity and Education.* https://doi.org/10.1080/13613324.2018.1511535.

13

"It's Better Now"

How Midwest Niceness Shapes Social Justice Education

BAILEY B. SMOLAREK AND GISELLE MARTINEZ NEGRETTE

Recently I (Bailey) was standing around a friend's kitchen table eating snacks and chatting with old pals, when our host interrupted us to bring to our attention that there was only one bite of smoked salmon left. He proceeded to look around the group and ask which of us would like to eat it. In response, everyone politely looked at him, then at the salmon, then at him again. Finally, after a bit of silence, we all resumed our conversations as if nothing had happened. A little while later, our host again asked, "Okay, now really, who wants the last piece of salmon?" He received the same response—silence and polite stares. Finally my friend exclaimed, "Well I guess it's easy to tell we're all from the Midwest!" At this, everyone broke into laughter and insisted that our host eat the last piece.

This brief anecdote begins to illustrate what "Midwest Niceness" means. We Midwesterners would never eat the last piece, nor would we even admit that we wanted to eat the last piece. To do that would be greedy and selfish or, even worse, it would bring attention to someone else's greed or selfishness. Instead, Midwesterners would much prefer to pretend that the last piece does not even exist; that way we can avoid any unwanted attention or misunderstanding. Still, perhaps the funniest thing about this anecdote is the fact that we were all aware that we do this. When my friend poked fun at us for not just eating the last piece, like we all wanted to, our response was to laugh because we all knew it was true. We all knew that eating the last piece would break the unspoken code of Midwest Niceness, something none of us would ever do.

While facilitating a teacher professional development (PD) series addressing issues in Latinx education in a suburban Midwestern school district, we started to notice the same sort of Midwest Niceness among our participating educators. Having two facilitators with different cultural backgrounds (Bailey is from the Midwest and Giselle is from Colombia) helped to bring up discussions about the topic as well as how Midwest Niceness was performed among our majority White teacher participants. One of the aspects of Midwest Niceness that we began to notice was how this particular performance of Niceness by teachers seemed to limit the conversations they were able to have about race, injustice, and inequality. This caused certain questions to circle in our minds: What is the role, if any, of Midwest Niceness in the willingness of (White) Midwest teachers to engage in meaningful discussions regarding race, injustice, and inequality? Is Midwest Niceness precluding teachers from engaging in deep conversations regarding these issues? If so, how?

Through semistructured interviews, observations, and artifact data, we explore the reflections and sense-making processes of educators involved in this PD series. One of the prominent themes that emerged in this research was how our White Midwestern teacher participants consistently minimized issues of race by avoiding racially charged topics and engaging in color-blind ideology (Bonilla-Silva 2017). For example, when confronted with direct quotes from Latinx students in the district discussing the racism they had experienced both during the 2016 presidential campaign and after the election, teacher participants employed optimistic, yet defensive, discourses (i.e., "It's better now") to argue that the racial backlash following President Donald Trump's victory was improving. We view these actions as part of performing Midwest Niceness and connect this behavior to what DiAngelo (2011) has termed "White fragility"—the notion that in White U.S. culture any amount of racial stress induces defensive emotions and responses.

Our goal with this chapter is neither to point a finger at White Midwestern teachers nor to offer prepackaged solutions. Rather, we aim to interrogate the possibilities and limitations of Midwest Niceness in social justice education, particularly given the current political climate toward culturally and linguistically diverse learners. We argue that while teachers can certainly still be "nice" and do social justice work, there must be a firm commitment to equity and justice that supersedes the Midwestern tendency to be overly agreeable and avoid uncomfortable topics. We end our chapter with a call to reconceptualize the taken-for-granted idea of "Niceness" in the Midwest to appropriately fit our current educational times.

What Is Midwest Niceness?

While underresearched and undertheorized, the U.S. Midwest is commonly associated with a "nice" and "friendly" demeanor.[1] Some have pointed to the source of this attitude as the dominant German and Scandinavian ancestry of present-day Midwesterners and their desire to live by the Golden Rule ("Do unto others as you would have them do unto you") (Gewirth 1978). According to the "Midwest Encyclopedia" from the Humanities Institute of Ohio State University, the Midwest is characterized as "the Heartland, the nation writ small, the great middle, lacking extremes, lacking diversity," and Midwesterners are characterized as "hard-working people, thrifty, devoted to family values, strong in character, middle-of-the-road, sedate, cautious" (Sisson, Zacher, and Cayton, 2007, n.p.). However, Ohio State's Encyclopedia also complicates the idea that the Midwest lacks "diversity" by arguing that the region is actually a "collection of disparate communities held together more or less by a civic culture that transcends (or at least ignores) differences, fashioned and buoyed by social engagement, and characterized by sustained public participation and philanthropic giving" (Sisson et al., 2007).

Indeed, while the popular conceptualization of Midwesterners is of polite, hardworking, generous, humble, Protestant, White, and somewhat boring people, nothing is ever that simple. For example Kix (2015) brings up some of the not-so-nice aspects of Midwest Niceness, arguing that in the Midwest, "humility permeates everything, helping to create the most remarkable facet of Midwestern Nice: the restraint from speaking ill of others, even if others should probably be ill-spoken of." Kix expands by arguing that this verbal restraint creates an emotionally repressive and subtly passive-aggressive environment. After its publication, the author was invited on Wisconsin Public Radio to discuss the article, where he acknowledged his discomfort discussing the topic in public, stating, "Midwesterners have a really hard time speaking blunt honesty about anything; we are taught to be nice, we are taught to think of others. These are great things. At the same time, because we are always trying to couch everything, there is a sort of hidden language that emerges making it so we can't speak to each other in ways how we honestly feel" ("The Sincere and Stifling Midwest 'Nice'" 2015).

Theoretical Background

Scholars have problematized the notion of Niceness in education by examining how good intentions and "nice" behavior can actually facilitate inequality (Castagno 2014; Lewis and Diamond 2015; Marshall and Theoharis 2007). This work illustrates the potential shortcomings of Niceness by demonstrating how educators can unintentionally perpetuate inequality through the avoidance of controversial topics. The notion of Niceness is a complex one; it involves the interplay of culture and Whiteness working together as a mechanism to maintain the status quo while rendering educators and school systems complicit in the preservation of injustice (Castagno 2014; Meadows and Lee 2002). According to Castagno (2014), Niceness is a "strategic element of whiteness," and "whiteness works through nice people" (8; emphasis in the original). Whiteness, Castagno (2014) explains, refers to "structural arrangements and ideologies of race dominance. Racial power and inequities are at the core of whiteness, but all forms of power and inequity create and perpetuate whiteness" (5). Whiteness is mainly concerned with legitimating the status quo while concurrently retaining an appearance of impartiality, fairness, and kindness (Castagno 2014). Within this frame, socially constructed ideologies embedded in culture work to produce and sustain material consequences that privilege some people and oppress others (McLaren 1998). In thinking about culture, we draw on Erickson's (2009) conceptualization of culture as "a sedimentation of the historical experience of persons and social groupings . . . all with differing access to power in society" (35) to understand how culture as a collective construction influences people's perceptions, and in this case, the engagement of teachers in racial dialogues.

By examining how the cultural behaviors and social norms of Midwest Niceness contribute to educators' responses to and interactions with racial injustice, we aim to unpack the intersecting sociocultural and epistemic dynamics that reflect its corollary Whiteness. For this purpose we draw on critical race scholarship (Bonilla-Silva 2017; Mills 1997; Omi and Winant 1994) to delve into a racial analysis beyond the intentions of single individuals. As Bonilla-Silva (2017) states, "individuals are not the ones who create larger systems such as 'capitalism,' 'patriarchy,' or 'racialized social systems,' but they are the 'cogs' that allow these systems to run" (221). To this end, we work on dissecting how Whiteness in the particular context that we analyze manifests in different ways. Sometimes it reveals itself as what DiAngelo (2011) has termed "White fragility," a state in which "even a minimum amount of racial stress becomes intolerable [for White people], triggering a range of defensive moves. These moves include the outward display of emotions such as anger, fear, and guilt, and behaviors such as argumentation, silence, and leaving the stress-inducing situation. These behaviors, in turn, function to reinstate White racial equilibrium" (54). Other times, the same construct of Whiteness is displayed through the use of what Sullivan and Tuana (2007) have described as epistemologies of ignorance; these can "take the form of the center's own ignorance of injustice, cruelty, and suffering such as contemporary white people's obliviousness to racism and white domination. Sometimes these 'unknowledges' are consciously produced, while at other times they are unconsciously generated and supported" (Sullivan and Tuana 2007, 1–2). These conceptual understandings guide our analysis as we investigate the role of Midwest Niceness in educators' engagement with and reactions to issues of racism, xenophobia, and inequality.

Methods

This study is based on a series of K–12 teacher PD workshops the authors of this chapter cocreated and cofacilitated. These workshops were held during the 2015–16 and 2016–17 school years in a suburban Wisconsin school district that we refer to as Springville.[2] The Springville School District is generally considered to be one of the best in the state, with modern facilities, consistently high state

Table 13.1. Springville School District Enrollment by Race, 2006–2017

	White	Hispanic	Asian	Black	Two or More Races	American Indian	Pacific Islander	Total Percentage of Students of Color
2016–17	72.2%	8.5%	9.2%	4.5%	5.2%	0.4%	0.1%	27.9%
2015–16	74.1%	8.4%	7.9%	4.5%	4.7%	0.3%	0.1%	25.9%
2014–15	75.8%	8.2%	7.4%	4.0%	4.2%	0.3%	0.1%	24.2%
2013–14	76.2%	8.3%	6.9%	4.2%	4.1%	0.3%	0.1%	23.9%
2012–13	77.6%	8.0%	6.3%	4.5%	3.3%	0.3%	0%	22.4%
2011–12	78.5%	7.3%	6.0%	5.3%	2.5%	0.2%	0.1%	21.4%
2010–11	80.2%	6.4%	5.6%	5.5%	2.0%	0.2%	0%	19.9%
2009–10	83.1%	5.4%	5.6%	5.5%	N/A	0.3%	N/A	16.8%
2008–9	84.2%	5.0%	5.0%	5.6%	N/A	0.3%	N/A	15.9%
2007–8	85.5%	4.5%	4.6%	5.2%	N/A	0.3%	N/A	14.6%
2006–7	86.4%	4.4%	4.0%	4.9%	N/A	0.2%	N/A	13.5%

Source: Wisconsin Department of Public Instruction 2017.

school report cards, and a generally affluent community. But Springville also consistently faces considerable disparities between its White students and its growing population of students of color. In the past ten years, the Springville School District, which served approximately seven thousand students in 2016–17, has seen its student of color population more than double, from 13.5 percent of the total student body to 27.9 percent (see Table 13.1), with Latinx enrollment increasing from 4.4 percent to over 8 percent during that same time period. In an effort to better serve these growing populations, in 2015 the Springville School District partnered with an area university to develop a series of equity-driven PDs aimed at addressing educational disparities through a racial justice lens.

This outreach eventually led to our partnership with the district to create and facilitate a PD centered on examining issues in Latinx education through a social justice lens. The series curriculum and instruction drew on critical pedagogy (Freire 1970; Giroux 2001; hooks 1994), culturally responsive pedagogy (Ladson-Billings 1995), Latino Critical Race Theory (Solórzano and Delgado Bernal 2001), racial microaggressions (Pérez Huber and Solórzano 2015), and social justice education (Banks and Banks 2003) in order to examine the historical and current experiences of Latinxs in the United States and to connect those experiences to students in the district.

Because of the implications of the 2016 presidential election, we began our 2017 PD by connecting larger narratives and policies concerning Latinxs to the experiences of students in Springville. We discussed President Trump's tweets targeting Latinxs, the executive orders regarding immigration, a video sharing the stories of undocumented students and families in the district, and a list of comments Latinxs and other students of color heard immediately following the election compiled by one of the vice principals. These comments included remarks from "Build a wall" to "I hope you get deported." In subsequent weeks, we dissected the dominant narrative of the "discovery of America," examined U.S. government intervention in Central and South America throughout the twentieth century, and explored the experiences of Latinx immigrants in the United States. We also emphasized the diversity found within the Latinx community and regularly pushed participants to question the roles of power, race, and language in a person's life experiences. Our last class asked participants to examine the role of microaggressions in their students' lives and the importance of culturally responsive teaching.

The PD consisted of five two-hour workshops, held twice in 2016 and twice in 2017, with seventeen to thirty-eight educator participants per workshop; the total number of participants was 105. The majority of participants were licensed K–12 teachers; there were also some paraeducators and student support staff. Course participation was voluntary but incentivized through graduate student credit and professional development points to earn a salary increase. Course participants were expected to attend class, read assigned articles, and participate in group discussions.

Data Collection and Analysis

In addition to our role as cofacilitators, we also conducted a qualitative study (Creswell 2007) aimed at examining how educators were responding to PD topics and activities in order to gain a better understanding of their sense-making processes. Data collected included participant observations, interviews, and artifacts. Field notes were taken during informal conversations with educators, planning meetings, and workshop sessions. During the first year of the study, three semistructured interviews were conducted with our two school district partners. The first two interviews were conducted individually before the PD workshops began and focused on the impetus of the PD series, the development of the partnership, and PD goals. The final interview was conducted jointly after the PD series had been completed and focused on perceived outcomes, lessons learned, and potential future collaborations. During the second year of the study, nine educators who participated in the PD were recruited to be focal participants and asked to participate

Table 13.2. Professional Development Series Focal Participants

Pseudonym	District Role	Race	Gender	Years in Education	Years in District	Home State
Darren	Springville School District administrator	Black	Male	20	3	Wisconsin
Nicole	Springville School District administrator	White	Female	17	17	Wisconsin
David	High school teacher	White	Male	4	3	Wisconsin
Laura	High school teacher	Latinx	Female	3	3	Wisconsin
Sara	High school teacher	White	Female	8	6	Wisconsin
John	Middle school teacher	White	Male	11	4	Wisconsin
Deborah	Middle school teacher	White	Female	25	3	Illinois
Erin	Middle school teacher	White	Female	2	1	Missouri
Jessica	Elementary school teacher	White	Female	14	2	Wisconsin
Amy	Elementary school teacher	Asian American	Female	2	2	Wisconsin
Hannah	Elementary school teacher	White	Female	2	1	Wisconsin

in one semistructured interview following the conclusion of the workshop series. These interviews focused on reactions to the workshops, impressions on issues of race and equity in the district, and personal comfort levels discussing such issues. Table 13.2 provides background on our focal participants, along with their self-reported demographic information. Additionally, artifact data included class materials, one-page reflection papers participants wrote midway through the PD, weekly exit slips, and pre- and postcourse surveys.

Throughout the workshops, researchers independently wrote field notes after each PD session and met often to discuss PD facilitation and the emerging themes of the research. Additionally, researchers conducted all twelve interviews together, met to discuss themes and content, and independently wrote research memos to later assist analysis. Once completed, interviews were transcribed and entered along with artifact data, field notes, research memos, and pre- and postcourse surveys into NVivo qualitative data analysis software. Analysts collaboratively developed a codebook of thematic and inductive codes that drew on various aspects of critical race scholarship (Bonilla-Silva 2017; Mills 1997; Omi and Winant 1994) to make sense of the data and create themed findings. The following section will discuss our key findings.

An Eye-Opening Experience

Multiple educators referred to the PD as an "eye-opening experience" that presented historical events, social issues, and cultural norms they had never heard of or thought about before. Many teachers commented that they had only been slightly aware or completely unaware of information regarding the history of Latinxs and/or immigrants in the United States prior to the PD. For example, high school teacher David stated in his reflection paper, "Before this class I really did not understand the Latino experience in America. I knew that this group needs to be accepted in our society, but I had no idea the struggles they go through just to get to the US, how much of a struggle it is for them here once they get here, and most importantly how the world has seen this group of people starting with the Conquistadors." Two other reflection papers also acknowledged that they knew Latinx immigrants' and other immigrant groups' struggles but not the full "extent" of that struggle. One educator wrote, "Before this class I was ignorant to what has really been going on with the immigration process. I've worked with people of the Latin@ culture and never thought once about their lives and how they got to the US." Another commented, "Prior to taking this class, I was aware of a small piece of the Latin@ history when it comes to immigration and how they've been treated. The video [Getzels and Lopez 2012] was an eye-opening experience that we were never privy to when I was going up. I knew that they have always been treated unfairly, but not to this extent."

White Ignorance

These narratives of being "ignorant" to the current and historical experiences of Latinx immigrant groups in the United States speak to both the White privilege these teachers possess (because they are not personally affected by these issues) and what Mills (2007) has termed "White ignorance." As Sullivan and Tuana (2007) explain, "White ignorance impacts social and individual memory, erasing both the achievements of people of color and the atrocities of white people. A collective amnesia about the past is the result, which supports hostility toward the testimony and credibility of non-white people" (3). We witnessed the manifestation of White ignorance through some participants' resistance to believing historical facts that did not conform to the dominant narratives of White supremacy. In fact, in some of the reflection papers, we noted examples of participants questioning credibility. One participant expressed feeling overwhelmed, noting, "I feel that I have to check the sources of everything that I am seeing and reading and trying to figure out what is true and honest. Finding an honest balanced view is seemingly hard to find, leaving me feeling frustrated and rather hopeless. I find myself waiting for something great or horrible to happen so that then the true intentions will maybe show themselves. This is not the way I am used to viewing the world. It doesn't feel good or right." An examination of that final sentence—"It doesn't feel good or right"—demonstrates the internal struggle some participants experienced in this PD series. Being confronted with an overwhelming amount of information regarding the racism and social inequities Latinxs face made this participant uncomfortable. It went against the Midwest Niceness norms of being pleasant, agreeable, and meritocratic; it did not feel "good." As a result, this participant (and others) displayed their White fragility (DiAngelo 2011) by becoming defensive and doubting the PD's accuracy and intentions. We argue that this display demonstrates how Midwest Niceness, and perhaps Niceness in general, can actually prevent social progress and equitable advances. Some White Midwestern teachers wanted everything to be "nice"—so much so that they were willing to discredit the lived experiences of their own Latinx students in order to preserve an agreeable and conflict-free environment for themselves. This finding also begs the question of whether these educators would have reacted differently if the dehumanization we discussed was experienced by White students rather than Brown ones.

Avoidance

Part of White privilege is the luxury to ignore issues of race, power, and oppression, and part of Midwest Niceness is a general preference toward pleasantness and nonconfrontation. We saw the two come together as White Midwestern teachers devised reasons to ignore, avoid, and/or discredit issues discussed in the PD in an attempt to maintain a pleasant environment that did not disrupt the norms of White privilege. Relatedly, we witnessed a similar situation during Black History Month, when many White Midwestern educators avoided lessons pertaining to Black history. In preparation for the month, Darren, a Springville administrator and one of the few staff members of color, had worked with several people in the district to develop lesson plans for the month to ensure that all students were hearing critical lessons on Black history. Many Springville teachers embraced the initiative and enthusiastically incorporated the new curricula, but others simply opted out. This resulted in a situation where some classes were receiving lessons related to Black history and others were hearing nothing related to the topic. Darren communicated his frustration about the situation to us and expressed his disappointment that the teachers who opted out had not attempted to discuss their concerns with him. He explained to us that Springville teachers are "so damn nice" that they do not come to him with their concerns in order to avoid conflict; thus, things often go unresolved. This example shows how the notion of Niceness interacts with culture and Whiteness to create a mechanism that maintains the status quo (Castagno 2014; Meadows and Lee 2002). By opting out without any discussion, these White teachers uphold their "nice" cultural disposition while continuing to reproduce racial structures by ignoring the significance of Black history. As Bonilla-Silva (2017) explains, "Since actors racialized as 'white'—or as members of the dominant race—receive material benefits from the racial order, they struggle (or passively receive the manifold wages of whiteness) to maintain their privileges" (9). This situation is the quintessential example of how *whiteness works through nice people*" (Castagno 2014, 8; emphasis in the original).

Emotional Processes and White Hesitancy

In our PD series, however, when White Midwestern educators did accept information concerning the historical and current oppression of Latinx peoples in the United States and the racialized experiences of their own students, it was not uncommon for them to cry or openly express deep sorrow for what has happened and is happening. We believe that this emotional process, while painful, actually helps educators along their path to critical consciousness (Freire 1970) by recognizing and reifying our mutual humanity. Nevertheless, when coupled with White fragility and Midwest Niceness, this emotional process can turn into guilt and avoidance. In our PDs, educators often expressed "feeling bad" or being "ashamed" for what has happened or is happening. While some educators reported to us that they had tried to turn these feelings into action by reading more about the topics we covered, looking for more culturally responsive resources, and reflecting more on their practice with diverse learners, other educators displayed significant hesitation to discuss with their students the historical facts and social issues that we discussed in the PD. These hesitations were often couched in excuses ranging from age appropriateness to parental disapproval to lack of time. For example, when we invited a 2016 participant to the 2017 workshop to discuss some of the social justice–oriented activities she employs in her class, she received pushback from several educators concerning fears about how parents *might* respond—despite the teacher stating she had not experienced any parental pushback.

Inappropriate for Whom?

While parental pushback toward social justice teaching is a legitimate concern that many districts around the country have dealt with, we saw the Springville School District not only supporting social justice teaching but advocating for it. Nevertheless, many of our teacher participants still claimed they worried how parents would respond and thus did not want to discuss certain topics. Likewise, some participants also claimed they were concerned about the age appropriateness of these issues, which eventually became a source of contention between participants and facilitators. For example, during one of our PDs, a kindergarten teacher expressed concern because she did not think it was appropriate to talk to young children about "unpleasant" historical facts such as the ones we were presenting. To this, our cofacilitator Darren, an African American, shared how he was only five years old when his family first sat him down to watch a documentary about slavery. He explained to the kindergarten teacher that he believed it was very important to talk with children at a young age about the histories that have greatly affected us. Scholars have also pointed to the importance of talking with children at an early age about race in order to promote equity and social justice (Doucet and Adair 2013). Still, some participants struggled to get past their own discomfort with discussing race and ethnicity, which prevented them from engaging in conversations about race within the PD or with their students in the classroom.

Similarly, another participant discussed how she was going to show a video we had watched in the PD to her class about minors migrating from Central America (Renaud and Renaud 2015), but ultimately decided not to because of images involving prostitutes and corpses and a fear that parents "would call." As facilitators we disagreed with this decision and pushed back on her comments by stating that her students are the exact same age as the unaccompanied minors traveling across Central America and through Mexico to ultimately get to the United States. We asked, "If those kids live this, why can't kids in Springville learn about it?" This example not only provides another instance of avoidance on the part of White Midwestern teachers to discuss social issues that have racial implications but also potentially points to the ways in which children of color are often viewed (consciously or not) as older or less innocent than their White peers (Goff et. al. 2014; Morris 2016).

Instead of embracing the opportunity to discuss social and racial justice issues, we witnessed many participants prioritize their own personal comfort levels as White middle-class Midwesterners. In fact, one participant told us during an informal conversation that she "didn't come here to feel uncomfortable," while another acknowledged how "guarded" and "politically correct" people in the Midwest can be and admitted that she was sometimes afraid that people will notice if she said the "wrong thing." While we understand the fear of being judged, we argue that making racial and social justice progress in the district and in the schooling experiences of Latinx students is much more important than one educator's momentary comfort level. The reluctance to engage in these conversations provides another illustration of how White Privilege and Midwest Niceness manifested in our PD. Many of our White Midwestern participants prioritized their own comfort levels over achieving social and racial justice for their students. Whether consciously or unconsciously carried out, the ignorance and avoidance expressed by some of our White Midwestern participants to engage in the "uncomfortable" demonstrates both a prioritization of the Midwest Nice value to maintain a pleasant environment at all costs and Castagno's (2014) categorization of Whiteness as legitimizing the status quo while simultaneously appearing impartial.

Outliers

While we have discussed the tendency of our educator participants to avoid, ignore, and/or disengage with discussions on race, we also want to share the examples of educators who were outliers to these patterns. In general we found that teachers of color or White Midwestern teachers who had significant relationships with people of color did not engage in the sort of behaviors of Midwest Niceness that we have described. Among our few Latinx educator participants, the majority expressed a strong identification with the themes and ideas we presented over the course of the PD series. For example, after the 2016 workshops, one of the Latinx teachers tearfully approached us to hug us and thank us for facilitating the PD. She stated how appreciative she was to have a space where she could share her background and feel like the expert. Amy, one of our Asian American PD participants, expressed how she strongly identified with many of the Latinx student experiences we presented. She explained that she grew up in a small Midwestern city and faced the same sort of prejudice and stereotypes faced by Springville's Latinx population. She expressed a strong desire to change attitudes and perceptions so that Springville's students of color would not have to endure what she had to. Similarly, Hannah, one of our White teacher participants, explained to us that her relationship with her partner, a first-generation Southeast Asian immigrant, has significantly pushed her "to consider more than [herself]" and to realize her privilege, which has helped her to recognize the needs of diverse students. Thus, we argue that while Whiteness is a dominant feature of Midwest Niceness and its desire to avoid unpleasant topics in order to maintain White privilege and comfort levels, not all White Midwesterners necessarily perform Midwest Niceness in this way. We saw that Midwesterners of color who have experienced racial injustice firsthand and White Midwesterners who had intimately witnessed racial injustice experienced by people they love were much more likely to engage in our social justice PD without fear. We also witnessed a few Midwestern educators of color performing Midwest Niceness in a way that was profoundly linked to Whiteness. We argue that while this was not the norm among our teacher participants of color, when it did occur it was an example of a person of color performing Whiteness through dominant Midwestern cultural sensibilities.

The Possibilities and Limitations of Equity-Driven PDs

Despite many White Midwestern educators' tendencies to avoid "unpleasant" topics and maintain a false sense of neutrality, we did see evidence of learning and growth in our PD participants. In both the 2016 and 2017 postcourse surveys, we received a considerable amount of comments expressing how much participants had learned and how much they had enjoyed the course. Educators told us that the PD helped them to become more open-minded, aware, and enlightened. While we find this feedback to be promising, we acknowledge that it is self-reported, and thus limits our ability to understand what is going on in the classroom from the students' perspective. Likewise, despite these very positive comments, there are limits to the difference a five-week equity PD can make. When we asked our participants about the potential of these sorts of workshops to reduce educational disparities, they usually responded by stating that it was a start, but "progress is slow." Moreover, because this PD and other PDs like it in the Springville School District are voluntary, the teachers who need it most may not be getting it.

Discussion

Our findings suggest that Niceness plays a significant role and can have stifling effects on addressing issues of social justice. We saw White Midwestern teachers inadvertently continue working to preserve inequality through the avoidance of unpleasant topics or contentious issues. Furthermore, our findings show how White Midwestern educators found themselves confronted epistemically and culturally during these PD sessions—for example, the reflection paper that expressed, "This is not the way I am used to viewing the world. It doesn't feel good or right." The "sincere fictions" (Bonilla-Silva 2017, 1) of these educators regarding the color-blind society we inhabit and their level of comfort in it were challenged. This often resulted in an apparent cognitive dissonance that made evident their "White fragility" (DiAngelo 2011). Here, it is important to point to the key function of White ignorance as it strengthens the construction and maintenance of White privilege, including how willing individuals are to step out of their comfort zones and how far they will do so. We met educators who held on to their Niceness and determined this "new" information was good, but not appropriate for their classrooms. This perspective, we argue, points to the "intimate relationship between power, knowledge and ignorance, and the relationship of all three to processes of racialized colonization" (Sullivan 2007, 154). The racial colonization still present in our classrooms today is not manifested through overt processes of physical and mental subjugation; it is a more subtle process established in White ignorance and perpetuated through privilege and Niceness.

The kind of ignorance that we witnessed during these PD sessions was not simply a lack of knowledge regarding Latinx issues and history. Rather, this type of ignorance revealed a more complex amalgamation of Whiteness, privilege, and power—couched in Niceness—that worked together to perpetuate particular types of knowledge about the "other." This type of ignorance allowed participants to continue believing the same histories and narratives they always had by casting doubt on anything that questioned those realities (e.g., teachers asking us for a more "balanced" view). Regarding this type of ignorance, Sullivan (2007) explains, "There is a dynamic interplay between ignorance and knowledge. The lack of knowledge about something allows people in power to fill that gap with a 'knowledge built on certain ways of not knowing them.' . . . This lack of knowledge about the other reinforces and legitimizes the paternalistic stance of Whites rendering the Other as incapable and in need of help. New types of ignorance are instituted in the form of a particular kind of knowledge" (160). Teachers, as part of an educational system that has been constructed on particular knowledge/ignorance about other people, constantly participate (often unknowingly) in the erasure of minoritized populations' knowledge and identities while also imposing on them "new" (read: colonized) ways of seeing themselves. This symbiotic relationship between ignorance and knowledge manages to perpetuate a particular lack of understanding because they believe already know everything that is worth knowing, and it imposes a specific type of knowledge onto the other. Thus, they first construct the other in a certain way, then tell the other "nicely" how to see him- or herself (Sullivan 2007). What is remarkable in this particular stance is how these educators manage to use Niceness to justify their ideological positions: "This is not the way I am used to viewing the world. It doesn't feel good or right." These words reveal the angst felt by one teacher at the possibility of losing her "paternalistic stance" over the other (Sullivan 2007).

After reading some of the data we have presented, some people may still think that the notion of Niceness, as we have theorized it in this chapter, may look at times as resistant behavior that wasn't necessarily racist. Yet it is precisely at this particular junction where we find the prowess of "new racism" practices (Bonilla-Silva 2017) at their best, because resistant behavior is never devoid of meaning. We argue that such resistance exposes deep-seated racial structures that people willingly or unwillingly support. Regarding this, Bonilla-Silva (2017) notes that "one reason why, in general terms, whites and people of color cannot agree on racial matters is because they conceive terms such as 'racism' very differently. Whereas for most whites racism is prejudice, for most people of color racism is systemic or institutionalized" (8). Whiteness functions to legitimate the status quo and new, "sophisticated," systems of social control. Additionally, when Whiteness is used in tandem with Niceness, it becomes a powerful tool to maintain an appearance of fairness (Castagno 2014). In so doing, Whiteness promotes the idea that relational reciprocity among different groups is not necessary. Hence, when these White Midwestern teachers come to acknowledge that they do not know the "full story" on Latin America and the histories of Latinxs, they begin to understand that there has to be a reciprocity in knowledge (Sullivan 2007) in order to disrupt the power hierarchy. It is at that point that they realize it is difficult for them to maintain their position of privilege while claiming to fight for social justice. This realization encouraged some of our PD participants to challenge themselves to genuinely rethink their worldviews and teaching practices, but it pushed others to create rationales for avoiding "unpleasant" histories that disrupted dominant norms of power.

Stirring Different Feelings

One phenomenon that we kept witnessing over and over again through the implementation of these PD workshops was the visible effect that the information we were presenting had on the teachers. We saw many of them with tears in their eyes at different points during the PD, and we knew that many feelings were being aroused in our audience. As we reflect back on those instances, now through a critical lens and trying to move beyond the tangible, two questions come to mind: What did those tears reveal? And what kind of feelings were they demonstrating? After thoughtful consideration, we tend to believe that the emotions fueling the tears were at least of two different kinds. The first was vindication: the few Latinx and other minority teachers who were part of the PD finally felt that their experiences were being taken into account and their voices heard. One of those Latinx teachers expressed, with tears in her eyes, "For once, I felt I was not simply the angry Latina, but I had something valuable to say." This educator had ultimately found the relational reciprocity she longed for in her district; her experiences and knowledge finally counted as worthy of being listened to.

The second type of tears, we argue, revealed realities being shaken and worldviews being disrupted. They epitomized the difficulty these White teachers were having in grappling with new understandings and examining their privilege; they embodied White fragility (DiAngelo 2011) and in some cases, we would venture to say, even "narcissism par excellence" (Leonardo and Porter 2010, 148). During those times, it was difficult for these White teachers to recognize themselves as the oppressor, especially when they had been raised to be "nice." Our hope is that those tears also reflected the acknowledgment that there is a coconstitutive relationship between them as White Americans and members of the Latinx community as their American equals. As Sullivan (2007) explains, "To be a White United Stater is to have a racial identity formed. . . . It is in my White-privileged interests to remain completely ignorant of that fact" (169). We want to believe that those instances were indications of deeper considerations of the complex relations the teachers have with other social groups and their roles in colluding with the systems that have formed their identities and empowered them with Niceness to continue perpetuating social injustice.

Moving Forward

As we consider where to go from here, we see glimpses of hope in the spaces that are opening to have these crucial conversations. The fact that we are naming constructs such as Niceness reveal significant steps toward the examination and deconstruction of particular ways of thinking and acting. In order to move forward we must go beyond simply finding a more "inclusive" way to present class materials or just "educate" White teachers, lest we forget our "tradition of treating others as mere objects of study for the colonizer's gaze" (Sullivan 2007, 169). Moving forward requires the willingness of individuals to question societal systems and power dynamics (Castagno 2014), to feel uncomfortable (Leonardo and Porter 2010), and to unpack the complexity and tangible effects of sociocultural notions such as Midwest Niceness. As Frye (1983) asserts, "White people do need to educate themselves about the lives and worlds of people of color, but to effectively tackle racism, they also need to turn their gaze upon themselves and simultaneously examine the active operation of their ignorance" (118).

As we point to conceptualizations of Niceness and identify their impact in our educational endeavors, the remaining challenge is to rework our cultural and social ideas in regard to this notion. It is time to move this concept beyond our living rooms and Thanksgiving dinner conversations in order to engage in constructing a notion that involves addressing injustice and naming social realities as part of that Niceness. The *Merriam-Webster Dictionary* includes in its definition of Niceness not only the words "pleasing" and "agreeable," but also "appropriate" and "fitting."[3] The question we ask as critical educators in an extremely polarized era is, What is appropriate and fitting in our current educational times? Unsurprisingly, the answer to this question does not come in the form of prepackaged materials. Our current educational responsibilities demand our utmost sense of self-awareness, which will help us to remain conscious of the limitations of knowledge, the power of ignorance, and the racial dynamics at work within "nice" frames in our society.

During the 2016 presidential campaign Kellyanne Conway, then campaign director for Donald Trump, expressed, "There's a difference for voters between what offends you and what affects you" ("Kellyanne Conway" 2016). These words resound in our minds as we reflect on the PD sessions and envision new possibilities. Living in a state (Wisconsin) visibly affected by the divisive sociopolitical rhetoric of our current times, we hope that the educators who participated in the PD sessions may continue to see that what offends them should not only affect them but also propel them to action, keeping in mind their responsibilities toward their diverse students and families. Most important, we hope that these teachers have realized that ignorance and color blindness are no longer viable excuses, because things are still not "better now." Midwest Niceness does not have to equate to "nice" oppression or diplomatic evasion; it can start to mean socially acute awareness of dissimilar realities. Our commitment to social justice is what will make the difference to overcome the timeworn idea of "Niceness."

Notes

1. While definitions of this region vary, for the purposes of this chapter we follow the U.S. Census's definition of the Midwest, which includes Illinois, Indiana, Iowa, Kansas, Michigan, Minnesota, Missouri, Ohio, Nebraska, North Dakota, South Dakota, and Wisconsin (U.S. Census Bureau, n.d.).

2. All names of places and people have been changed to maintain anonymity.

3. "Nice," *Merriam-Webster Online.* https://www.merriam-webster.com/dictionary/nice?utm_campaign=sd&utm_medium=serp&utm_source=jsonld.

References

Banks, J. A., and C. A. M. Banks, eds. 2003. *Handbook of Research on Multicultural Education.* 2nd ed. San Francisco: Jossey-Bass.

Bonilla-Silva, E. 2017. *Racism without Racists: Color-Blind Racism and the Persistence of Racial Inequality in America.* 5th ed. Lanham, Md.: Rowman and Littlefield.

Castagno, A. E. 2014. *Educated in Whiteness: Good Intentions and Diversity in Schools.* Minneapolis: University of Minnesota Press.

Creswell, J. W. 2007. *Qualitative Inquiry and Research Design: Choosing among Five Approaches.* 2nd ed. Thousand Oaks, Calif.: Sage.

DiAngelo, R. 2011. "White Fragility." *International Journal of Critical Pedagogy* 3, no. 3: 54–70.

Doucet, F., and J. K. Adair. 2013. "Addressing Race and Inequity in the Classroom." *Young Children* 68, no. 5: 88–97.

Erickson, F. 2009. "Culture in Society and in Educational Practices." In *Multicultural Education: Issues and Perspectives*, 7th ed., edited by J. Banks and C. A. M. Banks, 33–58. Hoboken, N.J.: Wiley.

Freire, P. 1970. *Pedagogy of the Oppressed.* Translated by M B. Ramos. New York: Continuum.

Frye, M. 1983. *The Politics of Reality: Essays in Feminist Theory.* Freedom, Calif.: Crossing.

Getzels, P., and E. Lopez, dirs. 2012. *Harvest of Empire: The Untold Story of Latinos in America.* http://www.harvestofempiremovie.com.

Gewirth, A. 1978. "The Golden Rule Rationalized." *Midwest Studies in Philosophy* 3, no. 1: 133–47.

Giroux, H. A. 2001. *Theory and Resistance in Education: Towards a Pedagogy for the Opposition.* 2nd ed. Westport, Conn.: Bergin and Garvey.

Goff, P. A., M. C. Jackson, B. A. L. Di Leone, C. M. Culotta, and N. A. DiTomasso. 2014. "The Essence of Innocence: Consequences of Dehumanizing Black Children." *Journal of Personality and Social Psychology* 106, no. 4: 526–45.

hooks, bell. 1994. *Teaching to Transgress.* New York: Routledge.

"Kellyanne Conway: Clinton Campaign Opposed 'What Offends You,' Trump Opposed 'What Affects You.'" 2016, December 2. Breitbart. https://www .breitbart.com/politics/2016/12/02/kellyanne-conway-clinton-campaign-op posed-what-offends-you-trump-opposed-what-affects-you/.

Kix, P. 2015, October 22. "Midwestern Nice: A Tribute to a Sincere and Suffocating Way of Life." *Thrillist.* https://www.thrillist.com/lifestyle/nation /my-life-living-midwestern-nice.

Ladson-Billings, G. 1995. "Toward a Theory of Culturally Relevant Pedagogy." *American Educational Research Journal* 32, no. 3: 465–91.

Leonardo, Z., and R. Porter. 2010. "Pedagogy of Fear: Toward a Fanonian Theory of 'Safety' in Race Dialogue." *Race Ethnicity and Education* 13, no. 2: 139–57.

Lewis, A., and J. Diamond. 2015. *Despite the Best Intentions: How Racial Inequality Thrives in Good Schools.* New York: Oxford University Press.

Marshall, J. M., and G. Theoharis. 2007. "Moving Beyond Being Nice: Teaching and Learning about Social Justice in a Predominantly White Educational Leadership Program." *Journal of Research on Leadership Education* 2, no. 2: 1–31. DOI:10.1177/194277510700200203.

McLaren, P. 1998. "Whiteness is . . . The Struggle for Postcolonial Hybridity." In *White Reign: Deploying Whiteness in America*, edited by J. Kincheloe and S. Steinberg, 63–75. New York: St. Martin's.

Meadows, M., and J. H. Lee. 2002. "The Challenge of Using Multicultural Education in Predominately White Early Childhood Classrooms." *International Journal of Early Childhood Education* 8, no. 2: 105–24.

Mills, C. W. 1997. *The Racial Contract*. Ithaca, N.Y.: Cornell University Press.

Mills, C. W. 2007. "White Ignorance." In *Race and Epistemologies of Ignorance*, edited by S. Sullivan and N. Tuana, 11–38. Albany: State University of New York Press.

Morris, M. 2016. *Pushout: The Criminalization of Black Girls in Schools*. New York: New Press.

Omi, M., and H. Winant. 1994. *Racial Formation in the United States*. 2nd ed. New York: Routledge.

Pérez Huber, L., and D. G. Solórzano, 2015. "Visualizing Everyday Racism: Critical Race Theory, Visual Microaggressions, and the Historical Image of Mexican Banditry." *Qualitative Inquiry* 21, no. 3: 223–38.

Renaud, B., and C. Renaud, dirs. 2015, October 6. *Between Borders: American Migrant Crisis*. New York: Times Films. https://www.nytimes.com/video /world/americas/100000003901101/central-america-child-migrants.html.

"The Sincere and Stifling Midwest 'Nice.'" 2015, November 5. *The Joy Cardin Show*. Wisconsin Public Radio. https://www.wpr.org/shows/sincere -and-stifling-midwest-nice.

Sisson, R.; Zacher, C., and Cayton, A., eds. 2007. *The American Midwest: An Interpretive Encyclopedia*. Bloomington, IN: Indiana University Press. Retrieved from https://huminst.osu.edu/encyclopedia.

Solórzano, D. G., and D. Delgado Bernal. 2001. "Examining Transformational Resistance through a Critical Race and Latcrit Theory Framework: Chicana and Chicano Students in an Urban Context." *Urban Education* 36, no. 3: 308–42.

Sullivan, S. 2007. "White Ignorance or Colonial Oppression: Or, Why I Know So Little about Puerto Rico." In *Race and Epistemologies of Ignorance*, edited by S. Sullivan and N. Tuana.. Albany: State University of New York Press.

Sullivan, S., and N. Tuana. 2007. "Introduction." In *Race and Epistemologies of Ignorance*, edited by S. Sullivan and N. Tuana, 1–10. Albany, NY: State University of New York Press.

U.S. Census Bureau. N.d. "Census Regions and Divisions of the United States." https://www2.census.gov/geo/pdfs/maps-data/maps/reference/us_regdiv.pdf.

Wisconsin Department of Public Instruction. 2017. WISEdash Web Portal. https://dpi.wi.gov/wisedash.

14

Schooling, Structural Niceness, and Not-Nice White Girls

SABINA VAUGHT AND DEIRDRE JUDGE

> Niceness breaks down when it can be framed as telling "hard truths" about the deficiencies of *other people*. Niceness obfuscates power, and it absolves individuals from needing to address what are actually deficiencies in the system. While the norms of niceness are acceptably broken in these cases, the influence of niceness to protect one's in-group and one's institution is unwavering. In other words . . . the actions and beliefs are always nice in relation to institutional and structural power because niceness masks structural dominance.
> —Angelina E. Castagno, *Educated in Whiteness: Good Intentions and Diversity in Schools*

Castagno (2014) offers "Niceness" as a complex practice of Whiteness and theorizes the ways it works to mask supremacist *structural dominance*, protecting and normalizing a system of racialized inequity or repression. In this chapter we take up a small portion of her framework to consider how the unwavering feature of Niceness—its commitment to group and institution—is central to the intra-White practice of structural dominance. Specifically, we observe this intra-White practice at sites where White supremacy and heteropatriarchy are interknit: through Niceness they coconstruct and buttress one another. We explore here how school-based treatment of White girls is one window into the ways in which state educational institutions hone a racialized Niceness that is contingent on and reified by paternalism. In line with Castagno's conceptualization, we suggest that state Niceness does not necessarily follow the interpersonal norms of Niceness, but rather facilitates and adheres to the patterned institutional protection of benevolence.

Drawing on brief ethnographic vignettes from Deirdre Judge's study of a comprehensive public high school's summer school, this chapter theorizes how the disciplining of four White girls by White teachers, policies, practices, and institutional organization reflects state Niceness in relation to its own race and gender domination. We argue that the state exerts Niceness to discipline White girls who are perceived as outside dominant White femininity and girlhood, largely through combined class and gender presentation. This discipline is both a means of bolstering what nice Whiteness is and should be, and also a means of entangling White misogyny and control with racial supremacy. While we recognize the ample evidence of Niceness inflicted on girls across race and sexual/gender identity, our specific attention here is an effort to understand a cluster of power constructions internal to Whiteness. In this chapter we look at how the state school uses White girls to draw boundaries around Whiteness and to silently *demark the deficiencies of other people*—a fundamental task of state benevolence.

The State, Benevolence, and Niceness

We approach "public" schooling as the state's most extensive compulsory apparatus (Vaught 2017). Along with Brown (1992), we understand the state as a "paradox that . . . is at once an incoherent, multifaceted ensemble of power relations and an apparent vehicle if not agent of massive domination" (12). Moreover, the state is featured by its imbricate colonizing mechanisms (Brayboy 2005; Jung 2011), racialist organizations (Bell 2004; Bonilla-Silva and Mayorga 2011; Bracey 2015), capitalist marketizations (Robinson 2000; Somers 2008), and heteropatriarchal structures (Bettie 2003; Canaday 2009), among others factors that are endemic to its founding (Bell 1992; Fraser 1990; Guinier 2004; Harris 1993) and enmeshed in its ongoing project of hierarchy and domination. Moving fluidly among these mechanisms, state paternal protection operates as a benevolent feature of the social contract (Brown 1992; Collins 2009; Harris 2006).

Benevolence is a capacious state rubric, a defining characteristic of the state's self-imagined magnanimity. Specifically, we conceptualize state benevolence here as both the ideologies and mechanizations of the liberal, Western state as it reproduces its original violent authority to make contractual, protective laws and systems that it presents as neutral and democratic (Agamben 2005; Anderson 2006; Robinson 2000). Differentiating among those who should be variously included and excluded is axial to its function. Benevolence is the endemic deep structure of the U.S. state.

Castagno (2014) encourages us to consider a feature of this paternal benevolence: Niceness. Niceness, we argue, is a fixture of that defining characteristic, a distinct mechanism by which just one part of the state's malignantly benevolent capacity is realized. Niceness functions as an analytically precise relational or transactional instrument. As transactional, Niceness can be understood as a semiotics of benevolence—an articulation, conveyance, or narration that has reifying and reproducing functions. Niceness bridges the vast and often shrouded apparatuses of benevolence to the daily, mundane exertions of state authority. It tells the structural "'hard truths' about the deficiencies of *other people*" (Castagno 2014, 167; emphasis in the original). Such structural forms of Niceness create the ongoing foundational narrative for state benevolence. In light of this, we ask the following questions: What is the relationship between state Niceness and nice individual interactions in the context of state schools? And how does that relationship help us to understand how heteropatriarchal Whiteness makes and masks power?

Niceness offers a mechanistic and conceptual view of the ways in which state heteropatriarchal Whiteness internally re-creates itself. Here we take up a feminist approach to the state.[1] Countering Michel Foucault's suggestion that the state's centrality is diminished in the disciplinary age, Brown (1992) argues that "male social power and the production of female subjects appears to be increasingly concentrated in the state" (29). As Brown (1992) also notes, "Domination, dependence, discipline, and protection, the terms marking the itinerary of women's subordination in vastly different cultures and epochs, are also characteristic effects of state power" (12). These effects of state power are particularly evident in compulsory state schooling, where youth are conditioned or coerced into various future citizenships or noncitizenships—inclusions and exclusions—through the gatekeeping practice of belonging and unbelonging fundamental to state paternalism (Harris 1993; Somers 2008; Williams 1991).

The school's characteristic as a benevolent paternal institution serves to camouflage the brute race–gender power differentials it helps to discipline and produce. As Meiners (2015) points out, "The category child masks the transactions that ultimately decide who has access to innocence, sentience, and full humanity" (124; see also Berlant 1997). In this chapter, it is through the transactions of structural Niceness that we see state paternal benevolence work out its ongoing heteropatriarchal Whiteness against a group of White girls the school treats as deficient and in need of protection through intraschool exclusion and unbelonging.

"Niceness," writes Castagno (2014), "compels us to reframe potentially disruptive or uncomfortable things in ways that are more soothing, pleasant, and comfortable" (9). That state schooling is in part an uncomfortable site in which heteropatriarchal Whiteness carries out intraracial gender discipline through structural Niceness and in service of benevolence is not evidenced only via the disciplining expectation that women and girls be nice in interpersonal contexts. It can also be observed in the dexterity of heteropatriarchal Niceness as it organizes around the enforcement of race-specific gender roles and conduct. In some cases, adult women are too unjust, unfair, or unkind to effectuate structural Niceness. As Castagno (2014) writes of Niceness, "The actions and beliefs are always nice in relation to institutional and structural power because niceness masks structural dominance"

(167). While on the surface the school most overtly carries out this gender-race protection in relation to White girls by discursively and structurally pretending to protect them from girls of Color and from all boys, we look here at the ways in which the school produces and protects Niceness by creating and disciplining deficient White girls. This maneuver protects the school itself.

Our examination of Niceness thus moves among several of its interlocking features and functions: the overt practice of smoothing over or being paternalistic; the quiet disciplining of some White students in order to maintain the façade of Niceness; the microenactments of Niceness—by teachers, principals, counselors, and others—that protect the macroinstantiations of Niceness; and compulsory schooling and state claims to democracy through punishment. Therefore individuals, schools, and the state constantly coproduce and protect White Niceness, masking the fact that membership in Whiteness is exclusive—even to its own possible members. Whiteness is not inclusive and inviting to all Whites, but rather structurally Nice through its relations to them, including marginalization, captivity, or exclusion. Whiteness sacrifices some Whites, in part through Niceness, in order to make Whiteness itself—as the state, as culture, as norm, and so on—benevolent.

We recognize at least two limitations of this chapter: The state is not consistently present or forceful in people's lives, and people as individuals and collectives resist and/or negotiate the state in a variety of strategic, agentive ways. Our effort here is to consider just one race-gender function of state Niceness within schooling and so to map that very particular but fundamentally partial terrain.

Methodology and Context

This chapter draws data from Judge's larger qualitative study of school-year Saturday school and summer school, both of which took place at the same urban rim, New England comprehensive public high school. Saturday school ran from 8:00 a.m. to 10:00 a.m., one or two Saturdays each month—during which time students were required to remain completely silent—and was housed in a math classroom on the second floor of the high school. Situated in the back wing of the school, summer school ran for six weeks, from 8:00 a.m. to 12:00 noon, Monday through Friday. Summer school students had to use a back entrance to enter the school and were prohibited from entering other areas of the school.

According to state categories, the high school student body of approximately fifteen hundred students was 61 percent White, 17 percent African American, 10 percent Asian, 9 percent Hispanic, and about 3 percent multiracial. While the school did not keep demographic data on Saturday and summer school, Judge made observations based on both student identification of race and ethnicity and her own assumptions. These assumptions and self-definitions at times conflicted and were far more complex than state categories. Judge approximated that during summer and Saturday schools over 40 percent of students were White, over 20 percent were Black, around 30 percent were Latinx, and a small number were multiracial. The administrator in charge of summer school confirmed that of the one administrator, six summer school teachers, and four administrators monitoring Saturday school, all but one were White; one was Asian American. Of the teachers, four were male and two were female; of the administrators, two were male and two were female. The school police officer on staff for the summer was a White man.

An assistant principal explained that students were "referred to" Saturday school by grade-level administrators for a variety of behavioral infractions, including excessive tardiness (more than five days in a row), missing a detention, and swearing at a teacher. Students who received a course grade below 70 percent and above 50 percent were identified for summer school and were informed of their ability to self-enroll for the summer session, the fee for which was $250 per course. Students who had received a grade below 50 percent were ineligible for summer school and forced to repeat the course the following year. In order to pass summer school, students were required to receive a grade of 70 percent or above. These sites articulated that part of Saturday school was to "avoid" summer school. Administrators in Saturday school told Judge she would see many of the same students in summer school, which proved to be true.

Judge's study was motivated by questions about the convergence of alternative instructional contexts with disciplinary practices as they shape the schooling experiences of girls. She situated her research within critical feminist qualitative traditions, which take up gender as an intersectional phenomenon and examine its multidimensional mechanisms (Abu-Lughod 1993; Davis and Craven 2016; Fine et. al. 2003; Mohanty 1988; Narayan 1993; Pillow and Mayo 2012). With particular attention to the daily sites of mundane power, Judge mobilized feminist practices of listening and reflexivity that disrupt dominant and individualistic narratives of power. Specifically, she attended to the ways in which both her institutional position as a White woman and as one who grew up and went to public schools in the same region impacted the way that participants interacted with her. These positions both potentially forged and ruptured communication. Despite Judge's clearly communicated purpose in the school as a researcher, she was often characterized by staff as a "teacher in training" or "future teacher," fitting into the institutional narrative about White women in schools. This alignment was uneven, however. For instance, one administrator at summer school sarcastically remarked of Judge, "I didn't know we let tattooed women work here." At times Judge shared her own challenging experiences with school discipline and was deliberate about how those shaped her lines of questioning and her understanding of school events. She interviewed and observed teachers, administrative staff, and students around questions of gender, race, class, and other functions of school and social organization. Her primary interview population was students, whom she interviewed individually and in groups. The stories of the four young women herein emerge from a constellation of stories of state disciplinary practices.

Feeding the Hungry

Saturday and summer school were sites of structural Niceness that did not have to internally abide by the interpersonal norms of Niceness (Castagno 2014). Their Niceness was produced through their structural purpose and externally narrated. Administrative and teaching staff described summer school as a "second chance" or an "opportunity" for students who individually failed to take advantage of the school year. This opportunity was imagined against the backdrop of student and family deficit. In describing Saturday school, one White female senior administrator, Ms. Hunter, said, "I'll never forget this. I used to work at [high school with majority low-income students of Color]. I started my career there. The principal of the school taught me a lot and he told me, you know, 'These kids crave structure.' I'll never forget it. They do. They have these chaotic home lives, and they won't say it, but these kids actually like the discipline and structure we provide because they don't get it at home . . . they need it, it helps them." Here Ms. Hunter discursively narrates state structural Niceness by describing "structure" as responsive and generous. Through the transactions of Niceness, she lays the ongoing narrative foundation for state benevolence. As Castagno (2014) writes, "These types of discursive strategies are nice ways to talk about the sorting and selecting mechanisms in schools. The niceness serves to deflect attention and responsibility away from the fact that schools and teachers are engaged in such processes" (69). Discursively positioning students as "craving" the sorting and selecting that Saturday school bolsters was "nice." Moreover, Ms. Hunter's nice and deflecting narration of schools as fulfilling this craving positioned the disciplinary structures of Saturday schooling as benevolently paternalistic. To that end she attached the benevolence of disciplinary schooling to deficient home lives and, more specifically, pathologically deficient families. Niceness tells and retells the ongoing fiction of deficiency to reproduce the foundation for state benevolence: deficient subjects who require paternal protection and from whom fit subjects require protection.

This supremacist undergirding of individual inadequacy and home deficiency, and the production of the school as nice, was structured into the official discourse of Saturday and summer schooling. Summer school itself was designated "credit recovery" in policy and institutional discourse. Specifically, students were informed about the ways in which they could "recover" their credits—as if they individually had lost them, failed to keep track of them, been incompetent to earn them on time, discarded them, or mishandled them. Summer school was a site at which students were to recover what home had not supported during the academic year. Ms. Hunter described Saturday school as an "opportunity" for students to be doing homework when they would not otherwise be doing so on a Saturday morning at home or had not done so at home during the week, when required. Home as the "hard truth" counterpart to school was degraded and unfit. School was the state institutional iteration and expression of state Niceness, providing a space for "good" student behavior. The nice discourse of recovery bolstered the larger discourse of benevolent paternalism.

This structural Niceness buttressed the construction of the broken subject required to maintain the fiction of a benevolent state (Collins 2009; Harris 2006; Smith et al. 2004; Stein 2004). The broken, unfit subject needs correction, but must undertake this correction outside the calendar and context of the fit subject. This separation of the unfit subject highlights the punitive aspect of this state service and physically and temporally sequesters the unfit student from the fit student, who is understood to need the breaks of weekends and summers that come with good future citizenship. The unfit student is expected to pay a debt of gratitude by accepting the loss of these times (which are used for labor, family care and support, relaxation, personal health, social engagement, and artistic projects, among others) as part of his or her debt owed for failing. This feature of debt of gratitude to state Niceness was compounded by the fact that neither Saturday school nor summer school were designed for or made possible academic acceleration or excellence but rather signaled deceleration or mediocrity at best. The contexts of Saturday and summer school were therefore also the context of state semantic, transactional, and structural organizations of belonging and not belonging, inclusion and exclusion. Our context is these two school sites, where we consider how unfitness gets specifically structured in intra-White race-gender practices.

Not-Nice Girls

The state use of Niceness to construct certain White girls as deviant or deficient is a mechanism we can access by looking at the institutional experiences of such girls—that is, "not-nice" girls.

Discomfort and Nice White Guys

We start with Mareena, who told Judge she was in summer school for complex reasons stemming from difficult interactions with school staff. During summer school class times, Mareena often sat quietly in the back of the room, part of the social interactions of other students but not animatedly engaged in their conversations; yet during class discussions about race, gender, and sexuality, Mareena was confidently outspoken. She described herself as "a little harsh" and was often brash, sarcastic, and seemingly sure of her righteous defense of marginalized people. Mareena frequently wore an oversize sweatshirt and jeans, with her cropped hair feathered out in careful layers. She told Judge that her appearance and her interest

Structural Niceness and Not-Nice White Girls   245

in the school's metal shop consistently led people to see her as a lesbian, but she self-identified as straight.

In a hot, cramped guidance counselor's office nestled in the corner of the summer school wing of the high school, Judge and Mareena sat together with two other girls, good friends of Mareena. The girls began talking about why they thought they were in summer school. One girl talked about not doing her homework. Then Mareena began talking, and suddenly she seemed unsure. Her voice rising in question at the end of her sentence, she said, "Well, I was put in a class where I told the teacher—well, not even the teacher, I couldn't really talk to the teacher because I wasn't, like, comfortable with him." Trying to understand, Judge asked, "Why weren't you comfortable with the teacher?" Mareena struggled to characterize the situation and her feelings: "The classroom made me really anxious, like, I don't know the setup and where I was put, and, like, I had asked him if I could move my seat and he said no—just a flat out no. And that really never got fixed until, like, fourth quarter." The other two girls were captivated, listening quietly and nodding as if to say, *that's the way this works.*

Unable to get support from her teacher, Mareena went to her guidance counselor. With sudden clarity, Mareena said, "I talked to my guidance counselor at the beginning of the year and I said, like, 'I'm not comfortable in the class,' and I didn't really know how to explain it." With a mocking tone of flippancy, Mareena added, "And so she was like, 'Well, I can't really do anything for you.'" The guidance counselor illustrates Castagno's suggestion that Niceness protects the institution and obfuscates power. In this instance, the guidance counselor was interpersonally not nice—perhaps even rude. But as Mareena's story unfolds, we see this instance as part of the counselor's "telling 'hard truths'" (Castagno 2014, 167) to and about Mareena and the White male teachers in the building.

Mareena began to fall behind in the class. She said to the group, "I wasn't understanding things so I wasn't even doing the homework, 'cause I didn't know what to do. I don't really like staying after, *alone* with a teacher. It—I don't know—it makes me uncomfortable. So I, like, didn't feel like I could." While Mareena shared with Judge in another conversation that she had always felt comfortable around boys because she has older brothers, she consistently stood far away from male teachers—especially one who was considered a "favorite" and "nice" teacher at summer school.

Mareena's brief story illustrates one exercise of state Niceness in schooling, highlighting its narratives and their reproduction of exclusion or unbelonging. Unable to articulate a reason that fit the state's narrative of why a student would need to be switched out of a class—particularly away from a teacher—Mareena was denied the ability to make a decision that would support her academic efforts. First in this interaction was the message that Mareena could not simply dislike her class. This reasoning sits within a larger logic that high school students are assigned to, and do not choose, most of their classes. Yet exceptions to this logic are made all the time. The logic itself masks the reasons adults in a building choose to follow or not follow the logic. In this case, Mareena's discomfort with a White male teacher was stalled in part by paternalistic notions of White male teachers as good guys, notions that place them outside the fray of heteropatriarchal power. White male teachers' institutional role as benevolent state agents in the large "democratic" project of schooling generally protects them from scrutiny around powered gendered interactions that might be recognized elsewhere between an adult male and a female minor, and makes the standard for legitimate discomfort in a girl who is already excluded or marked as deficient impossibly high. Such men are often understood to have sacrificed more lucrative, status-rich careers in order to altruistically serve in a White female–dominated profession, marking the paternal state as noble by proxy.

In this instance Mareena felt she was sanctioned for being a not-nice girl. According to Castagno (2014), "A nice person is not someone who creates a lot of disturbance, conflict, controversy, or discomfort. Nice people avoid potentially uncomfortable or upsetting experiences, knowledge, and interactions" (9). Mareena was punished for creating a "controversy" or "disturbance": being "not nice." Specifically, she was not nice for privileging her upsetting interactions with a White male teacher and for seeking redress or remedy. Any doubt of White male teachers' Niceness—particularly from White girls who do not possess dominant gender-race capital, are positioned as natural wards or daughters and, in the logics of heteropatriarchy, expected to be grateful for the attentions of men in the "caring professions"—is suspicious and not nice. Nice White girls do not complain about nice White men who are serving the greater good. Mareena did not possess or perform a White female gender identity that accrued greater institutional status, value, or empathic qualities (Bettie 2003). Not-nice White girls are often compelled into structural quietness, a core feature of structural Niceness.

Also at play in Mareena's interaction with the guidance counselor was that if her reason to leave the class was that she was "anxious," she was faced with the decision of whether or not to state that her discomfort stemmed from her own very individual difficulties—namely, anxiety and mental health. This pathologization of Mareena, even if narrated by her, was a function of the state protecting its own Niceness. White girls' discomfort with nice White men can be nicely attributed to the girls' psychological or behavioral deficiencies—again, their unfitness or unbelonging. Moreover, anxiety retells the hard truth about some White girls in that it plots out their imagined, gendered, psychological conditions of frailty and eclipses any view of school-based patriarchal violences that might be seen through the lens of very real anxiety. In this narrative of structural Niceness, Mareena would have had to present herself as someone in need of repair, correction, or treatment in order to escape a negative classroom situation. School-based treatment furthers the state's confidence in its Niceness. Specifically, the state can offer to support, treat, or accommodate a girl by converting her anxiety, produced by a male teacher, into a pathology in need of some repair. The repair may entail the girl going back and being appropriately, submissively nice in relation to the White male teacher or accepting heteropatriarchal structures and practices of predation and subordination that uphold Whiteness. Mareena's Whiteness matters especially here, as White male state benevolence hinges on the quiet, even if coerced, acquiescence of White girls.

Judge learned that a third feature of this interaction was that several of the girls who identified themselves as struggling with mental health faced the coerced relinquishment of privacy at school. Mareena did not use her very real anxiety as a strategy, because like many of the other girls in summer and Saturday school she had learned from her own experience and others' that the consequence would be school invasion into her private life. She said she was unwilling to surrender what privacy she had.

State Concern: The Nice Invasion of Privacy

In a separate conversation, another White female student, River, described this invasive ruse of care: "I think that my *therapist* and my *mom* should be worrying about me, and myself. I don't think, like, they [school staff] *care* . . . they jus', like, want me to get good grades and get outta high school. That's it." River captured the material irony of this nice, invasive uncaring. She said "the school," especially the counselors, consistently insisted on talking to her therapist. When she responded to this insistence with anger, counselors then told her that her anger was an individual problem through which she was impairing her own ability to succeed. The school weaponized River's real struggles in order to accomplish its nice and unsupportive goals of grades and graduation for White girls.

For Mareena, protecting her privacy meant in part removing herself from the uncomfortable classroom situation, given that she was unwilling to submit to it. The consequence of structural Niceness was that Mareena stopped going to that class. As a result, she was issued a non-credit-bearing grade and referred to summer school. Her protection of her own privacy against the nice state made her seem an unfit subject who was not afforded inclusion, largely because of her failure to accept the gendered hierarchies of Whiteness.

In discussing these negotiations of privacy, another White girl in the group, Morgan, jumped in and described a White female teacher who would reprimand her for missing class. As Morgan, an impeccably dressed young woman who was quiet in class but very outspoken outside it, explained,

> If I didn't show up or like I was absent, the next day she would be
> like, "Oh, you're here." And she would kinda like make me feel bad

about, like, not being there. Like, certain days, I know last year I had
a lot of days I was like out because doctor's office visits and stuff. So,
um, like, I'd bring in, like, the note and I had her during second
period, so during second period I'd asked to go to the office to
give them the note. Um, so I would ask her to, like, go, and she's like,
"Oh, your note's not real." She would just kinda say, I shouldn't have
been out, even if I had a note.

Then, her voice trailing off, Morgan said, as if in resignation, "And it was like,
'Okay.'" "Okay" stood in sharp contrast to Morgan's very agentive personality. In
fact, in her conversations with Judge, she mentioned events, times, and school practices most often through nonchalant descriptions of physical altercations she
had—specifically those she engaged in to stand up for herself or others. She was
seemingly fearless. As she said "Okay," she shook her head, gesturing defeat.

Morgan's truancy and unabashed confidence marked her as noncompliant and
thus not grateful for the Niceness of the school. Therefore, her private medical
needs—those rights of belonging through bodily health that denote future
citizenship—were dismissed. Her teacher was able to deny the legitimacy of the
physician's notes and put Morgan in a situation without recourse: further unexcused
truancy, this time without a physician's note. Therefore, the teacher's protection
of the integrity of the school—as a place that should not be manipulated or
mistreated by false claims—produced a condition for Morgan in which she
could make no claim except for the unrecognized claim of discomfort.

When Morgan finished telling this story, Mareena turned to her and said,
"In that situation, that's none of her business how long you're there and how long
you're not. That's something to put up with, like, the office, and, like, the principals
and stuff. I feel like teachers are very nosey, like, they like to stick their nose in
everything. And, like, they do notice a lot." Mareena distinguished for Morgan
who it was that should have the institutional purview over truancy. She also challenged one feature of the nice White heteropatriarchal state: White maternalism
and the quiet ability for White female teachers to socialize White girls into White
womanhood. Those girls who did not want that socialization were automatically
suspicious, cast as deceitful and liars. Nice White girls took their illnesses to the
school, for support. Again, nice White girlness required the abdication of privacy
and the invitation of state intervention and parental usurpation. Not-nice White
girls did not have believable medical needs; they lacked the right to belong to the
community of people who deserve bodily care. The rhetorical positioning conveyed
not-nice White girls as in need of more care (but only through school-sanctioned
treatment apparatuses) that at once bolstered the structural Niceness of the school
and further reproduced the not-Niceness of the White girls who refused this
benevolent invasion.

Trade and the Vocation of Niceness

The quiet disciplining Niceness of parental usurpation, violation of privacy, and the slow unbelonging of White girls was amplified by the structures of schooling. These four White girls, sent to summer school, were also enrolled in the institution's trade school, which shared a building and some core content curriculum with the comprehensive school. Trade school students were 12 percent Whiter, 12 percent more low-income, and 21 percent more often labeled with a disability than students at the comprehensive high school. The trade school comprised 65 percent male and 35 percent female students; the programs in cosmetology, nursing, and child care leaned more heavily female, while the programs in auto body work, metal shop work, automotive technology, engineering, carpentry and construction, robotics, and electrical work, among others, leaned more heavily male. As with most institutions in the state, the school did not keep demographic data broken down by race *and* gender, nor did it keep track of data for programs.

River sat on the edge of her seat, leaning her body forward emphatically as she expressed frustration about the skewed racial dimensions of the cosmetology program. She explained that while cosmetology was entirely female, only a very small number of students were girls of Color. "It focused more on the White—the White people," she explained. "It was a bunch of bull," she said as she explained how they only learned how to do "White hair." The state failure to keep program demographic records by race and gender in a school disproportionately White and male causes us to wonder why. What could these records reveal about the race and gender organization of the school?

Students enrolled in the trade school did weekly rotations across the programs to fulfill an elective requirement; these were the only times that the gender sorting of the school was disrupted. This elective rotation highlighted the rigid gender boundaries the school organization produced, as one student's story illustrates. Brooke's experience was a small window into the gender boundaries of the trade school and the function of Niceness in producing such rigid organization. Brooke looked and sounded tired all summer. Her deep brown eyes were generally fixed on something in the distance, and she rarely made direct eye contact. In class she was often a few seconds behind everyone else, seemingly off in her own world, disengaged from the interactions around her. She spoke with a strong accent attached to regional White working-class cultures. In reflecting on her school experiences, Brooke described herself as having struggled with depression and anxiety for some time, but she also highlighted her class status in thinking through her gendered experiences: "I feel like, between, like, the rich people and the *not*-so-rich people—and they get, like, treated better and we don't. 'Cause, like, if you don't have money then yer, like, *nobody*. If yer not pretty, yer nobody. That's how, like, society is nowadays, and it sucks." Even so, Brooke tried to perform as the nice girl—a girl inherently not poor, not depressed or anxious, not unattractive, and not failing.

Brooke explained calmly, "Every year I try my hardest to be like one of those [teachers' favorites], but it never happens."

"What do you do to try?" asked Judge.

"Like, I do all my work. And, like, I even help. I don't go to lunch, 'cause, like, the people, so I stay in, like, classrooms and, like, clean their rooms. I still don't be their favorite." Brooke paused. Dismayed, she said, "But, like, one kid, like the smahtest kid, gets the favorite, and he doesn't do nothin.'"

Brooke saw herself as categorically poor and responded in part by trying to be a good girl—a helper. She was not able to actually do the work of school, however—only the helping on the side. Poor helpers are imagined as fit to be assistants, custodians, lunch ladies, and so on, but not future citizens of the professions or the wives thereof, and therefore not nice White girls. Moreover, her location as a trade school student signaled her deficiency and not-Niceness. Nice girls, or what some administrators called "good girls," were in the aspirational, honors academic tracks, regardless of their future relationship to heteropatriarchal structures. The trade school was not preparing people for the upper echelons of White supremacy but was rather a more explicit social reproduction, a tracking mechanism, perhaps creating a student pipeline into employment, but not further education and not high-status employment. The Whiteness of the trade school helped to mask this sorting and excluding function, which was only further evident in the school's predominance of low-income, disability-labeled students. It was a structural site of the making of "other" Whites, those whose blue-collar success undergirded dominant White heteropatriarchal power, in part by producing rigid gender tracks and punishments through its programs.

Brooke's experience at the trade school further integrated White male freedom from scrutiny and the school's structural Niceness. In the same guidance counselor's office where Judge interviewed Morgan, Mareena, and another girl, Brooke and Judge met one morning with two other students. The three students were not close friends, but rather classmates for the summer. Brooke sat in the middle, her hands resting gently on her floral-patterned tank-top dress, rarely leaving her lap except to occasionally tuck a stray hair behind her ear. The group was talking about students reporting racist incidents to one of the assistant principals, and how he did not respond to these complaints but rather seemed to protect teachers who had been there "for a long time." Brooke talked about reporting a teacher at the trade school for what we identify as sexual harassment.

"There's this auto body teacher," said Brooke. "We were doin' rotations [required electives], and I remember goin' up to [the assistant principal, a White woman] 'cause he would not stop looking at me and I felt so uncomfortable." As she spoke, her voice faltered and trailed off. Like Mareena, Brooke expressed being uncomfortable with a White male teacher. Discomfort was an inherent condition of these girls' schooling, because it was something the school could produce but refused to recognize or ameliorate. It placed the girls in a constant state of distress and partial self-doubt that negatively mediated their learning. As one girl said, capturing the expressions of many others, "So, I didn't really like him, I wasn't comfortable and I couldn't focus." All four girls shared their experiences of ceasing their attendance in stressful classes, and it had obvious impact on their grades.

Brooke said, "Like, I tried to get switched out of that rotation. He [the teacher] would keep staring at me. And, like, I would wear—like, not low, but, like, you could see, like, the line [pointing to her bra line], and he would stare, and I was like, 'Oh, no.'" She said "Oh no" not with aggression, but instead with a mixture of fear, anticipation, and despair. Brooke continued: "Like, I'd be doin' this every second [holding her dress neckline up to her collarbone], and when we would, like—I don't know, for the cars, you hadda, like, clean the cars. And I would be doin' that, and he would still be looking, and I'm like, uh . . ." She was visibly disgusted in recounting his actions, but also talking freely with the group, as if this was so commonplace and such common knowledge that there was no secrecy or privacy about it among students.

"So I asked to go—every day I think I asked to go to the bathroom, but I would just skip that period. I would, like—I would still go, but I would, like—once I got one look and I would, like, leave. He's *still there*, and, like, he sees me in the hall, but I don't think he remembers my name. Which is good." While Brooke was glad to be anonymous to the predatory teacher, her sense that this was "good" revealed something about the discipline of not-nice White girls: the opposite of objectification and harassment was anonymity and namelessness, not agency, protection, retribution, or remediation. Judge heard this from all the White girls she interviewed. The desire for anonymity, for just wanting it to stop, for wanting to be recognized for good deeds—cleaning up, helping out—for not wanting to drop out, tells us something about Brooke and her peers, but also about state conditioning of certain White girls. Schooling conditions such girls to move just under the radar, to make no waves, but in doing so they gain little; they merely manage to function. Their quietly and systematically produced discomfort is a repressive feature of Niceness, one that hinges on their staying present bodily, but without agency.

Brooke went on to describe the conditions at the trade school: "Even the culinary teacher, he's so weird. Like, he comes in cosmo [cosmetology] and looks at all the girls. All the girls in cosmo, like, talks, like, 'Oh he's so weird.' Even the teachers—we, like, talk to the teachers about him. And, like, he would, like, take pictures of people without, like, permission." In spite of her having reported this to the assistant principal, and many students having complained to teachers, nothing ever came of the complaints.

This pattern of school nonresponse to these girls' discomfort with White male teacher behavior echoed the pattern in the main school, where Mareena had complained. It was exaggerated by the structure of the trade school, where students were funneled into school-identified gender-appropriate programs. As River explained during a different one-on-one interview, "I honestly don't think the people that are in nontraditional shops, like the girls in the guy shop and the guys in the girl shops, I don't think that [the] trade [school] wants that to happen, because they always try to stop it." Niceness at the trade school was built into gender separation along dominant notions of appropriate learning and vocation. Future roles in labor and society were delineated along traditional skill lines, and any disruption of the status quo was seen as not being nice to a state offering the generous, free preparation for blue-collar belonging.

Brooke's experience of harassment went unacknowledged by the school because she was not meant to be a permanent member of the class. She was temporarily in the wrong place, taking a brief elective class that was a sort of nice gesture toward exposure to other programs. The teacher's sexual harassment was school-based instruction to Brooke, teaching her where she should and should not be learning. The auto shop was a White man's space, and such spaces are only thought of as unsafe to women if women "wrongly" choose to enter them—survivors of sexual assault, for instance, being blamed for attendance at the party where they were assaulted. So nice White working-class girls take up Niceness in schooling by staying in appropriate skill-based programs such as cosmetology.

Additionally, according to Brooke, the cosmetology teachers, who were White women, were involved in conversation with students about the predatory auto body teacher. While they listened to the girls and did not defend the male teacher, Brooke said they did not report his behavior. This, too, was instructive. We wonder here about their institutional location as female teachers of cosmetology: What is the expectation for race and gender Niceness in state schooling in this track of the trade school? What is the expectation in relation to other teachers or in relation to the administration? How do these teachers compare to White female teachers in the main school who are certified to teach in the core content, or "academic," areas? We are curious about how their institutional location models and constructs a subordinate White female identity featured by quiet discomfort in students. What does the absolute absence of female teachers on the male side of the trade school teach young women about the gendered power relations of Whiteness?

Moreover, we see resonances with White hair salons and auto shops in the world of private business. The former is imagined in popular culture as a site where women—as customers and hairdressers—might get together to talk and complain about bad male behavior in order to trade confidential advice but perhaps not to collectively take action. The auto shop is imagined as a site of White male domination, depicted as decorated with nude centerfold calendars and lewd jokes, maybe a beer can or two in the trash—not a domain to be regulated by *anyone*. We wonder, then, if there are pedagogical and curricular matches between society, the trade school, and the main school that resulted in a disproportionate number of the girls in summer school coming from the trade school side. Judge observed that the trade school girls were particularly conditioned into the excuse of Niceness leveraged in favor of White male teachers.

As we consider excuse as a feature of structural Niceness, we turn to Castagno's (2014) suggestion, "Niceness functions to at once neutralize dominance and maintain it. Dominance, inequity, and fundamentally whiteness are neutralized through niceness" (174). This neutralization of dominance was evident in the excuse-laden protection of White male administrators and teachers. In summer school, students from both the main school and the trade school complained repeatedly in particular about one White male administrator. Summer school students described him as "the worst," "harsh," and "unfair." In a group with Brooke, one student said many students had complained to this administrator about racism and he "didn't do anything." A White male summer school teacher said that the students thought there was no follow-up to their complaints, but they did not know what "goes on behind the scenes." This teacher struggled to be structurally nice, both to the students and this administrator. He said the administrator was just trying to "protect confidentiality" and that the students did not understand the complexity of the follow-up to their complaints. He said, "He's a nice guy." The teacher's mobilization of the "nice guy" trope also animated state Niceness. As Castagno (2014) writes, nice people "do not point out failures or shortcomings in others but rather emphasize the good, the promise, and the improvement we see. . . . This avoidance and reframing are done with the best intentions, and having good intentions is a critical component of niceness. In fact, as long as one means well, the actual impact of one's behavior, discourse, or action is often meaningless" (9). Here, the administrator's nice-guyness made the hidden and mysterious policies and practices of the school nice; it made lack of transparency nice; it made failure to follow up nice, and positioned students as ungrateful and naive—not just to the administrator but more so to the benevolent state. It also aligned the White male teacher with the structure and practice of the school.

While Brooke, River, Morgan, and Mareena were critical of the practices and alignments of structural Niceness, they were variously conditioned by their punishments for not behaving nicely in the context of the trade school, and so were generally resigned. Detailing the previous school year's exhausting struggle over her schedule and curriculum with the administration, River said of the administrator's unfairness, "I'm too tired to fight. It's tiring."

Exhaustion

River's tiredness came from constantly battling her location outside nice White girlness. Standing no taller than five feet, she regularly wore large T-shirts and sweatshirts that swallowed her frame and were adorned with images of heavy metal bands and zombie faces. She affected a nervous half smile that was disjointed from her sometimes-shaved, sometimes-dyed (blue or orange) hair and her bold confidence.

When River started high school, she was the only girl in the auto shop program, which she described as a "passion." During summer school, both Mareena and River spoke about the difficulty navigating the male spaces of the trade school shops; there was "a lot of goofing around," "jokes about other girls in the school," and teachers and boys consistently underestimating the girls' abilities. River switched to cosmetology in part because of these structural issues that made the environment not serious enough and overtly hostile.

As River explained, "No matter how many times I would talk to [the shop teacher] about me doing on-field work, he—he would say yes, but then he would give it to the high school kids and the other trade kids that were guys, and I would be—and I would get stuck doing, like, the computer work. Which is like, um, putting the bills in and stuff like that. So I know the whole system, but—." She was frustrated. She was tired. And she was sad. Disappointment characterized her descriptions. As Brown (1992) states, "Male power, like state power, is real but largely intangible except for the occasions when it is expressed as violence, physical coercion, or outright discrimination" (15). We suggest that Niceness highlights the structurally powered White male characteristics of interpersonal interactions that might otherwise go undetected as benevolent state power.

The quiet marginalization of certain White girls and the maintenance of their roles allows the ongoing construction of female instability and reconstitutes the school's role as care provider through gendered control and subordination. Such paternalist White maneuvers draw from the benevolent "protection codes" that Brown (1992) identifies as "key technologies in regulating privileged women as well as in intensifying the vulnerability and degradation of those on the unprotected side of the constructed divide between light and dark, wives and prostitutes, good girls and bad ones" (9)—and, in the internal state construction of Whiteness, we would add, nice and not nice. Schools exercise an intraracial gendered Niceness that quietly degrades some White girls, building the unbelonging necessary for the fortification of the nice White heteropatriarchal state. We imagine a rich investigation into this very specific exercise of Niceness as part of a critical project in understanding and thus disrupting supremacist race and gender organizations of power. "Neither state power nor male dominance are unitary or systematic," argues Brown (1992), so a "feminist theory of state will be less a linear argument than a mapping of an intricate grid of often conflicting strategies, technologies, and discourses of power" (14).

Structural Niceness in schooling is a semiotics of intra-White narratives that reproduce the materiality of state race-gender domination. These narratives are mechanized transactions that undergird and convey paternal benevolence. Further study of structural Niceness might aid in mapping the perniciously mundane and evasive stories of how benevolence works itself out through the making of deficient Whites through class and gender *failures* at nice Whiteness—that is, not-Niceness—and how all of this serves to discipline students of color. This state-structured storytelling of the imagined inherent unbelonging of certain White girls is one site of the spectacular normalization of White heteropatriarchal dominance.

Note

1. In this chapter, we touch on the rich theoretical traditions of the state. For further reading on feminist analyses of the state, see the work of, among many others, Sara Ahmed, Wendy Brown, Kimberlé Crenshaw, Nancy Fraser, Inderpal Grewal, Angela Harris, Joy James, Chandra Mohanty, and Patricia Williams.

References

Abu-Lughod, L. 1993. *Writing Women's Worlds: Bedouin Stories.* Berkeley: University of California Press.

Agamben, G. 2005. *State of Exception.* Translated by K. Attell. Chicago: University of Chicago Press.

Anderson, B. 2006. *Imagined Communities.* Rev. ed. New York: Verso.

Bell, D. 1992. *Faces at the Bottom of the Well: The Permanence of Racism.* New York: Basic Books.

Bell, D. 2004. *Silent Covenants: Brown v. Board of Education and the Unfulfilled Hopes for Racial Reform.* Oxford: Oxford University Press.

Berlant, L. G. 1997. *The Queen of America Goes to Washington City: Essays on Sex and Citizenship.* Durham, N.C.: Duke University Press.

Bettie, J. 2003. *Women without Class: Girls, Race, and Identity.* Berkeley: University of California Press.

Bonilla-Silva, E., and S. Mayorga. 2011. "On (Not) Belonging: Why Citizenship Does Not Remedy Racial Inequality." In *State of White Supremacy: Racism, Governance, and the United States,* edited by M.-K. Jung, J. H. Costa Vargas, and E. Bonilla-Silva, 77–91. Stanford, Calif.: Stanford University Press.

Bracey, G. E. 2015. "Toward a Critical Race Theory of State." *Critical Sociology* 41, no. 3: 553–72.

Brayboy, B. M. 2005. "Toward a Tribal Critical Race Theory in Education." *Urban Review* 37, no. 5: 425–46.

Brown, W. 1992. "Finding the Man in the State." *Feminist Studies* 18, no. 1: 7–34.

Canaday, M. 2009. *The Straight State: Sexuality and Citizenship in Twentieth-Century America.* Princeton, N.J.: Princeton University Press.

Castagno, A. E. 2014. *Educated in Whiteness: Good Intentions and Diversity in Schools.* Minneapolis: University of Minnesota Press.

Collins, P. H. 2009. *Another Kind of Public Education: Race, Schools, the Media, and Democratic Possibilities.* Boston: Beacon.

Davis, D., and C. Craven. 2016. *Feminist Ethnography: Thinking through Methodologies, Challenges, and Possibilities.* Lanham, Md.: Rowman and Littlefield.

Fine, M., L. Weis, S. Weseen, and L. Wong. 2003. "For Whom? Qualitative Research, Representations, and Social Responsibilities." In *The Landscape of Qualitative Research*, 2nd ed., edited by N. K. Denzin and Y. S. Lincoln, 167–207. Thousand Oaks, Calif.: Sage.

Fraser, N. 1990. "Rethinking the Public Sphere: A Contribution to the Critique of Actually Existing Democracy." *Social Text* 25–26: 56–80.

Guinier, L. 2004. "From Racial Liberalism to Racial Literacy: *Brown v. Board of Education* and the Interest-Divergence Dilemma." *Journal of American History* 91, no. 1: 92–118.

Harris, A. P. 2006. "From Stonewall to the Suburbs? Toward a Political Economy of Sexuality." *William and Mary Bill of Rights Journal* 14, no. 4: 1539–1629.

Harris, C. 1993. "Whiteness as Property." *Harvard Law Review* 106, no. 8: 1709–91.

Jung, M.-K. 2011. "Constituting the US Empire-State and White Supremacy." In *State of White Supremacy: Racism, Governance, and the United States*, edited by M.-K. Jung, J. H. Costa Vargas, and E. Bonilla-Silva, 1–23. Stanford, Calif.: Stanford University Press.

Meiners, E. R. 2015. "Trouble with the Child in the Carceral State." *Social Justice* 41, no. 3: 120–44.

Mohanty, C. T. 1988. "Under Western Eyes: Feminist Scholarship and Colonial Discourses." In *Feminist Theory: A Reader*, 3rd ed., edited by W. K. Kolmar and F. Bartkowski, 319–27. New York: McGraw-Hill.

Narayan, K. 1993. "How Native is a 'Native' Anthropologist?" *American Anthropologist* 95, no. 3: 671–86.

Pillow, W. S., and C. Mayo. 2012. "Feminist Ethnography: Histories, Challenges, and Possibilities." In *Handbook of Feminist Research: Theory and Praxis,* 2nd ed., edited by S. N. Hesse-Biber, 187–205. Thousand Oaks, Calif.: Sage.

Robinson, C. 2000. *Black Marxism: The Making of the Black Radical Tradition.* Chapel Hill, N.C.: University of North Carolina Press.

Smith, M. L., L. Miller-Kahn, W. Heinecke, and P. F. Jarvis. 2004. *Political Spectacle and the Fate of American Schools.* New York: RoutledgeFalmer.

Somers, M. R. 2008. *Genealogies of Citizenship: Markets, Statelessness, and the Right to Have Rights.* New York: Cambridge University Press.

Stein, S. J. 2004. *The Culture of Education Policy.* New York: Teachers College Press.

Vaught, S. E. 2017. *Compulsory: Education and the Dispossession of Youth in a Prison School.* Minneapolis: University of Minnesota Press.

Williams, P. J. 1991. *The Alchemy of Race and Rights.* Cambridge, Mass.: Harvard University Press.

15

"She's Such a Nasty Woman"

Nice and Nasty as Gendered Tropes

Frances J. Riemer

During the final debate in the 2016 candidacy for the U.S. presidency, Donald Trump famously referred to his opponent, Hillary Rodham Clinton, as "such a nasty woman." Clinton was answering the moderator's question concerning taxes when Mr. Trump muttered the phrase into his microphone. His "nasty woman" comment immediately went viral on social media and became a hashtag and a slogan emblazoned across T-shirts and protest placards. The phrase was reclaimed in a poem read at the 2017 Women's March on Washington and in *The Nasty Woman Project: Voices from the Resistance* (Passons 2017), a compilation of women's stories written in response to Trump's presidential election win. "Nasty Woman" has a Wikipedia entry. *People* magazine (Quinn 2016) asserted that Trump's reproach became "a battle cry," and *HuffPost* (Gray 2016) called the term a "badge of honor." As one of *HuffPost*'s interviewees explained, "If she's nasty, I want to be a nasty woman too."

Both the "nasty woman" reprimand and the co-opted meme provide an opportune entry point to a discussion about the gendered tropes of nasty and nice. After all, everyone knew what Trump was suggesting. "A nasty woman" runs counter to Western beliefs about gender norms. The English nursery rhyme tells us that little girls are made of "sugar and spice and everything nice." If anyone is nasty, it will be boys, who are made of "snips and snails and puppy-dogs' tails." Drawing on empirical studies, cultural analyses, and literary sources, this chapter examines the ways Niceness and the antipodal mean girl and nasty woman tropes are gendered and racialized. Employing a feminist lens, this critical cultural analysis queries the gendered nature of Niceness discourse and practices as enacted across race, class, sexuality, and culture.

If You Don't Have Anything Nice to Say, Just Smile

The elder of two daughters in a first-generation white European immigrant American family, I grew up hearing a good deal about Niceness. We were taught to be polite; we were told to be nice. "If you don't have anything nice to say, just smile," was my mother's unquestioned and unquestioning mantra, and "Play nice, girls" was a much-repeated refrain. Being good, being nice, was to be an essential part of the ways my sister and I were to interact with the world.

In her cultural history, Bramen (2017) argues that Niceness has been an indispensable part of the American character. Niceness, Bramen explains, plays a role in "a particular fantasy of American exceptionalism, one based not on military and economic might but on friendliness and openness." Niceness, she asserts, defined the attitudes of the settler nation, and intersects with femininity, Native American hospitality, and Black amiability. In our immigrant family, Niceness related to a desire for acceptance and membership. We were to be American girls, and in American society, girls' behavior in particular is shaped by expectations of Niceness. A wide range of researchers argue that in the contexts of compulsory heterosexuality, one performs one's girlness by being nice—that is, being good, caring, nurturing, sexually innocent, and respectable (Hey 1997; Kehily 2002; Renold 2005; Walkerdine 1997).

One facet of Niceness is the use of a smile in interaction. Nice girls smile, and in their meta-analysis of 162 research reports on smiling, LaFrance, Hecht, and Paluck (2003) found that starting from early childhood, girls learned to disguise unhappiness, defuse anger, and alleviate pain with a smile. By five years of age, girls are more likely than boys to smile when they receive a disappointing gift (Cole 1985). Among adults, men said that they smiled less than women (Korzenny, Korzenny, and Sanchez de Rota 1985); both men and women agreed with that assessment (Briton and Hall 1995; Kramer 1977). Studies have also shown that nonsmiling women are judged more negatively than nonsmiling men (Deutsch, LeBaron, and Fryer 1987) and smiling men are perceived to be less effective than nonsmiling men (Kierstead, D'Agostino, and Dill 1988). In addition, women more than men anticipate that others will think less well of them if they do not smile in response to a friend's good news (LaFrance 1997). Across the studies, women and adolescent girls not only smile more than men and adolescent boys but are also expected to do so. Gender norms for smiling, like gender norms more broadly, appear to be imposed by self (Fiske and Stevens 1993) and others (Fischer 1993).

Smiling is a social requirement for women. While Wierzbicka (1995) has observed that cheerfulness is mandatory in many cultures, Hochschild (2003) has noted that some workers are required to smile as part of their jobs. Airline flight attendants, for example, must smile and smile well. According to Hochschild (2003), a flight attendant is trained to "really work on her smiles" and is expected to "manage her heart" in such a way as to create a smile that seems both "spontaneous and sincere" (105). Hartley (1993, 135) differentiated smiling professions (on-screen media personalities, teachers, therapists, and caregivers) from nonsmiling professions (in law, medicine, and science, which "have retained a straight faced craggy-jawed masculism, especially in the higher echelons"). This professional bifurcation suggests that normative women's professions require smiling, while men's work involves straight-faced seriousness.

Smile, Honey, You're Such a Pretty Girl

In 2016, articles began to appear in the popular press addressing women and smiling. *Atlantic* magazine (Smith 2016) collected readers' stories on the sexism of women being told to smile by strangers and male colleagues. Female college professors complained that "fewer smiles would mean lower student evaluations," and business administrators admitted being "infuriated" by constant admonishments to smile. "Don't Tell Me to Smile" has become a slogan on T-shirts sold by feminist apparel websites, and the phrase has garnered a page on Pinterest—both sure signs that the sentiment has morphed into a campaign.

Feminist theorists have complicated expectations around gender, providing the groundwork for this critique of norms of Niceness and related expectations to smile. Situating gender as social construct (Beauvoir 1989), organizing principle (Acker 1992), and performative practice (Butler 1990), feminists are well positioned to examine Niceness and nastiness as a "stylized repetition of acts" through which one constitutes a gendered self (Butler 1988).

Writing at the height of liberal feminism, Fox (1977) described Niceness as a "normative restriction" (805) of particular societies internalized by women themselves. Niceness, Fox argued, is a Western form of control over the social behavior of women, requiring women to be "chaste, gentle, gracious, ingenuous, good, clean, kind, virtuous, noncontroversial, and above suspicion and reproach" (807). And unlike confinement and protection practices found in non-Western societies, normative control extends over women's entire lives, regardless of marital status, sexual orientation, or age. Since Niceness is an *achieved rather than ascribed status*, "every woman can learn to be a lady, every woman is expected to act like one" (809). Niceness ascribes behavior (e.g., nice girls don't hitchhike), particular locations (e.g., nice girls don't visit bars unaccompanied), and temporal restrictions (e.g., nice girls don't go out alone at night). Fox's anthropological lens suggests that Niceness as normative construct "has the virtue of subtlety; it gives the appearance of nonrestriction and noncontrol, thus reducing the potential for resistance" (816).

In the subsequent four decades, feminist writers have become far more explicit in their naming of Niceness and the requisite smile as tyrannical mechanisms of control (Brown and Gilligan 1992; Sommers 2005; Waldman 2013). Brown and Gilligan (1992) argue that Niceness is a quality girls work hard to develop rather than being innate or automatic. Niceness is a form of social control, they assert, that appears as self-control, restrains women's voices, and is "a means of controlling and being controlled" (45). Sommers (2005) calls the outcome a "tyranny of Niceness" that translates to both a "deference and obedience to authority" and a "denial of the need to speak" (21). Going one step further, Sommers applies a disease model to the effects of this tyranny, referring to a story in O magazine in which Jane Fonda confessed to being afflicted with the "disease"—one that Oprah Winfrey herself professes to be suffering from. Nice girl has become a syndrome (Engel 2010), complete with inspirational stories and a recipe of prescriptions for curing the condition that include expressing one's anger, standing up for oneself, and putting others' feelings first.

Indeed, some semblance of nice girl syndrome also plays out in women's apprehension around salary negotiations. In experimental studies, Bowles, Babcock, and Lai (2007) found that women were more reluctant to negotiate wage levels. When they did, male evaluators tended to punish them for negotiating. Society rewards women for feminine ideals of modesty, Niceness, warmth, and sensitivity to others, and often penalizes women for engaging in the kind of competitive, self-promoting behaviors that are accepted as appropriate for men. As lower-status group members making claims to the privileges of higher-status group members, women are likely to appear inappropriately demanding if they attempt to negotiate for higher levels of compensation.

But for some girls, Niceness can be a "subversive strategy" (Hains 2008, 77). Girl studies, an interdisciplinary field that gained prominence in the 1990s, offered a reframing of Niceness. Drawing on the concept of girl power, acting nice can "make intelligence and power acceptable, even though broader social forces encourage girls' passivity and apparent disinterest in book smarts." Stressing that girls can be nice, "strong, smart, and capable," girl power cartoons offer supergirl characters that show strong, intelligent girls as "culturally valuable" (70). Girl power, in Goffmanesque fashion, positions Niceness as a strategy for intelligent girls' impression management.

An Intersectionality of Niceness

Niceness as impression management also appears in Dollard and Davis's (1940) classic study of young African American men and women in the urban South. There Niceness corresponded with a morality that emulated white middle-class standards of self-control and cleanliness. The webbing of class, race, and social responsibility suggests that Niceness may be not only a gendered norm but also one that is racialized and classed. The equating of girls and Niceness has been critiqued as overessentializing a first world, Anglocentric frame (Griffin 2004). In introducing intersectionality to the methodological and theoretical lexicon, feminist theorists argue that an analysis of the social and cultural requires a focus on overlapping constructs of gender, race, class, sexuality, and age within a larger political and sociocultural context (Collins 1990; Crenshaw 1991). Considering Niceness, then, as a set of gendered and racialized, as well as classed (and even age-based) practices, becomes a requisite complexity.

For African American and Creole girls in New Orleans (Simmons 2015), being nice meant staying in school, keeping a distance from boys, and abstaining from sex, fights, and alcohol. Nice girls could come from any neighborhood or class background in the city, as long as they followed the rules. "There was a certain cachet, a self-respect, afforded to nice girls, which provided a positive self-identity where one was not always available. To be a nice Black girl meant retaining dignity in a segregated world" (124). Yet since Niceness also meant being "cleaner and more refined" (132), in reality the pursuit of Niceness was far more difficult for girls from families with fewer resources and supports than for those from middle-class homes.

Niceness also plays a salient role for Hawaiian girls in Yano's (2016) study of beauty pageants and the Hawaiian Cherry Blossom Festival (CBF). For festival participants, Niceness is a public performance. An ethnic festival celebrating young women of Japanese heritage, its festival queen contestants are chosen based on their "commitment to the perpetuation of Japanese culture," community service, and continuing education (Genegabus 2017). In this context, Niceness looks like middle-class politeness with a Hawaiian spin: "The girl next door of the CBF rewards humility over ambition, self-effacement over self-aggrandizement, and blending in over standing out" (Yano 2016, 4). In both examples, Niceness plays a crucial role in signaling merit in racialized communities. Niceness communicates a desire to be accepted by the larger society, and is what Yano calls "public proof of assimilation" (5).

So What about Nice Men?

We like nice men; think Alan Alda, Hugh Grant, Tom Hanks, and Jimmy Stewart. These counters to normative masculinity (Pfell 2002) offer boyishness, decency, and virtuousness. These nice guys illustrate "the social tactics of Niceness, compliance, and liberal tolerance" (Rutherford 1997, 46). They are dependable but not threatening, and illustrate both traditional charm and modern feminist values. But because gender is performance, Niceness tends to be incompatible with typical male activities. Clark and Paechter's (2007) study of football and masculinity, for example, provides a compelling instance of sports as performance of masculinity. Playground football works through highly gendered dynamics that exclude girls. Niceness is positioned as opposed to the qualities needed to play well.

Nice guys have also become a syndrome, one that speaks to the gendering of Niceness. According to popular nomenclature, *nice guy syndrome* describes a man whose kindness to a woman leads to romantic feelings on the part of the man but not the woman. When the feelings are not reciprocated, the man then blames his Niceness for the rejection ("Nice Guy Syndrome," n.d.). This stereotype of male Niceness, rejection, and subsequent resentment plays into a narrative of masculinity that suggests that nice men finish last. Research (Herold and Milhausen 1999; Urbaniak and Kilmann 2003) conducted on women's dating and mating preferences, however, complicates this narrative. In reality, nice guys don't finish last. While women value both physical appearance and Niceness, they seek out nice men for long-term relationships.

Bad Girls and Nasty Women

If Niceness is a control mechanism, then bitchiness and meanness are an expected counterpoint (Chesney-Lind and Irwin 2004; Ringrose and Renold 2010). Bad girl, dirty girl, bitchy female, and nasty woman become the antipode of nice. Bad girls disrupt the social order and, in particular, they upend feminine norms. Faludi (1991) argues that society's framing of women consists of these opposing "instructional pairs." In this case, Niceness functions as a carrot, nastiness as stick. Following this line of thought, Trump's "nasty woman" was as close to a gendered punch to his female opponent as the pugilist candidate could throw on national television.

Badness as a category is punitive. It suggests deviance, a character defect. Good girls follow the rules. Bad girls disregard gender conventional expectations, formal or informal. Bad girls are a problem. They get into trouble in school, fight with other girls. They are disruptive, delinquent, and at risk. Bad girls are criticized by parents and teachers and silenced by boys' ridicule (Lloyd 2005). As Young (2005) argues,

> The stereotypes of the bitchy female "on the rag" accompany the construction of women as abject, monstrous, out of control. We are oversensitive, unpredictable, verbally unpleasant because of our womanly natures; we are most likely to erupt, so the imagery goes, at that time of the month. . . . [T]hese judgments can be and often are used against us as women whether we are menstruating at any given moment or not. . . . We try to conform to a modern norm of dispassionate reasons and proper niceness, a norm that allows the expression of emotion only in a narrow range. (118)

Both identifiers in this "instructional pair," good girl and bad girl, nice woman and nasty woman, are about "the surveillance and control of girls' bodies, minds, and spirits; a story that varies with social context, with race, class, and sexual orientation" (Brown 2003, 2). Feminist theorists and, in particular, theorists of girls studies, problematize the labels themselves, asserting that the signifiers are negotiated through gendered processes. Much of that work analyzes mass media representations of bad girls, illustrating media's linking of violence with girls of color (Chesney-Lind and Irwin 2004) and bad girls with sexuality (McRobbie 1997).

The 1990s girl power movement (Cowan and Kaloski 1998–99, Dibben 1999, Gonick 2006, Ringrose 2013) rehabilitated the concept of bad girls, reclaiming the reproach. These young, mainly White, middle-class women, many identifying as queer, embraced punk rock, combat boots, and a "girls rule" identity. Entering the mainstream through popular movies, television shows, and mainstream rock 'n' roll, bad girl discourse has also been rehabilitated. "How to Be a Bad Girl" (n.d.), an article at the internet to-do guide WikiHow, includes a long list about "the look" (which emphasizes a low-maintenance appearance that includes the right shoes, strategic use of makeup, sunglasses, black leather, and a small but meaningful tattoo); the attitude (creating a look rather than following a trend; being comfortable with sex appeal; exuding confidence, mystery, independence, fun, and passion; showing leadership; making no apologies); and adventurousness (picking the right "ride," traveling, showing courage, participating in sports, drinking the right way, listening to rock 'n' roll). By this definition, bad girls are cool. They're hip, they're rock 'n' roll. They're the most interesting people in the room.

Queering Niceness

Niceness takes a range of forms in the queer community. Lesbians are the only women named by their sexuality. And since nice women do not openly reflect their sexuality, lesbians by nature belong to that category of bad women. "Lesbians generally aren't such nice girls," writes Chapkis (1998, 71). "We are ugly women who pursue sexual pleasure. In fact, lesbian and bisexual women are the only categories of women defined by the pursuit of pleasure." Lesbians are equated with sex, which makes them bad girls.

A second theme complicates this total ban. Mirroring the heteronormative nice/nasty bifurcation, not all lesbians are bad—only those that aren't amply feminine. Here apolitical lesbian chic—that is, "good" lesbians—are positioned as a counterpoint to political, unfashionable, feminist lesbians (McKenna 2002). Drawing on Foucault's (1977) work on the production of docile female bodies, Nguyen (2008) develops this argument. She contends that butch lesbians, who dress and act as men, are less invested in female compliance and thus are less obliged to smile and enact Niceness. With their strut and swagger performance, they reject "the disciplinary practices of femininity" that "maintain women's subordination" (673).

"She's Such a Nasty Woman"   265

These characterizations of good and bad lesbians have shaped public policy around parenting. Historically, lesbians and gay men have met challenges to adoption because they have been seen as a threat to heteronormative parenting (Hicks and McDermott 1999, Pollack 1987, Skeates and Jabri 1988). Yet even when lesbians are legally permitted to adopt a child, adoption agencies and adoption panels still utilize a set of narrative heuristics to determine "good enough" applicants. Not surprisingly, the discourse of social workers and adoption panel judges mirrors gendered practices of Niceness (i.e., the applicants are discrete, quiet, and provide male role models) that police and reproduce heteronormativity (Hicks 2000).

A final line of discussion queers the conflation of Niceness and good in the larger community and society. As one blogger notes, "Our enemies are not only the people holding 'Fags Die God Laughs' signs, they are the nice people who just feel like marriage should be between a man and a woman, no offense, it's just how they feel!" (Rachel 2012). This line of discourse asserts that for allies, Niceness is not enough. Here we see another feminist critique of Niceness. Niceness not only serves to reproduce gendered norms of the heteropatriarchy but also sanctions social inequity. Resisting institutional oppression with Niceness is ineffective, these writers assert, since resistance requires questioning the very dominant social norms and structures that pressure girls to be nice.

Reclaiming Nastiness

We women are reclaiming nastiness on our T-shirts and in our everyday practices. From Beyoncé's alter ego Sasha Fierce to Hillary Rodham Clinton's presidential runs, we proclaim strength and capability. Standing on the shoulders of Anita Hill, and armed with funds from Emily's List, women have followed in the footsteps of Barbara Mikulski, the longest-serving woman in the U.S. Congress. And yet women in the United States are underrepresented in both the governmental and private sectors (Brown 2017). In fact, the United States ranks seventy-eighth in gender equity in national legislatures, behind both Afghanistan and China (Inter-Parliamentary Union 2019). According to Boschma (2017), the problem is not financial challenges, party bureaucracies, or sexism; the problem is that women in the United States simply don't consider running for office. Lawless and Fox (2013) argue that these political aspirations—or lack thereof—relate to childhood sports, parental encouragement, political activity in college, self-confidence, and particular professional networks, all of which are weighted heavily toward men.

Even so, after the 2016 election of Trump, women found themselves politically mobilized—many for the very first time. In Washington, D.C., and in cities across the United States, 4.2 million women marched in protest. In the aftermath, a women's movement has been growing not only on college campuses but also in

U.S. cities and suburbs. Women say they are also paying increased attention to politics. Fifty-eight percent of women surveyed, compared with 46 percent of men, stated they are more interested in politics since Trump was elected ("Since Trump's Election" 2017). A growing number of women considered running for political office, as reflected in a countless training events across the country, where women learn what's involved in getting elected (Walters 2017). And in what has been called "Year of the Woman," a record 117 women were elected to Congress and governorships in the 2018 midterms (Salam 2018).

The term *badass woman* has also resurfaced in popular discourse. Formerly a term used interchangeably for a bully and later for swaggering men, a few years ago *badass* became "a term of acclamation and aspiration" for strong, cool, "swaggerly" women like Beyoncé, Ruth Bader Ginsberg, Jennifer Lawrence, Malala, Nicki Minaj, and Amy Schumer (Garber 2015). According to the online *Urban Dictionary*, the badass woman "radiates confidence" and "carves her own path" ("Badass Women," n.d.). Badass women reclaim language, space, and voice. In January 2017 CNN introduced a seven-part digital series, *Badass Women of Washington*. "What makes a badass woman, at the core of it, is somebody, at least in Washington I think, who has broken barriers and along with that has done something extraordinary," explains CNN political correspondent Dana Bash (Kurtz 2017). While the women—Democratic senator Dianne Feinstein and Republican representative Jaime Herrera Beutler, among others—cross political party lines, the series makes clear they are all models of "accomplished" women.

Pledging Niceness

During the time of a combatant, bombastic president, we're talking a good deal about Niceness. But while the conversation is playing out both around Niceness and gender and Niceness and citizenship writ large, we see even more clearly the role Niceness plays in silencing critics. Niceness is currently employed to obscure political discontent in a way that mirrors its use in gender politics. In his first speech to his employees in March 2017, Ben Carson, the new secretary of housing and urban development, asked them to take a "Niceness Pledge": "Just raise your hand, everybody raise your hand. Now what did you just pledge to do? Be nice to every single person you encounter for one week, including your spouse!" (Levitz 2017). In May 2017 Ryan Zinke, then secretary of the interior, publicly admonished a Native American tribal liaison during a four-day listening tour when the liaison asked when the secretary would meet with tribal leaders: "Be nice. Don't be rude" (D'Angelo 2017). In each very public case, Niceness was employed by new administrators whose competency has been questioned in the national press. The goal in both cases was to quell potential complainants. Niceness functioned as admonition; it served as shorthand for "Be quiet, don't be a problem, don't speak out."

Figuratively speaking, teachers (along with nurses, secretaries, and airline flight attendants) take a Niceness pledge. In those positions, employees—the majority of whom are women—agree to be good, caring, nurturing, and respectable. These characteristics are not a surprise. We already know that women, often involved in relational work, do the emotional labor in both the home and the workplace (Hochschild 2003). Niceness is expected of women, and it translates seamlessly to the labor force. The problem is that Niceness constrains women's professional lives and careers. Being nice means neither asking questions nor disrupting the status quo. Niceness discourages sticking up for oneself, and encourages following the directives of those in positions of power. Specifically, Niceness prevents many women from negotiating for salaries, asking for raises, and seeking promotions (Babcock and Laschever 2007; Bowles, Babcock, and Lai 2007). Following this line of inquiry, female employees translate to a lower-paid and less expensive workforce.

In addition, when Niceness is stressed, orders can also be masked as personal requests, making it difficult for women to dispute or refuse them. Teaching, in particular, has been assigned as women's work (Acker 1989, Apple 1989, Biklen 1984, Lather 1987), and we see this submissiveness play out in public discourse over schooling in the United States. The organizational structure of schools—largely male administrators and lower-status female teachers—has made it easier to wage what Giroux (2012) calls "the war against teachers as public intellectuals." During the last two decades of curricular standardization and school privatization, teachers' pedagogical skills, expertise, and motivation have come under constant attack. Trained in Niceness, teachers have long been a compliant labor force.

Reclaiming Voice

We are, however, seeing teachers fight back and claim their voices. The Chicago Teachers Union has taken a strident stance against corporate educational reform, and has positioned itself on the front line in the neoliberal attack on public education (Gutstein and Lipman 2013, Uetricht 2014), providing training in organizing tactics, hosting book groups, and working with community members to organize protests against school closures. The Badass Teachers Association, founded in 2013 to give voice to teachers in the fight against corporate-driven reform efforts, is another example of fighting back. Using Facebook as a platform, more than fifty-six thousand "badass teachers" across all fifty states have taken a stance against educational privatization and standardized testing. They are fighting in their own defense, staging protests and hosting educational forums. As Naison (2013) notes,

"It is significant that there are clearly thousands of teachers in this country who are fed up with polite, respectful appeals to policy makers who hold them in contempt and are ready to fight fire with fire."

But it's not only teachers who are "fed up with polite." In what Pollitt (2018) calls the "post-Trump awakening," women across the country have moved into the political fray in notable ways. With women's marches of historic magnitude in January 2017, accusations of sexual harassment and molestation against a long list of powerful men, and the Me Too Movement that came about in the fall of 2017, women have begun to voice anger. Beginning with a public accusation and culminating with public fury, women are troubling the gendered tropes of nice and nasty.

References

Acker, J. 1992. "From Sex Roles to Gendered Institutions." *Contemporary Sociology* 21, no. 5: 565–69.

Apple, M. W. 1989. *Teachers and Texts: A Political Economy of Class and Gender.* New York: Routledge.

Babcock, L., and S. Laschever. 2007. *Women Don't Ask: The High Cost of Avoiding Negotiation—and Positive Strategies for Change.* New York: Bantam.

"Badass Women." N.d. Urban Dictionary. http://www.urbandictionary.com /define.php?term=badass%20women.

Beauvoir, S. de. 1989. *The Second Sex.* Translated by H. M. Parshley. New York: Vintage.

Biklen, S. K. 1994. *School Work: Gender and the Cultural Construction of Teaching.* New York: Teachers College Press.

Boschma, J. 2017. "Why Women Don't Run for Office." *Politico.* http://www .politico.com/interactives/2017/women-rule-politics-graphic/.

Bowles, H. R, L. Babcock, and L. Lai 2007. "Social Incentives for Gender Differences in the Propensity to Initiate Negotiations: Sometimes It Does Hurt to Ask." *Organizational Behavior and Human Decision Processes* 103, no. 1: 84–103.

Bramen, C. T. 2017. *American Niceness: A Cultural History.* Cambridge, Mass.: Harvard University Press.

Briton, N. J., and Hall, J. A. 1995. "Beliefs about Female and Male Nonverbal Communication." *Sex Roles* 32:79–90.

Brown, A. 2017, March 20. "Despite Gains, Women Remain Underrepresented among U.S. Political and Business Leaders." Pew Research Center. http://www .pewresearch.org/fact-tank/2017/03/20/despite-gains-women-remain-underrep resented-among-u-s-political-and-business-leaders/.

Brown, L. M. 2003. *Girlfighting: Betrayal and Rejection among Girls.* New York: New York University Press.

Brown, L. M., and C. Gilligan. 1992. *Meeting at the Crossroads: Women's Psychology and Girls' Development.* Cambridge, Mass.: Harvard University Press.

Butler, J. 1988. "Performative Acts and Gender Constitution: An Essay in Phenomenology and Feminist Theory." *Theater Journal* 40, no. 4: 519–31.

Butler, J. 1990. *Gender Trouble: Feminism and the Subversion of Identity.* New York: Routledge.

Chapkis, W. 1998. "The Ugly Dyke." In *Looking Queer: Image and Identity in Bisexual, Gay, and Transgender Communities,* edited by D. Atkins, 69-72. New York: Haworth.

Chesney-Lind, M., and K. Irwin. 2004. "From Badness to Meanness: Popular Constructions of Contemporary Girlhood." In *All About the Girl: Culture, Power, and Identity,* edited by A. Harris, 45–58. New York: Routledge.

Clark, S., and C. Paechter. 2007, July 27. "'Why can't girls play football?' Gender Dynamics and the Playground." *Sport, Education, and Society* 12, no. 3: 261–76.

Cole, P. M. 1985. "Display Rules and the Socialization of Affective Displays." In *The Development of Expressive Behavior: Biology–Environment Interactions,* edited by G. Zivin, 269–90. Orlando: Academic Press.

Collins, P. H. 1990. *Black Feminist Thought: Knowledge, Consciousness, and the Politics of Empowerment.* New York: Routledge.

Cowan, K., and A. Kaloski. 1998–99. "Spicing Up Girls' Lives." *Trouble and Strife* 38:3–11.

Crenshaw, K. 1991. "Mapping the Margins: Intersectionality, Identity Politics, and Violence against Women of Color." *Stanford Law Review* 43, no. 6: 1241–99.

D'Angelo, C. 2017, May 9. "Interior Secretary Orders Protestor to 'Be Nice' during Visit to Bears Ears." *HuffPost.* http://www.huffingtonpost.com/entry /ryan-zinke-bears-ears-be-Nice_us_59120315e4b05e1ca202516f.

Deutsch, F. M., LeBaron, D., and Fryer, M. 1987. "What Is in a Smile?" *Psychology of Women Quarterly* 11, no. 3: 341–52.

Dibben, N. 1999. "Representations of Femininity in Popular Music." *Popular Music* 18, no. 3: 351–55.

Dollard, A., and J. Davis. 1940. *Children of Bondage: The Personality Development of Negro Youth in the Urban South*. Washington, D.C.: America Council on Education.

Engel, B. 2010. *The Nice Girl Syndrome: Stop Being Manipulated and Abused and Start Standing Up for Yourself*. Hoboken, N.J.: Wiley.

Faludi, S. 1991. *Backlash: The Undeclared War against American Women*. New York: Broadway.

Fischer, A. H. 1993. "Sex Differences in Emotionality: Fact or Stereotype?" *Feminism and Psychology* 3, no. 3: 303–18.

Fiske, S. T., and Stevens, L. E. 1993. "What's So Special about Sex? Gender Stereotyping and Discrimination." In *Gender Issues in Contemporary Society*, edited by S. Oskamp and M. Costanzo, 73–196. Newbury Park, Calif.: Sage.

Foucault, M. 1977. *Discipline and Punish: The Birth of the Prison*. Translated by Alan Sheridan. New York: Pantheon.

Fox, G. L. 1977. "'Nice Girl': Social Control of Women through a Value Construct." *Signs* 2, no. 4: 805–17.

Garber, M. 2015, November 22. "How 'Badass' Became a Feminist Word. *Atlantic*. https://www.theatlantic.com/entertainment/archive/2015/11/how -badass-became-feminist/417096/.

Genegabus, J. 2017, January 10. "65th Cherry Blossom Festival Queen Contestants Announced."t *Honolulu Star Advertiser*. http://www.staradvertiser .com/2017/01/10/features/briefs-features/65th-cherry-blossom-festival-queen -contestants-announced/.

Giroux, H. A. 2012. "The War against Teachers as Public Intellectuals in Dark Times." *Truthout*. http://www.truth-out.org/opinion/item/13367-the-corporate -war-against-teachers-as-public-intellectuals-in-dark-times.

Gonick, M. 2006. "Between 'Girl Power' and 'Reviving Ophelia': Constituting the Neoliberal Girl Subject." *NWSA Journal* 18:1–23.

Gray, E. 2016, October 20. "How 'Nasty Woman' Became a Viral Call for Solidarity." *HuffPost*. http://www.huffingtonpost.com/entry/nasty-woman -became-a-call-of-solidarity-for-women-voters_us_5808f6a8e4b02444efa20c92.

Griffin, C. 2004. "Good Girls, Bad Girls: Anglocentrism and Diversity in the Constitution of Contemporary Girlhood." In *All About the Girl: Culture, Power, and Identity*, edited by A. Harris, 29–44. New York: Routledge.

Gutstein, E. R., and P. Lipman. 2013. "The Rebirth of the Chicago's Teachers Union and Possibilities for a Counter-hegemonic Education Movement." *Monthly Review* 65, no. 2. https://monthlyreview.org/2013/06/01/the-rebirth -of-the-chicago-teachers-union-and-possibilities-for-a-counter-hegemonic-edu cation-movement/.

Hains, R. C. 2008. "'Pretty Smart': Subversive Intelligence in Girl Power Cartoons." In *Geek Chic: Smart Women in Popular Culture*, edited by S. Inness, 65–84. London: Palgrave Macmillan.

Hartley, J. 1993. *The Politics of Pictures: The Creation of Public in the Age of the Popular Media*. New York: Routledge.

Herold, E. S., and R.R. Milhausen. 1999. "Dating Preferences of University Women: An Analysis of the Nice Guy Stereotype." *Journal of Sex and Marital Therapy* 25, no. 4: 333–43.

Hey, V. 1997. *The Company She Keeps: An Ethnography of Girls' Friendships*. Philadelphia: Open University Press.

Hicks, S. 2000. "'Good Lesbian, Bad Lesbian . . .': Regulating Heterosexuality in Fostering and Adoption Assessments." *Child and Family Social Work* 5, no. 2: 157–68.

Hicks, S., and J. McDermott. 1999. *Lesbian and Gay Fostering and Adoption: Extraordinary Yet Ordinary*. London: Kingsley.

Hochschild, A. R. 2003. *The Managed Heart: Commercialization of Human Feeling*. Berkeley: University of California Press.

"How to Be a Bad Girl." N.a. WikiHow. http://www.wikihow.com/Be-a-Bad-Girl.

Inness, S. 2008. *Geek Chic: Smart Women in Popular Culture*. London: Palgrave Macmillan.

Inter-Parliamentary Union. 2019. "Women in National Parliaments." http:// www.ipu.org/wmn-e/classif.htm.

Kehily, M. J. 2002. *Sexuality, Gender and Schooling: Shifting Agendas in Social Learning*. New York: Psychology Press.

Kierstead, D., P. D'Agostino, and H. Dill. 1988. "Sex Role Stereotyping of College Professors: Bias in Students' Ratings of Instructors." *Journal of Educational Psychology* 80, no. 3: 342–44.

Korzenny, B.A.G., F. Korzenny, and G. Sanchez de Rota. 1985. "Women's Communication in Mexican Organizations." *Sex Roles* 12, nos. 7–8: 867–76.

Kramer, C. 1977. "Perceptions of Male and Female Speech." Language and Speech 20:151–61.

Kurtz, J. 2017, June 6. "CNN Launches New Digital Series 'Badass Women of Washington,'" *The Hill*. http://thehill.com/blogs/in-the-know/in-the-know/336497-cnn-launches-new-digital-series-on-badass-women-of-washington.

LaFrance, M. 1997. "Pressure to Be Pleasant: Effects of Sex and Power on Reactions to Not Smiling." *International Review of Social Psychology* 2, no. 198: 95–108.

LaFrance, M., M. A. Hecht, and E. L. Paluck. 2003. "The Contingent Smile: A Meta-analysis of Sex Differences in Smiling." *Psychological Bulletin* 129, no. 2: 305–34.

Lather, P. 1987. "Patriarchy, Capitalism and the Nature of Teacher Work." *Teacher Education Quarterly* 14, no. 2: 25–38.

Lawless, J., and R. L. Fox. 2013. *Girls Just Wanna Not Run: The Gender Gap in Young Americans' Political Ambition*. Washington, D.C.: School of Public Affairs, American University. https://www.american.edu/spa/wpi/upload/girls-just-wanna-not-run_policy-report.pdf.

Levitz, E. 2017. "Ben Carson Makes HUD Employees Take the 'Niceness Pledge.'" *New York*. http://nymag.com/daily/intelligencer/2017/03/ben-carson-makes-hud-employees-take-the-Niceness-pledge.html.

Lloyd, G., ed. 2005. *Problem Girls: Understanding and Supporting Troubled and Troublesome Girls and Young Women*. New York: Routledge.

McKenna, S. E. 2002. "The Queer Insistence of *Ally McBeal*: Lesbian Chic, Postfeminism, and Lesbian Reception." *Communication Review* 5, no. 4: 285–314.

McRobbie, A. 1997. "Bridging the Gap: Feminism, Fashion, and Consumption." *Feminist Review* 55, no. 1: 73–89.

Naison, M. 2013. Badass Teachers Association. http://www.badassteacher.org/category/history/.

Nguyen, A. 2008. "Patriarchy, Power, and Female Masculinity." *Journal of Homosexuality* 55, no. 4: 665–83.

"Nice Guy Syndrome." N.d. Urban Dictionary. http://www.urbandictionary.com/define.php?term=Nice Guy Syndrome.

Passons, E., ed. 2017. *The Nasty Women Project: Voices from the Resistance*. Columbus, Ohio: Gatekeeper.

Pfell, F. 2002. "Getting Up There with Tom: The Politics of American 'Nice.'" In *Masculinity Studies and Feminist Theory: New Directions*, edited by J. K. Gardiner, 119–40. New York: Columbia University Press.

Pollack, S. 1987. "Lesbian Mothers: A Lesbian–Feminist Perspective on Research." In *Politics of the Heart: A Lesbian Parenting Anthology*, edited by S. Pollack and J. Vaughn, 316–24. Ithaca, N.Y.: Firebrand.

Pollitt, K. 2018. "We Are Living Through the Moment When Women Unleash Decades of Pent-Up Anger." *Nation.* https://www.thenation.com/article/we -are-living-through-the-moment-when-women-unleash-decades-of-pent-up -anger/.

Quinn, D. 2016, October 20. "Nasty Women! Thousands Turn Trump's 'Nasty' Debate Diss of Hilary Clinton into a Battle Cry." *People.* http://people.com /politics/nasty-women-thousands-turn-trumps-nasty-debate-diss-of-hillary -clinton-into-a-battlecry/.

Rachel. 2012, April 26. "The Revolution Will Not Be Polite: The Issue of Nice versus Good." *Social Justice League* (blog). https://socialjusticeleaguenet.word press.com/2012/04/26/the-revolution-will-not-be-polite-the-issue-of-nice-versus -good/.

Renold, E. 2005. *Girls, Boys and Junior Sexualities: Exploring Children's Gender and Relations in Primary School.* New York: Routledge.

Ringrose, J. 2013. *Postfeminist Education? Girls and the Sexual Politics of Schooling.* London: Routledge.

Ringrose, J., and E. Renold. 2010. "Normative Cruelties and Gender Deviants: The Performative Effects of Bully Discourses for Girls and Boys in School." *British Educational Research Journal* 36, no. 4: 573–96.

Rutherford, J. 1997. *Forever England: Reflections on Masculinity and Empire.* London: Lawrence and Wishart.

Salam, M. 2018. "Reshaping America's Leadership." *New York Times.* https:// www.nytimes.com/2018/11/07/us/elections/women-elected-midterm-elections .html.

Simmons, L. M. 2015. *Crescent City Girls: The Lives of Young Black Women in Segregated New Orleans.* Gender and America Culture. Chapel Hill: University of North Carolina Press.

"Since Trump's Election, Increased Attention to Politics–Especially among Women." 2017, July 20. Pew Research Center. http://www.people-press .org/2017/07/20/since-trumps-election-increased-attention-to-politics-espe cially-among-women/.

Skeates, J., and D. Jabri. 1988. *Fostering and Adoption by Lesbians and Gay Men.* London: London Strategic Policy Unit.

Smith, R. I. 2016. "What It's Like When a Coworker Tells You to Smile." *Atlantic*. https://www.theatlantic.com/notes/all/2016/10/ the-sexism-of-telling-women-to-smile-your-stories/503309/.

Sommers, E. 2005. *Tyranny of Niceness: Unmasking the Need for Approval.* Toronto: Dundurn.

Uetricht, M. 2014, March 6. "Uncommon Core." *Jacobin.* http://www.jacobin mag.com/2014/03/uncommon-core-chicago-teachers-union/.

Urbaniak, G. C., and P. R. Kilmann. 2003. "Physical Attractiveness and the 'Nice Guy Paradox': Do Nice Guys Really Finish Last?" *Sex Roles* 49, nos. 9–10: 413–26.

Waldman, Katy. 2013, June 18. "The Tyranny of the Smile." *Slate.* http://www .slate.com/articles/double_x/doublex/2013/06/bitchy_resting_face_and_female _Niceness_why_do_women_have_to_smile_more.html.

Walkerdine, V. 1997. *Daddy's Girl: Young Girls and Popular Culture.* Basingstoke, England: Macmillan.

Walters, J. 2017. "Trump Victory Spurs Women to Run for Office across US: 'Our Time Is Coming.'" *Guardian.* https://www.theguardian.com/world/2017 /jan/02/women-politics-us-election.

Wierzbicka, A. 1995. "Emotion and Facial Expression: A Semantic Perspective." *Culture and Psychology* 1, no. 2: 227–58.

Yano, C. R. 2005. *Crowning the Nice Girl: Gender, Ethnicity, and Culture in Hawai'i's Cherry Blossom Festival.* Honolulu: University of Hawai'i Press.

Young, I. M. 2005. *On Female Body Experience: "Throwing Like a Girl" and Other Essays.* Oxford: Oxford University Press.

Acknowledgments

I am honored and humbled that the chapter authors chose to share their work for this book. I have learned so much from the ways they are engaging the concept of Niceness in their research and their professional lives. The collective rendering that this book produces is inspiring, compelling, and smart. My deepest gratitude goes to each of you.

Many colleagues provided peer reviews of early drafts of the chapters in this book, and the final iterations of these chapters would not be what they are without the expert feedback of these individuals: Tara Affolter, Lesley Bartlett, Keffrelyn Brown, Katie Elliott, Melvin Hall, Gretchen McAllister, Sarah Robert, and Sofia Villenas. Peer review is so important to the process of creating publishable, accessible, and compelling work, and I am grateful for the time you each contributed to this collective project. Additional thanks to the two anonymous reviewers of the initial book idea and the final full manuscript; your feedback helped mold this project into a stronger book. And finally, I am grateful to Pieter Martin at the University of Minnesota Press, and to Peter Demerath at the University of Minnesota, for their ongoing interest in and advocacy of my work.

Finishing a book project somehow has the effect of causing me to reflect on the multiple and varied relationships, experiences, and intersections that contributed to the final product. Certainly, there are far too many to properly acknowledge, as this book has been in the making for quite some time. A full genealogy would likely take me back to my childhood—complete with expectations of Niceness paired with frequent displays of the strong adult women in my life who stood up and spoke out when necessary. Unbeknownst to my friends, family, and colleagues, I have been studying Niceness on a daily basis for at least the past decade. I suppose that's what happens when a concept monopolizes the mind of someone who is already primed to observe and analyze social and institutional interactions. Scholarly work can thrive only when one is supported and engaged in every aspect of her life, so I am indebted to the many people who have helped keep me (mostly) centered.

Contributors

SARAH ABUWANDI is majoring in justice studies and political science at Arizona State University.

COLIN BEN (Navajo Nation) is a doctoral candidate in the Educational Leadership and Policy program at the University of Utah and a predoctoral research fellow in the Center for Indian Education at Arizona State University.

NICHOLAS BUSTAMANTE is a research associate at the Center for Indian Education at Arizona State University and a doctoral student in justice studies at Arizona State University.

ANGELINA E. CASTAGNO is a professor in the College of Education at Northern Arizona University and director of the Diné Institute for Navajo Nation Educators. She is author of *Educated in Whiteness: Good Intentions and Diversity in Schools* (Minnesota, 2014) and coeditor of *The Anthropology of Educational Policy: Ethnographic Inquiries into Policy as Sociocultural Practice* and *Postsecondary Education for American Indian and Alaska Native Students: Higher Education toward Nation Building.*

AIDAN/AMANDA J. CHARLES majored in sociology and criminal justice at Northern Arizona University.

JEREMIAH CHIN is a postdoctoral research fellow at the Center for Indian Education at Arizona State University.

SALLY CAMPBELL GALMAN is a professor of child and family studies at the College of Education at the University of Massachusetts–Amherst. She is author of *Wise and Foolish Virgins: White Women at Work in the Feminized World of Primary School Teaching* and Shane, the Lone Ethnographer, an illustrated research methods series.

FREDERICK W. GOODING JR. is an honors professor of African American and media studies at Texas Christian University. He is author of *You Mean, There's RACE in My Movie? A Complete Guide to Understanding Race in Mainstream Hollywood* and coeditor of *Stories from the Front of the Room: How Higher Education Faculty of Color Overcome Challenges and Thrive in the Academy.*

DEIRDRE JUDGE holds an MA in educational studies from Tufts University.

Katie A. Lazdowski is a project manager for the Institute for Training and Development, a nonprofit organization based in Amherst, Massachusetts.

Román Liera is a postdoctoral research associate in the Pullias Center for Higher Education at the USC Rossier School of Education.

Sylvia Mac is assistant professor of special education at the University of La Verne.

Lindsey Malcom-Piqueux is senior institutional research analyst at the California Institute of Technology. She is coeditor of *Confronting Equity Issues on Campus: Implementing the Equity Scorecard in Theory and Practice*.

Giselle Martinez Negrette is assistant professor in the Department of Curriculum and Instruction at the University of Illinois at Urbana-Champaign.

Amber Poleviyuma (Hopi Tribe) is majoring in community health at Arizona State University.

Alexus Richmond is studying speech and hearing science with a concurrent degree in psychology at Arizona State University.

Frances J. Riemer is professor of educational foundations at Northern Arizona University. She is author of *Working at the Margins: Moving off Welfare in America* and coeditor of *Qualitative Research: An Introduction to Methods and Designs*.

Jessica Sierk is assistant professor of education at St. Lawrence University.

Bailey B. Smolarek is an assistant researcher at the Wisconsin Center for Education Research at the University of Wisconsin–Madison.

Jessica Solyom is assistant research professor at the Center for Indian Education at Arizona State University. She is coauthor of *Postsecondary Education for American Indian and Alaska Natives: Higher Education for Nation Building and Self-Determination*.

Megan Tom (Navajo Nation) is studying English literature at Arizona State University.

Sabina Vaught is professor of educational studies and chair of the Department of Educational Leadership and Policy Studies in the Jeannine Rainbolt College of Education at the University of Oklahoma. She is author of *Racism, Public Schooling, and the Entrenchment of White Supremacy: A Critical Race Ethnography* and *Compulsory: Education and the Dispossession of Youth in a Prison School* (Minnesota, 2017).

Cynthia Diana Villarreal is a PhD candidate in urban education policy at the University of Southern California's Rossier School of Education.

Kristine T. Weatherston is associate professor of instruction in the Department of Media Studies and Production at Temple University. She is the producer and director of the documentaries *American Boy* and *Under Pressure: The Hidden Story of Pregnancy and Preeclampsia.*

JOSEPH C. WEGWERT is associate professor in the College of Education at Northern Arizona University.

MARGUERITE ANNE FILLION WILSON is assistant professor of human development at Binghamton University of the State University of New York.

JIA-HUI STEFANIE WONG is assistant professor of educational studies at Trinity College.

DENISE GRAY YULL is associate professor of human development at Binghamton University of the State University of New York.

Index

anti-intellectualism, 91, 92, 95, 104
appearance, 74, 77, 79–81, 111, 117, 118, 221, 232, 244, 260, 263, 264
assimilation, x, 51, 157, 262
authoritarianism, 92, 105

Badass Teachers Association, 267, 272
badass women, 266, 268, 272
Banks, J., 33, 234, 235
Baptiste, I., ix, xii, xxi
beauty, 72, 76, 118, 262
Bell, D., 41, 50, 148, 159, 164, 179, 181, 201, 215, 239, 255
benevolence, xx, 54, 55, 57, 59, 63, 238–40, 243, 247, 254, 255
Bissonnette, J. D., xii, xiii, xxi, 91, 92, 95, 99, 105
Brown, W., 95, 106, 239, 240, 254, 255, 256
Brown v. Board of Education, 50, 54, 187, 199, 255, 256

campus climate, 141, 142, 146, 147, 157, 160, 163
Castagno, A. E., xi, xiii, xxi, 3, 18, 20–24, 33, 46, 50, 55, 67, 91, 94, 102, 104, 106, 114, 118, 124, 139, 140, 145, 146, 158, 159, 174–79, 185, 199–202, 214, 216, 217, 220, 221, 227, 229, 232–34, 238–46, 253, 256, 277

charter school, 7, 54–56, 67–69
civil rights movement, xvii, 17, 21, 54, 78, 80, 161
Clinton, Hillary Rodham, 82, 258, 265, 273
code-switch, xv, 138, 146, 157
colorblindness, 33, 201, 202, 214
compliance, 96, 99, 104, 262, 264
controversy, x, 14, 15, 20, 91, 93, 96, 100, 104, 146, 246
counterstory, xv, 145–48, 155–58, 162, 164, 176
critical discourse analysis, 188, 200, 202, 216, 217
critical ethnography, 33, 35, 204
critical pedagogy, 35, 36, 86, 216, 222, 234
Critical Race Theory, xi, 15, 40, 50, 51, 56, 66, 67, 145, 147, 159–64, 177–81, 186, 199, 201, 216, 217, 222, 236, 255, 256
critical Whiteness studies, 19, 20

deficit ideology, 103, 104, 107
deficit thinking, 62, 63, 65, 104, 176
demographic change, 37, 38, 40, 49
DiAngelo, R., xvi, 202, 209, 214, 216, 219, 221, 226, 230, 232, 234
disability, 56–69, 215, 249, 250
discourse analysis, 188, 200, 202, 204, 216, 217

discrimination, 22, 28, 120, 122, 128, 129, 133, 136, 145, 147, 169, 171, 179, 254, 270
DisCrit, 56, 59, 65, 66, 67
disproportionality, 86, 201, 202, 203, 215, 217
diversity, x, xi, xiii, 5, 15, 17, 22, 32, 33, 35, 38, 41, 42, 48, 50, 53, 67, 68, 85, 102, 106, 108, 114, 115, 122, 124, 127–29, 133–44, 147, 149, 153, 158, 159, 168–70, 176, 178, 179, 185, 199, 216, 220, 223, 234, 238, 256, 270, 277

equity, ix, xii, xv, xx, xxii, 18, 22, 33, 46, 67, 68, 76, 110, 114, 123, 127, 128, 132, 134, 140, 187, 188, 190, 197, 198, 201, 203, 216, 219, 222, 224, 228, 230, 265, 278
ethnography, 19, 23, 33, 35, 204, 256, 257, 271, 278

feminism, 73, 84, 86, 179, 260, 269, 270, 272, 273
feminization, xvii, 70, 71, 85, 86

gender, xiv, xv, xvi, xix, xx, 23–25, 35, 41, 51, 68, 70–73, 84–86, 93–97, 99, 101, 103, 105–8, 110, 111, 113–15, 117–26, 132, 142–46, 162–64, 168, 175, 180, 224, 239–55, 258–60, 262–74
gendered, xix, xx, 71, 86, 91, 93, 98, 99, 106, 110, 111, 113, 119, 121–23, 125, 246, 247, 249, 252, 254, 258, 260–65, 268
gender performance, 95, 96
girl power, 85, 261, 264, 271
girl studies, 261, 264
Giroux, H. A., 20, 34, 92, 95, 98, 106, 107, 222, 235, 267

global knowledge economy, 66, 69, 111, 112
Golden Rule, 97, 101–3, 219, 235
good intentions, x, xiii, xxiv, 18, 21, 32, 33, 46, 50, 55, 59, 65–67, 104, 106, 124, 140, 159, 179, 185, 195, 199, 201, 205, 208, 209, 214, 216, 220, 234, 238, 256, 277
Goodman, J., xiii, 120, 125
grades, 56, 72, 112, 116, 206, 247, 251, 254
grading, xvi, 112, 117, 120
Grant, C., 18, 22, 23, 31, 35
Guinier, L., 187, 199, 239, 256

harassment, 11, 27, 84, 147, 181, 250–52, 268
heteropatriarchy, 238, 265
higher education, xv, xvi, xix, xx, 16, 66, 89, 110, 111, 114, 124–26, 128, 130, 139–46, 155, 159, 160–62, 164, 167–70, 173, 174, 177, 179, 188, 199, 277, 278

ideal femininity, 71, 76, 79
identity, xv, xvi, xvii, xix, xx, 8, 11, 34, 35, 38, 50–52, 56, 71, 72, 77, 83, 84, 86, 93, 94, 96, 103, 104, 110, 115, 121, 122, 138, 145, 164, 194, 233, 239, 246, 252, 255, 262, 264, 269, 270
inclusion, ix, x, 47, 54, 57, 58, 59, 66, 68, 102, 109, 169, 196, 240, 244, 247
individualism, xvii, 92–95, 98, 102, 103
inequity, x, xii, xiii, xiv, xvi, xvii, xix, xx, xxi, xxii, 18–22, 27, 29, 31, 32, 37, 38, 55, 66, 118, 121, 123, 127, 128, 136, 138, 139, 158, 162, 167–70, 174, 176, 177, 185, 199, 201, 215, 220, 234, 238, 253, 265

institutional racism, 139, 141, 193, 194, 196, 202
intersectionality, xx, 41, 51, 177, 181, 261, 269

Ladson-Billings, G., xi, xii, 22, 34, 41, 51, 129, 141, 164, 170, 180, 201, 216, 222, 235
language, xii, xvi, xix, 10, 22, 38, 41–44, 50, 52, 65, 67, 97, 105, 109, 125, 130, 134–36, 163, 164, 175, 188, 205–7, 210–16, 220, 223, 266, 271
Latino Critical Race Theory, 162, 164, 177, 180, 181, 222
Leonardo, Z., 20, 27, 31, 34, 38, 41, 48, 51, 52, 61, 67, 81, 86, 185, 199, 201, 216, 232, 233, 235
Lewis, A., xiii, xxiv, 18, 21, 24, 34, 185, 186, 199, 220, 235
Lortie, D., 92, 93, 106, 108

mean girl, 154, 258
meanness, xvi, xvii, xviii, 13, 26, 146, 263, 269
Meiners, E., 70, 86, 240, 256
mental health, 181, 246, 247
mentors, 128, 153, 157, 158
meritocracy, xix, 59, 60, 92–98, 102, 105, 176, 214
microaggression, 129, 137, 139, 146, 153, 160, 176, 177, 179, 181, 222, 223, 236
Midwest Niceness, 218–21, 226–30, 233, 234
multicultural education, 18–22, 31, 33–36, 49, 52, 55, 236

nasty woman, 81, 82, 85, 258–73
neutrality, 18, 22, 28, 31, 32, 80, 92–94, 99, 116, 145, 176, 185, 230
New Latino Diaspora, 37, 39, 51, 52

nice guy, 253, 262, 263, 271, 272, 274
not-nice, xviii, xix, xxi, 5–7, 11, 13, 19, 23–27, 43, 45, 46, 49, 98, 100, 101, 118, 120, 137, 158, 186, 189, 196, 197, 202, 205, 214, 215, 238–57

organizational culture, 127, 128, 130, 132, 133, 135, 138, 139, 143

paternalism, 51, 54, 55, 63, 238, 240, 244
patriarchy, 82, 91, 92, 93, 94, 95, 99, 100, 105, 107, 108, 272
Pollock, M., xxi, xxiv, 4, 16, 18, 21, 24, 35, 196, 197, 199, 201, 202, 214, 217
poverty, 25, 62–65, 87, 92, 97, 98, 103, 106, 108, 202, 203, 213

race, xi, xiii, xiv, xv, xviii, xix, xx, xxi, 4–6, 15, 16, 20, 21, 23, 25–27, 31, 34, 35, 37, 40–56, 62–70, 77, 83–86, 91, 93, 94, 101–3, 106, 108, 122, 123, 129, 131, 132, 137, 140–49, 158, 159, 160, 162, 164, 167–71, 174–81, 185–87, 192, 194, 196–209, 214–29, 234–46, 249, 252, 254, 255–58, 261, 262, 264, 277, 278
racial battle fatigue, 157, 158, 160, 173, 178, 181
racial bias, 47, 65, 129, 131, 210
racial inequity, 127, 136, 138, 139, 167, 168, 185, 199, 201, 238
racial literacy, xiv, 186–88, 192–95, 197, 199, 200, 256
racially minoritized faculty, 127–29, 131–37, 139, 141, 143
racial microaggressions, 129, 160, 177, 181, 222

284   *Index*

racism, x, xiii, xvi, 10–13, 16, 20–27, 33–48, 52, 59, 62, 65, 78, 80, 87, 98, 127–29, 133, 137, 139, 141, 142, 145–60, 164, 167–69, 177, 181, 185–88, 190–202, 214, 215, 217, 219, 221, 226, 231–36, 255, 256, 278

school board, xx, 202–8, 210–14
school discipline, 17, 201, 217, 242
silence, xiii, xvi, 4, 33, 45, 47, 49, 50, 52, 62, 95, 108, 128, 129, 135–39, 141–43, 146, 148, 157, 175–77, 204, 205, 212–21, 263
Sleeter, C., 18, 22, 23, 31, 35, 36
smile/smiling, xv, xvi, 81, 82, 112, 117, 123, 133, 150–52, 175, 253, 259, 260, 264, 269, 272, 274
social justice, xxi, xxiv, 18–33, 49, 54, 55, 76, 81, 82, 93, 196, 218, 219, 222, 227–35, 256, 273
social justice education, 18–22, 32, 33, 218, 219, 222
solidarity, 48, 49, 52, 198, 270
Solórzano, D., 156, 157, 158, 160, 179, 181, 222, 236
Sommers, E., xiii, xxiv, 260, 261, 274
special education, xxi, 22, 54–69, 215, 278
state, x, xi, xii, xiv, xvi, xvii, xviii, 3, 8, 12, 14–17, 21–29, 35–47, 51, 54–85, 101, 106, 109, 114, 116, 131, 133, 137, 144, 146–70, 177, 178, 185–89, 192, 198, 203, 206, 210, 215, 217, 219–29, 233–56, 265–67, 277–79
stereotype, 5, 28, 29, 32, 44, 63–65, 111, 114, 115, 117, 118, 124, 137, 147, 168, 169, 174, 177, 229, 263, 270, 271
student behavior, 205, 207, 210, 214, 244

Tatum, B., 73, 78, 87
teacher preparation, xx, 49, 71, 73, 105
teachers, ix, xi–xiv, xviii, xxi, 3–16, 18, 21–39, 43, 45, 46, 47, 49, 52, 53, 57–83, 86, 87, 91–112, 122, 146, 160, 189, 199, 201–9, 212–34, 239–54, 257, 260, 263, 267, 268, 271, 272, 274
tenured faculty, 15, 110, 136, 163
tolerance, xii, xv, xvi, 40–45, 52, 119, 196, 201–2, 207, 210, 211, 215, 262
toxic masculinity, 94, 95, 107
Tribal Critical Race Theory, 147, 159, 179, 256
Trump, Donald, 26, 82, 86, 167, 219, 233, 258
tyranny of niceness, xiii, 261, 274

Ward, I., xii, xxiv, 119, 120, 123, 126
White fragility, xv, xvi, 209, 214, 216, 219, 221, 226, 227, 232, 234
White girls, 71, 84, 212, 238–57
Whiteness, xi, xii, xiii, xiv, 3–5, 10–39, 43, 47, 49–52, 67, 76, 77, 84–86, 91, 93, 94, 104, 106, 124, 139, 140, 145, 146, 148, 155–70, 174, 176, 179, 185–87, 189, 192, 195, 196, 199, 202, 214–17, 220, 221, 227–41, 247, 250–56, 277
White privilege, 26, 29, 35, 49, 73, 76, 78, 85, 192–201, 225, 226, 229–31, 233
White supremacy, 20, 38, 39, 91–96, 104, 105, 145, 146, 148, 155, 157, 167, 170, 177, 185, 187, 202, 226, 238, 250, 255, 256, 278

Young, I., 97, 109, 263, 274

Printed and bound by CPI Group (UK) Ltd, Croydon, CR0 4YY
17/06/2024